Copyright © 2024 Jessie ....

All rights reserved. No part of this publication may be reproduced, distributed, or transmitted in any form or by any means, including photocopying, recording, or other electronic or mechanical methods, without the prior written permission of the publisher, except in the case of brief quotations embodied in critical reviews and certain other noncommercial uses permitted by copyright law.

PTCB Exam Study Guide 2024-2025: UPDATED All in One PTCB Exam Prep 2024 for the Pharmacy Technician Certification Board Examination. Includes Exam Review Material and 949 Practice Test Questions.

ISBN: 978-1-964079-24-0

PTCB EXAM PREP:

DISCLOSURE: This publication is intended for educational and informational purposes only and is not intended as medical or legal advice. While the content herein is designed to provide accurate and authoritative information regarding the subject matter covered, it is provided with the understanding that the publisher and author are not engaged in rendering legal, medical, or other professional services. If legal or other expert assistance is required, the services of a competent professional should be sought.

The information in this book is based on sources believed to be reliable and accurate at the time of publication, but no warranty or fitness is implied. The information contained within is subject to change due to rapidly evolving regulatory environments and advancements in medical and pharmaceutical research.

The publisher and author specifically disclaim any liability, loss, or risk, personal or otherwise, which is incurred as a consequence, directly or indirectly, of the use and application of any of the contents of this book. It is the responsibility of the reader to consult with a professional familiar with their particular factual situation for advice or service.

The scenarios, case studies, and examples provided in this book are for illustrative purposes only and are not intended to represent or guarantee that anyone will achieve the same or similar results. Readers should use their discretion and consider their individual circumstances when applying the information contained within this publication.

Any trademarks, service marks, registered trademarks, or registered service marks mentioned in this book are the property of their respective owners and are used for identification purposes only. Such use should not be construed as an endorsement of this book by the trademark owners.

This publication is not affiliated with, nor has it been authorized, sponsored, or otherwise approved by the Pharmacy Technician Certification Board (PTCB) or any other governmental agency. The content and opinions expressed within this publication are solely those of the author and do not reflect the views or opinions of the PTCB or any other certifying agency or governmental body.

Table of Contents

INTRO:

Okay, picture this: you're at the pharmacy counter, a little nervous, trying to get a handle on all the medication names, the instructions, possible side effects...it's overwhelming. Now, imagine yourself on the other side of that counter - calm, knowledgeable, and ready to help someone navigate that complicated world of prescriptions. That's the power of becoming a Pharmacy Technician.

This study guide isn't just about memorizing drug names or passing the PTCB exam (though it'll help you rock both!). This is about becoming that trusted professional who makes a difference in people's lives. We'll cover everything from the basics of how medications work to the nitty-gritty of dosage calculations, deciphering prescriptions, and all the safety stuff you need to keep patients healthy.

I know some of this might seem dry or intimidating, but we'll break it down step-by-step. Think of it like learning a new recipe – sure, the ingredient list looks long at first, but once you get the hang of each step, you'll be whipping up those chocolate chip cookies (or life-saving prescriptions) like a pro.

So, if you're ready to step behind the counter and start this exciting journey, let's get going! This guide is your roadmap, and with a little dedication, you'll reach your destination as a Certified Pharmacy Technician.

Picture yourself as the backbone of a bustling pharmacy. You're not just filling bottles; you're a vital part of the healthcare team. Let's break down the wide-ranging world of a Pharmacy Technician:

Core Responsibilities:
- **Dispensing:** You'll become a pro at accurately reading prescriptions, selecting the right medication, counting out pills, and preparing labels. It's about precision and double-checking to make sure patients get the right medication at the right dose.
- **Inventory Management:** Think of yourself as the stockroom detective. You'll keep track of what medications are on hand, make sure nothing is expired, and place orders to replenish supplies. It's about ensuring the pharmacy never runs out of what patients need.
- **Compounding:** This is where science meets precision. You might be mixing custom ointments, solutions, or capsules based on specific patient needs and the doctor's instructions.
- **Data Entry and Insurance:** You'll master the art of entering patient information into the pharmacy system, verifying insurance coverage, and troubleshooting any billing issues, making sure patients can access their medication.

Where You Can Work:
- **Retail Pharmacy:** The familiar neighborhood pharmacy – you're the multitasker, juggling prescriptions, over-the-counter advice, and phone calls with a friendly smile.
- **Hospital Pharmacy:** Think teamwork in a fast-paced setting. You'll prepare IV medications, stock medication supplies for different hospital units, and likely get involved in emergency situations.
- **Specialty Pharmacy:** This is focused care. You'll handle complex medications for chronic conditions, working closely with patients to manage their prescriptions and side effects.

The Dream Team: Pharmacists & Patients
- **The Pharmacist's Right Hand:** You become a trusted partner, providing essential support to the pharmacist. Your attention to detail allows them to focus on counseling patients and providing clinical expertise.

- **Patient Advocate:** You're the bridge between the prescription and the patient. You'll translate medication instructions, answer questions, and build trusting relationships with the people you serve.

This is just a taste of the possibilities. As a pharmacy technician, you have the power to make a real impact, whether it's making a patient's day brighter at the retail counter or ensuring lifesaving medications are delivered on time in the hospital.

Achieving PTCB Certification opens a gateway to numerous advantages, elevating your professional standing, potential for higher earnings, and opportunities for career progression. It also bestows a mark of excellence recognized by employers and the public, affirming your commitment to the highest standards in pharmacy technician practice.

Eligibility Criteria: To embark on this path, you must meet specific prerequisites:

1. **High School Diploma or Equivalent**: A foundational requirement, ensuring all candidates possess a standard level of education.
2. **Full Disclosure**: Transparency about any criminal history and State Board of Pharmacy registration or licensure actions is essential.
3. **Completion of a PTCB-Recognized Education/Training Program or Equivalent Work Experience**: Whether you've completed a formal education program in pharmacy technology or accumulated equivalent work experience, both pathways are valid. The PTCB offers a detailed list of recognized programs, ensuring diverse avenues to meet this criterion.
4. **Passing the PTCE**: The final hurdle, the Pharmacy Technician Certification Exam (PTCE), is a comprehensive assessment of your knowledge and skills.

Application Process:

1. **Preparation**: Begin with gathering information and resources. Understanding the exam's scope and format is crucial, so consider investing time in a study guide or course.
2. **Eligibility Verification**: Ensure you meet all eligibility requirements. This may involve gathering documentation or verifying your educational program's recognition by the PTCB.
3. **Application Submission**: Complete the application through the PTCB website. This step includes submitting any required documentation and paying the examination fee.
4. **Scheduling the Exam**: Once your application is approved, you'll receive instructions to schedule your exam at a nearby testing center.
5. **Preparation and Study**: Dedicate time to study and review, focusing on areas outlined in the PTCE content outline. Utilize practice exams to gauge your readiness.
6. **Taking the Exam**: Approach the exam with confidence, armed with thorough preparation and knowledge.
7. **Certification and Beyond**: Upon passing, you'll receive your certification, opening doors to enhanced career opportunities and recognition in your field.

This guide is designed to navigate you through each of these steps, providing the knowledge, strategies, and confidence needed to achieve your PTCB certification. Embrace this journey with dedication and focus, and the rewards of your effort will be manifold and lasting.

Acing the PTCB exam isn't just about knowing the information – it's about studying smarter, not harder. Let's create a study strategy that works for you:

Study Techniques with Science on Their Side:

- **Active Recall: Don't Just Reread:** Quiz yourself! Flashcards, practice questions, and even explaining concepts out loud force your brain to actively retrieve information, making it stick better than simply staring at your notes.

- **Spaced Repetition: Beat the Forgetting Curve:** Instead of cramming, spread your studying over time with shorter, focused sessions. This helps your brain solidify the knowledge and avoid last-minute overload.

Time Management: Make Every Minute Count

- **The Pomodoro Technique:** This is your focus superpower. Set a timer for 25 minutes of uninterrupted study, followed by a short 5-minute break. Repeat this cycle a few times, then take a longer break. This helps combat procrastination and keeps your brain fresh.
- **Prioritize & Conquer:** Break down your study topics into bite-sized chunks. Tackle the most challenging or heavily-weighted subjects first when you're most alert.
- **Find Your Study Zone:** Is it a quiet corner in the library? A cozy coffee shop? Discover where you focus best and make that your study sanctuary.

Real-Life Scheduling

- **Analyze Your Time:** Be honest about how much free time you *realistically* have each week. Block out those dedicated study slots in your calendar and treat them like unbreakable appointments.
- **Be Flexible but Persistent:** Life throws curveballs. If you miss a study session, don't give up! Rearrange your schedule and squeeze it in somewhere else. Consistency is key.
- **Small Wins Matter:** Don't aim for marathon study sessions right off the bat. Start with shorter bursts and gradually increase the time as your focus builds.

Additional Tips:

- **Study Groups:** Find like-minded peers for collaboration and motivation.
- **Reward Yourself:** Set mini-goals and celebrate your progress along the way!

Now Here's how to break down PTCB questions and stay calm under pressure:

Question Analysis: Decode the Ask

- **Keywords matter:** Focus on words like "EXCEPT," "MOST," or "BEST." These words guide you to the core of what the question is asking.
- **Case-Based Questions:** First, identify the key patient information (age, medical conditions, allergies). Then, focus on what the question specifically asks about that scenario.

Eliminating the Obvious

- **Outliers Beware:** If an answer seems wildly out of range or contradicts basic pharmacy knowledge, it's likely a red flag.
- **Common Sense is Key:** Sometimes the most straightforward answer is the correct one. Don't overthink it.

Time Management: Pace Yourself

- **Know Your Sections:** Be aware of how many questions are in each section of the PTCB exam and the allotted time. Don't dwell too long on any one question.
- **Mark and Return:** If you're stumped, flag the question and move on. Come back to it with a fresh perspective once you've tackled the rest of the section.
- **Educated Guesses:** If you're truly unsure, eliminate the obviously wrong choices and make your best guess between the remaining options.

Taming those Test-Day Jitters

- **Deep Breaths for Focus:** Before the exam starts, take a few slow, deep breaths. Inhale for a count of 4, hold for 2, and exhale for 4. Repeat. This helps calm your nervous system.
- **Positive Self-Talk:** Remind yourself of all the hard work you've done. Instead of "I'm going to fail," tell yourself, "I've prepared for this, and I'm ready to give it my best."

- **One Question at a Time:** Don't let your mind race ahead. Focus solely on the question in front of you.

Additional Tips:
- **Practice Tests:** Simulate the exam experience to build stamina and identify areas where you need to brush up.
- **Good Night's Sleep:** Being well-rested is essential for clear thinking on test day.
- **Fuel Your Brain:** Eat a balanced breakfast and stay hydrated to keep your mind sharp.

Remember, the PTCB exam tests your knowledge and your ability to think critically. Approach it with confidence and those strategic techniques in your toolkit!

I. Pharmacology for Technicians:

Get ready to unlock the fascinating world of medications! The 'Pharmacology for Technicians' section is your foundation for understanding how drugs work, why they're prescribed, and your crucial role in ensuring patients use them safely and effectively.

Here's a taste of what we'll be exploring:
- **The ABCs of Drugs:** We'll decode medication names (generics vs. brands), learn how to navigate those long leaflets in medicine boxes (drug package inserts), and understand how to advise patients about those pesky auxiliary labels.
- **It's All About Action:** We'll explore how drugs travel through the body, the different ways they work their magic (or cause side effects), and why some medications just don't mix well with others.
- **Calculations for Safety:** You'll sharpen your dosage calculation skills, making sure those prescriptions get filled with the utmost accuracy.
- **High-Alert Medications:** Learn about those extra-important drugs, like insulin and chemotherapy, where your attention to detail plays a vital role in keeping patients safe.
- **Beyond the Pharmacy Counter:** Discover how medication knowledge translates to different settings, from the bustling community pharmacy to the fast-paced hospital environment.

Think of this section as your guide to transforming medication names from mysterious jargon into tools of healing. By the time we're finished, you'll be ready to assist pharmacists in ensuring patients understand their medications and use them with confidence. Let's dive in!

While generic substitutions often save patients money and provide the same therapeutic effect, there are instances where "Dispense as Written" (DAW) is critical for patient safety. Let's explore those scenarios:

Narrow Therapeutic Index (NTI) Drugs:
- **Tiny Changes, Big Consequences:** NTI drugs have a small window between a safe dose and a dangerous one. Slight variations between generic and brand versions can push drug levels outside the effective range. Examples include:
  - Warfarin (blood thinner): Inconsistent blood clotting levels can lead to bleeding or dangerous clots.
  - Levothyroxine (thyroid hormone): Different formulations can cause fluctuations in thyroid function, making it harder to find the optimal dose.
  - Anticonvulsants (seizure control): Even subtle changes can trigger seizures or increase side effects.

Complex Formulations: It's Not Just the Active Ingredient

- **Fillers Matter:** The inactive ingredients (binders, fillers) impact how and where a drug breaks down and gets absorbed in the body. Some medications depend on this controlled release for effectiveness. Examples include:
    - Extended-release tablets: Designed to dissolve slowly over time. Switching to a generic could mean the drug is released too quickly or unevenly.
    - Modified-release capsules: These use special coatings or beads. A generic substitution might change the absorption profile unpredictably.

Beyond the Obvious:
- **Patient Allergies:** A generic might contain an inactive ingredient the patient is allergic to, even if the active drug itself is fine.
- **Patient Comfort:** If a patient has been stable on a brand-name medication and switching causes anxiety or distrust, this can negatively impact their health.

Important Things to Remember
- **The Pharmacist's Role:** Always discuss a DAW prescription with the pharmacist to confirm the medical necessity and to ensure patient safety.
- **Communication is Key:** If a generic substitution is considered, the pharmacist should have an open conversation with the prescriber.

Prescribing DAW, when necessary, is about prioritizing patient safety over cost savings. As a pharmacy technician, your understanding of these situations will make you an even more valuable asset to your team!

Now lets get into the world of extended-release and modified-release medications, where staying brand-name can make all the difference for your patients.

Extended-Release (ER): Slow and Steady
These are designed to release the drug gradually over time, minimizing peaks and valleys in blood levels.
- Example: Bupropion XL (antidepressant) - Switching to generic could lead to the medication wearing off sooner, affecting mood stability and potentially increasing depression symptoms.
- Example: Oxycodone ER (pain reliever): A generic might release the medication too quickly, leading to breakthrough pain and increased risk of overdose or side effects.

Modified-Release (MR): It's about Timing and Location
These modify how and where the medication is released in the body, often targeting specific conditions.
- Example: Mesalamine DR (for inflammatory bowel disease): The coating ensures the drug is released in the intestines, where it's needed. A generic might dissolve too early, reducing its effectiveness.
- Example: Venlafaxine XR (antidepressant): Special capsule beads control release. Switching could lead to faster absorption, causing increased nausea and other side effects.

Why This Matters for Patients
- Inconsistent Drug Levels: Generics might have different release rates than the brand. This impacts how much and how often the medication is available in the body.
- Treatment Failure: Unpredictable drug levels could mean less symptom control (e.g., worsening pain, or uncontrolled seizures).
- Increased Side Effects: Sudden peaks in drug concentration can intensify side effects, making patients less likely to continue the medication properly.
- Safety Risks: With some drugs, sudden spikes or drops in concentration could be dangerous (e.g., irregular heartbeats from certain blood pressure medications).

- Not all generics are created equal: Even with the same active ingredient, release mechanisms can significantly differ.
- Check the Label: Look for markings like "XL," "ER," "CR" (controlled-release), "DR" (delayed-release), or "SA" (sustained action). These signal potential issues with substitution.
- Patient-Centered Approach: Brand-name might be necessary for patients who have been stable on a specific formulation or have conditions particularly sensitive to changes in drug levels.

As a pharmacy technician, your vigilance helps ensure patients get the consistent therapy they need!

Tiered formularies are a structured system insurance companies use to categorize medications based on various factors, including cost, efficacy, and therapeutic necessity. Typically divided into multiple levels or "tiers," each tier represents a different cost-sharing obligation for the patient, influencing their out-of-pocket expenses.

Tier Structure:
- **Tier 1**: Usually includes the lowest-cost medications, predominantly generics. Patients pay the lowest co-payment.
- **Tier 2**: Generally covers preferred brand-name medications with moderate co-payments.
- **Tier 3**: Consists of non-preferred brand-name medications, often accompanied by higher co-payments.
- **Specialty Tiers**: May include high-cost or specialty medications, often requiring a percentage of the drug's cost rather than a fixed co-payment, leading to significant patient expenses.

Impact on Patient Costs: Patients are incentivized to choose lower-tiered, often generic, medications through lower out-of-pocket costs, promoting cost-effective prescribing practices. When a prescriber recommends a higher-tier medication, such as a specific brand-name drug without a generic equivalent or when a generic isn't therapeutically equivalent, patients may face higher costs. This system directly influences medication adherence, as the financial burden can lead to patients delaying or forgoing necessary treatments.

Pharmacy Technician's Role in Prior Authorizations: When a prescribed medication falls into a higher tier or is not covered by the patient's insurance plan, a prior authorization (PA) may be required. This is where the role of pharmacy technicians becomes crucial:
- **Initiating PAs**: Pharmacy technicians often take the lead in initiating the PA process, gathering necessary information from the patient's records and coordinating with the prescriber's office.
- **Communication**: They act as liaisons between the insurance company, the prescriber, and the patient, communicating the status of PAs and explaining the implications for medication costs and alternatives.
- **Alternative Solutions**: Technicians might assist in identifying lower-tier alternatives or generic medications that are therapeutically equivalent but more cost-effective, advising the prescriber on possible switches to ease the patient's financial burden.

Understanding tiered formularies and adeptly navigating the prior authorization process are essential skills for pharmacy technicians, ensuring patients receive their medications in a timely and cost-effective manner while maintaining the therapeutic integrity of their treatment plans. This nuanced understanding of insurance formularies directly impacts patient care and pharmacy operations, highlighting the critical role of pharmacy technicians in the broader healthcare system.

Rebates and pricing agreements between drug manufacturers and Pharmacy Benefit Managers (PBMs) play a significant role in shaping the landscape of medication costs within the healthcare system. These financial arrangements can have profound implications on drug pricing, insurance formularies, and ultimately, patient accessibility to medications.

Rebates and Pricing Agreements:
Manufacturers often provide rebates to PBMs in exchange for favorable placement of their drugs on insurance formularies, which are lists of medications that an insurance plan prefers and covers. These rebates are not discounts passed directly to consumers; instead, they are negotiated after the point of sale and are intended to influence the PBM's drug coverage decisions.

Impact on Medication Costs:

Formulary Placement: Drugs receiving favorable formulary placement due to rebates might not always be the most cost-effective or clinically effective option. This can lead to higher overall costs for both the healthcare system and patients, especially if lower-cost alternatives are placed on higher tiers or excluded from coverage.
Increased Insurance Premiums: While rebates can lower costs for insurance plans and PBMs, these savings are not always passed on to consumers. Instead, they may contribute to higher insurance premiums over time.
Conflict of Interest:
The rebate system can create conflicts of interest:

PBM's Financial Incentives: PBMs may have financial incentives to favor high-rebate drugs, regardless of their cost-effectiveness or clinical value for patients. This can skew formulary designs away from the most beneficial or economical medications.
Manufacturer Influence: Drug manufacturers might prioritize rebate strategies over research and development for more effective or affordable medications, potentially stifacing innovation and competition.
Impact on Patient Accessibility:

Access to Preferred Medications: Patients may face challenges accessing the most suitable medications if those drugs are not favorably listed on their plan's formulary due to the absence of rebates or pricing agreements.
Out-of-Pocket Costs: Patients may incur higher out-of-pocket expenses for medications that are placed on higher formulary tiers or are not covered, impacting adherence and outcomes.
Pharmacy Technician's Role:
Pharmacy technicians, at the intersection of healthcare delivery and patient care, often navigate these complexities firsthand. They may assist in managing formulary restrictions, communicating with prescribers about alternative medications, and helping patients understand their insurance coverage. Their role in facilitating medication access amidst the backdrop of rebate-driven formulary placements underscores the critical nature of their position in healthcare.

Understanding the intricate dynamics between rebates, PBMs, and medication costs is essential for healthcare professionals, including pharmacy technicians, to advocate for policies and practices that prioritize patient care and access over financial incentives.

Locating stability information for reconstituted medications is a critical task for pharmacy technicians, especially those involved in compounding and preparing medications. Stability data ensure that reconstituted medications maintain their efficacy, safety, and quality up to the point of administration. Here's how to find this information across various references and why understanding diluent type, storage temperature, and stability duration is essential.

Reference Sources:

Drug Package Inserts: Often the first go-to source, package inserts provided by manufacturers contain comprehensive information, including stability data for reconstituted products. Look for sections titled "Reconstitution," "Storage," or "Stability" for specific instructions on diluents, temperatures, and time frames.

Pharmacy Compounding References: Texts like the US Pharmacopeia (USP), especially chapters on compounding and stability, and the American Society of Health-System Pharmacists (ASHP) guidelines provide detailed stability information for a wide range of medications and compounding scenarios.

Online Databases and Tools: Platforms like Lexicomp, Micromedex, and the Trissel's™ Stability of Compounded Formulations offer up-to-date, searchable databases with stability information on numerous drugs, including those not directly provided by the manufacturer.

Peer-Reviewed Journals: Research articles and studies published in pharmacy and medical journals often contain stability studies conducted by researchers, providing data on various reconstitution aspects not available in standard references.

Key Factors to Consider:

Diluent Used: The type of diluent (e.g., sterile water, saline, dextrose) can significantly affect a drug's stability post-reconstitution. Certain drugs may only be stable with specific diluents, and incompatible diluents can lead to reduced potency or increased risk of adverse reactions.

Storage Temperature: Stability data will specify the optimal storage temperature range (e.g., refrigerated at 2-8°C, room temperature). Deviating from recommended temperatures can accelerate drug degradation, impacting its effectiveness.

Duration of Stability: This indicates how long the reconstituted medication remains stable and effective. Exceeding this period can result in a loss of drug potency, risking therapeutic failure or harm.

Implications for Pharmacy Technicians:

Understanding and applying stability information is paramount for pharmacy technicians to ensure patient safety and medication efficacy. Technicians must:

Accurately interpret stability data from reliable sources.
Apply this information during the reconstitution process, adhering to specified diluents, temperatures, and time limits.
Label reconstituted medications with the correct "use by" date and storage instructions to prevent misuse.
Educate patients or healthcare providers on proper storage and handling of reconstituted medications.

The ability to locate and apply stability information for reconstituted medications is a fundamental skill for pharmacy technicians, underpinning safe and effective medication preparation and use.

The FDA's pregnancy risk categories and the LactMed database offer crucial information for counseling women of childbearing potential about medication safety during pregnancy and lactation. Understanding the nuances between these resources is key for healthcare professionals, including pharmacy technicians, to provide accurate and comprehensive advice.

FDA Pregnancy Risk Categories: Historically, the FDA classified medications into five pregnancy risk categories (A, B, C, D, X) based on potential risks to the fetus:

- **Category A**: Controlled studies show no risk.
- **Category B**: Animal studies show no risk, but no controlled studies in women or animal studies have shown a risk that wasn't confirmed in women.
- **Category C**: Animal studies have shown a risk, no controlled studies in women, or studies in women and animals are unavailable.
- **Category D**: Evidence of human fetal risk exists, but benefits may warrant use in pregnant women despite risks.
- **Category X**: Risks clearly outweigh any possible benefits; contraindicated in pregnancy.

In 2015, the FDA began transitioning to a new labeling system to provide more detailed information about a drug's risks during pregnancy and lactation, moving away from the A-X system. This new approach includes a narrative summary of the risks, a discussion of the data supporting that summary, and relevant information to help healthcare providers make prescribing decisions.

LactMed Database: LactMed, part of the National Library of Medicine's TOXNET system, is a specialized database focusing on drugs and other chemicals to which breastfeeding mothers might be exposed. It provides detailed information on drug levels in breast milk and infant blood, potential effects on breastfeeding infants and lactation, and alternative drugs to consider. The key advantages of LactMed include:

- **Comprehensive Information**: Offers detailed summaries of studies related to lactation and drug safety, including quantitative data on drug concentrations in breast milk.
- **Updated Regularly**: Reflects the most current research findings, making it a dynamic and reliable resource.
- **Practical Recommendations**: Provides guidance on monitoring or whether an alternative medication is advisable, assisting healthcare providers in making informed decisions.

Importance of Counseling Women of Childbearing Potential: Counseling women of childbearing potential on medication use during pregnancy and lactation is vital due to the potential risks to fetal and infant health. Healthcare providers should:

- Evaluate the necessity of medication, considering the condition being treated and the potential risks and benefits.
- Discuss alternative treatments or medications that might be safer during pregnancy and breastfeeding.
- Emphasize the importance of consulting healthcare providers before starting, stopping, or changing any medication during pregnancy and lactation.

Pharmacy technicians, equipped with knowledge from resources like the FDA's pregnancy risk information and the LactMed database, play a supportive role in educating and guiding women of childbearing potential in making informed decisions about medication use, ensuring safety for both mothers and their children.

When a prescriber questions a potential drug-drug interaction flagged by pharmacy software, a pharmacy technician must take a systematic approach to validate and address the concern. Utilizing resources like Lexicomp and Micromedex allows for a comprehensive review of the interaction, its clinical significance, and the primary literature supporting the data. Here's how a technician can navigate this scenario:

1. Comparing Interaction Severity in Lexicomp and Micromedex:
Access Both Databases: Begin by accessing the drug-drug interaction information for the medications in question in both Lexicomp and Micromedex. These platforms categorize interactions by severity levels, such as "major," "moderate," and "minor" in Lexicomp, and "contraindicated," "major," "moderate," and "minor" in Micromedex.
Analyze Severity Ratings: Compare the severity ratings assigned to the interaction by both databases. Note any discrepancies or agreements in the classification, as this can influence the clinical decision-making process.

2. Analyzing Primary Literature Cited:
Locate References: Both Lexicomp and Micromedex provide references for their interaction data, often including primary literature, clinical guidelines, or expert consensus documents. Locate these references within the interaction detail sections.
Review Study Summaries: Briefly review the summaries or abstracts of the cited studies to understand the basis of the interaction, the population studied, and the clinical outcomes observed. Pay special attention to any recommendations or cautions mentioned in these studies.

3. Determining Next Steps:
Document Findings: Concisely document the severity levels from both databases and key points from the primary literature. Include any consensus or discrepancies found between the databases.
Consult with the Pharmacist: Present the documented findings to the supervising pharmacist, highlighting the interaction's severity levels, the evidence base, and any discrepancies between the databases. This will enable the pharmacist to make an informed decision on how to proceed.
Communicate with the Prescriber: Based on the pharmacist's assessment, assist in communicating the findings to the prescriber. This may involve explaining the basis of the interaction concern, the evidence reviewed, and any recommendations from the pharmacist, such as monitoring parameters, dosage adjustments, or alternative therapies.

4. Follow-Up Actions:
Document the Interaction and Resolution: Ensure that the interaction concern and the resolution decided by the pharmacist are documented in the patient's record. This is crucial for future reference and continuity of care.
Patient Counseling: If the decision involves changes to the patient's medication regimen, be prepared to assist in counseling the patient on these changes, emphasizing the importance of adherence to the new regimen and what to monitor for in terms of efficacy and side effects. By following these steps, a pharmacy technician can efficiently facilitate the review of drug-drug interactions, supporting the pharmacist in making evidence-based decisions to ensure patient safety and optimal therapeutic outcomes.

A black box warning signals a serious safety concern, so finding those missing monitoring details is crucial! Let's map out your investigation as a pharmacy technician:
1. Recognize the Red Flag:

- Understand what a black box warning means: It's the FDA's strongest warning, alerting prescribers and patients to potentially severe side effects or risks.
- Check the package insert thoroughly: Sometimes there's a basic mention of monitoring (e.g., "monitor blood counts"), but not the specifics you need.

2. Initiate Your Search:
- **Micromedex or Lexicomp:** These are your go-to comprehensive drug references. Search for the medication and head to the "Monitoring" or "Warnings/Precautions" sections. These databases often:
  - Detail the type and frequency of lab tests or other monitoring needed.
  - Explain why this monitoring is important and what changes might warrant contacting the prescriber.
- **Specialized References:** Depending on the medication, specialized resources might be helpful:
  - Oncology drugs: Resources detailing chemotherapy protocols or management of specific side effects.
  - Psychiatric drugs: Guides on monitoring for movement disorders or metabolic changes.
- **Trusted Websites:**
  - FDA Website: Search for recent safety alerts or updated prescribing information on the drug.
  - Manufacturer Website: Sometimes they provide patient education materials with additional monitoring details.

3. Collaboration is Key:
- Team Up with the Pharmacist: Don't hesitate to ask the pharmacist for guidance in finding the needed information and determining how best to counsel the patient.

Example Scenario:
- Medication: Atypical Antipsychotic
- Black Box Warning: Increased mortality in elderly patients with dementia-related psychosis.
- Monitoring Missing: How frequently to assess for cognitive changes or worsening behavior.
- Where to Look: Micromedex, FDA website (for safety alerts specific to this drug class), and guidelines for dementia care.
- Black box warnings are serious, but sometimes lack clear action steps.
- Don't just rely on the package insert – your research skills are vital for patient safety.
- Knowing where to search empowers you to provide the best possible patient care!

Federal requirements and individual state laws both play pivotal roles in determining the use of auxiliary labels on medication packaging, yet they often operate on different levels of specificity and stringency. Understanding the interplay between these regulations is crucial for pharmacy technicians to ensure compliance and safeguard patient health.

Federal Requirements:
At the federal level, regulations primarily focus on broad standards for medication labeling to ensure patient safety and drug efficacy. These include the Food and Drug Administration (FDA) mandates on labeling, which encompass:

Identification of the drug: Name, dosage form, and strength.
Usage instructions: Clear directions for the intended use, dosage, frequency, and route of administration.
Warnings and precautions: Information on potential drug interactions, side effects, and contraindications.

While federal guidelines establish the foundational requirements for medication labels, they often allow room for interpretation and flexibility, enabling states to adapt or expand these rules to address specific local needs or concerns.

State Laws:
Individual states may enact laws that require auxiliary labels for certain medications or conditions, often based on local public health priorities, historical incidents, or emerging health trends. These state-specific regulations can be more stringent than federal requirements, necessitating additional warnings or instructions. For instance:

Controlled Substances: Some states require specific auxiliary labels for opioids or other controlled substances, such as warnings about addiction risks or safe storage instructions to prevent misuse.
Allergy Alerts: Certain states might mandate explicit auxiliary labels for medications containing common allergens, like peanuts or sulfites, even if federal law doesn't require such specificity.
Environmental Concerns: In areas with specific environmental concerns, like water system contamination, states might require auxiliary labels advising against flushing medications down the toilet.
Navigating Federal and State Regulations:
Pharmacy technicians must be adept at navigating both federal and state requirements for auxiliary labels. This involves:

Staying Informed: Regularly updating their knowledge of state-specific pharmacy laws and regulations, as these can change more frequently than federal laws.
Software Utilization: Efficiently using pharmacy software systems that can flag the need for specific auxiliary labels based on the patient's location and medication prescribed.
Collaboration with Pharmacists: When discrepancies or uncertainties arise, technicians should consult with pharmacists to clarify the necessity and wording of auxiliary labels, ensuring they meet both federal and state mandates.
Implications for Practice:
Stricter state regulations necessitate a heightened level of diligence from pharmacy staff. Technicians, in collaboration with pharmacists, play a critical role in interpreting and applying these laws to ensure that every medication dispensed meets the requisite legal standards for labeling, thus safeguarding patient health and adherence to therapy. This proactive approach in managing auxiliary labels reinforces the pharmacy's commitment to patient education and safety.

Regulatory requirements for auxiliary labels on unit-dose repackaged medications are designed to ensure patient safety and medication efficacy, governed by guidelines from entities like the U.S. Food and Drug Administration (FDA) and the United States Pharmacopeia (USP). These standards stipulate that labels must provide critical information, even in a condensed format suitable for smaller, unit-dose packages, contrasting with the more comprehensive labeling found on multi-dose containers.

Essential Elements for Unit-Dose Repackaged Medications:

Drug Name and Strength: The generic or brand name of the medication and its potency must be clearly stated to avoid confusion with similar-sounding or looking drugs.
Lot or Batch Number: This identifier links the unit-dose package to a specific manufacturing batch, crucial for tracking in the event of a recall.

Expiration Date: Defined as the date until which the repackaged medication is expected to remain stable and effective, considering the original manufacturer's expiration date and any factors that might shorten it upon repackaging.

Manufacturer or Repackager Information: Identification of the original manufacturer or the entity responsible for repackaging, ensuring accountability.

Bar Code: Includes a scannable barcode that conforms to standards like the National Drug Code (NDC), facilitating accurate dispensing and inventory management.

Differences from Multi-Dose Container Labeling:

Condensed Information: Due to the limited space on unit-dose packaging, auxiliary labels must convey essential information concisely, focusing on what's most critical for safe administration.

Absence of Comprehensive Instructions: Unlike multi-dose containers, which often include detailed dosing instructions, precautions, and potential side effects, unit-dose packages typically omit this extensive detail. Instead, this information might be provided separately by the healthcare provider or in accompanying patient information leaflets.

Storage Conditions: While multi-dose containers might provide detailed storage instructions directly on the label, unit-dose packages may have more generalized storage information due to space constraints, relying on healthcare professionals to understand and apply appropriate storage practices based on their knowledge of the medication.

Regulatory Compliance:

Pharmacy technicians must ensure that repackaging practices for unit-dose medications comply with regulatory standards, maintaining the integrity and safety of the medication. This involves:

Regularly reviewing and adhering to guidelines from the FDA, USP, and relevant state pharmacy boards. Employing meticulous attention to detail when applying auxiliary labels to unit-dose packages, ensuring legibility and accuracy.

Staying informed about changes in regulations and best practices related to medication repackaging and labeling. Auxiliary labels on unit-dose repackaged medications must include critical information that ensures patient safety while adapting to the smaller packaging format. Pharmacy technicians play a vital role in ensuring these labels meet regulatory requirements, supporting safe medication use.

When dispensing medications adorned with multiple auxiliary warning labels, it's crucial to convey important information effectively without overwhelming the patient. Here's a structured checklist to guide pharmacy technicians and pharmacists in prioritizing and delivering counseling points succinctly:

Checklist for Counseling on Medications with Multiple Auxiliary Labels

1. Identify Critical Warnings:
- Highlight life-threatening warnings first (e.g., risk of anaphylaxis).
- Address warnings that significantly impact daily activities (e.g., drowsiness, dizziness).

2. Discuss Dosage and Administration:
- Confirm understanding of dosing schedule and route of administration.
- Emphasize instructions specific to the medication's form (e.g., with food, whole tablet).

3. Explain Side Effects:
- Briefly discuss common side effects.
- Prioritize severe side effects that require immediate medical attention.

4. Storage and Handling:
- Provide clear instructions on storage requirements.

- Discuss handling precautions, if applicable (e.g., wear gloves, don't cut or crush).

5. Interactions and Contraindications:
- Mention critical drug-drug and drug-food interactions.
- Highlight any contraindications based on patient's known medical history.

6. Special Instructions:
- Cover any unique auxiliary warnings (e.g., exposure to sunlight, alcohol consumption).
- Discuss the importance of adherence to therapy and not skipping doses.

7. Management of Missed Doses:
- Instruct on what to do if a dose is missed, avoiding double dosing.

8. Monitoring and Follow-up:
- Advise on any necessary monitoring (e.g., blood pressure, blood sugar).
- Encourage follow-up visits with their healthcare provider.

9. Disposal Instructions:
- Provide guidance on how to safely dispose of unused or expired medication.

Strategies to Prioritize Information Without Overwhelming the Patient
- **Simplify Language**: Use plain language and avoid medical jargon to enhance understanding.
- **Personalize the Counseling**: Tailor the information based on the patient's lifestyle, condition, and medication history.
- **Engage Visually**: Use the medication and its packaging as visual aids to reinforce points.
- **Empower with Questions**: Encourage the patient to ask questions to clarify doubts and engage them in the conversation.
- **Summarize Key Points**: Conclude with a brief summary of the most critical counseling points.
- **Provide Written Information**: Offer printed materials or direct them to reputable sources for additional reading.
- **Schedule Follow-ups**: Recommend follow-up consultations to address any emerging questions or concerns.

Employing this checklist and strategies ensures comprehensive and patient-centric counseling, enhancing medication safety and adherence while mitigating the risk of overwhelming the patient with information.

The phrasing of auxiliary warnings on medication labels plays a pivotal role in patient comprehension, adherence, and safety. Let's examine the auxiliary warning "May cause drowsiness" and its alternative "Do not drive or operate machinery," delving into how different wordings can influence patient behavior and understanding.

"May Cause Drowsiness"
Implications:
- **Perception of Possibility**: The word "may" suggests that drowsiness is a potential, not guaranteed, side effect. This can lead patients to believe they might not be affected, possibly underestimating the risk.
- **Focus on Side Effect**: This phrasing centers on the side effect itself, potentially lacking clear guidance on how to mitigate risk.

Patient Behavior:
- Patients might continue their activities, including driving, until they personally experience drowsiness, which could pose safety risks.

"Do not drive or operate machinery"
Implications:

- **Direct Instruction**: This version provides explicit behavioral guidance, leaving little room for interpretation and highlighting the severity of the risk.
- **Action-Oriented**: By focusing on the action to avoid, it directly addresses safety precautions patients should take.

Patient Behavior:
- Patients are more likely to heed the warning and avoid potentially dangerous activities, even if they don't immediately feel drowsy, reducing risk of accidents.

Impact on Patient Understanding and Adherence
- **Clarity and Directness**: Clear, action-oriented instructions tend to be more effective in guiding patient behavior. Patients are more likely to adhere to straightforward directives ("Do not drive") than interpret the implications of a side effect ("May cause drowsiness").
- **Risk Perception**: How a warning is worded can significantly impact a patient's perception of risk. Direct warnings can heighten perceived risk, encouraging more cautious behavior.
- **Empowerment vs. Fear**: While direct instructions can promote safety, they should be balanced to avoid instilling unnecessary fear. Patients need to feel empowered to manage their treatment effectively, not anxious about potential side effects.
- **Cultural and Linguistic Considerations**: The patient's cultural background and language proficiency can affect the interpretation of warnings. It's crucial to tailor the language to the patient's level of understanding, potentially offering translations or visual aids for clarity.

The wording of auxiliary warnings is not merely a matter of semantics but a critical component of patient care. Pharmacy professionals should strive for clarity, directness, and relevance in their communication, ensuring that patients are well-informed about their medications and can take necessary precautions to safeguard their health and well-being.

The combination of an Angiotensin-Converting Enzyme (ACE) inhibitor and a thiazide diuretic is a well-established therapeutic strategy for managing hypertension, particularly in patients with resistant hypertension, where blood pressure remains above target levels despite the use of multiple antihypertensive agents. This combination leverages the complementary mechanisms of action and synergistic effects of the two drug classes, offering several potential benefits.

Complementary Mechanisms:
ACE Inhibitors:

ACE inhibitors work by blocking the conversion of angiotensin I to angiotensin II, a potent vasoconstrictor, thereby decreasing vascular resistance and blood pressure.
They also reduce aldosterone secretion, leading to a decrease in sodium and water retention by the kidneys, albeit to a lesser extent.
Additionally, ACE inhibitors confer renal protective effects, particularly beneficial in hypertensive patients with diabetes or chronic kidney disease.
Thiazide Diuretics:

Thiazide diuretics reduce blood pressure primarily by decreasing the reabsorption of sodium and water in the distal convoluted tubule of the kidneys, leading to increased urine output (diuresis).
This diuretic effect results in a decrease in blood volume and, subsequently, a reduction in cardiac output and blood pressure.

Thiazides also have a vasodilatory effect on the peripheral vasculature, contributing further to their antihypertensive action.

Synergistic Effects:

Volume Reduction and Vasodilation: The initial diuretic effect of thiazides reduces blood volume, which can activate the renin-angiotensin system (RAS). ACE inhibitors counter this effect by inhibiting the RAS, enhancing the overall antihypertensive efficacy and mitigating compensatory mechanisms that can diminish the effectiveness of diuretic therapy.

Potassium Balance: Thiazide diuretics can lead to hypokalemia (low potassium levels), whereas ACE inhibitors can increase potassium levels by reducing aldosterone secretion. Together, they can help maintain potassium balance, reducing the risk of adverse effects associated with abnormal potassium levels.

Potential Benefits for Patients with Resistant Hypertension:

Enhanced Blood Pressure Control: The complementary actions of ACE inhibitors and thiazide diuretics can lead to more significant reductions in blood pressure compared to monotherapy, especially in resistant hypertension.

Cardiovascular and Renal Protection: ACE inhibitors offer protective effects against cardiovascular events and renal disease progression, benefits that are particularly important in patients with resistant hypertension who are at higher risk for cardiovascular morbidity and mortality.

Improved Adherence: The availability of fixed-dose combination pills containing both an ACE inhibitor and a thiazide diuretic can simplify treatment regimens, potentially improving medication adherence and patient outcomes. The combination of an ACE inhibitor and a thiazide diuretic for hypertension management, especially in resistant cases, capitalizes on their complementary mechanisms and synergistic effects, providing enhanced blood pressure control and additional cardiovascular and renal protective benefits. This strategic approach underscores the importance of understanding pharmacological interactions and patient-specific factors in optimizing hypertension therapy.

Calcium Channel Blockers (CCBs) are a diverse group of medications widely used in the management of hypertension. They function by inhibiting the entry of calcium ions into cardiac and smooth muscle cells, leading to vasodilation and decreased blood pressure. CCBs are broadly categorized into two main types: dihydropyridines and non-dihydropyridines, each with distinct pharmacological profiles and clinical applications.

Dihydropyridine-Type CCBs
Examples: Amlodipine, Nifedipine, Felodipine

Primary Effects:

Vasodilation: Dihydropyridines predominantly act on the vascular smooth muscle, causing significant vasodilation. This leads to a reduction in systemic vascular resistance and, consequently, lowers blood pressure.

Minimal Cardiac Effects: Unlike non-dihydropyridines, dihydropyridines have minimal direct effects on the heart, such as heart rate or contractility, making them suitable for patients with certain cardiac conditions.

Clinical Use:

Hypertension: They are widely prescribed for hypertension, particularly when systolic blood pressure reduction is a primary goal.

Angina: Some dihydropyridines, like amlodipine, are used in managing chronic stable angina due to their ability to decrease afterload and myocardial oxygen demand.

Non-Dihydropyridine-Type CCBs

Examples: Diltiazem, Verapamil

Primary Effects:

Cardiac Effects: Non-dihydropyridines exert significant effects on the heart, reducing heart rate and contractility, which can be beneficial in conditions like arrhythmias.

Vasodilation: They also cause vasodilation but to a lesser extent compared to dihydropyridines, contributing to their antihypertensive effect.

Clinical Use:

Hypertension: Used in hypertension, particularly in patients who may benefit from the added heart rate control.

Cardiac Conditions: Ideal for patients with supraventricular tachycardias, atrial fibrillation, or flutter due to their slowing effect on the atrioventricular (AV) node.

When One Might Be Preferred Over the Other

Dihydropyridines: Preferred in uncomplicated hypertension, especially when a significant reduction in systolic blood pressure is needed without impacting heart rate. They are also chosen for patients with concurrent stable angina.

Non-Dihydropyridines: Selected for patients with hypertension who require heart rate control or have specific supraventricular cardiac arrhythmias. Their use requires caution in patients with heart failure due to their negative inotropic effects. The choice between dihydropyridine and non-dihydropyridine CCBs in hypertension management is guided by the patient's overall cardiovascular profile and specific therapeutic goals. Understanding the distinct properties of these CCB subclasses enables healthcare professionals to tailor hypertension therapy to each patient's unique needs, optimizing outcomes while minimizing risks.

Calcium Channel Blockers (CCBs) are a diverse group of medications widely used in the management of hypertension. They function by inhibiting the entry of calcium ions into cardiac and smooth muscle cells, leading to vasodilation and decreased blood pressure. CCBs are broadly categorized into two main types: dihydropyridines and non-dihydropyridines, each with distinct pharmacological profiles and clinical applications.

Dihydropyridine-Type CCBs

Examples: Amlodipine, Nifedipine, Felodipine

Primary Effects:

- **Vasodilation**: Dihydropyridines predominantly act on the vascular smooth muscle, causing significant vasodilation. This leads to a reduction in systemic vascular resistance and, consequently, lowers blood pressure.
- **Minimal Cardiac Effects**: Unlike non-dihydropyridines, dihydropyridines have minimal direct effects on the heart, such as heart rate or contractility, making them suitable for patients with certain cardiac conditions.

Clinical Use:

- **Hypertension**: They are widely prescribed for hypertension, particularly when systolic blood pressure reduction is a primary goal.

- **Angina**: Some dihydropyridines, like amlodipine, are used in managing chronic stable angina due to their ability to decrease afterload and myocardial oxygen demand.

Non-Dihydropyridine-Type CCBs

Examples: Diltiazem, Verapamil

Primary Effects:

- **Cardiac Effects**: Non-dihydropyridines exert significant effects on the heart, reducing heart rate and contractility, which can be beneficial in conditions like arrhythmias.
- **Vasodilation**: They also cause vasodilation but to a lesser extent compared to dihydropyridines, contributing to their antihypertensive effect.

Clinical Use:

- **Hypertension**: Used in hypertension, particularly in patients who may benefit from the added heart rate control.
- **Cardiac Conditions**: Ideal for patients with supraventricular tachycardias, atrial fibrillation, or flutter due to their slowing effect on the atrioventricular (AV) node.

When One Might Be Preferred Over the Other

- **Dihydropyridines**: Preferred in uncomplicated hypertension, especially when a significant reduction in systolic blood pressure is needed without impacting heart rate. They are also chosen for patients with concurrent stable angina.
- **Non-Dihydropyridines**: Selected for patients with hypertension who require heart rate control or have specific supraventricular cardiac arrhythmias. Their use requires caution in patients with heart failure due to their negative inotropic effects.

In summary, the choice between dihydropyridine and non-dihydropyridine CCBs in hypertension management is guided by the patient's overall cardiovascular profile and specific therapeutic goals. Understanding the distinct properties of these CCB subclasses enables healthcare professionals to tailor hypertension therapy to each patient's unique needs, optimizing outcomes while minimizing risks.

Detail how to counsel a patient prescribed amoxicillin for an ear infection. Include information on administration with/without food, the importance of finishing the full course, common side effects, and when to seek medical attention.

PART 1: Study Guide Responses.

Counseling a patient prescribed amoxicillin for an ear infection involves providing comprehensive and understandable information to ensure effective treatment and minimize complications. Here's a structured approach to patient counseling:

Administration Instructions

- **With or Without Food**: Inform the patient that amoxicillin can be taken with or without food. However, taking it with food may reduce gastrointestinal side effects like stomach upset. Advise drinking a full glass of water with each dose to aid absorption.
- **Dosage Schedule**: Emphasize the importance of adhering to the prescribed dosing schedule. For example, if prescribed three times daily, explain the doses should be spaced evenly throughout the day to maintain optimal blood levels of the antibiotic.

Importance of Completing the Full Course

- Stress the necessity of finishing the entire course of amoxicillin, even if symptoms improve before the medication is finished. Explain that stopping early can lead to the infection not being fully treated and may contribute to antibiotic resistance.

Common Side Effects

- **Gastrointestinal Issues**: Mention that amoxicillin may cause mild stomach upset, nausea, or diarrhea. Suggest eating small, frequent meals to alleviate discomfort.
- **Allergic Reactions**: Advise patients to watch for signs of an allergic reaction, such as rash, itching, or difficulty breathing, and to seek immediate medical attention if these occur.
- **Oral and Vaginal Thrush**: Inform about the possibility of developing thrush, a fungal infection, as a side effect. Symptoms include white patches in the mouth or a change in vaginal discharge.

When to Seek Medical Attention
- **Worsening Symptoms**: Advise patients to contact their healthcare provider if symptoms of the ear infection worsen or do not start to improve within a few days of starting amoxicillin.
- **Severe Side Effects**: Instruct patients to seek immediate medical care for severe diarrhea, bloody stools, severe abdominal pain, or any signs of an allergic reaction.

Additional Tips
- **Storage**: Instruct on proper storage of amoxicillin, typically at room temperature away from direct light, moisture, and heat. If given as a liquid suspension, mention whether refrigeration is necessary and the expiration after reconstitution.
- **Missed Dose**: If a dose is missed, advise taking it as soon as remembered unless it's almost time for the next dose. Instruct not to double up on doses to make up for the missed one.

By providing clear, structured information on amoxicillin administration, potential side effects, and the importance of completing the treatment course, pharmacy technicians can empower patients to manage their ear infection effectively while minimizing the risk of complications.

When a prescriber orders a Z-Pak (azithromycin) for a patient taking warfarin, careful consideration of the potential drug-drug interaction is paramount due to the serious implications it could have on patient safety. Azithromycin, a macrolide antibiotic, and warfarin, an anticoagulant, can interact in a way that may enhance the anticoagulant effects of warfarin, increasing the risk of bleeding.

Mechanism of Interaction
The exact mechanism by which azithromycin affects warfarin is not fully understood, but it is thought to be related to the antibiotic's ability to alter the gut flora. The gut flora plays a role in the metabolism of warfarin; thus, changes in gut flora could potentially enhance the effects of warfarin by increasing its bioavailability. Additionally, azithromycin can inhibit hepatic cytochrome P450 enzymes, though to a lesser extent than other macrolides, potentially leading to decreased metabolism of warfarin and increased warfarin plasma levels.

Necessity for INR Monitoring
Given the potential for increased bleeding risk, it is crucial to monitor the patient's International Normalized Ratio (INR) more closely when starting azithromycin therapy. The INR is a standardized measure of how long it takes the blood to clot and is used to adjust warfarin doses to maintain a balance between preventing clots and minimizing bleeding risk. Patients on warfarin typically have a target INR range based on their specific clinical indications. When introducing azithromycin, the patient's INR may rise above this therapeutic range, necessitating a warfarin dose adjustment.

Prioritizing Safety with the Pharmacist
As a pharmacy technician, upon identifying the prescription for azithromycin in a patient taking warfarin, the following steps should be taken to prioritize patient safety:

Flag the Interaction: Immediately bring the potential interaction to the pharmacist's attention for a comprehensive review.

Communication with Prescriber: The pharmacist may decide to contact the prescriber to discuss the identified interaction, confirm the necessity of azithromycin, and explore alternative antibiotics if deemed appropriate.

Patient Counseling: Assist the pharmacist in providing thorough counseling to the patient about the signs of increased bleeding (e.g., unusual bruising, prolonged bleeding from cuts, increased menstrual flow, bloody or tarry stools, coughing up blood) and the importance of promptly reporting these symptoms.

INR Monitoring: Ensure the patient is aware of the need for more frequent INR monitoring during and possibly after azithromycin treatment. Coordination with the patient's healthcare provider for INR checks should be facilitated.

Documentation: Document the interaction alert and any actions taken in the patient's pharmacy record, ensuring a clear record of the intervention and monitoring plan.

By understanding the potential interaction between azithromycin and warfarin and taking proactive steps to manage it, pharmacy professionals play a critical role in maintaining patient safety and optimizing therapeutic outcomes.

Metformin is a cornerstone medication in the management of Type 2 diabetes, primarily due to its effectiveness, safety profile, and the additional benefits it offers beyond blood sugar control. Understanding its mechanism, side effects, and contraindications, as well as how it contrasts with sulfonylureas like glipizide, is crucial for optimal patient care.

Mechanism of Action:

Metformin primarily works by decreasing hepatic glucose production, a significant contributor to elevated blood sugar levels in Type 2 diabetes. It inhibits gluconeogenesis (glucose production in the liver), which leads to reduced fasting blood glucose levels. Additionally, metformin enhances insulin sensitivity in peripheral tissues, improving glucose uptake and utilization, particularly in muscle cells. Unlike sulfonylureas, metformin does not directly stimulate insulin secretion from the pancreas, thereby not causing hypoglycemia when used as monotherapy.

Potential Side Effects:

- **Gastrointestinal Issues**: The most common side effects are gastrointestinal, including nausea, diarrhea, bloating, and abdominal discomfort, which often improve over time or with dose adjustment.
- **Vitamin B12 Deficiency**: Long-term use of metformin has been associated with decreased vitamin B12 absorption, which can occasionally lead to deficiency if not monitored.
- **Lactic Acidosis**: Although rare, metformin can cause lactic acidosis, a serious condition characterized by the buildup of lactic acid in the body, particularly in situations where it accumulates, such as renal impairment.

Contraindications:

- **Renal Impairment**: Metformin is contraindicated in patients with significant renal dysfunction due to the risk of lactic acidosis. The risk increases as renal function declines, necessitating regular monitoring of kidney function.

- **Severe Liver Disease**: Impaired liver function can increase the risk of lactic acidosis.
- **Acute or Chronic Metabolic Acidosis**: Including diabetic ketoacidosis, with or without coma.

Differences from Sulfonylureas (e.g., Glipizide):
- **Insulin Secretion**: Sulfonylureas work by stimulating the beta cells of the pancreas to release insulin, which can lead to hypoglycemia as a side effect, especially if meals are skipped or delayed.
- **Weight Impact**: Sulfonylureas may lead to weight gain, whereas metformin is weight-neutral or may even contribute to slight weight loss.
- **Cardiovascular Effects**: Metformin is associated with potential cardiovascular benefits and is often preferred for patients with Type 2 diabetes who have a higher risk of cardiovascular disease. Sulfonylureas, especially older ones, have been linked to potential cardiovascular risks.
- **Secondary Failure**: Sulfonylureas may lose effectiveness over time as pancreatic beta-cell function declines, a phenomenon less commonly observed with metformin.

In counseling a patient prescribed metformin, it's important to emphasize the mechanism of action, the need to monitor for side effects, adherence to renal function monitoring, and lifestyle modifications that can enhance the drug's efficacy. Educating the patient about the differences between metformin and other antidiabetic medications like sulfonylureas enables informed decision-making and promotes better adherence to the treatment plan.

Newer diabetes drug classes, including GLP-1 agonists like liraglutide and SGLT-2 inhibitors like empagliflozin, have garnered attention not only for their glucose-lowering capabilities but also for their cardioprotective and renoprotective benefits. These additional advantages offer significant implications for patient care, particularly in individuals with Type 2 diabetes who are at increased risk for cardiovascular and renal complications.

GLP-1 Agonists (e.g., Liraglutide)
Cardioprotective Benefits:

GLP-1 agonists have been shown to reduce major cardiovascular events, including heart attack, stroke, and cardiovascular mortality. Liraglutide, for instance, has demonstrated efficacy in reducing these risks in adults with Type 2 diabetes and established cardiovascular disease.
Renoprotective Benefits:

These agents can also confer renal benefits, primarily through their effects on albuminuria and stabilizing kidney function. They may slow the progression of diabetic kidney disease by improving glucose control, reducing blood pressure, and promoting weight loss.
Patient Counseling Points:

Gastrointestinal Side Effects: Advise patients that nausea, vomiting, and diarrhea are common, especially during the initiation phase, and usually diminish over time.
Injection Site Reactions: Inform about potential injection site reactions and proper rotation of injection sites.
Hypoglycemia Risk: While lower than with insulin or sulfonylureas, the risk exists, especially when combined with other glucose-lowering medications.
Signs of Pancreatitis: Counsel on the rare but serious risk of pancreatitis, advising immediate medical attention if symptoms of severe abdominal pain, nausea, or vomiting occur.

SGLT-2 Inhibitors (e.g., Empagliflozin)

Cardioprotective Benefits:

SGLT-2 inhibitors have been associated with a reduction in heart failure hospitalization and cardiovascular death in patients with Type 2 diabetes, likely due to effects on heart function and arterial stiffness.

Renoprotective Benefits:

These drugs slow the progression of kidney disease by reducing hyperfiltration and albuminuria, offering protection against the decline in kidney function.

Patient Counseling Points:

Risk of Dehydration and Hypotension: Advise patients to stay well-hydrated, especially in hot weather or during illness, to mitigate the risk of dehydration and low blood pressure.

Ketoacidosis: Inform about the rare risk of diabetic ketoacidosis, even if blood sugar levels are not very high. Symptoms include nausea, vomiting, abdominal pain, and rapid breathing.

Genital Infections: Counsel on the increased risk of genital mycotic infections due to glycosuria, emphasizing the importance of personal hygiene.

Urinary Tract Infections: Alert patients to the potential for urinary tract infections and to seek medical attention for symptoms such as burning during urination, urinary urgency, or pain.

Incorporating these cardioprotective and renoprotective agents into the treatment regimen for appropriate patients with Type 2 diabetes can significantly impact long-term outcomes. It is crucial for healthcare providers to not only consider the glucose-lowering efficacy but also the broader cardiovascular and renal benefits these newer drug classes offer. Patient education on recognizing and managing potential side effects is vital to maximizing therapeutic benefits and ensuring patient safety.

Dose calculations based on Body Surface Area (BSA) are a critical aspect of administering chemotherapy, ensuring that patients receive a dosage that is both effective and safe, tailored to their individual physiological characteristics. This method takes into account the patient's size, which can significantly affect how they metabolize and respond to chemotherapy drugs.

Concept of BSA-Based Dosing:

BSA-based dosing is predicated on the principle that the metabolism of many chemotherapy agents correlates more closely with BSA than with body weight alone. This method aims to reduce the variability in drug plasma concentrations, thereby optimizing therapeutic effects while minimizing toxicity.

Steps Involved in BSA-Based Dose Calculations:

1. **Measure Height and Weight**: Accurately measure the patient's height in meters (m) and weight in kilograms (kg). These measurements must be as precise as possible to ensure the accuracy of the BSA calculation.

2. **Calculate BSA**: Use the Mosteller formula, one of the most common methods for calculating BSA:

$$\text{BSA } (m^2) = \sqrt{\frac{\text{Height (cm)} \times \text{Weight (kg)}}{3600}}$$

Other formulas like the DuBois formula also exist, but the Mosteller formula is widely used for its simplicity and accuracy.

3. **Determine Chemotherapy Dose**: Once BSA is calculated, multiply it by the drug's dosage per square meter (mg/m²) to determine the patient's specific dose.

$$\text{Dose (mg)} = \text{BSA } (m^2) \times \text{Drug dosage } (mg/m^2)$$

4. **Double-Check Calculations**: Due to the high stakes of chemotherapy dosing, it's critical to double-check all calculations. This can involve a second healthcare professional verifying the measurements, calculations, and final dose.

5. **Adjustments for Renal and Hepatic Function**: Consider any necessary dose adjustments based on the patient's renal and hepatic function, as these can affect drug clearance.

Importance of Accuracy and Double-Checks:

Minimizing Toxicity: Accurate BSA calculations and dosing are crucial to avoid overdosing, which can lead to severe and potentially life-threatening side effects due to the narrow therapeutic index of many chemotherapy agents.

Maximizing Efficacy: Underdosing can result in subtherapeutic drug levels, reducing the treatment's effectiveness against cancer cells.

Individual Variability: Given the significant variability in how individuals metabolize chemotherapy drugs, precise dosing is essential to tailor the treatment to the patient's specific needs.

Double-Checking: This practice is a safeguard against calculation errors and ensures that any discrepancies are caught and corrected before the administration of chemotherapy. It is a standard procedure in oncology pharmacy practice to have multiple checks at various stages of medication preparation and administration. BSA-based dosing for chemotherapy is a complex process that requires meticulous attention to detail and adherence to safety protocols. Accurate measurements, careful calculations, and stringent double-checking procedures are indispensable to provide optimal patient care in oncology settings.

Handling hazardous medications, such as chemotherapy agents and certain antivirals, requires strict adherence to safety protocols to minimize personal exposure and ensure a safe working environment. Pharmacy technicians play a crucial role in this process and must be well-versed in the use of appropriate personal protective equipment (PPE), containment strategies, and disposal procedures.

Personal Protective Equipment (PPE)

- **Gloves**: Use chemotherapy-tested nitrile gloves when handling hazardous drugs. Double gloving can provide an additional layer of protection.
- **Gowns**: Wear disposable, long-sleeved gowns made of low-permeability fabric with closed fronts and tight cuffs to protect the skin and personal clothing from contamination.
- **Eye Protection**: Use safety goggles or face shields when there is a risk of splashes or aerosolization of hazardous drugs to protect the eyes.
- **Respiratory Protection**: In scenarios where there is potential for inhalation of drug particles or vapors, wear an appropriate mask or respirator, such as an N95 respirator, especially during drug compounding or administration.

Containment Strategies

- **Closed System Drug-Transfer Devices (CSTDs)**: Utilize CSTDs when compounding or administering hazardous medications to prevent the escape of hazardous drug vapors or aerosols into the environment.
- **Biological Safety Cabinets (BSCs) and Compounding Aseptic Containment Isolators (CACIs)**: Perform all compounding activities within BSCs or CACIs specifically designed for handling hazardous drugs, ensuring that they are certified and functioning correctly.
- **Ventilation**: Ensure that the compounding area is well-ventilated with proper air filtration systems to remove any airborne contaminants.

Disposal Procedures

- **Hazardous Waste Containers**: Dispose of all used PPE, empty drug vials, syringes, and other contaminated materials in designated hazardous waste containers, which are typically yellow and labeled as "Hazardous" or "Chemotherapy Waste."
- **Spill Kits**: Be prepared for potential spills by having spill kits readily available in areas where hazardous drugs are handled. Spill kits should include absorbent materials, protective apparel, and waste disposal bags.

- **Documentation and Training**: Maintain clear documentation of hazardous waste disposal procedures and ensure all pharmacy staff handling these medications are adequately trained in these protocols.

Additional Precautions

- **Hand Hygiene**: Perform thorough hand hygiene before donning and after removing PPE.
- **No Eating or Drinking**: Prohibit eating, drinking, applying cosmetics, or handling contact lenses in areas where hazardous drugs are prepared or administered to prevent ingestion or mucosal exposure.
- **Pregnancy and Reproductive Health**: Staff who are pregnant, breastfeeding, or trying to conceive should be made aware of the potential risks and given the option to avoid handling hazardous drugs if possible.

By rigorously adhering to these guidelines for PPE, containment, and disposal, pharmacy technicians can significantly reduce the risks associated with handling hazardous medications, protecting themselves, their colleagues, and the environment from potential harm.

Converting between different opioid medications requires careful calculation of equianalgesic doses to ensure effective pain management while minimizing the risk of under- or over-dosing. Equianalgesic dosing involves using a standard reference to understand the relative potency of different opioids, allowing healthcare professionals to switch a patient from one opioid to another safely.

Steps for Converting Opioid Medications:
Determine the Total Daily Dose: Calculate the total daily dose of the current opioid medication the patient is taking. This might involve summing up multiple doses throughout the day.

Use Equianalgesic Dose Tables: Refer to a reliable equianalgesic dose table, which provides the equivalent dose of various opioids relative to a standard dose of morphine, considered the benchmark.

Calculate the Equivalent Dose: Identify the equivalent dose of the new opioid using the table. For example, if a patient is on 30mg of oral morphine daily and the plan is to switch to oxycodone, and the table suggests that morphine to oxycodone conversion is 1:1.5, the equivalent dose of oxycodone would be 20mg daily.

Consider Individual Factors: Adjust the calculated dose based on patient-specific factors such as opioid tolerance, age, renal and hepatic function, and the presence of comorbid conditions that may affect opioid metabolism or sensitivity.

Apply a Safety Margin: When switching opioids, it's common practice to reduce the calculated dose of the new opioid by a certain percentage (often 25-50%) to account for incomplete cross-tolerance. This provides an additional safety margin to prevent over-dosing.

Monitor and Titrate: Start the patient on the calculated equivalent dose of the new opioid, then closely monitor for effectiveness and side effects. Titrate the dose as needed to achieve the desired pain control while minimizing adverse effects.

Importance of Accurate Equianalgesic Dosing:
Preventing Under-dosing: Inadequate pain management can significantly impact a patient's quality of life and may lead to pain becoming chronic or intractable.

Avoiding Over-dosing: Over-dosing can lead to life-threatening respiratory depression, increased side effects, and the potential for opioid use disorder.

Managing Side Effects: Different opioids may have varying side effect profiles. Proper dosing helps manage these side effects effectively.

Personal Protective Equipment (PPE) and Precautions:

When handling opioid medications, especially potent opioids like fentanyl, pharmacy technicians should use appropriate PPE to avoid accidental exposure. This might include gloves and, in some cases, masks or gowns when handling powder forms or compounding.

Converting between opioid medications is a complex process that requires a thorough understanding of equianalgesic dosing principles, careful consideration of patient-specific factors, and close monitoring to ensure patient safety and effective pain management.

Counseling patients on the safe storage and disposal of opioids is crucial to prevent diversion, accidental ingestion, and overdose. It's also essential to educate patients and their families about the use of naloxone for overdose reversal. Here are key patient-focused counseling points:

Safe Storage

Secure Location: Store opioids in a locked cabinet or a secure location out of reach and sight of children, pets, and unauthorized individuals to prevent accidental ingestion and misuse.

Original Containers: Keep opioids in their original packaging with the label intact. This helps in identifying the medication, understanding its potency, and following the prescribed dosage.

Avoid Common Areas: Do not store opioids in common areas such as the kitchen or bathroom medicine cabinets, where they can be easily accessed by others.

Privacy: Be discreet about possessing opioid medications to avoid drawing attention and potential theft or misuse by visitors.

Safe Disposal

Follow Instructions: Adhere to any specific disposal instructions provided by the pharmacy or prescriber. If no instructions are given, utilize available drug take-back programs or authorized DEA-registered collectors.

DEA Take-Back Events: Participate in DEA National Prescription Drug Take-Back Day events, where unused or expired medications can be safely disposed of.

FDA Guidelines: If immediate disposal is necessary and no take-back options are available, follow the FDA's guidelines, which may involve mixing the medication with an unpalatable substance (such as dirt, cat litter, or used coffee grounds), placing the mixture in a sealed plastic bag, and disposing of it in the household trash.

Remove Personal Information: Before disposing of prescription bottles or packaging, ensure personal information is removed or obscured to protect privacy.

Preventing Diversion

Monitor Quantities: Regularly check the quantity of opioid medications to detect any discrepancies or unauthorized use.

Educate Household Members: Discuss the risks of opioid misuse with family members, emphasizing the importance of not sharing medications.

Travel Precautions: When traveling, keep opioids in carry-on luggage and maintain possession to prevent loss or theft.

Naloxone for Overdose Reversal
Availability: Inform patients and their families about naloxone, a medication that can rapidly reverse the effects of an opioid overdose. Discuss the availability of naloxone in pharmacies, often without a prescription.

Administration Training: Encourage patients and family members to receive training on the proper administration of naloxone, available through local health departments, pharmacies, or community organizations.

Recognition of Overdose Signs: Educate on recognizing the signs of an opioid overdose, such as difficulty breathing, extreme drowsiness, or inability to respond.

Emergency Response: Emphasize that naloxone is a temporary measure and that emergency medical assistance (calling 911) is critical after administering naloxone.

By providing comprehensive counseling on the safe storage, disposal, and handling of opioids, pharmacy professionals can play a pivotal role in mitigating the risks associated with opioid use, thereby safeguarding patients and the broader community.

II. Pharmacy Law and Regulations:

Welcome to the world of Pharmacy Law and Regulations, where rules aren't just meant to be followed, but are there to protect patients and ensure quality healthcare. Let's get ready to explore this essential foundation of your pharmacy practice.
Overview: What We'll Navigate
- The Big Picture: We'll understand how federal laws, like the Controlled Substances Act, and state regulations shape how a pharmacy operates. You'll learn about your state's Board of Pharmacy and their role.
- Behind the Counter: Prepare to handle prescription rules, from deciphering those hard-to-read prescriptions to knowing what refills are allowed (and when they aren't).
- Beyond Pills: We'll discuss regulations regarding sterile and non-sterile compounding to make sure those custom medications are prepared safely.
- Controlled Substances: Understand extra layers of security and record-keeping for handling high-risk medications like narcotics.
- Patient Privacy & Beyond: Get familiar with HIPAA, the rulebook designed to protect patient confidentiality and other ethical responsibilities of a pharmacy technician.
Why This Section Matters

Think of Pharmacy Law as your roadmap to a safe and efficient practice. Knowing these regulations will help you:

- Protect Patients: Avoid dispensing errors that could cause harm.
- Shield Yourself and the Pharmacy: Reduce the risk of legal trouble and fines.
- Build Patient Trust: Demonstrate your commitment to ethical and compliant practices.

Get ready to become the rule-abiding expert! By the end of this section, you'll feel empowered to handle any prescription situation with both knowledge and confidence.

DEA Form 224, DEA Form 222, and DEA Form 106 serve distinct yet crucial roles in the regulatory oversight of controlled substances within the United States. Understanding their purposes and proper usage is essential for pharmacy operations, compliance, and the safeguarding of these substances.

DEA Form 224: Initial Registration

Purpose: DEA Form 224 is used for the initial registration of practitioners, pharmacies, hospitals, clinics, and other entities authorized to handle controlled substances. This registration grants the legal authority to dispense, administer, or conduct research with controlled substances.

Usage:

- **Application**: Entities must apply for registration before engaging in activities involving controlled substances. The form requires information about the business, the responsible parties, and the schedules of controlled substances to be handled.
- **Renewal**: Registration with DEA Form 224 must be renewed every three years to maintain the authority to handle controlled substances.

DEA Form 222: Ordering Controlled Substances

Purpose: DEA Form 222 is specifically used for ordering Schedule I and II controlled substances. It ensures a documented chain of custody from the supplier to the registrant, facilitating the tracking and accountability of these substances.

Usage:

- **Order Forms**: Registrants with a DEA number receive official DEA Form 222 order forms, which are serialized and must be used in sequential order.
- **Completion**: The form requires details about the quantity and name of the controlled substances ordered, along with the registrant's information.
- **Submission**: A completed Form 222 is sent to the supplier, and upon receipt of the order, the supplier fills the request and maintains a copy of the form for their records, as does the purchaser.

DEA Form 106: Reporting Theft or Loss

Purpose: DEA Form 106 is utilized to report the theft or significant loss of controlled substances. It's a critical component of regulatory compliance and ensures that any diversion or loss is promptly and transparently communicated to the DEA.

Usage:

- **Discovery of Loss**: Upon discovering a theft or significant loss of controlled substances, registrants are required to immediately notify the local DEA office, typically via phone or online.
- **Detailed Information**: The form requires comprehensive details about the incident, including the date of loss, the type and quantity of substances lost, and any known circumstances or suspects.
- **Investigation and Follow-Up**: Submission of DEA Form 106 initiates a formal review process, which may involve further investigation by the DEA and possibly local law enforcement.

Contrast Between Forms

- **Initial Registration vs. Transactional Use**: DEA Form 224 is foundational, establishing the registrant's authority to handle controlled substances, whereas DEA Form 222 is transactional, used for each specific order of Schedule I and II drugs.
- **Operational vs. Incidental**: DEA Forms 224 and 222 are part of regular operations involving controlled substances, from initial registration to ordering. In contrast, DEA Form 106 is used incidentally, in response to unexpected events such as theft or significant loss.
- **Chain of Custody vs. Incident Reporting**: Form 222 ensures a secure chain of custody for high-risk controlled substances, while Form 106 serves as an incident report, crucial for accountability and regulatory compliance in the event of a breach.

Understanding and correctly utilizing these DEA forms is essential for the lawful management of controlled substances, ensuring both regulatory compliance and the protection of public health and safety.

DEA Form 41, DEA Form 363, and DEA Form 225 are integral components of the regulatory framework governing controlled substances in the United States, each serving distinct purposes related to disposal, narcotic treatment programs, and the activities of manufacturers and distributors. Understanding the application and implications of these forms is crucial for compliance and the safe management of controlled substances.

DEA Form 41: Disposal of Controlled Substances

Application: DEA Form 41 is utilized by registered entities to document the disposal and destruction of controlled substances. This form ensures that the disposal process is transparent and accountable, in line with DEA regulations.

Implications:

- **Procedure**: Registrants must seek DEA approval before disposing of controlled substances, detailing the substances and quantities intended for disposal. The DEA may require witnessing the disposal process to ensure compliance.
- **Record-Keeping**: Maintaining accurate records of disposal on DEA Form 41 is essential for audits and investigations, ensuring that controlled substances are accounted for from acquisition to disposal.

DEA Form 363: Registration for Narcotic Treatment Programs

Application: DEA Form 363 is required for entities seeking to operate narcotic treatment programs, including methadone clinics. These programs provide medically supervised treatment for individuals with substance use disorders.

Implications:

- **Specialized Requirements**: Obtaining approval involves stringent criteria to ensure the program meets federal standards for patient care, record-keeping, and security of narcotics used in treatment.
- **Ongoing Compliance**: Programs must adhere to specific operational and reporting requirements, emphasizing the safe administration and tracking of treatment medications to prevent diversion.

DEA Form 225: Registration for Manufacturers and Distributors

Application: DEA Form 225 is used by businesses and entities that manufacture or distribute controlled substances. This registration is critical for companies involved in the production, sale, or distribution of pharmaceuticals subject to DEA oversight.

Implications:

- **Supply Chain Integrity**: Registrants must implement robust security measures and maintain meticulous records to trace the movement of controlled substances through the supply chain.

- **Regulatory Scrutiny**: Manufacturers and distributors are subject to periodic inspections and audits by the DEA to ensure compliance with regulations governing the production, distribution, and security of controlled substances.

Discussion on Differences in Regulatory Requirements

- **Scope of Activity**: DEA Form 41 pertains to the end-of-life cycle of controlled substances, focusing on their secure disposal. In contrast, DEA Forms 363 and 225 are concerned with the beginning and middle stages of the controlled substance lifecycle, including treatment use and supply chain management, respectively.
- **Operational vs. Incidental Use**: DEA Form 41 is used incidentally, as needed for disposal, whereas DEA Forms 363 and 225 are part of the initial and ongoing operational requirements for entities engaged in narcotic treatment and the controlled substance supply chain.
- **Regulatory Focus**: The focus of DEA Form 363 on narcotic treatment programs emphasizes patient care and the therapeutic use of narcotics, requiring a different set of regulatory considerations compared to the broader manufacturing and distribution oversight associated with DEA Form 225.

Understanding the specific applications, implications, and regulatory distinctions of DEA Forms 41, 363, and 225 is essential for entities engaged in any aspect of controlled substance management, ensuring compliance, public safety, and the integrity of the pharmaceutical supply chain and treatment programs.

The Health Insurance Portability and Accountability Act's (HIPAA) Privacy Rule establishes national standards for the protection of individuals' medical records and other personal health information (PHI). It applies to health plans, health care clearinghouses, and health care providers that conduct certain health care transactions electronically. A crucial aspect of the Privacy Rule is regulating how PHI can be used and disclosed, with specific provisions for public health emergencies and research scenarios. Balancing patient privacy with public health needs is a nuanced aspect of these regulations.

PHI Disclosures in Public Health Emergencies:

During public health emergencies, such as pandemics, natural disasters, or bioterrorism events, the Privacy Rule permits covered entities to disclose PHI without individual authorization to entities legally authorized to respond to the emergency. These entities may include public health authorities, foreign government agencies, and persons at risk.

Key Provisions:

- **Minimum Necessary**: Disclosures must be limited to the "minimum necessary" to achieve the public health objective, except when disclosing to healthcare providers for treatment purposes.
- **Notification**: In certain situations, such as imminent threats, covered entities may disclose PHI to prevent or lessen a serious and imminent threat to health or safety, consistent with applicable law and ethical standards.

PHI Disclosures for Research:

The Privacy Rule also addresses the use and disclosure of PHI for research purposes, striking a balance between facilitating important research and protecting individual privacy.

Key Provisions:

- **Institutional Review Boards (IRB) or Privacy Boards**: Researchers can use or disclose PHI for research with the approval of an IRB or a Privacy Board, which reviews the research proposal to ensure privacy protections are in place.
- **Waiver of Authorization**: An IRB or Privacy Board may waive the authorization requirement for the use or disclosure of PHI for research if specific criteria are met, including minimal risk to privacy.

- **Preparatory to Research**: PHI can be used or disclosed to researchers preparing to conduct research, for example, to aid in study design or to assess the feasibility of a study, provided no PHI is removed from the covered entity's site.
- **De-identified Information**: The Privacy Rule does not restrict the use or disclosure of de-identified health information, as it is not considered PHI.

Balancing Privacy and Public Health Needs:

Balancing patient privacy with the need for public health interventions and research is complex. The Privacy Rule aims to ensure that individuals' health information is adequately protected while allowing the flow of health information needed to provide high-quality health care, protect public health, and conduct vital research.

Challenges:

- **Determining the "Minimum Necessary"**: Identifying what constitutes the minimum necessary information can be challenging, particularly in rapidly evolving public health emergencies.
- **Public Trust**: Ensuring that PHI disclosures for public health or research purposes do not erode public trust in health institutions is paramount. Clear communication and transparency about how PHI is used and protected can help maintain this trust.
- **Adapting to Technological Advances**: As health data collection and sharing technologies evolve, maintaining the balance between privacy and public health needs requires ongoing adaptation and vigilance.

The HIPAA Privacy Rule provides a framework for the protection of PHI while accommodating the critical needs of public health and research. Navigating the balance between individual privacy rights and collective health needs is an ongoing challenge that requires careful consideration, ethical standards, and regulatory oversight.

The Health Insurance Portability and Accountability Act's (HIPAA) Security Rule is a critical component of healthcare regulations, specifically designed to protect Electronic Protected Health Information (ePHI) within healthcare settings, including pharmacies. It mandates healthcare providers, including pharmacies, to implement a series of administrative, physical, and technical safeguards to ensure the confidentiality, integrity, and security of ePHI. The nuances of this rule, especially in the context of Electronic Health Records (EHRs) and pharmacy information systems, are pivotal in safeguarding sensitive patient data.

Administrative Safeguards

These are policies and procedures designed to clearly show how the entity will comply with the act. For pharmacies, this involves:

Risk Analysis and Management: Conducting regular assessments to identify potential risks to ePHI and implementing measures to mitigate these risks.

Training Programs: Implementing training programs for all employees to ensure they understand their roles in protecting ePHI.

Access Management: Ensuring that access to ePHI is granted on a need-to-know basis, limiting access to those who require it to perform their job functions.

Physical Safeguards

These safeguards are physical measures, policies, and procedures to protect electronic information systems and related buildings and equipment from natural and environmental hazards and unauthorized intrusion. In pharmacies, this might include:

Facility Access Controls: Implementing procedures to control and validate access to facilities housing ePHI systems, such as key card access.

Workstation and Device Security: Policies and procedures must be in place to specify the proper use of and access to workstations and electronic media. This includes how workstations should be transferred, removed, and disposed of when no longer needed.

Technical Safeguards

These are the automated processes used to protect data and control access to data. For EHRs and pharmacy systems, technical safeguards include:

Access Control: Implementing technical policies and procedures that allow only authorized persons to access electronic protected health information. This can involve unique user IDs, emergency access procedures, automatic log-off, and encryption and decryption.

Audit Controls: Hardware, software, and procedural mechanisms must be in place to record and examine activity in information systems containing or using ePHI.

Integrity Controls: Measures must be implemented to ensure that ePHI is not improperly altered or destroyed. Digital signatures could be a part of this safeguard.

Transmission Security: Measures must protect against unauthorized access to ePHI that is being transmitted over an electronic network.

Implications of Data Breaches

Data breaches can have severe implications, including financial penalties, loss of patient trust, and legal consequences. Breaches can result from various factors, including hacking, employee error, or theft of physical devices containing ePHI. The Security Rule mandates that covered entities must have breach notification procedures, including notifying affected individuals, the Secretary of Health and Human Services (HHS), and, in some cases, the media.

Required Safeguards to Protect ePHI

To protect ePHI, pharmacies and healthcare providers must implement a combination of the aforementioned safeguards. This includes conducting regular risk assessments, encrypting data, ensuring secure data transmission, and training staff on data privacy and security policies.

The HIPAA Security Rule's comprehensive requirements for administrative, physical, and technical safeguards are designed to protect ePHI, especially within EHRs and pharmacy information systems. Adhering to these regulations is essential not only for compliance but for maintaining the trust and safety of patients in the digital healthcare environment.

The technician-to-pharmacist ratio is a regulatory parameter set by state pharmacy boards to ensure safe and effective pharmacy practice. This ratio determines the maximum number of pharmacy technicians that can work under the supervision of a single pharmacist. These ratios vary significantly across different states, reflecting diverse perspectives on optimizing pharmacy workflow, safety, and efficiency.

Variation Across States

In some states, the ratio is as low as 1:1, meaning one technician per pharmacist, which is often the case in states with more stringent regulations. In contrast, other states may allow higher ratios, such as 3:1 or 4:1, and some states have no specified limit, leaving it to the discretion of the pharmacist in charge. For instance, states like Texas and California have specific ratios set by their pharmacy boards, whereas others may offer more flexibility depending on the pharmacy setting (retail, hospital, compounding) and the tasks being performed.

Impact on Workflow, Safety, and Efficiency
Positive Impacts:

Increased Efficiency: Higher technician-to-pharmacist ratios can lead to increased efficiency in pharmacy operations. Technicians can manage tasks like medication dispensing, inventory management, and administrative duties, allowing pharmacists to focus on clinical tasks, patient counseling, and medication management.
Cost-Effectiveness: Utilizing technicians for operational tasks can be more cost-effective for pharmacies, potentially leading to lower operational costs and savings for patients.
Potential Risks:

Safety Concerns: Higher ratios may put a strain on pharmacists' ability to effectively supervise all technicians' work, potentially increasing the risk of dispensing errors and compromising patient safety.
Workload and Stress: Pharmacists overseeing too many technicians might experience increased workload and stress, possibly impacting their ability to provide high-quality patient care.
Scenarios for Ratio Adjustments
Beneficial Adjustments:

High-Volume Pharmacies: In settings with high prescription volumes, slightly higher technician-to-pharmacist ratios might be beneficial to manage the workload efficiently, provided that there are systems in place to maintain safety and accuracy.
Specialized Pharmacy Services: Pharmacies offering specialized services such as compounding or clinical consultations might benefit from higher ratios, allowing pharmacists to dedicate more time to these complex tasks.
Detrimental Adjustments:

Complex Patient Populations: In settings serving complex patient populations, such as hospitals or specialty pharmacies, higher ratios might be detrimental, as pharmacists need to spend more time on clinical reviews, drug therapy management, and patient counseling.
Inadequate Training: Increasing the technician-to-pharmacist ratio without ensuring technicians have adequate training and competency can lead to operational inefficiencies and increased error rates. The technician-to-pharmacist ratio is a critical factor that influences pharmacy workflow, safety, and efficiency. While higher ratios can enhance operational efficiency and cost-effectiveness, they require careful implementation and oversight to ensure patient safety and care quality are not compromised. State regulatory bodies and pharmacy management must consider the specific needs and circumstances of their practice settings when determining the most appropriate ratios to maintain a balance between efficiency and safety.

Technician Check Tech (TCT) programs, where permitted, represent an innovative shift in pharmacy practice, allowing trained pharmacy technicians to assume additional responsibilities traditionally reserved for pharmacists, such as the final verification of medications prepared by other technicians. These programs are designed to optimize pharmacy workflow, enhance efficiency, and allow pharmacists to focus more on patient care activities. However, they also come with legal stipulations, specific qualifications for technicians, and practical considerations regarding the types of medications they can check.

Legal Implications

The allowance and scope of TCT programs are governed by state pharmacy boards, and regulations vary significantly. States that permit TCT programs have specific guidelines outlining the implementation, including technician training requirements, supervision levels, and types of medications that can be checked. Pharmacies must adhere to these regulations to ensure compliance and maintain the integrity of the pharmacy practice.

Technician Qualifications

For a technician to participate in a TCT program, stringent qualifications are typically required, which may include:

Certification: Technicians are often required to be certified by a recognized board, such as the Pharmacy Technician Certification Board (PTCB) or the National Healthcareer Association (NHA).

Experience: A specified minimum number of years of experience working as a pharmacy technician, often in the setting where the TCT program will be implemented.

Additional Training: Completion of a formal TCT training program, which may include modules on medication safety, error prevention, and specific procedures for the final check process.

Competency Assessment: Technicians might need to pass a competency assessment, demonstrating their ability to accurately and safely perform final medication verifications.

Types of Medications Checked

The scope of medications that a technician can check under a TCT program may be limited by state regulations or institutional policies. Common stipulations include:

Non-Sterile Preparations: Many TCT programs initially focus on non-sterile preparations, such as oral medications in unit-dose or multi-dose packaging.

Exclusions: High-risk medications, sterile preparations (e.g., IV admixtures), and controlled substances are often excluded from TCT programs due to their increased risk of harm if errors occur.

Potential Benefits

Increased Efficiency: TCT programs can free up pharmacists' time, allowing them to engage more in direct patient care activities, such as medication therapy management (MTM) and patient counseling.

Enhanced Job Satisfaction: For technicians, participating in TCT programs can lead to increased job satisfaction and professional growth opportunities.

Workflow Optimization: By redistributing tasks, pharmacies can optimize workflow and potentially reduce wait times for patients.

Drawbacks and Considerations

Safety Concerns: There may be concerns about maintaining the same level of medication safety, given that technicians, despite their training, might not have the same depth of pharmacological knowledge as pharmacists.

Liability Issues: Errors in medication checking could lead to liability issues, raising questions about supervision and accountability.

Training and Oversight: Implementing a TCT program requires significant investment in technician training and ongoing oversight to ensure continued competency and adherence to safety protocols. TCT programs, where permitted, offer a promising avenue to enhance pharmacy operations and patient care but must be approached with careful consideration to training, regulatory compliance, and the maintenance of high safety standards. Balancing the benefits of increased operational efficiency and technician engagement with the paramount importance of patient safety is crucial for the success of these programs.

Sterile compounding involves preparing medications in a sterile environment to prevent contamination and ensure patient safety, particularly for medications administered intravenously, intramuscularly, or through other routes where sterility is crucial. The scope of sterile compounding activities that pharmacy technicians are allowed to perform varies by state laws, but generally includes tasks such as preparing solutions, transferring medications to sterile containers, and labeling compounded sterile products under the supervision of a licensed pharmacist.

Required Certifications and Training

To participate in sterile compounding, pharmacy technicians typically need to undergo specialized training and obtain certain certifications, which may include:

- **Completion of a Pharmacy Technician Training Program**: Many states require pharmacy technicians to complete an accredited training program that includes specific coursework or modules on sterile compounding.
- **Certification**: Obtaining certification from a recognized organization, such as the Pharmacy Technician Certification Board (PTCB), which offers a Compounded Sterile Preparation Technician (CSPT) certification. This certification requires passing an exam and demonstrating hands-on experience in sterile compounding.
- **Continuing Education**: Technicians involved in sterile compounding are often required to complete continuing education focused on sterile compounding practices and aseptic techniques to maintain their certification and ensure they stay up-to-date with the latest standards and practices.

Scope of Activities

Under the oversight of a pharmacist, certified pharmacy technicians may be involved in various sterile compounding activities, including:

- **Weighing and Measuring Ingredients**: Accurately measuring the amounts of active pharmaceutical ingredients and excipients based on compounding formulas.
- **Mixing Ingredients**: Combining ingredients in a sterile environment, using techniques that maintain sterility and ensure homogeneity of the final product.
- **Filling Sterile Containers**: Transferring compounded medications into sterile containers, such as vials, syringes, or IV bags, in a way that maintains sterility.
- **Applying Labels**: Labeling compounded sterile products with the necessary information, including drug name, strength, quantity, and expiration date.
- **Quality Assurance**: Performing or participating in quality assurance checks, such as visual inspections and sterility tests, to ensure the compounded medications meet the required standards.

Potential Risks

Compounded sterile preparations carry inherent risks, primarily related to contamination and medication errors, which can lead to infections or adverse drug reactions. Risks include:

- **Microbial Contamination**: Improper aseptic techniques can introduce microorganisms into sterile preparations, posing serious infection risks to patients.
- **Dosage Inaccuracies**: Errors in measuring or mixing ingredients can lead to incorrect dosages, potentially resulting in underdosing or overdosing.
- **Cross-Contamination**: Using non-sterile equipment or containers can lead to cross-contamination between different medications.

Mitigating Risks through Stringent Oversight

To minimize these risks, stringent oversight and adherence to established protocols are essential:

- **Compliance with USP <797>**: Following the United States Pharmacopeia (USP) Chapter <797> guidelines for sterile compounding, which outline standards for personnel qualifications, environmental monitoring, and compounding processes.
- **Supervision by Pharmacists**: Ensuring that all sterile compounding activities performed by technicians are directly supervised by a licensed pharmacist who verifies the accuracy and sterility of compounded preparations.
- **Regular Training and Competency Assessments**: Conducting ongoing training and periodic competency assessments for pharmacy technicians to reinforce aseptic techniques and sterile compounding procedures.
- **Environmental Controls**: Maintaining strict environmental controls, including the use of cleanrooms, laminar airflow workbenches, and proper personal protective equipment (PPE), to ensure a sterile compounding environment.

By ensuring that pharmacy technicians are properly certified, trained, and supervised, and by strictly adhering to established sterile compounding protocols, pharmacies can effectively mitigate the risks associated with compounded sterile preparations and ensure patient safety.

Pharmacy technicians play a crucial role in the compounding of high-risk sterile preparations, including chemotherapy agents, which require meticulous attention to detail, adherence to strict protocols, and specialized training to ensure patient safety and medication efficacy. The compounding of these preparations is governed by specific regulations and guidelines, notably USP <797> and <800>, which set the standards for sterile compounding and handling hazardous drugs, respectively.

Role of Pharmacy Technicians in High-Risk Sterile Compounding
Pharmacy technicians involved in high-risk sterile compounding, such as chemotherapy preparation, are responsible for:

Weighing and Measuring: Accurately weighing and measuring chemotherapy agents and adjuvants under aseptic conditions.
Mixing and Compounding: Diluting and mixing chemotherapy drugs within biological safety cabinets or compounding aseptic containment isolators to maintain sterility and contain hazardous drug particles.
Final Product Verification: Ensuring the final compounded product matches the prescribed therapy, including drug type, concentration, and volume, under the supervision of a pharmacist.
USP <797> and <800> Guidelines
USP <797> focuses on the sterility aspects of compounding, providing guidelines on:

Environmental Standards: Requirements for clean rooms, laminar airflow workbenches, and other engineering controls.
Personnel Training: Mandates regular training and competency evaluation in aseptic techniques for anyone involved in sterile compounding.
Quality Assurance: Procedures for ensuring compounded sterile preparations meet expected standards, including sterility and potency.
USP <800> addresses the safe handling of hazardous drugs, with key provisions including:

Containment Strategies: Use of appropriate containment practices and engineering controls to minimize exposure to hazardous drugs, such as closed system drug-transfer devices (CSTDs) and proper ventilation systems.

Personal Protective Equipment (PPE): Requirements for specific types of PPE, such as gloves, gowns, and respiratory protection, when handling hazardous drugs.

Decontamination, Cleaning, and Disinfection: Detailed protocols for decontaminating compounding areas and equipment to prevent cross-contamination and ensure the safety of personnel.

Implications for Technician Training and Competency Assessment

Given the complexities and risks associated with compounding high-risk sterile preparations, pharmacy technicians must undergo rigorous training and regular competency assessments:

Specialized Training: Technicians must receive specialized training in handling hazardous drugs, aseptic technique, and the use of specific compounding equipment. Training often includes simulations and practical demonstrations in a controlled environment.

Competency Assessment: Regular assessments of a technician's competency in compounding practices are required, typically involving direct observation, written tests, and media-fill tests to simulate compounding processes using sterile media.

Continuing Education: Ongoing education on updates to USP <797> and <800>, new compounding techniques, and safety protocols is essential to maintain high standards of practice. The involvement of pharmacy technicians in the compounding of high-risk sterile preparations, such as chemotherapy agents, demands a high level of expertise, strict adherence to USP <797> and <800> guidelines, and a commitment to continuous learning and improvement. Through specialized training, rigorous competency assessments, and adherence to established safety protocols, pharmacy technicians can effectively contribute to the safe and effective preparation of these critical medications, ensuring the best possible outcomes for patients undergoing treatment.

III. Sterile and Non-Sterile Compounding:

Let's roll up our sleeves and dive into the world of sterile and non-sterile compounding, where precision, safety, and sometimes a dash of creativity, meet. Imagine becoming a compounding maestro, custom-crafting medications that go beyond what you find on pharmacy shelves.

What You'll Learn

Sterile Technique: Get ready to master cleanliness! We'll break down aseptic techniques, cleanroom rules, and the art of preparing those injectable medications (IVs, eye drops, etc.) free from contamination.

Beyond the Basics: Explore the different types of non-sterile compounds, from whipping up creams and ointments to customizing oral liquids for a child who can't swallow pills.

Calculations & Conversions: Sharpen those math skills! We'll ensure you can accurately convert measurements, determine doses, and understand those sometimes-tricky compounding formulas.

Rules and Regulations: Learn the guidelines for compounding to ensure your creations are not only effective but also safe and prepared to the highest standards.

Why Compounding Matters

Compounding empowers you to:

Personalize Medicine: Tailor treatments to a patient's unique needs when a one-size-fits-all medication won't do.

Overcome Shortages: Create essential medications that are out of stock, helping patients get the treatment they need.

Expand Your Skills: Compounding adds valuable tools to your pharmacy technician toolkit. Get ready to think both outside the box and safely within the guidelines. By the end of this section, you'll be equipped to transform ingredients into medications that make a difference!

Cleaning and maintaining a sterile environment within both Horizontal Laminar Airflow Workbenches (LAFWs) and Biological Safety Cabinets (BSCs) are critical for ensuring the safety and efficacy of compounded preparations. The cleaning procedures, while sharing some similarities, must account for the distinct airflow patterns and intended uses of each type of cabinet.

Horizontal Laminar Airflow Workbench (LAFW) Cleaning Procedure:
Preparation: Don appropriate Personal Protective Equipment (PPE) such as gloves, gowns, and masks. Ensure the LAFW is turned on and running for at least 30 minutes before cleaning to establish proper airflow.

Surface Cleaning: Starting from the back of the work area, clean all surfaces using a sterile, lint-free wipe saturated with an appropriate disinfectant. Use overlapping strokes and move from the cleanest area (furthest back) to the dirtiest area (closest to the operator) to avoid contaminating clean areas.

Side Walls and IV Bar: Clean the side walls and the IV bar (if present) using the same technique, moving from top to bottom.

HEPA Filter and Grille: Wipe the HEPA filter's protective grille gently without touching the filter itself, ensuring not to disrupt the integrity of the filter.

Equipment and Supplies: Clean and disinfect all equipment and supplies before placing them back into the LAFW.

Final Wipe: Perform a final wipe of all surfaces, starting from the back to the front, with a sterile 70% isopropyl alcohol wipe to ensure all residues from the previous disinfectant are removed.

Drying: Allow the workbench to air dry completely before use. Do not use the LAFW until all surfaces are dry to maintain the integrity of the sterile field.

Biological Safety Cabinet (BSC) Cleaning Procedure:
Preparation: As with the LAFW, wear appropriate PPE. Ensure the BSC has been running to establish proper airflow.

Starting from the Top: Clean the interior top surface first, using a disinfectant-soaked lint-free wipe, to prevent contamination from falling onto lower, already cleaned surfaces.

Rear Grille and Side Walls: Clean the rear grille where the HEPA filter is located, ensuring not to damage the filter. Proceed with the side walls using top-to-bottom strokes.

Work Surface: Clean the work surface from back to front to ensure that any contaminants are moved towards the area closest to the operator, which is considered the dirtiest.

Sash and Front Grille: Wipe down the interior of the sash and the front grille, maintaining the integrity of the airflow.

Equipment and Supplies: Disinfect all items before placing them back into the BSC.

Final Wipe and Drying: Use a 70% isopropyl alcohol wipe for the final pass over all surfaces and allow the cabinet to air dry.

Differences in Airflow Patterns and Implications:
LAFWs provide unidirectional, horizontal airflow from the back of the workbench towards the operator. This design is intended for compounding sterile preparations where product protection from contamination is the priority. The horizontal flow means that operators must be particularly cautious to work in a manner that doesn't obstruct the airflow, potentially introducing contaminants from their person or the environment into the sterile field.

BSCs, on the other hand, offer vertical laminar airflow and provide both product protection and operator/environment protection, making them suitable for handling hazardous substances like chemotherapy agents. The vertical airflow directs particles and contaminants downwards and away from both the operator and the work surface. This design minimizes the risk of operator exposure to hazardous drugs but requires careful placement of materials within the cabinet to avoid disrupting the downward airflow pattern.

Understanding and adhering to the specific cleaning protocols and recognizing the importance of airflow patterns in LAFWs and BSCs are essential for pharmacy technicians to maintain a sterile environment and ensure the safe compounding of medications.

Certifying an ISO Class 7 cleanroom involves a series of stringent evaluations to ensure that the environment meets the specific standards set by the International Organization for Standardization (ISO) for airborne particulate cleanliness in controlled environments. The process is critical for environments where small particles could significantly impact manufacturing processes, product quality, or research outcomes, such as in pharmaceutical compounding.

Parameters Tested in ISO Class 7 Cleanroom Certification:
Air Particle Counts: The primary parameter for ISO Class 7 certification is the concentration of airborne particles. For Class 7, the air cleanliness standard allows a maximum particle concentration of 352,000 particles sized 0.5 micrometers or larger per cubic meter of air. Testing involves using particle counters to measure the number of particles, ensuring they do not exceed the specified limit.

Room Pressurization: Proper pressurization is essential to prevent infiltration of unfiltered air. ISO Class 7 cleanrooms should maintain positive pressure relative to adjacent areas to ensure that any air flow is from the clean area outwards, thus preventing entry of contaminants.

Airflow Patterns and Velocity: Testing includes verifying the laminar airflow patterns (unidirectional flow) to ensure that air moves in a single direction at a uniform speed, effectively removing particles from the area. The airflow velocity must also be within a certain range to maintain the required cleanliness level.

Temperature and Humidity Control: Although not specifically defined by the ISO standard, maintaining consistent temperature and humidity levels is critical for operational processes within the cleanroom. These parameters are often tested to ensure they meet the specific requirements of the processes conducted in the cleanroom.

HEPA Filter Integrity: High-Efficiency Particulate Air (HEPA) filters are crucial for maintaining air purity. Testing involves checking for leaks or damage to the filters that could compromise their efficiency.

Frequency of Recertification:
Initial Certification: Occurs after the cleanroom is constructed and before it is put into operation to ensure that all design and construction criteria meet the ISO Class 7 requirements.

Periodic Recertification: ISO standards and industry best practices typically recommend that cleanrooms be recertified at least annually. However, the frequency can vary based on regulatory requirements, the type of activities conducted in the cleanroom, and any changes or upgrades to the cleanroom or its equipment.

After Major Changes: Recertification is also necessary after significant modifications to the cleanroom structure, HVAC system, or after replacing HEPA filters, to ensure that these changes have not adversely affected the cleanroom's performance.

Process of Certification and Recertification:
Preparation: Before the certification process, ensure that the cleanroom and all equipment are properly cleaned and functioning. Inform all personnel about the certification schedule.

Testing: A certified cleanroom testing professional conducts the tests using calibrated instruments. The process includes particle counting, measuring room pressurization, airflow velocity, temperature, and humidity, as well as inspecting HEPA filter integrity.

Documentation: The results of all tests are documented in a certification report, detailing the methods used, the findings, and any areas requiring remediation.

Remediation: If any parameters do not meet the required standards, corrective actions must be taken, followed by retesting to confirm compliance.

Certification: Once all parameters meet the ISO Class 7 requirements, the cleanroom is certified, and the certification documentation is provided, including the date and scope of the certification.

Regular monitoring and adherence to strict operational protocols complement the certification process, ensuring ongoing compliance with ISO Class 7 standards and maintaining the integrity of the cleanroom environment.

Alcohol-based hand sanitizers are widely used in healthcare settings for their effectiveness in reducing microbial populations on the skin, contributing significantly to infection control. However, in the context of compounding, especially sterile compounding, there are specific situations where alcohol-based sanitizers may not be appropriate for hand hygiene, necessitating alternative methods.

Scenarios Where Alcohol-Based Sanitizers Are Inadequate:
Presence of Spore-Forming Bacteria:

Alcohol-based sanitizers are effective against many types of bacteria, viruses, and fungi but have limited efficacy against spore-forming bacteria like Clostridium difficile and certain species of Bacillus. These spores are resistant to the alcohol's action and can remain viable on the skin even after sanitizer application. In compounding areas, particularly those involving high-risk sterile preparations, the presence of such spores poses a significant contamination risk.

When Full Sterile Scrub Procedure Is Required:

For high-risk compounding, especially preparations intended for routes of administration that bypass the body's natural barriers (e.g., intravenous, intrathecal), a more rigorous aseptic technique is required. This includes a full sterile scrub procedure using antimicrobial soap and water, followed by the donning of sterile gloves and garb. The mechanical action of scrubbing with soap and water is more effective in reducing microbial load, including spores, than alcohol-based sanitizers alone.

Visible Soiling or Contamination of Hands:

In instances where hands are visibly soiled or contaminated, particularly with substances that alcohol cannot dissolve (e.g., blood, body fluids, protein material), alcohol-based sanitizers are ineffective. The physical removal of contaminants through handwashing with soap and water is necessary to ensure hand hygiene.

Before Donning Sterile Gloves:

Prior to donning sterile gloves for compounding sterile preparations, a comprehensive hand hygiene protocol involving washing with antimicrobial soap, thorough rinsing, and proper drying is essential to minimize the risk of transferring microorganisms to the sterile field.

Best Practices for Hand Hygiene in Compounding:

Routine Handwashing: Regular handwashing with antimicrobial soap and water should be a standard practice before initiating any compounding activities, especially after any activity that could contaminate the hands.

Use of Alcohol-Based Sanitizers: While alcohol-based sanitizers can be used for interim hand hygiene, their use should be supplemental to, rather than a replacement for, traditional handwashing in compounding settings.

Aseptic Technique Training: Pharmacy personnel involved in compounding should receive comprehensive training on aseptic techniques, including proper hand hygiene, to ensure the sterility of compounded preparations.

Policy and Procedure Adherence: Pharmacies should have clear policies and procedures outlining hand hygiene protocols, including situations where alcohol-based sanitizers are insufficient, and full scrub procedures are mandated.

Understanding the limitations of alcohol-based sanitizers in specific compounding scenarios, particularly those involving spore-forming bacteria and the need for sterile procedures, is crucial for maintaining the sterility of compounded preparations and ensuring patient safety.

Environmental monitoring in sterile compounding environments, such as those adhering to USP <797> standards, is a critical aspect of ensuring the sterility and safety of compounded medications. This monitoring involves viable air sampling and surface sampling to detect the presence of microbial contaminants that could compromise the sterile conditions. These methods are essential for verifying the effectiveness of cleaning procedures, air filtration systems, and aseptic techniques employed by compounding personnel.

Viable Air Sampling

Purpose: Viable air sampling assesses the quality of the air in terms of microbial contamination. It helps identify potential airborne pathogens that could compromise the sterility of the compounding environment and the preparations.

Methods:

- **Active Air Sampling**: Uses devices like air samplers or impactors that actively pull a known volume of air over a culture media plate. The plate is then incubated, and any colonies that grow are counted and identified. This method quantifies the level of microbial contamination in the air.
- **Passive Air Sampling (Settle Plates)**: Involves placing open Petri dishes containing culture media in various locations within the compounding area. The plates are exposed to air for a specific period, then incubated to allow any microorganisms that have settled from the air to grow. This method provides an indication of the cleanliness of the environment but does not actively quantify airborne particles like active sampling does.

Surface Sampling

Purpose: Surface sampling is conducted to detect contamination on work surfaces, equipment, and other areas within the compounding environment. It helps identify potential sources of contamination that could transfer to sterile preparations.

Methods:

- **Contact Plates (Rodac Plates)**: These are agar plates with a convex surface that can be pressed directly onto surfaces to sample for contaminants. After incubation, microbial colonies are counted and identified.
- **Swab Sampling**: Involves using sterile swabs to collect samples from surfaces, especially from areas that are difficult to sample with contact plates. The swab is then applied to culture media and incubated to allow any collected microorganisms to grow.

Frequency of Environmental Monitoring

The frequency of environmental monitoring in sterile compounding environments is dictated by several factors, including the risk level of the compounding activities, the volume of compounding conducted, and any changes to the compounding environment or procedures. Generally, guidelines suggest the following:

- **ISO Class 5 Areas (Primary Engineering Controls)**: Viable air and surface sampling should be performed at least semiannually (every six months) for low and medium-risk compounding and at least monthly for high-risk compounding.
- **ISO Class 7 and 8 Areas (Buffer and Ante Areas)**: Sampling frequencies for these areas may vary but are typically performed in conjunction with ISO Class 5 area sampling, considering the risk levels and activities performed in these areas.

Purpose of Environmental Monitoring

The overarching goal of environmental monitoring in sterile compounding environments is to ensure that the controls in place (engineering, procedural, and personnel-related) effectively maintain a state of control over the environment, minimizing the risk of microbial contamination in compounded sterile preparations. Regular monitoring:

- Validates the effectiveness of cleaning and disinfection procedures.
- Ensures the proper functioning of HVAC and filtration systems.
- Assesses the aseptic technique of compounding personnel.
- Provides data for continuous quality improvement.

Environmental monitoring is a critical component of a comprehensive quality assurance program in sterile compounding, ensuring patient safety and adherence to compounding standards.

Beyond Use Date (BUD) is a critical aspect of compounded sterile preparations (CSPs), indicating the date or time beyond which a compounded preparation should not be used. Determining the BUD is crucial for ensuring the safety, stability, and efficacy of CSPs. The United States Pharmacopeia (USP) provides guidelines on assigning BUDs, which vary depending on the storage conditions (room temperature, refrigerated, frozen) and the risk level of compounding (low, medium, high).

Factors Influencing BUD Assignment

Sterility: The likelihood of microbial contamination or growth, which is influenced by the compounding environment, techniques, and duration of compounding.

Chemical Stability: The duration over which the chemical components of the CSP remain stable and effective, which can be influenced by factors such as light, temperature, and pH.

Risk Level: Defined by USP <797>, the risk levels (low, medium, high) are determined by the complexity of compounding, the number of ingredients, and the potential for microbial contamination.

BUD for Different Storage Conditions

Room Temperature (20 to 25°C):

Low-Risk CSPs: Typically assigned a BUD of up to 48 hours.

Medium-Risk CSPs: Generally limited to 30 hours.

High-Risk CSPs: Often restricted to a maximum of 24 hours due to the increased risk of contamination.

Refrigerated (2 to 8°C):

Low-Risk CSPs: Can be assigned a BUD of up to 14 days, reflecting the reduced rate of microbial growth at lower temperatures.

Medium-Risk CSPs: Typically assigned a BUD of up to 9 days.

High-Risk CSPs: Due to the higher initial risk of contamination, the BUD might be limited to 3 days.

Frozen (-20°C or colder):

For all risk levels, CSPs intended for freezing can be assigned a BUD of up to 45 days. Freezing halts microbial growth and can help preserve the chemical stability of the components, allowing for a longer BUD.

Considerations for BUD Assignment

Direct Compounding Area (DCA) Quality: The cleanliness and control over the DCA where compounding takes place directly influence the risk of contamination and, consequently, the assigned BUD.

Sterilization Methods: The method of sterilization (e.g., filtration, heat) can impact the BUD, with more reliable sterilization methods potentially allowing for longer BUDs.

Container-Closure System: The integrity of the system used to store the CSP can affect the BUD, with systems that better protect against contamination and permeation allowing for longer BUDs.

Published Data and Literature: When available, stability data from published studies or manufacturer information can be used to extend BUDs beyond default limits, provided there is sufficient evidence to support the extended duration.

Regulatory Compliance and Best Practices

It's essential for compounding pharmacies to adhere to USP <797> guidelines when assigning BUDs to ensure regulatory compliance. Additionally, pharmacies should implement best practices such as:

Regularly reviewing and updating compounding procedures based on the latest guidelines and evidence. Conducting stability testing for CSPs, especially when using extended BUDs.

Training compounding personnel on the factors affecting BUDs and the importance of adherence to assigned BUDs for patient safety.

By carefully considering the risk level, storage conditions, and other relevant factors, compounding pharmacies can assign appropriate BUDs to CSPs, ensuring their safety and efficacy for patient use.

Assigning a Beyond Use Date (BUD) to an infrequently prepared intravenous (IV) medication in a compounding pharmacy requires a meticulous process that combines regulatory guidelines, available stability data, and compounding best practices. Here's an outline of the steps involved in this critical aspect of compounding practice:

1. Review Regulatory Guidelines

- **USP <797> Standards**: Start by consulting the United States Pharmacopeia (USP) Chapter <797> for general guidelines on assigning BUDs for compounded sterile preparations (CSPs), considering factors like sterility and chemical stability.
- **State Regulations**: Check for any state-specific compounding regulations that might provide additional requirements or limitations on BUDs.

2. Analyze the Compounding Process

- **Risk Level Determination**: Assess the risk level of the compounding process (low, medium, high) based on factors such as the number of manipulations, sterility of starting ingredients, and complexity of the procedure.
- **Compounding Environment**: Consider the quality of the compounding environment, including the ISO class of the cleanroom or laminar airflow workbench where the medication will be prepared.

3. Gather Stability Data

- **Published Literature**: Look for stability data in pharmaceutical literature, peer-reviewed articles, and standard compounding references like the USP-NF, Trissel's Stability of Compounded Formulations, or the American Society of Health-System Pharmacists (ASHP) guidelines.
- **Manufacturer Information**: Consult the medication's manufacturer for any available stability data for the active pharmaceutical ingredient (API) or similar compounded formulations.
- **Professional Networks**: Reach out to professional compounding networks or forums that may have insights or shared experiences with the specific medication.

4. Consider Container-Closure System

- Evaluate the type of container (e.g., syringe, IV bag) and closure system to be used for the IV medication, as this can significantly impact the medication's stability and risk of contamination.

5. Assign Preliminary BUD

- Based on the gathered information and considering the most conservative data available, assign a preliminary BUD. This should account for the medication's stability while ensuring patient safety and efficacy of the preparation.

6. Stability Testing (if applicable)

- For medications with insufficient stability data or when an extended BUD is desired, consider conducting in-house stability testing or consulting with a laboratory that can perform such testing.

7. Documentation and Labeling
- Document the rationale for the assigned BUD, including references to stability data, compounding conditions, and risk assessments.
- Ensure that the assigned BUD is clearly labeled on the medication, along with the compound name, concentration, and storage instructions.

8. Continuous Quality Improvement
- Monitor outcomes and any stability issues with the compounded IV medication. Use this information to refine the BUD assignment process for future preparations.

9. Patient and Healthcare Provider Communication
- Communicate clearly with the healthcare provider and patient (if applicable) regarding the assigned BUD, storage conditions, and any other relevant information to ensure the safe use of the medication.

Assigning a BUD to an infrequently prepared IV medication is a complex process that requires careful consideration of multiple factors, including regulatory guidelines, stability data, compounding conditions, and container-closure systems. By adhering to a systematic approach and utilizing available resources, a compounding pharmacy can ensure the safety, stability, and efficacy of compounded sterile preparations.

Here's a practice problem that involves converting a weight-based dose to a volume-based concentration for a medication:

Practice Problem:

A pediatric patient weighing 22 kg requires a medication dosed at 5 mg/kg. The medication is available in a stock solution concentration of 10 mg/mL. You need to prepare the appropriate dose for this patient.

Task: Calculate the total dose required for the patient in milligrams (mg), and then determine the volume in milliliters (mL) of the stock solution needed to administer this dose.

Steps to Solve:
1. **Calculate the Total Dose Required**:
   - Use the weight-based dosing information to calculate the total dose needed for the patient.
   - Formula: Total Dose (mg) = Dose (mg/kg) × Patient's Weight (kg)
2. **Convert the Total Dose to Volume**:
   - Use the concentration of the stock solution to convert the total dose from mg to mL.
   - Formula: Volume (mL) = Total Dose (mg) / Concentration of Stock Solution (mg/mL)

Solution:
1. **Calculate the Total Dose**:
   - Dose required = 5 mg/kg
   - Patient's weight = 22 kg
   - Total Dose = 5 mg/kg × 22 kg = 110 mg
2. **Convert the Total Dose to Volume**:
   - Concentration of stock solution = 10 mg/mL
   - Volume needed = Total Dose / Concentration of Stock Solution = 110 mg / 10 mg/mL = 11 mL

Answer:

The patient requires a total dose of 110 mg of the medication, which corresponds to 11 mL of the stock solution at a concentration of 10 mg/mL.

This practice problem helps pharmacy technicians understand the process of converting weight-based dosing instructions into the practical volume of medication to be administered, ensuring accurate and safe medication preparation and administration.

Here's a practice problem that involves using the alligation method to prepare a specific concentration of a solution from two different stock solutions:

Practice Problem:

A pharmacist needs to prepare 500 mL of a 25% w/v dextrose solution for a patient's IV therapy. The pharmacy has in stock a 10% w/v dextrose solution and a 50% w/v dextrose solution. Using the alligation method, calculate how much of each stock solution is needed to prepare the required 500 mL of a 25% w/v dextrose solution.

Steps to Solve:

1. **Set Up the Alligation Grid:**
   - Place the concentration of the higher strength solution at the top and the lower strength solution at the bottom, with the desired concentration in the middle.
2. **Calculate the Differences:**
   - Subtract diagonally across the grid to find the parts of each solution needed.
3. **Determine the Total Parts:**
   - Sum the parts of the two solutions.
4. **Calculate the Volume of Each Solution:**
   - Use the proportion of each part relative to the total parts to determine the volume of each stock solution required to make up the total final volume.

Solution:

1. **Alligation Grid:**

50% (higher concentration) | 25% (desired concentration) | 10% (lower concentration)

2. **Calculate the Differences:**
   - Difference between 50% and 25% = 25 parts (of 10% solution)
   - Difference between 25% and 10% = 15 parts (of 50% solution)
3. **Determine Total Parts:**
   - Total parts = 25 parts + 15 parts = 40 parts
4. **Calculate Volume of Each Solution:**
   - Volume of 10% solution = (25 parts / 40 parts) × 500 mL = 312.5 mL
   - Volume of 50% solution = (15 parts / 40 parts) × 500 mL = 187.5 mL

Answer:

To prepare 500 mL of a 25% w/v dextrose solution, the pharmacist needs to mix 312.5 mL of the 10% w/v dextrose solution with 187.5 mL of the 50% w/v dextrose solution.

This practice problem illustrates the application of the alligation method in compounding, allowing pharmacy technicians and pharmacists to accurately mix solutions of different concentrations to achieve a desired final concentration.

To calculate the hourly flow rate (mL/hr) for a continuous infusion prescribed at a rate of micrograms per kilogram per minute (mcg/kg/min), given the concentration of the solution and the patient's weight, follow these steps:

Step 1: Calculate the Patient's Total Hourly Dose

1. **Convert the infusion rate to an hourly basis**:
    - Since the rate is given in mcg/kg/min, multiply by 60 minutes to convert it to mcg/kg/hour.
    - Formula: Total Hourly Dose (mcg/kg/hr) = Infusion Rate (mcg/kg/min) × 60 minutes
2. **Calculate the total dose needed per hour for the patient**:
    - Multiply the hourly dose (mcg/kg/hr) by the patient's weight in kilograms (kg).
    - Formula: Patient's Total Hourly Dose (mcg/hr) = Total Hourly Dose (mcg/kg/hr) × Patient's Weight (kg)

Step 2: Calculate the Hourly Flow Rate (mL/hr)
1. **Determine the concentration of the solution**:
    - The concentration of the solution will be given in mcg/mL.
2. **Calculate the volume of solution needed per hour**:
    - Divide the patient's total hourly dose (mcg/hr) by the concentration of the solution (mcg/mL) to find the flow rate in mL/hr.
    - Formula: Hourly Flow Rate (mL/hr) = Patient's Total Hourly Dose (mcg/hr) / Solution Concentration (mcg/mL)

Practice Problem:
A patient weighing 70 kg is prescribed an infusion at a rate of 0.05 mcg/kg/min. The medication is supplied in a concentration of 400 mcg/mL. Calculate the hourly flow rate (mL/hr).

Solution:
1. **Calculate the Total Hourly Dose**:
    - Infusion Rate: 0.05 mcg/kg/min
    - Convert to hourly dose: 0.05 mcg/kg/min × 60 min = 3 mcg/kg/hr
    - Patient's weight: 70 kg
    - Patient's Total Hourly Dose: 3 mcg/kg/hr × 70 kg = 210 mcg/hr
2. **Calculate the Hourly Flow Rate**:
    - Solution Concentration: 400 mcg/mL
    - Hourly Flow Rate: 210 mcg/hr ÷ 400 mcg/mL = 0.525 mL/hr

Answer:
The hourly flow rate for the continuous infusion is 0.525 mL/hr.
This calculation ensures the patient receives the prescribed dose based on their weight and the medication's concentration, critical for achieving the desired therapeutic effect while minimizing the risk of adverse reactions.

Analyzing a Total Parenteral Nutrition (TPN) order involves meticulous calculations and considerations to ensure the patient's nutritional and electrolyte needs are met safely. Here's a structured approach to break down a complex TPN order, focusing on dextrose, amino acids, electrolytes, and trace elements:

1. Dextrose Calculation (Calories from Carbohydrates)
- **Determine Total Caloric Needs**: Based on the patient's age, weight, height, and clinical condition (e.g., sepsis, trauma).
- **Calculate Dextrose Contribution**: Dextrose provides 3.4 kcal/g. If the TPN order specifies a certain percentage of dextrose (e.g., 10% dextrose), calculate the calories contributed by dextrose.
    - Example: For a 2,000 mL TPN solution with 10% dextrose: 2,000 mL × 0.10 = 200 g of dextrose. Total calories from dextrose = 200 g × 3.4 kcal/g = 680 kcal.

2. Amino Acids Calculation (Grams of Protein)

- **Protein Requirements**: Determine based on the patient's condition, typically 1.0 to 1.5 g/kg/day for adults.
- **Calculate Amino Acid Contribution**: If the TPN contains a specific percentage of amino acids (e.g., 2.5% amino acid solution), calculate the total grams of protein provided.
  - Example: For a 2,000 mL TPN solution with 2.5% amino acids: 2,000 mL × 0.025 = 50 g of amino acids (protein).

3. Electrolytes Calculation (mEq)

- **Assess Patient's Needs**: Based on serum electrolyte levels, renal function, and fluid balance. Common electrolytes in TPN include sodium, potassium, calcium, magnesium, and phosphorus.
- **Calculate Electrolyte Additions**: Electrolytes are added in milliequivalents (mEq) or millimoles (mmol). Ensure the ordered amounts are within safe limits and adjust based on the patient's ongoing labs.
  - Example: If the patient requires 40 mEq of potassium and the stock solution is 2 mEq/mL, the volume to add is 40 mEq ÷ 2 mEq/mL = 20 mL of potassium stock solution.

4. Trace Elements and Vitamins

- **Include Essential Trace Elements**: Such as zinc, copper, manganese, and selenium, based on standard recommendations or specific patient needs.
- **Ensure Compatibility**: Some trace elements or vitamins may not be compatible with other components of the TPN solution, leading to precipitation or degradation.

Double-Checking and Compatibility:

- **Double-Check Calculations**: Have another healthcare professional independently verify all calculations to minimize errors.
- **Compatibility Check**: Review all components for compatibility issues. Use compatibility charts or resources like Trissel's Handbook on Injectable Drugs to prevent interactions that could cause precipitation or decrease the efficacy of the TPN solution.
- **Osmolarity Consideration**: Ensure the final osmolarity of the TPN solution is appropriate for the intended vein of administration (peripheral vs. central).

Final Steps:

- **Final Review**: Before administration, review the TPN order comprehensively, including the patient's current clinical status, recent lab values, and any changes in medication or fluid requirements.
- **Monitoring**: Establish a monitoring plan for the patient, including regular checks of electrolyte levels, blood glucose, triglycerides, liver function tests, and any signs of complications like infection at the catheter site.

By systematically analyzing each component of the TPN order and emphasizing the importance of double-checking and compatibility, healthcare professionals can ensure safe and effective nutritional support for patients requiring TPN therapy.

Compounding an ophthalmic solution requires strict adherence to aseptic techniques and specific protocols to ensure the solution is sterile, safe, and effective for ocular use. The procedure involves several critical steps, from selecting the appropriate ingredients and containers to filtration and labeling. Here's a detailed overview of the compounding process for an ophthalmic solution:

1. Formulation and Ingredient Selection

- **Purity and Quality**: Use only high-purity, pharmaceutical-grade ingredients to minimize the risk of irritation or adverse reactions.

- **Isotonicity**: Ensure the solution is isotonic with tears to prevent ocular discomfort. This may involve the use of buffering agents and tonicity adjusters.

2. Aseptic Technique and Environment

- **Cleanroom or Laminar Flow Hood**: Prepare the ophthalmic solution in a certified cleanroom or under a laminar airflow hood to maintain a sterile environment.
- **Personal Protective Equipment (PPE)**: Wear appropriate PPE, including gloves, masks, and sterile gowns, to prevent contamination.

3. Dissolution and Mixing

- **Solubilization**: Dissolve all solid ingredients in a suitable solvent, often sterile water for injection (WFI), ensuring complete dissolution.
- **Mixing**: Use magnetic stirrers or gentle agitation to mix the solution without introducing air bubbles or contaminants.

4. Filtration Requirements

- **Sterilizing Filter**: Use a 0.22-micron sterilizing-grade membrane filter to remove any microbial contaminants. The filter should be pre-wetted with the same solvent used in the solution to ensure compatibility and prevent filter blockage.
- **Integrity Testing**: Perform integrity testing of the filter before and after filtration to ensure it is functioning correctly and has not been compromised during the process.

5. Choice of Containers

- **Sterile Containers**: Use sterile, single-use containers designed for ophthalmic solutions. Containers should be made of materials that do not interact with the solution's components.
- **Tamper-Evident and Dropper Tips**: Select containers with tamper-evident seals and compatible dropper tips that allow for precise administration without contamination.

6. Filling and Sealing

- **Aseptic Filling**: Fill containers under aseptic conditions, taking care not to touch the tip of the container or dropper to any surface.
- **Volume**: Fill containers with the appropriate volume, ensuring sufficient headspace to facilitate shaking before use if necessary.

7. Labeling Considerations

- **Patient Information**: Include the patient's name, if the solution is patient-specific.
- **Ingredients and Concentration**: List all active and inactive ingredients and their concentrations.
- **Directions for Use**: Provide clear instructions on the dosage, administration method, and frequency.
- **Storage Conditions**: Indicate the required storage conditions, typically "Store at room temperature away from light."
- **BUD**: Assign a beyond-use date according to USP <797> guidelines, typically not exceeding 14 days when stored at controlled room temperature.
- **Warnings**: Include any necessary warnings, such as "For external use only" and "Do not touch dropper tip to any surface, as this may contaminate the solution."

8. Final Inspection and Packaging

- **Inspection**: Visually inspect the final product for any particulate matter, discoloration, or phase separation.
- **Packaging**: Package the solution in a way that protects it from light and physical damage during transportation and storage.

9. Documentation and Verification

- **Compounding Record**: Maintain a detailed compounding record that includes all ingredients, quantities, compounding steps, and any quality control measures taken.
- **Pharmacist's Verification**: Have a pharmacist or another qualified individual verify the final product against the compounding record to ensure accuracy and adherence to the formulation.

Compounding ophthalmic solutions demands meticulous attention to sterility, formulation, and packaging to ensure the compounded medication is safe and effective for ocular use. Adhering to established compounding standards and guidelines is crucial throughout the process.

The preparation of chemotherapy infusions is a critical process that requires stringent safety measures to protect both the healthcare professionals involved in the preparation and the patients receiving the treatment. Due to the cytotoxic nature of many chemotherapy agents, special precautions, reconstitution techniques, and spill management protocols are essential.

Safety Precautions
Personal Protective Equipment (PPE):

Wear appropriate PPE, including double gloves (chemotherapy-rated), gowns resistant to permeation by chemotherapy drugs, eye protection, and face shields to protect against splashes.
Use respiratory protection if there's a risk of inhaling powdered forms of cytotoxic drugs.
Containment Hood:

Utilize a Class II Biological Safety Cabinet (BSC) or Compounding Aseptic Containment Isolator (CACI) specifically designed for handling hazardous drugs. These hoods provide a sterile environment and contain harmful aerosols and drug particles.
Ensure the hood is certified and functioning correctly, with regular airflow tests to maintain safety standards.
Reconstitution Techniques
Aseptic Technique:

Maintain strict aseptic technique throughout the reconstitution process to prevent microbial contamination.
Work at least six inches inside the hood to ensure the work is done within the clean air environment.
Dissolving the Drug:

Use the diluent recommended by the manufacturer, which is often provided with the chemotherapy agent. The volume required for reconstitution should be carefully calculated based on the manufacturer's instructions to achieve the desired concentration.
Swirl gently or invert the vial to dissolve the drug. Avoid vigorous shaking, which can create aerosols.
Withdrawal and Transfer:

Use a closed-system drug transfer device (CSTD) if available to minimize exposure to drug aerosols and spills during the transfer of the reconstituted solution from the vial to the infusion bag or bottle.
Prime the infusion set with the same solution that will be used for the patient's infusion to avoid incompatibilities and reduce the risk of air embolism.
Handling Spills and Contamination
Spill Kits:

Have a chemotherapy spill kit readily available in all areas where chemotherapy drugs are handled. The kit should include absorbent pads, protective apparel, gloves, a scoop for collecting solid spills, and a sealed container for hazardous waste.
Immediate Response:

In the event of a spill, don PPE immediately before attempting to manage the spill. Follow the spill kit instructions, which typically involve containing the spill, absorbing liquid spills with pads, and cleaning the area with a detergent followed by water.
Waste Disposal:

Dispose of all waste materials, including used PPE, absorbent pads, and any contaminated materials, in designated chemotherapy waste containers, which are usually yellow and labeled as hazardous or chemotherapy waste.
Reporting:

Report all spills or exposures to the appropriate department within the healthcare facility, such as occupational health, to ensure proper documentation and follow-up, including medical evaluation if necessary.
Training and Drills:

Regularly conduct training sessions and drills for pharmacy staff and healthcare workers who handle chemotherapy agents to ensure they are proficient in spill management and emergency procedures.
The preparation of chemotherapy infusions demands meticulous attention to safety protocols, including the use of appropriate PPE, containment hoods, and strict aseptic techniques. Additionally, having protocols in place for managing spills and contamination is crucial to ensure the safety of healthcare professionals and patients alike. Regular training and adherence to established guidelines are essential to maintain a safe environment for chemotherapy compounding.

IV. Medication Safety:

Welcome to the high-stakes world of Medication Safety! This section is your guide to ensuring a patient's care experience is healing, not harmful. Let's sharpen your error-prevention skills and boost your confidence in handling those critical medications.
What We'll Focus On:

- The Mistakes That Matter: Learn the most common medication errors (wrong drug, wrong dose, wrong route) and the devastating harm they can cause.
- System-Wide Safeguards: Explore how technology (e-prescribing, barcode scanning), teamwork, and clear labeling protocols help minimize those errors.
- Your Role as Guardian: Discover how your attention to detail at each stage of the process – from data entry to dispensing – protects patients from harm.
- When Things Go Wrong: Understand procedures for error reporting and analysis. It's about preventing future mistakes, not placing blame.
- Beyond the Pharmacy Walls: We'll discuss patient education techniques, empowering patients to be active partners in their safe medication use.

Why This is Critical:

- Patient Lives at Stake: Medication errors aren't just a slip-up; they can have life-altering consequences. Your knowledge directly contributes to preventing harm.
- Building Trust: The public expects their pharmacy to be a safe zone. Your vigilance in error prevention reinforces that trust.
- Professional Growth: Medication safety isn't just about following rules, it's about critical thinking, problem-solving, and continuous improvement.

Consider this section your shield against medication errors. By the end, you'll be equipped with the knowledge, strategies, and mindset to make patient safety your top priority!

Designing and implementing pharmacy workflows to minimize medication errors is a critical aspect of pharmacy operations, enhancing patient safety and the quality of care. Effective strategies such as minimizing interruptions during medication preparation and instituting a "read-back" verification process for telephone orders are vital components of such workflows. Here's a detailed exploration of these strategies:

Minimizing Interruptions During Medication Preparation

Interruptions during medication preparation can significantly increase the risk of errors, such as incorrect dosing or medication mix-ups. Implementing strategies to reduce these interruptions can enhance focus and accuracy.

Design Considerations:
- **Dedicated Preparation Areas**: Establish clearly designated medication preparation areas that are off-limits for non-urgent communication. These areas should be clearly marked and respected by all pharmacy staff.
- **Visual and Auditory Cues**: Use visual cues like signage or colored mats and auditory cues to signal that a pharmacist or technician is in a 'no interruption' zone.
- **Workflow Scheduling**: Schedule high-risk medication preparation tasks during lower-traffic times to reduce the likelihood of interruptions.

Implementation Strategies:
- **Staff Training and Awareness**: Educate all staff about the importance of minimizing interruptions and the proper protocols for approaching colleagues during medication preparation.
- **Use of Technology**: Implement technology solutions such as automated alerts or status indicators that inform others when a pharmacist or technician is engaged in medication preparation.

"Read-back" Verification Process for Telephone Orders

The "read-back" process involves repeating verbal or telephone orders back to the prescriber to ensure accuracy. This strategy is particularly crucial for telephone orders, where the risk of miscommunication is heightened.

Design Considerations:
- **Standardized Protocols**: Develop and implement standardized protocols for taking telephone orders, including a mandatory read-back step.
- **Documentation**: Ensure that all telephone orders and their read-back confirmations are documented promptly and accurately in the patient's record.

Implementation Strategies:
- **Training**: Provide comprehensive training to all pharmacy staff on the read-back protocol, emphasizing its importance in preventing medication errors.
- **Prescriber Engagement**: Engage prescribers in the process, informing them of the pharmacy's read-back policy to ensure their cooperation and patience during order verification.

- **Quality Assurance**: Regularly review telephone order processes as part of the pharmacy's quality assurance program, identifying areas for improvement and ensuring adherence to protocols.

Additional Strategies to Enhance Workflow and Reduce Errors
- **Barcoding and Scanning**: Implement barcoding systems for medication verification to reduce the risk of dispensing errors.
- **Double-check Systems**: Establish protocols requiring a second pharmacist or trained technician to verify high-risk medications before dispensing.
- **Technology Utilization**: Use pharmacy management systems with clinical decision support features, including drug interaction checks and allergy alerts, to provide an additional layer of error prevention.
- **Continuous Education**: Foster a culture of continuous learning and improvement, encouraging staff to stay updated on best practices in medication safety and error prevention.

Fostering a Culture of Safety
- **Non-punitive Error Reporting**: Encourage a culture where staff feel comfortable reporting errors or near-misses without fear of punitive action, facilitating learning and system improvement.
- **Regular Feedback and Communication**: Hold regular meetings to discuss workflow efficiency, medication safety concerns, and strategies for improvement, fostering open communication and team collaboration.

Designing pharmacy workflows to minimize medication errors requires a multifaceted approach that combines environmental, procedural, and cultural strategies. By minimizing interruptions, implementing read-back verification for telephone orders, and continuously engaging in error prevention practices, pharmacies can significantly enhance medication safety and patient care quality.

Technology plays a pivotal role in error prevention within the medication use process, offering innovative solutions that enhance accuracy, improve efficiency, and reduce the risk of medication errors. Key technologies such as barcoding systems, electronic medication administration records (eMARs), and automated dispensing machines have been instrumental in transforming pharmacy operations and patient care practices.

Barcoding Systems
Functionality: Barcoding systems involve attaching barcodes to medication packages, which can then be scanned at various points in the medication use process to verify the drug, dose, and patient information.

Error Prevention:

Verification at Dispensing: Scanning the barcode when dispensing ensures the correct medication is selected according to the prescription, reducing dispensing errors.
Bedside Scanning: In hospitals, scanning the patient's wristband and the medication barcode at the bedside ensures the "five rights" of medication administration (right patient, right medication, right dose, right route, and right time) are met, significantly reducing administration errors.
Electronic Medication Administration Records (eMARs)
Functionality: eMARs are digital versions of traditional paper-based medication administration records, integrated into healthcare systems to track and document medication administration electronically.

Error Prevention:

Real-time Documentation: eMARs provide real-time documentation of medication administration, reducing the likelihood of missed doses or duplicate administrations.

Alerts and Reminders: They can generate alerts for potential drug interactions, allergies, or deviations from the prescribed regimen, allowing healthcare providers to address issues before they lead to errors.

Audit Trails: eMARs create a comprehensive audit trail for each medication administration event, facilitating the monitoring of compliance and the identification of patterns that may indicate potential problems.

Automated Dispensing Machines (ADMs)

Functionality: ADMs are computer-controlled storage and dispensing devices used in healthcare settings to manage and dispense medications near the point of care, with built-in safeguards for verification.

Error Prevention:

Controlled Access: ADMs control access to medications, ensuring that only authorized personnel can retrieve drugs, and only the medications that have been ordered for a patient are accessible, reducing the risk of selection errors.

Inventory Management: These systems provide accurate, real-time inventory tracking, reducing the risk of stockouts or the use of expired medications.

Dose Accuracy: ADMs can dispense exact doses required for patient treatment, minimizing the risk associated with manual preparation, especially for high-risk medications like chemotherapy.

Integration and Interoperability

The greatest benefit of these technologies is realized when they are integrated and interoperable within the broader healthcare information system, including electronic health records (EHRs). Integration ensures that all parts of the medication use process are informed by consistent, up-to-date patient and medication information, further reducing the risk of errors.

The role of technology in error prevention in the medication use process is profound and multifaceted. By ensuring accurate medication selection with barcoding systems, enhancing the reliability of medication administration records through eMARs, and improving the safety and efficiency of medication dispensing with ADMs, technology significantly reduces the risk of medication errors. As these technologies continue to evolve and integrate, they promise to further advance the safety and quality of patient care in pharmacy practice and the broader healthcare landscape.

Adverse drug reactions (ADRs) are unwanted or harmful effects experienced following the administration of a medication. They are broadly categorized into two types: Type A (predictable) and Type B (unpredictable) reactions. Understanding the distinction between these two types is crucial for healthcare professionals to provide effective patient counseling and monitoring.

Type A (Predictable) Adverse Drug Reactions
Characteristics:

Mechanism: Type A reactions are an extension of the drug's pharmacological action and are often dose-dependent. They occur within the therapeutic dose range and are related to the known pharmacodynamics of the drug.

Frequency: These are more common, accounting for approximately 80% of all ADRs.

Preventability: Since they are related to the drug's known actions, Type A reactions are generally predictable and preventable with appropriate dosing and monitoring.

Examples:

Excessive Bleeding with Anticoagulants: Warfarin, used to prevent blood clots, can cause excessive bleeding if not properly monitored and dosed according to the patient's INR (International Normalized Ratio) levels.

Hypoglycemia with Insulin: Insulin and other hypoglycemic agents used in diabetes management can cause dangerously low blood sugar levels if the dose exceeds the patient's needs.

Type B (Unpredictable) Adverse Drug Reactions

Characteristics:

Mechanism: These reactions are not related to the drug's pharmacological action and are not dose-dependent. They often involve immune-mediated mechanisms (drug allergies) or are due to idiosyncratic responses.

Frequency: Less common than Type A, but they can be more severe and life-threatening.

Preventability: Type B reactions are inherently unpredictable, making them difficult to prevent based solely on the drug's pharmacology.

Examples:

Anaphylaxis to Penicillin: Some patients may have an unpredictable, severe allergic reaction to penicillin, characterized by anaphylaxis, which requires immediate medical intervention.

Stevens-Johnson Syndrome with Sulfa Drugs: A rare, severe disorder of the skin and mucous membranes that can occur as an idiosyncratic reaction to medications like sulfonamides.

Implications for Patient Counseling and Monitoring

For Type A Reactions:

Counseling: Educate patients on the expected side effects based on the drug's pharmacological action and advise them on how to manage or mitigate these effects.

Monitoring: Regular monitoring, dose adjustments, and therapeutic drug monitoring (TDM) where applicable (e.g., warfarin) are essential to prevent or minimize Type A reactions.

For Type B Reactions:

Counseling: Inform patients about the potential for unpredictable reactions and instruct them on the signs that require immediate medical attention, such as difficulty breathing, severe rash, or swelling.

Monitoring: Collect a detailed medication and allergy history to avoid drugs with known allergies. In some cases, genetic testing may be useful for predicting idiosyncratic reactions.

General Strategies:

Patient Education: Empower patients with information about their medications, including potential ADRs, and the importance of adherence to prescribed dosing regimens.

Encourage Reporting: Urge patients to report any adverse effects they experience, even if they are unsure whether the medication is the cause, to facilitate early intervention and management.

Distinguishing between Type A and Type B adverse drug reactions is vital for healthcare providers to implement appropriate preventive strategies, provide targeted patient counseling, and ensure careful monitoring, thereby enhancing patient safety and therapeutic outcomes.

Reporting systems play a crucial role in medication safety, serving as vital tools for collecting and analyzing data on adverse drug reactions (ADRs) and other medication-related problems. Two key reporting systems in the United States are the FDA's MedWatch and the Vaccine Adverse Event Reporting System (VAERS). These systems allow healthcare professionals, including pharmacy technicians, as well as patients and consumers, to report suspected ADRs and vaccine-related adverse events. The data collected contribute to national drug safety efforts by identifying potential safety signals and informing regulatory actions, such as updating drug labels, issuing safety alerts, or withdrawing drugs from the market.

MedWatch: The FDA Safety Information and Adverse Event Reporting Program

Purpose: MedWatch is designed for the reporting of adverse events and problems with medical products, including prescription and over-the-counter medications, biologics, medical devices, and dietary supplements.

How Pharmacy Technicians Can Use MedWatch:

- **Identifying and Reporting ADRs**: Pharmacy technicians, often being the first point of contact for patients experiencing medication-related issues, can identify potential ADRs during patient interactions or while dispensing medications.
- **Submitting Reports**: Technicians can submit reports online, by mail, or fax using the FDA Form 3500. Reporting can be done anonymously, and it's crucial to provide as much detail as possible about the adverse event and the product involved.
- **Educating Patients**: They can inform patients about the existence of MedWatch and encourage them to report any adverse experiences they suspect are related to the medications they are using.

Vaccine Adverse Event Reporting System (VAERS)

Purpose: VAERS is a national system for monitoring the safety of vaccines after they are licensed for use in the U.S. It collects information about adverse events that may occur after vaccination, ranging from mild side effects like arm soreness to more serious health problems that could be related to vaccination.

How Pharmacy Technicians Can Use VAERS:

- **Observation and Documentation**: With the increasing role of pharmacies in vaccine administration, pharmacy technicians are well-positioned to observe and document post-vaccination reactions.
- **Reporting Adverse Events**: Technicians should report any clinically significant, unexpected adverse events following vaccination to VAERS, even if the causal relationship to the vaccine is uncertain.
- **Patient Assistance**: They can assist patients or their caregivers in reporting adverse events to VAERS, providing the necessary information and guidance on completing the VAERS form.

Contribution to National Drug Safety Efforts

The information reported to MedWatch and VAERS is analyzed by safety experts to detect new adverse effects and safety trends, evaluate the seriousness of reported problems, and identify potential public health issues related to medical products and vaccines. By contributing data to these systems, pharmacy technicians help to:

- **Enhance Post-Market Surveillance**: Reporting ADRs and vaccine-related adverse events provide real-world data that complement clinical trial information, offering a more comprehensive view of the product's safety profile.
- **Inform Regulatory Actions**: Analysis of reports can lead to regulatory actions to improve product safety, such as updating labeling with new warnings, restricting the use of the product, or removing unsafe products from the market.
- **Improve Patient Care**: By identifying and reporting ADRs, pharmacy technicians play a direct role in preventing further occurrences of similar adverse events, thereby improving patient care and outcomes.

Pharmacy technicians are vital participants in medication safety efforts through their active use of reporting systems like MedWatch and VAERS. By recognizing and reporting adverse drug reactions and vaccine-related events, they contribute valuable information that supports the ongoing assessment of medication and vaccine safety, ultimately enhancing patient care and public health.

Controlling humidity in medication storage areas is crucial for maintaining medication stability and integrity. Humidity, along with factors like light and temperature, can significantly affect the physical and chemical properties of medications, potentially compromising their efficacy and safety.

Impact of Humidity on Medication Stability and Integrity

1. **Hygroscopicity**: Many medications are hygroscopic, meaning they can absorb moisture from the air. Excessive humidity can lead to the absorption of moisture by these medications, causing them to degrade, lose potency, or undergo undesirable physical changes such as clumping or dissolution.
2. **Chemical Degradation**: Certain medications may undergo hydrolysis, where water molecules break chemical bonds within the drug molecule, leading to degradation and loss of efficacy.
3. **Microbial Growth**: High humidity can promote the growth of mold, fungi, and bacteria, especially in non-sterile medications such as creams, ointments, and suspensions, posing a risk of contamination.
4. **Packaging Integrity**: Excessive moisture can damage packaging materials, compromising the protective barrier against contaminants and further exposure to adverse conditions.

Guidelines for Storing Medications Sensitive to Humidity, Light, or Temperature

Humidity Control:

- Maintain the relative humidity (RH) within medication storage areas at recommended levels, typically between 30% and 60%. Use dehumidifiers or HVAC systems to regulate humidity.
- Store medications in airtight, moisture-resistant containers to protect them from humidity. Desiccants can be used within containers to absorb excess moisture.
- Regularly monitor humidity levels with hygrometers to ensure they remain within the safe range.

Light Protection:

- Store light-sensitive medications in amber-colored or opaque containers to block or reduce light exposure.
- Avoid storing medications near windows or under direct artificial light sources. Use UV-protective window films and lighting fixtures if necessary.
- Review the manufacturer's storage recommendations for specific light protection requirements for each medication.

Temperature Regulation:

- Maintain storage areas at room temperature, typically between 15°C and 25°C (59°F and 77°F), unless otherwise specified by the medication's storage requirements.
- Refrigerate medications that require lower storage temperatures, typically between 2°C and 8°C (36°F and 46°F). Use dedicated medication refrigerators that allow for precise temperature control.
- Avoid storing medications in areas prone to temperature fluctuations, such as near radiators, vents, or in vehicles.

Additional Considerations

- **Documentation and Labeling**: Clearly label storage areas and containers with the appropriate storage conditions for each medication. Maintain records of storage conditions, including temperature and humidity logs.
- **Staff Training**: Educate pharmacy staff on the importance of proper storage conditions for medications and how to monitor and adjust environmental parameters.

- **Regular Inspection**: Periodically inspect medication storage areas and the medications themselves for signs of degradation, contamination, or damage due to humidity, light, or temperature.

Controlling environmental conditions, including humidity, light, and temperature, in medication storage areas is essential for preserving medication stability and integrity. Adhering to these guidelines helps ensure that medications remain effective and safe for patient use throughout their shelf life.

Safety Data Sheets (SDS) are essential resources that provide comprehensive information about the properties of hazardous drugs, including their potential health and safety risks. For pharmacy technicians working with these substances, understanding and adhering to the guidelines outlined in the SDS is crucial for ensuring safety and compliance with regulatory standards, such as USP <800>.

Handling Precautions
- **Safe Handling Practices**: The SDS outlines specific practices for safely handling hazardous drugs, such as avoiding direct skin contact, not eating or drinking near hazardous drugs, and using appropriate engineering controls like biological safety cabinets.
- **Storage Requirements**: Information on proper storage conditions to maintain drug stability and prevent contamination, including requirements for temperature, light, and humidity, as well as segregation of hazardous drugs from non-hazardous items.

Personal Protective Equipment (PPE) Requirements
- **Type of PPE**: The SDS specifies the types of PPE required when handling the drug, which may include gloves, gowns, respiratory protection, and eye/face protection. It is essential to use PPE that is rated for protection against the specific hazards of the drug.
- **Proper Use and Disposal**: Instructions for correctly donning and doffing PPE to avoid contamination, as well as proper disposal procedures for used PPE, to minimize exposure to hazardous drug residues.

Spill Management Procedures
- **Immediate Actions**: Step-by-step instructions for responding to spills, including initial actions to protect oneself and others, such as evacuating the area and donning PPE.
- **Containment and Clean-up**: Detailed procedures for containing the spill to prevent further spread, safe methods for cleaning up the spill, and appropriate decontamination procedures to ensure complete removal of hazardous residues.
- **Disposal**: Guidelines for the safe disposal of spill materials and contaminated PPE, including the use of designated hazardous waste containers and compliance with local, state, and federal waste disposal regulations.

Using SDS for Safety and Compliance
- **Accessibility**: Pharmacy technicians should ensure that SDS for all hazardous drugs they handle are readily accessible in the work area, either in a physical binder or through an electronic system.
- **Familiarity**: Technicians should familiarize themselves with the critical information in the SDS, especially the handling precautions, PPE requirements, and spill management procedures, for each hazardous drug they work with.
- **Training**: Participate in regular training sessions that include reviewing SDS information, practicing safe handling techniques, and conducting spill response drills.
- **Compliance with USP <800>**: Adhering to the safety practices outlined in the SDS is integral to complying with USP <800> standards, which provide detailed guidance on handling hazardous drugs in healthcare settings to protect personnel, patients, and the environment.

Safety Data Sheets are invaluable tools for pharmacy technicians in managing the risks associated with hazardous drugs. By thoroughly understanding and applying the information contained in the SDS, including handling precautions, PPE requirements, and spill management procedures, pharmacy technicians can ensure their safety and maintain compliance with regulations like USP <800>. Regular review and training on SDS content, along with adherence to established safety protocols, are essential for minimizing the health risks posed by hazardous drugs in the pharmacy setting.

V. Pharmacy Inventory Management:

Think of Pharmacy Inventory Management as a well-choreographed dance. It's about ensuring the right medications waltz onto the shelves at the right time, creating a seamless experience for patients. Get ready to master the art of stock balancing, forecasting, and keeping those shelves organized and efficient. Here's a glimpse into what we'll cover:

- Just-In-Time Pharmacy: Explore strategies to maintain optimal stock levels, preventing both frustrating shortages and wasteful overstocking.
- Behind the Order Button: Understand the world of wholesalers, contracts, and how to place those crucial orders that keep your pharmacy running smoothly.
- Technology Tango: Discover how pharmacy inventory software helps you track expiration dates, recall alerts, and gives you real-time stock information.
- Counting and Control: Learn the ins and outs of periodic controlled substance inventories as well as safeguarding other high-value medications.
- It's Not Just About Refills: We'll look beyond patient demand to consider factors like seasonal illness patterns and drug recalls that can impact your inventory.

Why Inventory Management Matters:

- Happy Patients, Smooth Operations: A well-managed inventory allows you to fill prescriptions promptly, avoid frustrating backorders, and minimize patient wait times.
- It's About the Money: Efficient inventory practices reduce waste due to expired medications, and help control the pharmacy's bottom line.
- Regulatory Compliance: You'll learn the records to keep and procedures to follow to stay on the right side of state and federal regulations.

Get ready to become the inventory ninja! By the end of this section, you'll feel empowered to take charge of the pharmacy's stock, ensuring a seamless flow of medications for the patients you serve.

The National Drug Code (NDC) is a unique identifier assigned to medications in the United States by the Food and Drug Administration (FDA). The NDC serves as a universal product identifier for human drugs and provides specific information about the medication, including the manufacturer, the specific product, and the packaging. An NDC number is typically displayed in a 10-digit format, divided into three segments: the labeler code, the product code, and the package code, which are separated by hyphens. It's important to note that the NDC can be displayed in different formats, such as 5-4-2 or 5-3-2, depending on the number of digits in each segment.

Components of an NDC Number
1. **Labeler Code (Manufacturer Code)**:
   - **Digits**: The first segment contains 4 or 5 digits.
   - **Represents**: This segment identifies the manufacturer or labeler of the product. The FDA assigns this code to the labeler, and it remains a constant identifier for the labeler in all their products' NDC numbers.

- **Example**: If the labeler code is "12345", it indicates the specific manufacturer registered with the FDA.

2. **Product Code**:
   - **Digits**: The second segment consists of 3 or 4 digits.
   - **Represents**: This segment identifies a specific strength, dosage form, and formulation for a particular drug. Each unique formulation and dosage form of a drug produced by the same labeler will have a distinct product code.
   - **Example**: In the NDC "12345-6789-XX", "6789" would represent a specific drug's formulation, strength, and dosage form, such as 20mg tablets of a particular medication.

3. **Package Code**:
   - **Digits**: The third segment is made up of 1 or 2 digits.
   - **Represents**: This segment indicates the package size and type. It identifies how the product is packaged and sold, which can vary from single units to bulk packages.
   - **Example**: In the NDC "12345-6789-01", "01" might represent a specific package type, such as a bottle containing 30 tablets.

Understanding NDC Formats

The NDC can be represented in different formats, primarily based on the number of digits in each segment. The most common formats are:

- **5-4-2 Format**: Used when the labeler code has 5 digits, the product code has 4 digits, and the package code has 2 digits (e.g., "12345-6789-01").
- **5-3-2 Format**: Used when the labeler code has 5 digits, the product code has 3 digits, and the package code has 2 digits (e.g., "12345-678-01").

The FDA does not dictate the format, so the presentation of the NDC number can vary. However, the total number of digits should always be 10.

Practical Implications

Understanding the NDC is crucial for healthcare professionals, including pharmacists and pharmacy technicians, as it allows them to:

- **Verify Medications**: Ensure the correct medication, dosage form, strength, and quantity are dispensed.
- **Manage Inventory**: Facilitate the accurate ordering, stocking, and inventory management of pharmaceutical products.
- **Billing and Reimbursement**: Use NDC numbers for billing and insurance claims to specify the exact medication provided to the patient.

The NDC number is a vital identifier in the pharmaceutical industry, offering a systematic way to identify drug products from manufacturing through distribution to dispensing. Familiarity with the NDC format and its components enhances medication safety, inventory management, and billing processes in healthcare settings.

Scenario: Substituting a Medication for a Patient with Hypertension
Background:
A pharmacy technician named Alex is working in a community pharmacy when a regular patient, Mrs. Johnson, comes in to refill her prescription for Lisinopril 20 mg tablets, used to manage her hypertension. Mrs. Johnson has been stable on this medication and dosage for several years. However, upon checking the inventory, Alex notices that the specific brand and NDC number (e.g., "12345-6789-01") of Lisinopril 20 mg tablets that Mrs. Johnson usually receives are out of stock due to a temporary supply issue.

Task:
Alex needs to locate a suitable alternative product for Mrs. Johnson's Lisinopril 20 mg prescription, ensuring continuity of care and avoiding any potential disruption in Mrs. Johnson's hypertension management.

Factors to Consider When Making Substitutions:
Identical Active Ingredient:

The alternative must contain Lisinopril as the active ingredient to ensure therapeutic consistency.
Dosage Form:

The substitute should be in tablet form, as Mrs. Johnson's prescription and her familiarity are with Lisinopril tablets.
Strength:

The strength of the alternative Lisinopril must be 20 mg to match her current prescription and maintain the effectiveness of her hypertension management.
Package Size:

Alex should consider the package size of the alternative product. If Mrs. Johnson's original prescription was for a 30-tablet package, the substitute should ideally be in a similar or convenient package size to maintain her dosing schedule without interruption.
Manufacturer Reputation and Drug Formulary Considerations:

The reputation of the alternative product's manufacturer for quality and reliability should be considered. Additionally, Alex should check the pharmacy's drug formulary or insurance coverage to ensure the substitute is covered for Mrs. Johnson.
Patient Counseling and Notification:

Alex will need to inform Mrs. Johnson about the substitution, explaining the reason for the change and reassuring her that the alternative medication has the same efficacy and safety profile as her usual brand.
Execution:
After considering these factors, Alex locates an alternative product with NDC "54321-9876-05" that matches the required active ingredient (Lisinopril), dosage form (tablet), strength (20 mg), and comes in a package of 30 tablets, which is suitable for Mrs. Johnson's monthly supply.

Before finalizing the substitution, Alex consults with the pharmacist on duty to verify the suitability of the chosen alternative. The pharmacist approves the substitution and advises Alex to update Mrs. Johnson's medication profile to reflect the change for this refill.

Alex then prepares the Lisinopril 20 mg tablets from the alternative NDC, labels the medication, and includes a note in the system to check the availability of Mrs. Johnson's usual brand for her next refill. When Mrs. Johnson arrives to pick up her medication, Alex takes the time to explain the temporary substitution, highlighting that the alternative has the same active ingredient, strength, and dosage form as her usual medication. Alex reassures Mrs. Johnson that her treatment effectiveness will remain unchanged and confirms Mrs. Johnson understands the substitution before completing the transaction.

In this scenario, pharmacy technician Alex successfully navigates a medication substitution by carefully considering the essential factors such as the active ingredient, dosage form, strength, and package size. By doing so, Alex ensures Mrs. Johnson's treatment continuity and contributes to the overall goal of maintaining optimal patient care in the pharmacy setting.

Managing drug shortages is a complex challenge that requires proactive and strategic approaches to ensure patient care is not compromised. Pharmacy technicians, in collaboration with pharmacists, play a crucial role in navigating these situations. Here are some strategies to effectively manage drug shortages:

Locating Alternative Suppliers
Wholesaler and Distributor Networks: Regularly communicate with your primary and secondary wholesalers or distributors to check the availability of the drug in shortage. Sometimes, alternative suppliers might have stock available, even if it's limited.

Manufacturer Direct Purchases: Contact the drug manufacturer directly for information on availability and potential direct purchase options. Manufacturers can sometimes allocate products to healthcare providers during shortages.

Pharmacy Networks and Collaborations: Reach out to other pharmacies in your network or area to see if they have surplus stock they can share or sell. Pharmacy networks can be invaluable during shortages for resource sharing.

Therapeutic Substitutions
Pharmacist Consultation: Always consult with a pharmacist before making any therapeutic substitutions. Pharmacists can assess the clinical appropriateness of substituting a medication based on the patient's health status and the therapeutic equivalence of alternatives.

Evidence-Based Alternatives: Use evidence-based resources, such as clinical guidelines and formulary recommendations, to identify suitable therapeutic alternatives. Ensure that the alternative medication has a similar mechanism of action, efficacy, and safety profile.

Communication with Prescribers: Inform the prescriber of the drug shortage and suggest therapeutic alternatives. Obtain a new prescription if a substitution is agreed upon, ensuring legal and regulatory compliance.

Prioritizing Dispensing for Patients with Urgent Needs
Assess Clinical Urgency: Work with pharmacists to prioritize patients based on the clinical urgency of their need for the medication. Patients for whom the medication is life-sustaining or critical for maintaining quality of life should be prioritized.

Partial Fills: In some cases, providing a partial fill of the medication can be a temporary solution, allowing the patient to continue their therapy while more of the drug is sourced. This approach requires clear communication with the patient and prescriber about the plan for obtaining the remainder of the medication.

Patient Communication: Communicate transparently with patients about the shortage, the steps being taken to resolve the issue, and the expected timeline. Offer support and guidance on how they can manage their condition during the shortage.

Documentation and Monitoring
Shortage Log: Maintain a log of all drug shortages, including the actions taken, suppliers contacted, and any substitutions made. This record can be valuable for future reference and for identifying patterns that might inform better long-term strategies.

Regular Review: Regularly review the status of drug shortages and the effectiveness of implemented strategies. This can help in adjusting approaches as the situation evolves and in preparing for future shortages.

Policy Development: Develop or contribute to the development of pharmacy policies on managing drug shortages, ensuring there are standardized procedures that all staff can follow.
Effectively managing drug shortages requires a multifaceted approach, involving diligent monitoring of supply chains, strategic collaboration with healthcare professionals, and clear communication with patients. By employing these strategies, pharmacy technicians, in collaboration with pharmacists, can mitigate the impact of drug shortages on patient care, ensuring that therapeutic needs are met even in challenging circumstances.

Handling drug backorders is a critical aspect of pharmacy operations, and the approach can vary significantly depending on whether the pharmacy is dealing with a wholesaler or ordering directly from the manufacturer. Both methods have their unique processes, lead time differences, order minimums, and implications for inventory decisions.

Ordering from a Wholesaler
Process: Pharmacies typically order most of their inventory from wholesalers, who aggregate products from various manufacturers. When a drug is on backorder, the pharmacy can place the order with the wholesaler, who then fulfills it once the stock becomes available.

Lead Time Differences: Wholesalers usually have shorter lead times compared to manufacturers because they might have multiple sources for the same drug or have stock in different locations. However, during widespread shortages, lead times can increase significantly.

Order Minimums: Wholesalers often have lower order minimums or none at all, making it easier for pharmacies to order small quantities. This flexibility is beneficial for managing inventory levels without overstocking.

Inventory Decisions: Ordering from wholesalers allows pharmacies to maintain a leaner inventory, relying on the wholesaler's broader network to source products. However, reliance on wholesalers during backorders might require pharmacies to seek alternative drugs or suppliers if the lead time extends too long.

Ordering Directly from the Manufacturer

Process: Ordering directly from the drug manufacturer is less common for routine inventory but can be an alternative during backorders. This process involves contacting the manufacturer's sales or customer service department and placing an order for the drug in shortage.

Lead Time Differences: Lead times can be longer when ordering directly from the manufacturer, especially if the drug is in production or if there are allocation issues. However, obtaining information directly from the manufacturer about the expected availability can sometimes offer more certainty.

Order Minimums: Manufacturers may have higher order minimums compared to wholesalers, which can be a barrier for smaller pharmacies or those not wanting to hold excessive inventory. This can lead to higher upfront costs and potential overstock issues.

Inventory Decisions: Ordering directly from the manufacturer might necessitate larger, less frequent orders, affecting inventory turnover and cash flow. Pharmacies need to balance the risk of stockouts against the cost of holding excess inventory.

Considerations and Strategies
Diversification: Pharmacies should consider diversifying their sourcing strategies, using both wholesalers and direct manufacturer orders to mitigate risks associated with backorders.
Communication: Regular communication with both wholesalers and manufacturers is key to staying informed about backorder statuses, expected lead times, and potential alternatives.
Alternative Sourcing: Exploring alternative drugs or therapeutic substitutions (with prescriber approval) can be a strategy to manage patient care during backorders.
Contingency Planning: Developing a contingency plan for handling backorders, including criteria for when to order from wholesalers versus manufacturers, can help pharmacies respond more effectively to supply disruptions. While ordering from wholesalers is generally more convenient and allows for more flexible inventory management, direct manufacturer orders can sometimes provide more certainty during backorders, albeit with potential challenges like longer lead times and higher order minimums. Pharmacies should weigh these factors and adopt a strategic approach to inventory management that accommodates the nuances of each ordering method.

The 340B Drug Pricing Program, established by the U.S. government in 1992, is designed to enable eligible healthcare facilities to purchase outpatient drugs at significantly reduced prices. The program aims to stretch scarce federal resources, reduce medication costs for patients, and provide more comprehensive services. Eligible entities include certain types of hospitals serving a high number of low-income patients, as well as specific clinics and healthcare centers receiving federal grants.

Impact on Drug Pricing for Eligible Healthcare Facilities
1. **Reduced Costs**: Eligible healthcare facilities can purchase medications at prices significantly lower than the average wholesale price, allowing them to save on drug costs.
2. **Expanded Services**: The savings from the 340B Program can be used to enhance patient services, such as by offering more free or discounted medications or expanding healthcare services offered to underserved populations.
3. **Financial Sustainability**: For many participating facilities, the program helps maintain financial sustainability, enabling them to serve vulnerable populations effectively.

Role of Pharmacy Technicians in Verifying Patient Eligibility
Pharmacy technicians play a crucial role in the operational aspects of the 340B Program, particularly in verifying patient eligibility and maintaining compliance with program requirements:

1. **Eligibility Verification**:
   - Technicians verify that patients meet the criteria for receiving 340B discounted drugs, ensuring that medications are dispensed in accordance with program guidelines. Eligibility criteria can include patient status (e.g., outpatient), the healthcare service provided, and the relationship between the service and the eligible healthcare facility.
2. **Maintaining Compliance**:
   - Technicians must be familiar with the specific compliance requirements of the 340B Program to avoid diversion (providing 340B drugs to ineligible patients) and duplicate discounts (where a rebate is claimed for a drug already purchased at the 340B discounted price).
3. **Coordination with Prescribers**:
   - Technicians may need to coordinate with prescribers to ensure prescriptions are written and documented in a manner that meets 340B eligibility requirements.

Record-Keeping Requirements

Maintaining accurate records is essential for compliance with the 340B Program and for audits conducted by the Health Resources and Services Administration (HRSA), which oversees the program:

1. **Documentation of Eligibility**:
   - Pharmacy technicians must ensure that all dispensed 340B medications have corresponding documentation proving patient eligibility, including medical records and documentation of the service provided.
2. **Inventory Management**:
   - Accurate records of 340B drug inventory must be maintained, including purchasing records, dispensing logs, and any other documentation that tracks the flow of 340B drugs through the pharmacy.
3. **Audit Readiness**:
   - Technicians should assist in maintaining records in an audit-ready state, ensuring that documentation can support compliance with 340B Program requirements during an HRSA audit or internal compliance check.
4. **Software and Reporting**:
   - Many 340B eligible facilities use specialized software to manage 340B prescriptions and compliance. Pharmacy technicians may be responsible for managing or inputting data into these systems, ensuring accurate reporting and compliance.

Pharmacy technicians are vital to the successful implementation and management of the 340B Program in eligible healthcare facilities. Their roles in verifying patient eligibility, maintaining compliance, and ensuring accurate record-keeping are critical for maximizing the benefits of the program and ensuring that it continues to serve vulnerable populations effectively.

The 340B Drug Pricing Program, while beneficial in many respects, does have its limitations and complexities that can influence the cost-effectiveness of drug procurement for participating pharmacies and healthcare facilities. Understanding these limitations is crucial for making informed purchasing decisions.

Limitations of the 340B Program

Administrative Complexity: The management of 340B pricing within a pharmacy's inventory system can be complex, requiring meticulous tracking and segregation of 340B drugs from non-340B inventory. This complexity can increase operational costs and reduce the net benefit.

Compliance and Audit Risks: Strict compliance with 340B Program requirements, including patient eligibility and prevention of drug diversion, places a significant administrative burden on participating facilities. Non-compliance can lead to financial penalties and repayment of discounts, negating the cost savings.

Variable Savings: The discounts offered through the 340B Program can vary widely depending on the drug and the manufacturer. In some cases, the 340B price might not be significantly lower than prices available through other purchasing arrangements, such as group purchasing organizations (GPOs) or direct manufacturer discounts.

Market Dynamics: The pharmaceutical market is dynamic, with frequent changes in drug prices, availability, and manufacturer promotions. These changes can occasionally make non-340B purchasing options more cost-effective.

Contract Pharmacy Arrangements: Some 340B eligible entities use contract pharmacies to dispense 340B drugs. The contractual agreements and fees associated with these arrangements can diminish the financial benefits of the program.

Situations Influencing Pharmacy Purchasing Decisions
Lower Prices Elsewhere: Pharmacies might find certain medications at lower prices through alternative sources, such as GPOs, especially for generic drugs where the market is competitive, and prices can fluctuate significantly.

Manufacturer Shortages or Allocations: During drug shortages or when manufacturers allocate specific quantities to different channels, the 340B price might not be the most advantageous, or the drug might not be available through 340B at all, necessitating alternative sourcing.

Special Promotions and Discounts: Manufacturers or wholesalers might offer promotions, rebates, or additional discounts that make non-340B purchasing more appealing for specific drugs at certain times.

Overhead Costs of Compliance: For some drugs, the overhead costs associated with maintaining 340B compliance, including software, staffing, and auditing, might outweigh the cost savings, leading pharmacies to consider non-340B sources.

Decision-Making and Best Practices
Regular Price Comparisons: Pharmacies should regularly compare 340B prices with those available through other channels to ensure they are obtaining the best possible deal for each medication.

Compliance Cost Analysis: Evaluate the total costs of compliance with 340B Program requirements against the savings to determine the net benefit for each drug.

Flexible Sourcing Strategies: Maintain flexibility in sourcing strategies to adapt to market changes, ensuring that patient care remains uninterrupted and cost-effective.

Transparency with Patients: When the cost-savings from 340B are minimal or negative, pharmacies should consider the implications for patient charges, especially for uninsured or underinsured patients who might benefit from 340B savings. While the 340B Program offers significant opportunities for cost savings and expanded patient services, pharmacies must navigate its limitations and complexities carefully. By continually evaluating purchasing strategies and remaining adaptable to market changes, pharmacies can maximize the benefits of the 340B Program while ensuring the most cost-effective procurement of medications.

The storage requirements for controlled substances in the United States, as defined by the Drug Enforcement Administration (DEA), vary between Schedule II medications and those classified as Schedules III-V. These regulations are designed to reduce the risk of diversion and misuse while ensuring that these medications are available for legitimate medical needs.

Storage Requirements for Schedule II Medications

Schedule II medications include drugs with a high potential for abuse and dependence, such as oxycodone, fentanyl, and amphetamines. The storage requirements for these substances are more stringent:

- **Secure Storage**: Schedule II drugs must be stored in a substantially constructed, securely locked cabinet or safe. The security measures should be robust enough to deter or prevent unauthorized access.
- **Limited Access**: Access to the storage area should be restricted to authorized personnel only. Pharmacies often maintain a log of individuals who have access to ensure accountability.
- **Inventory Management**: Pharmacies are required to maintain accurate inventory records for Schedule II drugs, including documentation of all receipts, dispenses, thefts, or losses. Inventories must be conducted at least every two years, with records kept for a minimum of two years.

Storage Requirements for Schedules III-V Medications

Schedules III-V medications have a lower potential for abuse compared to Schedule II drugs and include substances such as codeine-containing products, certain stimulants, and sedatives. The storage requirements allow for more flexibility:

- **Dispersed Storage**: Unlike Schedule II medications, Schedules III-V drugs can be stored throughout the pharmacy's inventory in a method known as "dispersed storage." This approach integrates these controlled substances with non-controlled medications on shelves or in other storage areas.
- **Security Measures**: While a dedicated safe or locked cabinet is not explicitly required for Schedules III-V medications, pharmacies must still implement adequate security measures to prevent theft or diversion.
- **Inventory Tracking**: Accurate inventory records are still necessary for Schedules III-V drugs, including documentation of receipts, dispenses, and losses. Periodic inventories are required, with the same record-keeping duration as Schedule II medications.

Impact of Dispersed Storage on Inventory Tracking

- **Enhanced Oversight**: Dispersed storage can facilitate better oversight by integrating controlled substance monitoring into the broader pharmacy inventory management processes.
- **Challenges in Tracking**: While dispersed storage can deter theft by making it less obvious where controlled substances are kept, it may complicate inventory tracking, as these drugs are not centralized.
- **Adoption of Technology**: To manage the challenges of dispersed storage, many pharmacies utilize technology solutions like electronic inventory systems, which can track medication movement and usage across various storage locations.

- **Regular Audits**: Pharmacies may conduct more frequent audits or cycle counts for controlled substances stored in a dispersed manner to ensure accuracy and identify discrepancies promptly.

Best Practices

- **Comprehensive Training**: Pharmacy staff should receive comprehensive training on the specific storage requirements for controlled substances and the importance of adhering to DEA regulations.
- **Leverage Technology**: Utilize advanced inventory management systems that provide real-time tracking of controlled substances, support compliance, and facilitate quick responses to discrepancies or potential diversion.
- **Security Enhancements**: Even with dispersed storage for Schedules III-V medications, consider additional security measures such as surveillance cameras, alarm systems, and restricted access areas to enhance overall security.

While Schedule II medications require secure, locked storage, Schedules III-V controlled substances offer the option of dispersed storage within the pharmacy, presenting both opportunities and challenges for inventory management. Adopting robust inventory tracking systems and regular audits can help pharmacies maintain compliance with DEA regulations and ensure the safe handling of these medications.

A periodic controlled substance inventory is a regulatory requirement for pharmacies to account for all controlled substances on hand. This process is crucial for ensuring compliance with regulations set forth by the Drug Enforcement Administration (DEA) and for maintaining the integrity of the pharmacy's controlled substance management practices. The inventory must be conducted at least every two years, though more frequent inventories are encouraged to ensure tighter control and oversight.

Required Documentation for Periodic Controlled Substance Inventory
When conducting a periodic inventory of controlled substances, specific details must be meticulously recorded to meet regulatory requirements:

Date of Inventory: The exact date the inventory is conducted must be documented. Pharmacies have the flexibility to choose any date for the inventory, provided it does not exceed two years since the last inventory date.

Time of Inventory: The inventory can be taken at the start or the end of the business day. The specific time must be noted in the inventory records, as this determines which transactions need to be included or excluded from the inventory count.

Inventory Method: The documentation should specify whether the inventory was a complete "actual count" or an "estimated count." For Schedule II controlled substances, an exact count is mandatory. For Schedules III-V, an estimated count is permissible unless the container holds more than 1,000 tablets or capsules, in which case an exact count is required.

Name of the Controlled Substances: The inventory must list each controlled substance by its name. This includes the brand name or generic name along with the dosage form and strength.

Quantity of Each Substance: The total quantity of each controlled substance must be accurately recorded. For Schedule II substances, this involves an exact count of all units. For Schedules III-V, an exact count is required for containers with more than 1,000 units, while an estimate is acceptable for smaller quantities.

Form of Substance: The form of each controlled substance (e.g., tablet, capsule, liquid) must be documented, along with the concentration if applicable.

Location of Substances: If controlled substances are stored in multiple locations within the pharmacy, the inventory must specify these locations for each drug.

Handling Discrepancies
Discrepancies discovered during the inventory process must be addressed promptly and thoroughly:

Investigation: Any discrepancy between the inventory count and what should theoretically be on hand, based on dispensing records, must be investigated immediately to determine the cause.

Documentation: The details of the discrepancy, the investigation findings, and any corrective actions taken must be documented. This documentation is crucial for regulatory compliance and may be required in the event of an audit.

Reporting: Significant losses or thefts of controlled substances must be reported to the DEA using Form 106 (Report of Theft or Loss of Controlled Substances). Minor discrepancies should still be documented internally but may not require DEA notification unless a pattern emerges that suggests ongoing issues.

Corrective Measures: Based on the investigation's findings, the pharmacy should implement corrective measures to prevent future discrepancies. This might include additional staff training, changes in storage or security practices, or modifications to inventory management procedures.

Review and Update Policies: The pharmacy's controlled substance policies and procedures should be reviewed and updated in light of the discrepancy investigation to strengthen controls and prevent recurrence.

Properly conducted and documented periodic controlled substance inventories are essential for regulatory compliance, safeguarding against diversion, and ensuring the responsible management of controlled substances within the pharmacy setting.

Certain medications require special storage conditions, such as protection from light or freezing temperatures, to maintain their stability, potency, and efficacy. These requirements are based on the medication's chemical and physical properties and how they interact with environmental factors. Failure to adhere to these conditions can lead to drug degradation, reduced potency, or changes in medication form, which can compromise patient safety and treatment effectiveness.

Protection from Light
Rationale: Many drugs are photosensitive, meaning they can undergo chemical changes when exposed to light (especially UV light). These changes can lead to the formation of harmful degradation products, loss of drug potency, or alterations in the drug's therapeutic properties.

Examples:

Nitroglycerin: Used for angina pectoris, nitroglycerin is highly light-sensitive and can lose potency when exposed to light, necessitating storage in dark, amber-colored bottles.

Amphotericin B: An antifungal medication that is light-sensitive. Exposure to light can lead to degradation, reducing its efficacy.
Consequences: Exposure to light can cause some medications to degrade, reducing their effectiveness. In some cases, the degradation products can be harmful, leading to adverse effects.

Protection from Freezing
Rationale: Certain medications can undergo physical changes or degradation when frozen, which can alter their solubility, stability, and efficacy. Freezing can cause the separation of components in emulsions, crystallization of solutions, or damage to the integrity of drug delivery systems.

Examples:
Vaccines: Many vaccines are sensitive to freezing temperatures, which can affect their immunogenicity and potency. For instance, the varicella vaccine can lose effectiveness if frozen.
Insulin: Freezing can cause insulin to precipitate or form aggregates, affecting its potency and pharmacokinetic properties.
Consequences: Freezing can irreversibly alter the physical state or stability of medications, rendering them ineffective or unsafe for use. Patients may receive suboptimal or inactive doses, leading to therapeutic failure or adverse outcomes.

General Guidelines for Special Storage Conditions
Adherence to Manufacturer's Instructions: Always follow the storage instructions provided by the medication's manufacturer, as they are based on stability testing under various conditions.

Use of Appropriate Containers: Store light-sensitive medications in opaque or amber-colored containers to minimize light exposure. Ensure containers are airtight to protect against humidity and air oxidation.

Proper Refrigeration: Medications requiring refrigeration should be stored at temperatures typically between 2°C and 8°C (36°F and 46°F). Pharmacies should use dedicated medication refrigerators with temperature monitoring and alarms.

Avoiding Freezing: For medications sensitive to freezing, ensure they are stored in a refrigerator that does not reach freezing temperatures or in a part of the refrigerator away from the cooling element where freezing is less likely.

Staff Training and Awareness: Pharmacy staff should be trained on the importance of special storage conditions and the potential consequences of improper storage.

Regular Monitoring: Implement a system for regular monitoring and recording of storage conditions, including temperature logs and checks for light exposure.

Proper storage of medications is a critical aspect of pharmacy practice and patient care. Failure to store medications under recommended conditions can compromise their efficacy and safety, potentially leading to therapeutic failures or adverse drug reactions. Pharmacists and pharmacy technicians play a vital role in ensuring that all medications are stored appropriately, adhering to guidelines and manufacturer instructions.

The use of inventory management software in pharmacies plays a crucial role in efficiently tracking expiration dates of medications and generating alerts for short-dated products. This technological approach enhances the accuracy and efficiency of inventory control, ultimately optimizing stock rotation and minimizing waste. Here's how it contributes to more effective inventory management:

Tracking Expiration Dates
Automated Monitoring: Inventory management software automates the tracking of expiration dates for all medications in stock. It maintains a database with the expiry information of each item, eliminating manual tracking errors and ensuring that the data is always up-to-date.

Prioritization of Short-Dated Products: The software can prioritize medications that are approaching their expiration dates, ensuring they are dispensed or used first before newer stock. This "first-expiry, first-out" (FEFO) approach is critical in managing pharmaceutical products where the expiration date directly impacts the medication's safety and efficacy.

Alerts for Short-Dated Products
Automated Alerts: The software generates automated alerts for products nearing their expiration dates, allowing pharmacy staff to take timely action. These alerts can be set to notify staff well in advance, providing ample time to adjust ordering and dispensing practices.

Customizable Notification Settings: Pharmacies can customize the alert settings based on their specific needs, such as setting different alert thresholds for different types of medications, based on how critical they are or how fast they typically move.

Optimizing Stock Rotation
Data-Driven Decision Making: Inventory management software provides valuable data that help in making informed decisions about stock rotation. By analyzing patterns of medication usage and turnover rates, pharmacies can adjust their ordering practices to ensure a steady flow of inventory without overstocking.

Integration with Dispensing: The software can be integrated with the pharmacy's dispensing system, ensuring that the oldest stock is dispensed first, according to the FEFO principle. This integration ensures seamless operation between inventory management and patient service.

Minimizing Waste
Reduced Expiry-Related Waste: By effectively rotating stock and dispensing medications based on their expiration dates, pharmacies can significantly reduce the amount of waste due to expired medications. This not only has financial benefits but also contributes to environmental sustainability.

Strategic Ordering: With advanced insights from inventory management software, pharmacies can make more strategic decisions about order quantities and frequencies, reducing the likelihood of overstocking medications that may not be used before their expiration.

Return and Credit Management: For medications that are unlikely to be used before expiration, the software can facilitate the process of returning eligible products to suppliers for credit, further reducing potential waste. The implementation of inventory management software in pharmacies revolutionizes how expiration dates are tracked and managed. By automating the monitoring of expiry dates, generating timely alerts for short-dated products, and optimizing stock rotation, pharmacies can significantly minimize waste and ensure that medications dispensed are within their effective shelf life. This not only enhances operational efficiency but also ensures patient safety and contributes to the pharmacy's economic sustainability.

Insurance claim rejections are a common challenge in pharmacy operations, often leading to delays in medication dispensing and requiring additional administrative work to resolve. Understanding the common reasons behind these rejections is crucial for pharmacy staff to streamline the claims process and enhance patient satisfaction. Here are some of the most prevalent causes of insurance claim rejections:

Incorrect Patient Information
Data Entry Errors: Mistakes in entering patient details, such as misspelled names, incorrect date of birth, or wrong insurance policy numbers, can lead to claim rejections. These errors often arise from manual data entry or misinterpretation of handwritten prescriptions or insurance cards.

Outdated Information: Claims can be rejected if the patient's insurance information has changed but the pharmacy's records have not been updated. This includes changes in insurance providers, policy numbers, or patient demographics.

Prior Authorization Requirements
Unmet Criteria: Many insurance plans require prior authorization for certain medications, especially those that are high-cost, have a safer or more cost-effective alternative, or are used for non-traditional indications. If the prescriber has not obtained approval before the prescription is filled, the claim may be rejected.

Incomplete Documentation: Even if prior authorization is sought, incomplete submission of the necessary clinical information or justification for the prescribed medication can result in rejection.

Formulary Restrictions
Non-Formulary Drugs: Insurance formularies list the drugs that are covered under a particular plan. If a prescribed medication is not on the patient's formulary, the claim may be denied. Insurers encourage the use of formulary drugs by offering lower copays or by not covering non-formulary medications at all.

Therapeutic Substitution: Some insurance plans implement therapeutic substitution policies, where a prescribed medication is substituted with a therapeutically equivalent but more cost-effective alternative. If the original medication is dispensed without addressing this substitution, the claim may be rejected.

Step Therapy Requirements: Certain insurance plans require step therapy, where patients must try one or more specified medications and prove they are not effective before a more expensive medication is approved. If this protocol is not followed, the claim for the higher-tier medication may be rejected.

Dosage or Quantity Limits
Exceeding Limits: Insurance plans often have limits on the quantity or dosage of medication that can be dispensed within a certain period. Claims for quantities exceeding these limits are likely to be rejected unless justified and approved through an exceptions process.
Copayment or Coverage Issues

Deductibles and Copays: Claims can be rejected if there is confusion or a lack of clarity about the patient's responsibility for deductibles or copayments, especially at the beginning of a new insurance cycle.

Coverage Termination: If a patient's insurance coverage has been terminated or suspended, any claims processed during the period of inactivity will be rejected.

Addressing Claim Rejections
To mitigate these issues, pharmacy staff can take several proactive steps:

Verification: Regularly verify and update patient insurance information.
Education: Educate patients about their insurance plan's formulary, prior authorization, and step therapy requirements.
Communication: Maintain open lines of communication with prescribers to address prior authorizations, formulary issues, and therapeutic substitutions efficiently.
Technology: Utilize pharmacy management systems that can flag common issues before claim submission, reducing the likelihood of rejections.
Understanding and addressing these common reasons for insurance claim rejections can significantly improve the efficiency of pharmacy operations, reduce administrative burdens, and enhance patient care and satisfaction.

Troubleshooting a rejected insurance claim is a multi-step process that requires attention to detail, effective communication, and problem-solving skills. Pharmacy technicians play a vital role in this process, ensuring that patients receive their medications in a timely manner. Here's a detailed outline of the steps involved in troubleshooting a rejected insurance claim:

1. Identifying the Reason for Rejection

- **Review the Rejection Notice**: Begin by carefully reviewing the rejection notice or electronic rejection message provided by the insurance company. These notices typically include specific codes and descriptions that explain why the claim was rejected.
- **Common Rejection Codes**: Familiarize yourself with common rejection codes related to patient information errors, formulary issues, prior authorization requirements, dosage or quantity limits, and other plan-specific rules.

2. Verifying Patient and Prescription Information

- **Double-Check Patient Information**: Confirm the accuracy of the patient's information, including name, date of birth, insurance policy number, and group number. Ensure that this information matches what is on file with the insurance company.
- **Review Prescription Details**: Verify the prescription details, such as drug name, dosage, quantity, and prescriber information, to ensure they were entered correctly and match the insurance company's formulary requirements.

3. Communicating with Relevant Parties

- **Insurance Company**: Contact the insurance company's pharmacy help desk using the contact information provided on the rejection notice or the patient's insurance card. Be prepared to provide the claim details and ask for clarification on the rejection reason and how to resolve it.
- **Prescriber**: If the rejection is due to formulary restrictions, prior authorization, or therapeutic substitution requirements, contact the prescriber to discuss alternative options or to initiate the prior authorization process.

- **Patient**: Keep the patient informed throughout the troubleshooting process, especially if there are delays or if additional information is needed from them.

4. Resolving Specific Issues
- **Prior Authorization**: If prior authorization is needed, work with the prescriber's office to submit the necessary documentation to the insurance company. Follow up to ensure the authorization is processed.
- **Formulary Issues**: For non-formulary drugs, discuss alternative formulary options with the prescriber or seek approval for an exception from the insurance company.
- **Dosage or Quantity Limits**: If the claim was rejected due to exceeding dosage or quantity limits, consult with the prescriber to adjust the prescription or request an override from the insurance company.

5. Resubmitting the Claim
- **Correction of Errors**: Make any necessary corrections to patient information, prescription details, or insurance billing codes based on the information gathered.
- **Electronic Resubmission**: Use the pharmacy's software system to electronically resubmit the corrected claim to the insurance company. Ensure that all changes are accurately reflected in the new submission.
- **Confirmation of Processing**: After resubmitting the claim, confirm that it has been received and processed by the insurance company. This may require checking the status electronically or following up by phone.

6. Documentation and Follow-Up
- **Record-Keeping**: Document all steps taken to troubleshoot the rejected claim, including communications with the insurance company, the prescriber, and the patient. This documentation is essential for future reference and in case of audits.
- **Finalizing the Dispensing Process**: Once the claim is approved, finalize the dispensing process, inform the patient of any copayment or coverage details, and provide the medication with appropriate counseling.

Troubleshooting rejected insurance claims is an integral part of pharmacy operations that requires meticulousness, effective communication, and an understanding of insurance policies. By systematically identifying the error, engaging with the insurance company and prescriber, and making informed corrections, pharmacy technicians can efficiently resolve claim rejections, ensuring patients receive their medications without unnecessary delays.

VI. Pharmacy Quality Assurance:

Get ready to become a quality control detective! The Pharmacy Quality Assurance Section trains you to spot potential errors, identify system weaknesses, and ensure your pharmacy delivers the highest level of care to every patient.

What We'll Discover:
- Errors – The Good, the Bad, and How to Stop Them: We'll explore different types of medication errors, common causes, and how technology (like barcode scanning) helps reduce them.
- Reporting for a Safer Tomorrow: Understand the importance of error and near-miss reporting, both within your pharmacy and to national organizations. Learn how analyzing these incidents leads to improvements.
- Problem-Solving Superpowers: Develop strategies for troubleshooting issues that pop up in the dispensing process, like insurance rejections and prescription conflicts.

- Continuous Improvement: Learn about quality improvement tools (like those fishbone diagrams) that help your team identify root causes and create lasting solutions, not just temporary fixes.
- Going Beyond Safety: We'll touch upon quality control throughout the pharmacy – from keeping the shelves tidy to providing top-notch patient counseling.

Why Quality Assurance is Key:

- It's All About the Patients: Every error prevented is a potential harm avoided. Quality assurance safeguards your patients' health.
- Trust and Reputation: A pharmacy known for its accuracy and attention to detail earns the trust of both patients and the healthcare community.
- Professional Excellence: Quality assurance isn't just about following rules – it's about a mindset of continuous learning and improvement.

Think of this section as your toolkit for creating a culture of quality within your pharmacy. By the end, you'll be equipped to take an active role in ensuring every prescription that leaves your counter promotes safety and patient wellbeing.

E-prescribing, or electronic prescribing, is a technology that allows prescribers to send prescriptions directly to a pharmacy's computer system, bypassing the traditional methods of handwritten or faxed prescriptions. This advancement significantly reduces various types of medication errors, enhancing patient safety and the efficiency of the prescribing process. Here's how e-prescribing addresses specific medication error concerns:

Legibility Issues

- **Handwritten Prescriptions**: One of the most common sources of medication errors with handwritten prescriptions is poor legibility, which can lead to misinterpretation of the drug name, dosage, or directions by pharmacy staff.
- **E-Prescribing Solution**: E-prescribing eliminates legibility issues by providing clear, electronically generated text for all prescription details. This clarity ensures that pharmacy staff can accurately interpret and dispense the correct medication.

Look-Alike/Sound-Alike Drug Confusion

- **Traditional Prescriptions**: Look-alike/sound-alike (LASA) drug names are a significant source of medication errors. Similarities in drug names, when handwritten or faxed, can easily be mistaken for one another, leading to the dispensing of the wrong medication.
- **E-Prescribing Solution**: E-prescribing systems often incorporate alert mechanisms that notify prescribers if the entered drug name closely resembles another drug name, reducing the risk of selecting the wrong medication. Additionally, the electronic transmission of the prescription minimizes the chance of pharmacy staff misinterpreting similar drug names.

Dosing Unit Errors

- **Unit Misinterpretation**: With handwritten prescriptions, dosing units can be misread or misinterpreted, especially if abbreviations are used or if the handwriting is unclear. This can lead to errors in medication strength or quantity dispensed.
- **E-Prescribing Solution**: E-prescribing systems typically use standardized dosing units and require prescribers to select from predefined options, reducing the risk of dosing errors. The electronic format also helps ensure that dosing instructions are clearly communicated to the pharmacy, minimizing the chance of misinterpretation.

Additional Benefits of E-Prescribing

- **Direct Integration**: E-prescribing systems are often integrated with electronic health records (EHRs), allowing prescribers to have immediate access to a patient's medication history, allergies, and potential drug interactions at the point of prescribing.
- **Real-Time Information**: E-prescribing enables real-time transmission of prescriptions, allowing for quicker dispensing and the ability to address any issues or clarifications immediately, further reducing the risk of errors.
- **Audit Trails**: Electronic prescriptions create an electronic audit trail, providing a record of the prescribing and dispensing process that can be reviewed in case of discrepancies or for quality assurance purposes.

E-prescribing addresses many of the common pitfalls associated with handwritten or faxed prescriptions, such as legibility issues, look-alike/sound-alike drug confusion, and dosing unit errors. By leveraging technology to standardize and clarify prescription information, e-prescribing enhances medication safety, reduces the likelihood of errors, and improves the overall efficiency of the medication dispensing process.

Barcode-Assisted Medication Administration (BCMA) is a technology-driven process designed to enhance the safety and accuracy of medication administration in healthcare settings. It involves the use of barcoding on patient identification bands and medication packaging to verify the 'Five Rights' of medication administration: the right patient, the right medication, the right dose, the right route, and the right time.

Role in Verifying the 'Five Rights'
Right Patient: BCMA systems require healthcare providers to scan the barcode on the patient's identification band, ensuring that the medication is administered to the intended patient.

Right Medication: Scanning the barcode on the medication package confirms that the correct medication is being administered, reducing the risk of medication errors.

Right Dose: The BCMA system checks the medication dosage against the prescriber's orders to ensure the correct dose is administered.

Right Route: The system verifies the route of administration (e.g., oral, intravenous) specified in the medication order, ensuring that the medication is delivered correctly.

Right Time: BCMA systems help ensure medications are administered at the correct times, adhering to the prescribed schedule, and avoiding missed or duplicate doses.

Potential Limitations of BCMA and Addressing Them
Despite the significant benefits of BCMA in enhancing medication safety, there are potential limitations that healthcare facilities must address:

Barcode Scanning Failures: Barcodes can be damaged or poorly printed, leading to scanning failures. To address this, regular checks and maintenance of barcode printers and scanners are essential, and backup procedures should be in place for manual verification when necessary.

Workarounds by Staff: Healthcare staff may develop workarounds that bypass BCMA protocols due to workflow inefficiencies or time constraints. Addressing this requires continuous training, emphasizing the importance of adherence to BCMA protocols for patient safety, and engaging staff in workflow design to reduce the need for workarounds.

Alert Fatigue: BCMA systems can generate numerous alerts, leading to alert fatigue among healthcare providers, who may then ignore important warnings. To mitigate this, it's crucial to regularly review and optimize alert settings to ensure they are meaningful and actionable.

Integration with Electronic Health Records (EHRs): In some cases, BCMA systems may not be fully integrated with EHRs, leading to discrepancies in medication orders. Ensuring seamless integration and real-time communication between BCMA systems and EHRs can help overcome this challenge.

Training and User Competency: Effective use of BCMA systems requires comprehensive training for all healthcare staff involved in medication administration. Regular training sessions and competency assessments can help ensure that staff are proficient in using the system and understanding its importance.

Patient and Medication Exceptions: Some patients (e.g., emergency admissions) or medications (e.g., topical applications) may not be immediately compatible with BCMA protocols. Developing clear guidelines for handling such exceptions is necessary to maintain safety and efficiency.

BCMA is a valuable tool in enhancing medication administration safety by verifying the 'Five Rights.' However, its effectiveness depends on addressing potential limitations through regular system maintenance, staff training, workflow optimization, and ensuring integration with other healthcare information systems. By proactively addressing these challenges, healthcare facilities can maximize the benefits of BCMA in improving patient safety and care quality.

Automated dispensing systems, including carousels and robots, represent significant advancements in pharmacy technology, offering substantial improvements in dispensing accuracy and operational efficiency. These systems are designed to minimize human error in the medication dispensing process, thereby enhancing patient safety. They work by automating the storage, retrieval, and dispensing of medications, and when integrated with pharmacy management software, they provide a comprehensive solution that ensures accuracy and safety in medication dispensing.

Improving Dispensing Accuracy
Precision in Dispensing: Automated systems are programmed to dispense the exact dose and quantity prescribed, reducing the risk of human error associated with manual counting and dispensing. This precision is particularly crucial for medications that require exact dosing, such as anticoagulants or chemotherapy drugs.

Reduction of Selection Errors: Automated carousels and robots use barcoding and other identification technologies to ensure that the correct medication is selected for dispensing. This technology significantly reduces the risk of look-alike/sound-alike medication errors.

Controlled Access: These systems restrict access to medications, allowing only authorized personnel to operate them. This controlled access minimizes the risk of unauthorized handling and dispensing of medications.

Types of Errors Minimized
Dispensing Wrong Medication: Automated systems use sophisticated algorithms and scanning technologies to match prescriptions with the correct medication, thereby minimizing the risk of dispensing the wrong medication.

Incorrect Dosing: The precision of automated systems ensures that medications are dispensed in the correct dosage form and quantity, reducing dosing errors.

Inventory and Expiry Management Errors: Automated dispensing systems track inventory levels in real-time and monitor expiration dates, reducing the risk of dispensing expired or out-of-stock medications.

Integration with Pharmacy Software for Additional Safety Checks
Real-Time Data Synchronization: Automated dispensing systems are often integrated with pharmacy management software, ensuring that medication orders are updated in real-time. This integration allows for immediate verification of prescriptions against patient records, allergy alerts, and potential drug interactions.

Decision Support Tools: Pharmacy software can provide clinical decision support, offering alerts and reminders about drug interactions, duplicate therapies, and patient-specific contraindications based on the patient's medication history and health records.

Audit Trails and Reporting: Integration with pharmacy software allows for comprehensive audit trails of medication dispensing activities, enhancing traceability and accountability. This feature is crucial for identifying and analyzing dispensing errors, should they occur.

Customizable Alerts: Pharmacy software can be configured to generate customizable alerts for specific medications or situations, such as when a medication requires special handling or when a patient's medication history indicates a potential issue with the prescribed medication. Automated dispensing systems, when integrated with pharmacy software, offer a multi-layered approach to improving dispensing accuracy and minimizing medication errors. These technologies complement each other, with automated systems ensuring precise dispensing and physical handling of medications, while pharmacy software provides the necessary clinical checks and balances. Together, they form a robust defense against common dispensing errors, significantly enhancing patient safety and the quality of care provided by pharmacies.

Think of a prospective drug utilization review (DUR) as your computerized safety net, catching potential medication problems before they reach the patient. Let's dive into how it works and your role in the process:
How DUR Flags Potential Issues:
- Patient Profile Power: The DUR system analyzes a patient's medication profile against the new prescription, searching for red flags like:
  - Drug-Drug Interactions: Medications that might clash with each other, causing side effects, reduced effectiveness, or even dangerous reactions.
  - Allergies: Detects if a patient is allergic to the prescribed drug or ingredients.
  - Duplicate Therapy: Identifies overlapping medications, which could lead to overdosing.

- Incorrect Dosage: Alerts to doses outside the usual range, especially for age or kidney/liver function.
- Drug-Disease Conflicts: Checks if a new medication is inappropriate for a patient's medical condition (e.g., some heart medications are dangerous with asthma).

The Technician's Role:

1. Alert the Pharmacist:** When the DUR flags a potential issue, you are often the first to be notified. Bring the alert to the pharmacist's attention for review.
2. Gather Information: Assist the pharmacist by providing any relevant patient details:
   - Confirm allergies and current medications (including over-the-counter or supplements).
   - Recent medical history updates (new diagnoses, hospitalizations).
3. Resolution Support: Depending on the alert, you might:
   - Contact the prescriber's office for clarification under the pharmacist's guidance.
   - Prepare patient counseling materials about potential interactions or necessary monitoring.

Important Points

- DUR is a Tool, Not a Fail-Safe: It relies on the accuracy of the patient's profile; therefore, double-checking information is vital.
- Pharmacist is the Final Decision-Maker: They assess the severity of the alert, consider patient-specific factors, and determine how to proceed.

Your attention to those DUR alerts makes you a key player in preventing medication errors and ensuring patient safety!

Let's break down the difference between proactive and reactive error detection using DURs:

Prospective DUR: The Gatekeeper

- Real-Time Prevention: Catches potential problems *before* the medication reaches the patient.
- Focus on the Individual: Each prescription is analyzed against the patient's specific profile.
- Technician's Role: Alerts the pharmacist to potential issues, aiding in prompt resolution.

Retrospective DUR: The Sleuth

- Looks Back for Patterns: Analyzes dispensing data over time (like a month or quarter).
- The Bigger Picture: Identifies trends like frequently overridden alerts, problematic drug combinations, or prescribers with a higher error rate.
- Technician's Role: May assist in gathering and sorting DUR data for the pharmacist's analysis.

Retrospective DUR's Value for Quality Improvement

- Targeted Education: If specific prescribers repeatedly override alerts for certain drug interactions, focused education on those medications can be provided.
- Proactive Problem-Solving: Patterns in errors might reveal flaws in pharmacy workflow – maybe confusing drug names cause frequent mis-picks. This data guides system improvements.
- Overprescribing Trends: Retrospective DUR helps track if certain medications (like opioids) are being overprescribed in your community, allowing for targeted interventions.

Example Scenario

- Prospective DUR: Catches a potentially dangerous drug interaction for a specific patient. The pharmacist contacts the prescriber and suggests an alternative medication.
- Retrospective DUR: Reveals the same interaction alert is overridden repeatedly, often for short-term use. This prompts pharmacist-led education for prescribers on safer options for short-term situations.

Key Points

- Complementary, not Competitive: Both types of DUR are essential for a comprehensive quality assurance strategy.
- Retrospective DUR isn't about blaming individuals, but rather improving the system to prevent future errors.

Think of it like this: Prospective DUR prevents accidents at a specific intersection, while Retrospective DUR analyzes accident data to recommend a redesign of the entire road for smoother traffic flow.

Think of the FDA's MedWatch program as a vital safety network after a medication hits the market. Your reports can help identify unforeseen issues and protect patients. Let's break down how it works and your role as a pharmacy technician:

Why Post-Marketing Surveillance Matters:

- Clinical Trials Have Limits: While pre-approval studies are rigorous, they can't fully predict how a drug will perform within diverse populations or over long-term use.
- New Risks Emerge: Sometimes rare side effects or problematic interactions only become apparent once hundreds of thousands of patients are taking the drug.

The MedWatch Mission:

- Early Warning System: MedWatch collects reports about suspected adverse events or product quality issues from healthcare professionals, patients, and manufacturers.
- Data Detectives: The FDA analyzes these reports, looking for patterns that might signal a safety risk.
- Taking Action: Based on MedWatch data, the FDA might:
  - Require label changes with new warnings.
  - Issue safety communications to health professionals.
  - In severe cases, restrict the use of a drug or even remove it from the market.

What Pharmacy Staff Should Report:

- Focus on Serious & Unexpected:
  - Severe side effects: Hospitalization, disability, birth defects, life-threatening events.
  - Unexpected reactions: Side effects not listed on the drug label, or occurring at lower doses than expected.
- Product Quality Problems:
  - Contamination, incorrect dosage, mislabeling, medication not working as intended.
- It's OK to be Unsure: Report even if you're not positive the medication is the cause. Your report adds a piece to the puzzle.

Important Points:

- Include Patient Details (anonymized), the medication, suspected side effects, and any other relevant info.
- You're Protecting Patients: Even a single report could contribute to uncovering a safety issue affecting thousands.

As a pharmacy technician, you have front-line insights into how patients respond to medications. Your vigilance in reporting to MedWatch helps keep medications safe for all!

Beyond the FDA's MedWatch, there's a network of organizations dedicated to medication safety. Here's a breakdown of some key players and how reporting systems might be specialized:

National Organizations

Institute for Safe Medication Practices (ISMP): Focuses on analyzing medication errors and disseminating prevention strategies. They run the National Medication Errors Reporting Program (ISMP MERP):

Accepts reports from healthcare professionals and consumers
Broader scope than MedWatch, includes errors that didn't reach the patient (close calls)
Analysis leads to industry-wide recommendations and safety alerts.
The Joint Commission: Accredits hospitals and other healthcare organizations.

Sentinel Event reporting: Mandatory for serious adverse events, including those related to medications. Focuses on root cause analysis within the hospital setting to prevent future errors.
State-Specific Reporting

State Boards of Pharmacy: Many states have their own reporting programs focused on errors occurring in community pharmacies.
Patient Safety Organizations (PSOs): Contracted by the federal government to collect and analyze error data. They provide a confidential, non-punitive environment for reporting, encouraging open sharing to improve safety.
Specialized Error Reporting

Pediatric Focus: Organizations like the Children's Hospital Association and the Pediatric Pharmacy Advocacy Group (PPAG) often have specialized reporting mechanisms for medication errors in children, recognizing the unique risks in this population.
Chemotherapy Errors: Oncology-specific organizations offer reporting channels and analysis for chemotherapy errors, which can have severe consequences and require expert knowledge to address.
How Technicians Can Utilize These Systems

Know Your Options: Familiarize yourself with reporting systems applicable to your type of pharmacy practice.
Reporting Isn't Just for Pharmacists: Technicians often have first-hand knowledge of errors or potential problems. Empower yourself to report!
Learn from the Data: Many organizations publish newsletters and alerts based on error reports. Utilize these to enhance your pharmacy practice.
Remember, reporting medication errors isn't about assigning blame, it's about identifying system weaknesses and driving improvements to protect patients!

Anonymous reporting in a pharmacy is like a safety shield. It encourages open sharing of mistakes, which is essential for learning and preventing future harm. Let's explore why this matters:
Why Fear is a Barrier to Improvement:
- Blame Game: When the focus is on finding someone to punish, people are less likely to admit mistakes for fear of job repercussions or embarrassment.
- Hiding the Problem: Sweeping errors under the rug means missing the chance to analyze what went wrong and how to prevent it from happening again.
- Damaged Trust: A culture of fear erodes trust between colleagues and can even discourage patients from openly discussing medication concerns.
How Anonymous Reporting Changes the Game:

- Safety, Not Scapegoats: Anonymizing reports shifts the focus from individual blame to system-level improvement.
- Honest Data = Better Solutions: When people are free to report without fear, you get a more accurate picture of where errors are occurring and the true underlying causes.
- Learning from the Near Misses: Anonymous reporting encourages sharing even those close calls, which hold valuable lessons for prevention.

How It Works in Practice:
- Secure Channels: Anonymous reporting systems could be via online forms, a dedicated suggestion box, or external reporting bodies (ISMP, state agencies).
- Removing Identifiers: Reports focus on the factual details of the error: medication, setting, what happened, without including staff names or other identifying patient information.

Additional Benefits of Anonymity:
- Protects Reporters: Encourages more hesitant staff to speak up, potentially revealing trends that might have otherwise been hidden.
- Focus on Prevention: Allows the pharmacy team to collectively analyze patterns and work on solutions without getting bogged down in personal defensiveness.

Remember, a pharmacy that emphasizes learning from mistakes over punishment fosters a safer environment for both patients *and* staff. Anonymous reporting is a key tool in building this type of culture!

Think of a root cause analysis (RCA) as a detective investigation – it's about digging deeper than just "whodunnit" to understand *why* a medication error occurred. Here's how it unfolds and where a pharmacy technician plays a crucial role:

Step-by-Step RCA Process:
1. Gather the Facts:
   - Start with the error report itself: What medication, wrong dose/route/patient, when did it happen, was the patient harmed?
   - Interview involved staff: Get their perspective on what happened, but focus on facts and sequence of events, not placing blame.
2. Ask "Why?" Repeatedly:
   - Why did they select the wrong drug? Keep asking why until you reach the root issue. Example: Mistakenly grabbed a similar-looking drug --> Why? They were stored next to each other on the shelf --> Why? Workflow led to restocking without double-checking labels.
3. Broaden Your Lens: Use RCA tools to look for contributing factors:
   - Fishbone Diagram: Visually map out categories (people, equipment, environment) and how they might have led to the error.
   - 5 Whys: Starting with the error, ask "Why?" five times to drill down to underlying issues.

Where Technicians Shine:
- Frontline Insights: You witness the day-to-day workflow, the potential distractions, and the medication 'look-alikes' that cause trouble.
- System Thinker: Can you spot where technology glitches cause problems, or where confusing labeling contributes to picking the wrong medication?
- No Detail is Too Small: Sometimes the root cause lies in a seemingly minor issue – outdated auxiliary labels, a cluttered work area, etc. Your attention to detail matters!

Example Scenario:

- Error: Wrong dose of insulin pen dispensed.
- Individual Focus: Blaming the staff member for inattention.
- RCA reveals: Pharmacy recently switched to a new insulin pen with different dosage markings leading to confusion.
- Solution: Training for ALL staff on the new pens, plus extra visual cues on shelves to distinguish pens.

RCA is a team effort! Your contributions help shift the focus from fixing a person to fixing the system, preventing future errors and protecting patient safety.

Let's picture a fishbone diagram as your x-ray for medication errors. It helps you see the skeleton of the problem, revealing all the potential weak points in your pharmacy's system. Here's how it works:

How to Build a Fishbone Diagram
1. The Head: This is your specific error. Example: Patient received an antibiotic they were allergic to.
2. The Main Bones: These are the broad categories of contributing factors. Typical ones include:
    o People: Knowledge gaps, miscommunications, distractions
    o Equipment: Computer glitches, faulty labeling
    o Materials: Outdated drug information, confusing look-alike medications
    o Environment: Pharmacy layout, noise levels, workflow
    o Process: Unclear procedures, insufficient double-checks
3. The Smaller Bones: Drill down within each category. For our allergy example:
    o People: Did the technician miss the allergy alert? If so, was it fatigue, or alert overload?
    o Process: Is there a standard step to verbally confirm allergies with every patient?
    o Environment: Was the pharmacy extremely busy causing rushed workflow?

Example in Action:
- The completed fishbone diagram reveals that while the technician bears some responsibility, it was a combination of factors:
    o New patient profile not fully completed with allergies.
    o DUR alert was present but overridden due to workload pressure.
    o Verbally confirming allergies was not routine practice.

Why the Fishbone is Powerful:
- It's Visual: Makes it clear that errors are rarely due to a single issue, but rather a tangle of causes.
- Team Collaboration: Analyzing the diagram together prevents finger-pointing and fosters a solution-oriented mindset.
- Prioritizes Action: Helps you see what changes would have the greatest impact on preventing similar errors.

Remember, the fishbone diagram isn't about blame, but a tool for making your pharmacy safer for everyone!

Let's break down how the Plan-Do-Study-Act (PDSA) cycle provides a structured approach for quality improvement in your pharmacy, turning problems into positive change.

Scenario: Your pharmacy has noticed an increase in patients returning with missed refills, leading to gaps in medication therapy.

Step 1: Plan
- Define the Problem: Quantify the issue - how many missed refills? Which medications are most common? This gives you a baseline to measure against.

- Assemble Your Team: Include pharmacists, technicians, perhaps even front-end staff who interact with patients as they pick up meds.
- Root Cause Brainstorm: What might be causing missed refills? Cost, forgetfulness, lack of reminders, complex regimens? Analyze any existing data.
- Set a Goal: Be specific. Example: Decrease missed refills of chronic medications by 20% in 3 months.
- Propose a Solution: Based on your root cause theories, design an intervention. Example: Develop an automated refill reminder system (call/text) a few days before the due date.

Step 2: Do
- Small-Scale Test: Pick a few patients or a single medication for a trial run. This allows you to refine your solution before going full-scale.
- Document Everything: How you contacted patients, their responses, any hiccups with the new process.

Step 3: Study
- Did It Work? Compare the refill rate for your test group to the baseline data.
- Get Feedback: Talk to patients who did refill on time – was the reminder helpful? Ask those who still missed it why.
- Tweak as Needed: Did the timing of the reminder need adjusting? Is a phone call better than text for some patients?

Step 4: Act
- Full-Scale or Abandon? Based on your study, decide:
  - Implement: The reminder system worked! Roll it out to all eligible patients with your refinements.
  - Revise: Results were mixed. Modify your solution further and run another PDSA cycle.
  - Ditch the Idea: Sometimes you learn the wrong solution was tackled. Back to the drawing board!

Ongoing PDSA:
- Continue Monitoring: Track your refill rates to ensure the improvement is sustained.
- Next Target: Success with one problem inspires you to tackle another!

The PDSA cycle excels because it's about rapid, focused experiments. It's OK if your initial solution isn't flawless – you'll iterate your way to a better, data-driven system!

VII. Order Entry and Processing:

Welcome to Order Entry and Processing, the nerve center of pharmacy operations! Think of yourself as the mastermind translator, turning doctors' scribbles and patient requests into accurate, actionable medication orders that ensure patients receive the right treatments.

Here's a Taste of What You'll Master:
- Decoding Prescriptions: Learn to decipher those notoriously messy prescriptions, identify different dosage forms (tablets, eye drops, etc.), and understand the abbreviations doctors love to use.
- Mastering the Patient Profile: Discover how to create and update those all-important medication records, checking for allergies, drug interactions, and duplicate therapies.
- Tech Tools: Become fluent in pharmacy software, from entering basic prescriptions to navigating those critical DUR alerts and insurance billing processes.

- Prioritizing Like a Pro: Handle a mix of walk-in prescriptions, medication refill requests, and even those urgent calls from doctor's offices with speed and accuracy.
- Data Accuracy is Everything: Understand the consequences of even small entry errors, and how double-checking and attention to detail protect patients.

Why This Section is Crucial

Think of order entry and processing as the foundation of a safe and efficient pharmacy. Here's what's at stake:

- Avoiding Errors, Saving Lives: Mistakes at this stage can lead to wrong medications, dangerous interactions, or incorrect dosages. Your accuracy is the first line of defense.
- Efficiency Matters: A streamlined order process means patients get their needed medications faster, improving their experience and treatment outcomes.
- Team Player: You're the bridge between the patient, the pharmacist, and the insurance company. Strong communication and collaboration skills are essential.

Get ready to enter the fast-paced world of prescriptions! By the end of this section, you'll be an expert in transforming prescription information into safe and timely medication dispensing.

A prescription for a compounded suppository requires specific and detailed information to ensure the medication is compounded accurately and meets the patient's therapeutic needs. Compounded medications are tailored to individual patients, often because commercially available drug forms do not meet those patients' needs. Here's what needs to be included on a prescription specifically for a compounded suppository:

1. Patient Information

- **Full Name**: The patient's full name to ensure the medication is personalized and correctly identified.
- **Date of Birth**: To verify the patient's identity and for pharmacists to consider age-related dosing and contraindications.

2. Medication and Active Ingredient(s)

- **Drug Name**: The specific active ingredient(s) to be included in the suppository. If multiple active ingredients are needed, each should be clearly listed.
- **Strength per Suppository**: The exact amount of each active ingredient per suppository, typically in milligrams (mg) or other appropriate units. This is crucial for dosing accuracy.

3. Base Composition

- **Suppository Base**: The type of base material to be used, such as cocoa butter (theobroma oil), glycerinated gelatin, or polyethylene glycol (PEG), which can affect the medication's release rate and patient comfort.

4. Quantity and Dosage

- **Quantity to be Dispensed**: The total number of suppositories to be compounded and dispensed, which should align with the dosing instructions.
- **Dosage Instructions**: Detailed instructions on how the suppositories are to be used by the patient, including the frequency of administration (e.g., "Insert one suppository rectally at bedtime") and duration of the therapy.

5. Prescriber Information

- **Prescriber's Name**: The full name of the healthcare provider prescribing the compounded suppository.
- **Signature and Credentials**: The prescriber's signature and professional credentials (e.g., MD, DO, NP) to verify the prescription's authenticity.

- **Contact Information**: Including the prescriber's phone number, and possibly fax or email, for clarification or consultation if needed.

Considerations for Compounded Suppositories
- **Patient Allergies and Sensitivities**: Information on any known allergies or sensitivities, especially to potential base ingredients, to avoid adverse reactions.
- **Intended Use**: The therapeutic purpose of the suppository, which can influence the choice of base and additives (e.g., for local vs. systemic effect).
- **Storage Instructions**: Specific storage conditions required to maintain the stability and efficacy of the compounded suppositories, which the pharmacy should communicate to the patient upon dispensing.

Additional Instructions
- **Labeling Requirements**: Instructions for labeling, which should include all the above information, plus storage instructions and any warnings or precautions.
- **Special Instructions**: Any additional compounding instructions or considerations, such as the need for specific molds or packaging to maintain stability and efficacy.

Compounded suppositories offer a personalized medication solution for patients, but they require detailed prescriptions to ensure safety and effectiveness. Clear communication between the prescriber, pharmacist, and patient is crucial in the compounding and use of these specialized medications.

The route of administration significantly influences the instructions (SIG) for a troche or lozenge, both of which are solid preparations designed to dissolve or disintegrate slowly in the mouth. Troches and lozenges are commonly used for localized effects in the oral cavity or pharynx, but some are formulated for systemic absorption through the buccal or sublingual mucosa. The unique characteristics of these dosage forms, including their dissolving time, play a crucial role in determining the frequency of use and other usage instructions.

Factors Influencing SIG for Troches and Lozenges
1. **Dissolving Time**:
   - Troches and lozenges are formulated to dissolve slowly over a period, typically ranging from a few minutes to half an hour. The dissolving time is formulated based on the drug's intended effect and its absorption rate.
   - Instructions must clearly state that the troche or lozenge should not be chewed or swallowed whole but allowed to dissolve slowly in the mouth to ensure the medication is released gradually and absorbed properly.
2. **Intended Effect**:
   - For medications intended to exert a local effect in the mouth or throat (e.g., local anesthetics, antiseptics), the SIG will emphasize keeping the medication in contact with the affected area for as long as possible while it dissolves.
   - For systemic effects, instructions may specify placing the troche or lozenge under the tongue (sublingual) or in the buccal pouch to facilitate absorption directly into the bloodstream, bypassing the first-pass metabolism.
3. **Frequency of Use**:
   - The dissolving time and the medication's pharmacokinetics and pharmacodynamics dictate how frequently a troche or lozenge can be used. For example, a troche intended for pain relief in the oral cavity may be prescribed more frequently than one used for systemic hormone replacement therapy.

- The SIG will specify the frequency, such as "Use one troche every 4 hours as needed for pain," taking into account the maximum daily dose and potential for systemic absorption.

Example SIG Instructions for Troches and Lozenges
- **Local Effect**: "Dissolve one lozenge slowly in the mouth every 2 hours as needed for sore throat pain, not to exceed 5 lozenges in 24 hours."
- **Systemic Absorption**: "Place one troche under the tongue and allow to dissolve completely, once daily at bedtime."

Additional Considerations
- **Food and Drink**: Instructions may advise avoiding eating or drinking for a specific period before and after using the troche or lozenge to ensure optimal absorption and effectiveness, especially for those intended for systemic absorption.
- **Storage**: Some troches or lozenges may require specific storage conditions to maintain their stability and efficacy, which should be communicated to the patient.
- **Side Effects**: Patients should be informed about possible side effects, such as local irritation or systemic effects, depending on the medication's action.

The route of administration for troches and lozenges critically influences the SIG instructions provided to the patient, with factors such as dissolving time, intended effect, and frequency of use being key determinants. Clear, precise instructions are essential to ensure that the patient uses these medications effectively and safely, achieving the desired therapeutic outcomes while minimizing potential side effects.

Prescriptions with SIGs such as "Take 1 tablet every 6-8 hours as needed for pain" can potentially lead to patient misinterpretation due to the flexibility in dosing intervals. This ambiguity might result in patients taking the medication less effectively—either too frequently, risking overdose and side effects, or too infrequently, leading to inadequate pain management.

Potential Areas of Misinterpretation
Dosing Frequency: The range provided (6-8 hours) might confuse patients about the optimal or maximum frequency for dosing. Some might wonder if they should always wait 8 hours, or if taking a dose every 6 hours is preferable for managing pain.

"As Needed": The term "as needed" (prn) introduces subjectivity into when to take the medication, relying on the patient's judgment of pain severity. This can lead to underuse (patients enduring pain without taking the medication) or overuse (patients taking the medication at the slightest discomfort).

Maximum Daily Dose: The prescription does not specify a daily maximum, which could lead to patients consuming more than recommended within a 24-hour period, especially when opting for the 6-hour dosing interval.

Technician's Role in Clarification
A pharmacy technician, upon noticing a prescription with such potentially ambiguous instructions, would take the following steps to ensure clarity and patient safety:

Reviewing Pharmacy Records: First, the technician might review the patient's medication history and previous instructions for similar medications to understand the prescriber's intent based on past practices.

Consulting the Pharmacist: Before contacting the prescriber, the technician would discuss the ambiguity with a pharmacist to confirm that clarification is needed. The pharmacist might provide insights based on their professional experience or knowledge of the patient's medication history.

Clarification with the Prescriber: The technician, under the pharmacist's guidance, would then contact the prescriber's office for clarification. The request would be specific: to define a clearer dosing interval, confirm the intended maximum daily dose, and understand the pain severity level warranting medication use.

Documenting the Interaction: The technician would document the communication with the prescriber's office, including who provided the clarification and the specific instructions received.

Ensuring Patient Understanding
Once the prescription's instructions are clarified, the technician would ensure that:

The clarified instructions are accurately entered into the pharmacy system for dispensing.
The patient is counseled on the correct use of the medication, emphasizing the clarified dosing schedule, the criteria for "as needed" use, and the importance of not exceeding the maximum daily dose.
The patient knows to monitor their response to the medication and to contact their healthcare provider if their pain is not adequately controlled or if they experience adverse effects. Prescriptions with flexible or subjective SIGs require careful handling to prevent patient misinterpretation. Pharmacy technicians play a crucial role in identifying potential ambiguities, facilitating clarification with prescribers, and ensuring that patients receive clear, understandable instructions for safe medication use. This collaborative approach helps optimize therapeutic outcomes while minimizing risks.

Tapered dose prescriptions require extra diligence when entering them into the pharmacy system. Here's why accuracy is key, and how to navigate these unique orders:
Understanding Tapered Doses
- Gradual Reduction: A tapered dose involves decreasing the medication dosage over a set period, often to prevent withdrawal symptoms or allow the body to adjust.
- Example: Prednisone tapers are common for treating inflammation. The dose might start high and decrease gradually over several days or weeks.

How to Enter the Prescription
1. Individual Strengths: Often, each dosage change requires dispensing a different strength of the medication.
   o Example: Prednisone 20mg x 6 days, then 10mg x 5 days, then 5mg x 4 days.
2. Break It Down: Enter each dosage change as a separate line on the prescription within the pharmacy software. This ensures accurate dispensing and labeling.
3. Day Supply is Crucial: Calculate the correct day supply for each strength to prevent the patient from running out or getting too much medication.
   o Example: If the prescription is written for a 15-day total taper, ensure the day supplies for each strength add up to 15.

Why Accurate Day Supply Matters
- Patient Adherence: Clearly marking how many tablets to take each day is crucial for a successful taper. Running out mid-taper can worsen the condition.

- Safety: Giving too much medication for too long increases side effect risks. An accurate day supply ensures the taper ends on schedule.
- Inventory: Incorrect day supplies can lead to overstocking those odd quantities of tapered medications or frustrating shortages for the patient.

Tech Tips & Teamwork

- Pharmacy Software Help: Some systems may have special fields for entering tapered dose instructions. Learn if yours does!
- Check and Double-Check: Have the pharmacist verify both your day supply calculations and the prescription entry before dispensing.
- Clear Counseling: Explain the taper schedule carefully to the patient. Providing a written calendar can be a lifesaver.

Remember, attention to detail with tapered prescriptions ensures patients get the correct dose at the correct time, crucial for a safe and effective treatment plan!

Let's dive into specific scenarios where prescribing "Dispense as Written" (DAW) isn't just about cost but about patient safety and ensuring the correct form of the medication.

Narrow Therapeutic Index (NTI) Medications:

- Levothyroxine (thyroid replacement): Even minor variations between generic brands can cause significant fluctuations in thyroid hormone levels, leading to complications.
- Warfarin (blood thinner): Inconsistent blood clotting levels from switching between brands can increase bleeding or clot risks.
- Antiseizure medications: Slight differences in absorption between generics could provoke seizures or increase medication side effects.

Unique Formulations:

- Extended-release/Modified-release: These are designed to release the medication slowly. Examples:
  - Bupropion XL (antidepressant): Switching to a generic immediate-release version could cause a spike in drug levels, leading to increased side effects.
  - Oxycodone ER (pain reliever): A generic without the controlled-release mechanism could provide inadequate pain control or lead to overdose.
- Special Delivery Systems: Switching from brand to generic can lead to drastically different absorption or local effectiveness. Examples:
  - Inhalers: Generic and brand inhalers may have slightly different propellant systems, meaning the patient wouldn't receive the same dose per puff.
  - Topical Patches: Fillers and adhesives in the generic version might alter how much medication is delivered through the skin.

Additional Instances for DAW:

- Patient Allergies: Even if the active ingredient is the same, a generic might contain a filler that the patient is allergic to.
- Proven Patient Stability: If a patient has been doing well on a specific brand for an extended period, changing can potentially introduce unnecessary risks.
- It's Not Just About Brand Loyalty: DAW in these cases is about prioritizing the precise dose and delivery of the drug, which directly impacts treatment success.
- Pharmacist's Role: The pharmacist is the expert, responsible for confirming the DAW is medically necessary.

- Technician's Eye for Detail: Noticing a DAW code prompts you to double-check the prescription and alerts you to a potentially crucial patient need.

As a pharmacy technician, understanding these DAW scenarios empowers you to safeguard your patients and contribute to the best possible treatment outcomes.

While the "Dispense as Written" (DAW) code signals important medical considerations, there are situations where, after careful evaluation, the pharmacist might override it in the patient's best interest. Let's explore those scenarios:

1. Financial Hardship:
- High Brand-Name Copay: If the cost of the brand-name medication creates a significant financial burden for the patient, the pharmacist might discuss a generic substitution with the prescriber to find a less expensive, therapeutically equivalent option.
- Lack of Insurance Coverage: In some cases, the patient might completely lack insurance coverage for the specific brand-name drug. A switch to a more affordable generic becomes essential for the patient to access the medication.

2. Formulary Restrictions:
- Preferred Alternatives: Insurance formularies often favor certain generic equivalents or even alternative medications within the same drug class. The pharmacist might contact the prescriber to consider a substitution that aligns with the patient's coverage.
- Prior Authorization Hurdles: Obtaining approval for a brand-name drug often involves time-consuming paperwork. Switching to a formulary-preferred generic might expedite access to the needed medication for the patient.

3. Shortages & Discontinued Medications:
- Limited Supply: When there's a shortage of a specific brand-name drug, finding a therapeutically equivalent substitute becomes crucial for providing the patient with their necessary treatment.
- Manufacturer Changes: Sometimes a specific brand and formulation of a medication is permanently discontinued. The pharmacist would work with the prescriber to determine a suitable alternative.

Important Considerations:
- Prescriber Consultation: The pharmacist always consults with the prescriber before overriding a DAW code to ensure the switch is clinically appropriate.
- Patient Communication: Transparency with the patient about the reasons for substitution and any potential differences between the medications is vital.
- Documentation: Any DAW override and its rationale should be carefully documented in the patient's record.

Remember, the goal is always to provide the best care for the patient. DAW overrides, when done judiciously, help balance patient safety with accessibility and affordability of medications.

Data entry errors have the potential to slip through the cracks, causing serious medication errors. Let's break down common mistakes and how technology acts as your safety net:

Common Data Entry Errors:
- The Look-Alike Trap: Confusing similarly named medications (like Hydralazine and Hydroxyzine) due to a rushed selection or misreading the prescription.

- Quantity Confusion: Mistyping the quantity or misinterpreting the prescriber's handwriting (was that 30 tablets or 80?).
- Dosage Snafus: Entering incorrect dosage strength (e.g., 5mg instead of 50mg) or misreading dosage instructions on the prescription.

How Pharmacy Software Can Help

1. Tall Man Lettering:
- What it is: Visually highlighting differences in look-alike drug names (hydroCHLOROthiazide vs hydroXYzine)
- How it helps: Draws your attention to similar names, forcing you to double-check your selection.
2. Dose Range Alerts
- What it is: Software flags doses that fall outside typical or safe ranges for a specific medication, age, or medical condition.
- How it helps: Catches potential errors in dosage entry or even mistakes on the prescription, prompting a double-check with the pharmacist.
3. Additional Safety Features:
- Drug Interaction Alerts: Warns of potentially harmful interactions with other medications in the patient's profile.
- Allergy Alerts: Provides a visual warning when a medication conflicts with a known patient allergy.
- Duplicate Therapy Alerts: Flags if the same or similar medication has been recently filled, preventing accidental overdosing.

Technician's Role:
- Technology Isn't Perfect: Never fully rely on software alerts. Careful attention to detail during data entry remains crucial.
- Question the Unexpected: If you get an alert, don't automatically override it. Investigate with the pharmacist.
- Learning from Mistakes: Report any near-misses or errors that occur so the pharmacy can further improve its software systems and safety protocols.

Remember, pharmacy software is a powerful tool, but your vigilance and knowledge form the ultimate line of defense against data entry errors that could harm patients!

Picture those pharmacy software 'hard stops' as your digital guardians, but sometimes they need help deciphering the situation. Let's strategize when to tackle them yourself or call in the pharmacist for backup:

Resolving Hard Stops: Your Troubleshooting Toolbox

1. Understand the Message:
- Read the alert carefully! Is it about an allergy, drug interaction, incorrect dosage, etc.? This guides your next steps.
- Decipher the Code: Some software uses specific codes that you'll learn. Does it point to an insurance issue or a clinical concern?
2. Gather Information:
- Double-Check the Prescription: Verify the medication, dosage, and directions against the original prescription. Look for potential errors.
- Review Patient Profile: Check for allergies, recent medications that could be interacting, or any relevant medical notes.

Situations You Can Likely Handle:

- Refill Too Soon: Often caused by insurance refill restrictions. Check the patient's recent fill history and insurance rules (some allow early refills with overrides).
- Incorrect Days Supply: If the calculated days supply doesn't match the prescriber's intent, a quick adjustment can sometimes resolve it.
- Outdated Information: If an old allergy is triggering an alert, verify with the patient (if present) that it's no longer relevant and update the profile (pharmacist might need to confirm).

Call in the Pharmacist:

- Drug Interactions: Even if the alert seems minor, the pharmacist needs to assess the severity and determine if contacting the doctor is necessary.
- Dosage Issues: Alerts about doses outside the usual range, especially for high-risk medications or specific patient populations (children, the elderly) always warrant pharmacist evaluation.
- Unclear Prescriber Intent: If the prescription is illegible or ambiguous, the pharmacist needs to clarify with the prescriber.
- New/Unfamiliar Patient: If the patient is new and has several medications on their profile, the pharmacist might do a comprehensive medication review.

Key Points:

- Know Your Limits: Never be afraid to escalate to the pharmacist when unsure. Patient safety always comes first!
- Document Everything: Keep records of alerts you resolve, the actions taken, and situations referred to the pharmacist.
- Learn with Each Alert: Resolving those hard stops increases your knowledge and helps you proactively prevent errors in the future.

Think of it as teamwork – your tech skills paired with the pharmacist's clinical expertise create a robust safety net for your patients!

Working in the wrong patient profile is like mailing a letter to the wrong address – it can have serious consequences! Here's how meticulous technicians ensure they've got the right digital "file" open:

The Verification Triad:

Name:

Full Name Match: Verify the patient's first and last name are entered correctly in the pharmacy software. Beware of Nicknames and Spelling Variations: If the patient goes by a different name than their legal one, confirm that it's documented. Be alert for common misspellings.
Date of Birth (DOB):

The Unique Key: DOB is often the most reliable identifier as many people have the same or similar names. Confirm the Format: Double-check you've entered the DOB correctly (especially those tricky month/day/year variations!).
Address:

Secondary Check: While less reliable (people move!), the address provides an extra layer of verification.

Catching Transposition Errors: Addresses are prone to number mix-ups. A quick mental "read back" before proceeding can catch errors.
Resolving Discrepancies: STOP & Investigate

Never Assume: If any of the identifiers don't match perfectly, don't proceed with data entry or prescription filling.
Clarify with the Patient: Discrepancies can mean multiple patient profiles exist, or there might be an error on the prescription.
Double-Check Sources: Verify that you've typed in the information from the prescription and patient intake forms correctly. Mistakes happen!
Alert the Pharmacist: Sometimes resolving the issue requires the pharmacist to further investigate or potentially create a new patient profile.
Why Taking it Seriously Matters:

Medication Mix-Ups: Working in the wrong profile can lead to adding medications to a different patient's record, causing drug interactions or allergies to be missed.
Confidentiality Breaches: Entering data into the wrong profile means that person's private medical information isn't secure.
Patient Harm: Incorrect profiles can cause delays in patients getting needed medications, or worse, receiving the wrong drug or dose.
Remember, accuracy starts at the very beginning! Your attention to detail with patient identifiers protects patient safety and ensures everyone gets the personalized care they deserve.

Think of a patient profile as a map with flashing warning signs designed to keep your patient safe. Let's break down the most critical alerts you might encounter:
1. Drug Allergies:
- Severity Matters: Alerts range from mild rash to life-threatening anaphylaxis. Pay close attention to the severity level.
- Cross-Sensitivities: Some alerts warn about allergies to drugs within the same class as the prescribed medication.
- Why It's Crucial: Alerts prevent dispensing a medication that could trigger a dangerous allergic reaction.
2. High-Risk Drug Interactions:
- Combo Trouble: Identifies medications that, when taken together, can cause serious side effects, reduce drug effectiveness, or increase drug levels to dangerous amounts.
- Levels of Severity: Some interactions warrant caution, while others are absolutely prohibited.
- Why It's Crucial: Alerts help prevent unintended harm caused by interacting medications.
3. Potential Duplicate Therapies:
- Overlapping Medications: Flags if the patient has recently filled a similar medication or one within the same drug class.
- Purposeful vs. Accidental: Sometimes duplicates are intentional, but often they reveal a prescribing error or lack of communication between doctors.
- Why It's Crucial: Prevents unintentional overdosing or unnecessary side effects from multiple medications doing the same thing.
4. Gaps in Adherence (Overdue Refills):

- Spotting Red Flags: Alerts when a patient is late for refilling a chronic medication (e.g., blood pressure, diabetes drugs).
- Beyond Forgetfulness: Can indicate the patient is experiencing medication side effects, cost issues, or lack of understanding about their condition.
- Why It's Crucial: Allows for proactive outreach by the pharmacy to ensure continuity of care and prevent worsening health for the patient.

A Note on Technician's Role:

- Alert Doesn't Equal Action: You bring these alerts to the pharmacist's attention for clinical assessment and decision-making.
- Ask Questions, Learn More: Each alert you resolve teaches you about potential drug problems, making you a more knowledgeable and safety-focused pharmacy technician.

Patient profiles with thorough alerts are your early warning system. Your sharp eyes on those alerts contribute to a safer, more effective medication experience for the patients you serve!

While federal regulations provide a baseline for prescription labeling, individual states often add their own little twists and turns. Since I don't know your specific state, here's a guide on how to find those state-specific labeling requirements and some common examples:

Your Research Mission:

1. State Board of Pharmacy Website: This is your goldmine!
    - Search for terms like "labeling requirements," "prescription regulations," or "pharmacy practice act."
    - Look for downloadable PDFs or sections within the state rules dedicated to prescription labeling.
2. Reach Out Directly:
- Consider calling your State Board of Pharmacy. They can direct you to the right resources or answer specific questions you have.

Common State-Specific Labeling Extras:

- Pharmacy Address Fine Print: Some states mandate a specific format for displaying the pharmacy's address (street vs. PO box, etc.) or require including the city or ZIP code.
- Beyond the Feds: States might require additional auxiliary warning labels not mandated by federal regulations. Examples could be more specific warnings about drowsiness or specific food/drink interactions.
- Font Size Matters: While the federal law sets a minimum font size, some states might have a slightly larger minimum requirement on prescription labels for improved readability.
- Unique State Identifiers: Some states require a unique identifier, either for the pharmacy or the dispensing pharmacist, to be included on the prescription label.

Why States Do This:

- Patient Safety: Tailored auxiliary labels might address specific concerns within that state (e.g., substance abuse warnings for certain medications).
- Clarity & Readability: Larger font sizes or specific address formatting helps patients, especially the elderly, easily identify where their medication came from.
- Accountability: State identifiers increase traceability in case of a dispensing error investigation.

Important Note: Remember, state regulations always take precedence when they are stricter than federal laws. Stay updated by checking with your State Board of Pharmacy periodically for any changes or updates!

Patient Information Leaflets (PILs) are your patient's portable knowledge nugget regarding their medication. Let's explore when they're mandatory and how to ensure every patient gets the information they need, regardless of the language they speak.

When PILs Are a Must:

- Federal Mandate: The FDA requires PILs to be dispensed with certain high-risk or complex medications. Examples include:
    o Oral contraceptives
    o Estrogens and Progesterone Hormone Replacement
    o Certain Antidepressants
- State Specifics: Some states expand the list of medications that mandate the inclusion of PILs with every dispensing.

How PILs Are Provided:

- With Each Fill: Anytime a medication requiring a PIL is dispensed (new prescription or refill), the latest version of the PIL should be included.
- Sources:
    o Pharmacies often have pre-printed stock of common PILs.
    o FDA Website: Provides downloadable PILs for many medications ([invalid URL removed])

Addressing Language Barriers:

- Translated PILs: The FDA works to provide PILs in multiple languages, particularly for those mandated medications. You can often find these on their website.
- Pharmacy Resources:
    o Some pharmacy software systems have links to translated PILs.
    o Pharmacies may partner with translation services to provide written translations for patients when needed.
- Patient-Focused: Encourage patients to ask if they need a PIL in their preferred language and guide them to available resources.

Why PILs Matter:

- Beyond the Label: PILs provide more in-depth information about potential side effects, interactions, proper usage, and storage of the medication.
- Empowering Patients: PILs help patients become active participants in their healthcare and understand how to safely manage their medications.

As a pharmacy technician, knowing your PIL requirements and helping patients access them in the language they understand is essential for promoting medication safety and patient-centered care!

PRACTICE TEST QUESTIONS:

Get ready to put your knowledge to the test! This practice exam section is designed to simulate the types of questions you might encounter on the real PTCB exam and to help you identify areas where you might need a little more review. To maximize your learning experience, we've placed the answer and a detailed explanation directly after each question. This immediate feedback approach is intended to reinforce your understanding of the subject matter, clarify any misconceptions, and elucidate the reasoning behind the correct answer.

How It Works:

- Questions & Answers: Each question will be followed by the correct answer along with a brief explanation of why it's the right choice.
- Focus on Understanding: Don't just memorize answers. Read the explanations carefully to reinforce core concepts and apply them to similar scenarios.
- Realistic Simulation: These questions mirror the style and content areas of the PTCB exam, building your confidence for test day.

Tips for Success:

- Time yourself: Try answering a set number of questions within a timeframe. This helps you gauge your speed and manage time efficiently on the real exam.
- Difficult Questions: Mark those that stump you for later review. Identify whether it's the topic or question style that gives you trouble.
- Analyze the Rationale: Even if you get a question right, read the explanation. It might highlight a concept you hadn't considered.

Remember, practice isn't just about acing these questions; it's about sharpening your critical thinking skills and mastering the knowledge that will make you an excellent pharmacy technician. Let's get started!

1. A patient arrives at the pharmacy with a new prescription for amoxicillin 500mg capsules. The instructions are to take one capsule by mouth three times a day for 10 days. What is the total quantity of capsules to be dispensed?
a. 10
b. 20
c. 30
d. 50

Answer: c. 30 capsules. Explanation: The patient takes 3 capsules per day for 10 days, requiring a total of 30 capsules (3 x 10 = 30).

2. A patient with a history of chronic heart failure is prescribed digoxin. Which electrolyte imbalance should be monitored due to its potential to increase the risk of digoxin toxicity?
a. Hypernatremia
b. Hypokalemia
c. Hypercalcemia
d. Hypomagnesemia

Answer: b. Hypokalemia. Explanation: Hypokalemia increases the risk of digoxin toxicity because both digoxin and potassium compete for the same binding sites on the Na+/K+ ATPase pump; low potassium levels allow more digoxin to bind to the pump, enhancing its pharmacological effects and potential toxicity.

3. In the context of antibiotic stewardship, why is it important to distinguish between bacterial and viral infections when prescribing antibiotics?
a. Antibiotics increase the risk of viral mutation
b. Antibiotics are only effective against bacterial infections
c. Viral infections are self-limiting and do not require medication
d. Bacterial infections are always more severe than viral infections

Answer: b. Antibiotics are only effective against bacterial infections. Explanation: Antibiotics target specific components of bacterial cells, such as cell wall synthesis, protein synthesis, nucleic acid synthesis, and metabolic pathways, which are not present in viruses. Prescribing antibiotics for viral infections contributes to antibiotic resistance without providing any therapeutic benefit.

4. A pharmacy technician receives a prescription for Isotretinoin. What specific procedure must be followed due to the medication's teratogenic risk?
a. Refrigeration after dispensing
b. Enrollment in the iPledge program
c. Double-counting the tablets
d. Use of child-resistant packaging

Answer: b. Enrollment in the iPledge program. Explanation: The iPledge program is a risk management program designed to prevent fetal exposure to isotretinoin, which is highly teratogenic. Both male and female patients, as well as pharmacies dispensing the medication, must be registered and comply with the program's requirements.

5. A patient on warfarin therapy has a salad high in vitamin K. What effect might this have on their INR (International Normalized Ratio) value?
a. Increase the INR, leading to a higher risk of bleeding
b. Decrease the INR, leading to a higher risk of clot formation
c. No effect, as dietary vitamin K does not affect INR
d. Increase the INR, leading to a higher risk of clot formation

Answer: b. Decrease the INR, leading to a higher risk of clot formation. Explanation: Vitamin K is a crucial factor in the synthesis of clotting factors. Warfarin works by inhibiting the vitamin K-dependent clotting factors. A high intake of vitamin K can counteract the effect of warfarin, leading to a lower INR and a higher risk of clot formation.

6. When converting a patient's medication from IV to oral form, which principle is important to consider for ensuring therapeutic equivalence?
a. Half-life of the medication
b. Bioavailability differences

c. The pH level of the stomach

d. The patient's weight

Answer: b. Bioavailability differences. Explanation: Bioavailability refers to the extent and rate at which the active drug ingredient is absorbed and becomes available at the site of action. Oral medications often have lower bioavailability than their IV counterparts due to the first-pass metabolism, thus requiring dose adjustments.

7. A pharmacy technician is asked to prepare a 1:200 w/v solution. How many grams of solute are needed to prepare 100 mL of this solution?

a. 0.5 grams

b. 2 grams

c. 0.2 grams

d. 5 grams

Answer: a. 0.5 grams. Explanation: A 1:200 w/v solution means 1 gram of solute per 200 mL of solution. For 100 mL (half of 200 mL), half the amount of solute is needed, hence 0.5 grams.

8. For a medication known to be a CYP3A4 enzyme inducer, what potential interaction should be closely monitored?

a. Increased effects of medications metabolized by CYP3A4

b. Decreased effects of medications metabolized by CYP3A4

c. Increased risk of allergic reactions to medications

d. Decreased bioavailability of orally administered medications

Answer: b. Decreased effects of medications metabolized by CYP3A4. Explanation: CYP3A4 inducers increase the metabolic activity of the enzyme, leading to faster metabolism of drugs that are CYP3A4 substrates. This can reduce the plasma levels and effects of these medications, potentially leading to therapeutic failure.

9. A patient presents a prescription for a topical corticosteroid for eczema. Which of the following factors is NOT important in selecting the appropriate formulation?

a. The specific type of eczema

b. The location of the eczema on the body

c. The patient's preference for cream or ointment

d. The patient's blood type

Answer: d. The patient's blood type. Explanation: The patient's blood type is irrelevant to the selection of a topical corticosteroid for eczema. Important factors include the type and severity of eczema, the affected body area, and patient preferences regarding the formulation, as these can influence the absorption and effectiveness of the medication.

10. A pharmacy technician is calculating the dose of amoxicillin for a pediatric patient. The prescription indicates 20 mg/kg/day divided into three doses. If the child weighs 15 kg, what is the total daily dose?
a. 300 mg
b. 100 mg
c. 900 mg
d. 450 mg

Answer: a. 300 mg. Explanation: The calculation for the total daily dose is 20 mg/kg * 15 kg = 300 mg. This total dose is then divided into three doses to be administered throughout the day.

11. A patient is prescribed a medication that follows first-order kinetics. What does this imply about the medication's elimination from the body?
a. The rate of elimination is constant regardless of concentration.
b. The rate of elimination is directly proportional to the drug's concentration.
c. The drug is eliminated at a variable rate that is not dependent on its concentration.
d. The drug is eliminated at a faster rate as its concentration decreases.

Answer: b. The rate of elimination is directly proportional to the drug's concentration. Explanation: First-order kinetics means that the rate of drug elimination is directly proportional to the concentration of the drug in the bloodstream. As the concentration decreases, the rate of elimination also decreases, which is characteristic of most medications.

12. A patient with a history of atrial fibrillation is prescribed a new medication for rate control. You notice the prescription is for diltiazem. Which of the following should be brought to the pharmacist's attention before dispensing?
a. Diltiazem can worsen heart failure symptoms.
b. The patient's heart rate is already low.
c. Diltiazem is contraindicated in patients over the age of 75.
d. The medication should be taken on an empty stomach.

Answer: b. The patient's heart rate is already low. Explanation: Diltiazem is a calcium channel blocker that slows heart rate and AV conduction, making it useful for rate control in atrial fibrillation. However, it should be used cautiously in patients with bradycardia (low heart rate) as it can worsen this condition.

13. A patient picking up metformin extended-release tablets asks why they shouldn't crush or chew their medication. Which explanation is most accurate?
a. Crushing the tablets will increase the risk of nausea and vomiting.
b. The extended-release mechanism will be disrupted, leading to a rapid spike in blood sugar levels.
c. The medication will have a bitter, unpleasant taste.
d. Crushing the tablets will cause the active ingredient to become inactive.

Answer: b. The extended-release mechanism will be disrupted, leading to a rapid spike in blood sugar levels. Explanation: Extended-release formulations are designed to release the medication slowly over time. Crushing or chewing disrupts this mechanism, potentially causing a rapid release of the drug leading to side effects or ineffective treatment.

14. A technician receives a prescription for amoxicillin oral suspension 250mg/5mL. The instructions are for 1 teaspoonful twice daily for 10 days. Which of the following auxiliary labels should be added to the prescription vial?
a. Shake well before using.
b. May cause drowsiness.
c. Take with food.
d. Do not refrigerate.

Answer: a. Shake well before using. Explanation: Suspensions need to be shaken well before each dose to ensure the medication is evenly distributed, as the active ingredient can settle over time.

15. A patient with type 2 diabetes reports frequent episodes of hypoglycemia (low blood sugar). Upon reviewing their medication list, which of the following medications is the most likely contributor?
a. Metformin
b. Pioglitazone
c. Glipizide
d. Liraglutide

Answer: c. Glipizide. Explanation: Glipizide is a sulfonylurea, a class of medications that stimulates insulin secretion. This can lead to hypoglycemia, especially in elderly patients or those with irregular eating habits.

16. A patient taking warfarin for atrial fibrillation asks about over-the-counter pain relief options. Which of the following is the safest choice?
a. Ibuprofen
b. Naproxen
c. Acetaminophen
d. Aspirin

Answer: c. Acetaminophen. Explanation: NSAIDs (ibuprofen, naproxen, aspirin) increase the risk of bleeding, especially when combined with warfarin, an anticoagulant. Acetaminophen is generally a safer option for pain relief in this case.

17. A physician calls the pharmacy asking about reversing the effects of heparin for a patient experiencing excessive bleeding. Which medication would you expect to prepare?
a. Vitamin K
b. Aminocaproic acid
c. Tranexamic acid
d. Protamine sulfate

Answer: d. Protamine sulfate. Explanation: Protamine sulfate directly binds and inactivates heparin, quickly reversing its anticoagulant effects.

18. A hospital pharmacist asks you to prepare a dobutamine infusion. Which of the following best describes the primary effect of this medication?
a. Decreases blood pressure and heart rate
b. Increases cardiac contractility
c. Dilates coronary arteries
d. Prevents irregular heart rhythms

Answer: b. Increases cardiac contractility. Explanation: Dobutamine is a positive inotropic agent, primarily used to increase the force of heart contractions in conditions like heart failure or cardiogenic shock.

19. A patient with chronic kidney disease presents with hyperkalemia. Their medication list includes lisinopril. Which of the following actions is most appropriate?
a. Continue the lisinopril as prescribed.
b. Hold the lisinopril and notify the prescriber.
c. Switch the lisinopril to losartan.
d. Reduce the dose of lisinopril by half.

Answer: b. Hold the lisinopril and notify the prescriber. Explanation: ACE inhibitors (like lisinopril) can worsen hyperkalemia (high potassium), especially in patients with kidney dysfunction. Holding the medication and notifying the prescriber is essential for patient safety.

20. A patient requests a refill for their zolpidem (Ambien) prescription. It has been 9 months since their last refill, and they have one refill remaining. Which of the following actions is most appropriate?
a. Refill the prescription as requested.
b. Inform the patient that controlled substance prescriptions cannot be refilled after 6 months.
c. Contact the prescriber to request a new prescription.
d. Advise the patient the prescription can be refilled, but they'll need to pay out-of-pocket.

Answer: c. Contact the prescriber to request a new prescription. Explanation: Schedule IV controlled substance prescriptions may expire after 6 months or the maximum number of refills, whichever comes first. The pharmacist needs a new prescription from the prescriber to dispense additional refills.

21. A pharmacy receives a subpoena requesting patient records as part of a legal investigation. What is the most appropriate first step for the pharmacy technician?
a. Provide the requested records immediately to comply with the subpoena.
b. Shred the patient records to protect confidentiality.

c. Consult with the pharmacist in charge or legal counsel for guidance.
d. Contact the patient to inform them about the subpoena.

Answer: c. Consult with the pharmacist in charge or legal counsel for guidance. Explanation: Subpoenas require careful handling to balance legal compliance and patient privacy. The pharmacist or legal counsel will advise on the proper procedure, which might involve verifying the subpoena's validity and potentially redacting sensitive information.

22. A new pharmacy technician notices that some expired medications are still on the shelf. The technician brings this to the pharmacist's attention, who says, "We're short-staffed, just put them in the back for now." How should the technician respond?
a. Follow the pharmacist's instructions to avoid conflict.
b. Remove the expired medications from the shelf immediately.
c. Inform the patient about expired medications if they are dispensed.
d. Explain the risks of dispensing expired medications and advocate for their proper disposal.

Answer: d. Explain the risks of dispensing expired medications and advocate for their proper disposal. Explanation: While respecting the pharmacist's authority, patient safety is paramount. Expired medications may have reduced potency or become unsafe. The technician should voice their concerns professionally and advocate for following proper disposal procedures.

23. A patient taking levothyroxine for hypothyroidism reports difficulty obtaining their medication due to a recent shortage. Which of the following actions may be permissible within pharmacy regulations?
a. Substitute the patient's prescription with a similar thyroid medication at a different strength.
b. Dispense a partial fill of the levothyroxine prescription to ration the available supply.
c. Refer the patient to a compounding pharmacy to prepare a custom formulation.

d. Contact the patient's prescriber to discuss alternative treatment options.

Answer: d. Contact the patient's prescriber to discuss alternative treatment options. Explanation: Drug shortages create complex situations. Pharmacies cannot independently substitute medications with different active ingredients or strengths. Consulting the prescriber is essential for finding a safe and effective solution for the patient, whether it's a temporary dosage change or switching to a different therapy.

24. A hospital pharmacy technician receives an urgent order for a medication not stocked in their automated dispensing cabinet. The technician locates the medication in a locked narcotics cabinet requiring a nurse's access code. Which action is most appropriate in this situation?
a. Use the nurse's code they overheard earlier to access the medication for the urgent need.
b. Wait for a nurse to become available to unlock the cabinet and retrieve the medication.
c. Inform the pharmacist that the medication is not available.
d. Contact the nurse manager to request a temporary override of the cabinet's security.

Answer: b. Wait for a nurse to become available to unlock the cabinet and retrieve the medication. Explanation: Accessing controlled substance cabinets requires adherence to strict security protocols. Using someone else's access code is a violation, even in urgent situations. Collaborating with nursing staff is the safest and most appropriate course of action.

25. A pharmacist dispenses a 30-day supply of hydrocodone-acetaminophen tablets to a patient. Ten days later, the patient requests an early refill claiming they lost their medication. Which of the following raises the most significant red flag?
a. The patient is requesting a refill earlier than expected.
b. The prescribed medication has a high potential for abuse.
c. The patient does not have a police report documenting the lost medication.
d. The prescriber is located in a different state than the pharmacy.

Answer: b. The prescribed medication has a high potential for abuse. Explanation: While all options raise potential concerns, the high abuse potential of Schedule II opioids warrants extra caution. Early refill requests could signal medication misuse or diversion, necessitating further assessment and collaboration with the prescriber.

26. A patient presents a prescription for warfarin, a medication known for its narrow therapeutic index. The pharmacy technician must be aware of the importance of monitoring which of the following laboratory values to prevent adverse effects?
a. Blood glucose levels
b. Serum creatinine
c. International Normalized Ratio (INR)
d. Blood urea nitrogen (BUN)

Answer: c. International Normalized Ratio (INR). Explanation: Warfarin therapy requires close monitoring of the INR to ensure the patient remains within the therapeutic range, minimizing the risk of bleeding (if too high) or thrombosis (if too low). This reflects the principle of medication safety and monitoring in pharmacology.

27. A pharmacy technician receives a prescription for azithromycin 500 mg on the first day, followed by 250 mg for the next four days. How many total milligrams of azithromycin will the patient take over the 5-day course?
a. 1000 mg
b. 1250 mg
c. 1500 mg
d. 1750 mg

Answer: c. 1500 mg. Explanation: The patient takes 500 mg on day 1 and then 250 mg for the next four days. The total dosage is 500+(250×4)=1500 mg. This question tests the technician's ability to calculate cumulative dosages, a crucial skill in pharmacology and dispensing.

28. When advising a patient on the use of an albuterol inhaler for asthma, which of the following is crucial information to impart regarding its pharmacological action?
a. It provides immediate relief by suppressing the immune response.
b. It reduces inflammation in the airways and should be used daily.
c. It relaxes bronchial muscles, providing quick relief from bronchospasm.
d. It rebuilds the damaged airway tissue and requires consistent use.

Answer: c. It relaxes bronchial muscles, providing quick relief from bronchospasm. Explanation: Albuterol is a short-acting β2-adrenergic agonist that works by relaxing bronchial smooth muscle, leading to bronchodilation and providing quick relief from bronchospasm, a principle of respiratory pharmacotherapy.

29. A patient on lisinopril for hypertension complains of a persistent dry cough. This side effect is commonly associated with which class of antihypertensive drugs?
a. Beta-blockers
b. Calcium channel blockers
c. Angiotensin-converting enzyme (ACE) inhibitors
d. Diuretics

Answer: c. Angiotensin-converting enzyme (ACE) inhibitors. Explanation: ACE inhibitors, such as lisinopril, can cause a persistent dry cough in some patients, a result of the accumulation of bradykinin in the lungs. Understanding drug side effects is key in pharmacology.

30. A pharmacy technician notes that a medication has a half-life of 8 hours. If a patient takes a 160 mg dose, how much of the drug remains in the body after 24 hours?
a. 20 mg
b. 40 mg
c. 80 mg
d. 160 mg

Answer: a. 20 mg. Explanation: After 8 hours (1 half-life), 80 mg remains; after 16 hours (2 half-lives), 40 mg remains; and after 24 hours (3 half-lives), 20 mg remains. This question assesses the technician's understanding of pharmacokinetics, specifically half-life calculations.

31. A patient has been prescribed a medication that is a known substrate of CYP3A4. Which of the following dietary changes could potentially increase the drug's plasma levels?
a. Consuming more vitamin C-rich foods
b. Reducing intake of fatty foods
c. Increasing grapefruit juice consumption
d. Drinking more green tea

Answer: c. Increasing grapefruit juice consumption. Explanation: Grapefruit juice is known to inhibit CYP3A4 enzymes, potentially increasing the plasma levels of drugs metabolized by this pathway, an important consideration in drug-food interactions.

32. A pharmacy technician is preparing an intravenous (IV) admixture under a laminar flow hood. Which of the following techniques is critical to maintain sterility?
a. Using a filter needle when withdrawing medication from a vial
b. Swabbing the injection port with alcohol for at least 30 seconds
c. Keeping all materials within a 6-inch area inside the hood
d. Practicing first air principle by not obstructing the HEPA filter airflow

Answer: d. Practicing first air principle by not obstructing the HEPA filter airflow. Explanation: The first air principle ensures that the sterile products are exposed to unobstructed HEPA-filtered air, minimizing contamination risk, a fundamental aseptic technique in pharmacy practice.

33. For a medication that follows zero-order kinetics, which of the following statements is true regarding its elimination?
a. The drug is eliminated at a constant rate regardless of its concentration.
b. The rate of elimination is directly proportional to the drug's concentration.
c. The half-life of the drug decreases as the dose increases.
d. The drug's elimination rate increases with increasing plasma levels.

Answer: a. The drug is eliminated at a constant rate regardless of its concentration. Explanation: Zero-order kinetics implies that a drug is eliminated at a constant rate regardless of its concentration, a concept crucial in understanding the pharmacokinetics of certain drugs like phenytoin.

34. A pharmacy receives a prescription for clindamycin topical gel. The patient's profile indicates a history of ulcerative colitis. What is the most appropriate action for the pharmacy technician to take?
a. Dispense the medication as prescribed; topical formulations have minimal systemic absorption.
b. Recommend an alternative antibiotic due to the risk of pseudomembranous colitis.
c. Consult with the pharmacist to review the patient's history and potential medication risks.
d. Suggest over-the-counter probiotics to mitigate any potential gastrointestinal side effects.

Answer: c. Consult with the pharmacist to review the patient's history and potential medication risks. Explanation: Given the history of ulcerative colitis and the risk of pseudomembranous colitis with clindamycin (even though less likely with topical formulations), consulting with the pharmacist is prudent to ensure patient safety, highlighting the importance of understanding drug-disease interactions.

35. A pharmacy is updating its inventory system for controlled substances. Which of the following is an essential feature to include for regulatory compliance?
a. Automatic refill reminders for all Schedule II medications
b. Real-time tracking of medication quantities against prescription orders

c. A built-in calculator for converting opioid dosages to morphine milligram equivalents

d. Periodic automatic orders to restock popular controlled substances

Answer: b. Real-time tracking of medication quantities against prescription orders. Explanation: Real-time tracking of controlled substances ensures accurate, up-to-date inventory management, essential for regulatory compliance and preventing diversion, reflecting the principles of pharmacy operations and law.

36. Under the Drug Supply Chain Security Act (DSCSA), what information must be provided with drug products to ensure traceability?

a. Product name, lot number, and expiration date

b. Transaction history, transaction information, and a transaction statement

c. Manufacturer's name, active ingredients, and NDC

d. DEA number, pharmacist's signature, and date of transaction

Answer: b. Transaction history, transaction information, and a transaction statement. Explanation: The DSCSA requires the provision of transaction history, transaction information, and a transaction statement to ensure a secure supply chain and facilitate the traceability of pharmaceutical products, enhancing the ability to detect and respond to counterfeit and other illegitimate drugs in the supply chain.

37. When repackaging bulk medications into unit-dose packaging, which USP chapter provides the standards for beyond-use dating?

a. USP <795>

b. USP <797>

c. USP <800>

d. USP <1160>

Answer: d. USP <1160>. Explanation: USP <1160> (Pharmaceutical Calculations in Prescription Compounding) provides guidance on assigning beyond-use dates when repackaging bulk medications into unit-dose formats. This is critical for ensuring that repackaged medications maintain their stability, potency, and safety up to the point of administration.

38. A pharmacy receives a prescription for a Schedule II drug with no refills. The patient requests to fill only half of the prescribed quantity. What is the pharmacy's obligation regarding the remaining quantity?

a. The remaining quantity must be dispensed within 72 hours.

b. The remaining quantity may be dispensed within 30 days with prescriber authorization.

c. The remaining quantity is forfeited and cannot be dispensed.

d. The pharmacy may hold the remaining quantity for the patient indefinitely.

Answer: c. The remaining quantity is forfeited and cannot be dispensed. Explanation: For Schedule II drugs, if a partial fill is requested by the patient, the remaining portion of the prescription cannot be dispensed and is forfeited. This regulation ensures strict control over the distribution of highly regulated substances and prevents potential misuse.

39. In accordance with HIPAA, under what circumstance can a pharmacy disclose protected health information (PHI) without patient consent?
a. For marketing purposes
b. When requested by a family member
c. For public health activities
d. For online testimonials

Answer: c. For public health activities. Explanation: HIPAA allows the disclosure of PHI without patient consent for specific public health activities, including the prevention or control of disease, injury, or disability. This provision supports public health surveillance and interventions while maintaining patient privacy in other contexts.

40. What is the primary purpose of the Combat Methamphetamine Epidemic Act (CMEA) in pharmacy practice?
a. Regulate the sale of opioid medications
b. Limit the quantities of pseudoephedrine products sold
c. Increase the availability of naloxone
d. Mandate child-resistant packaging for all medications

Answer: b. Limit the quantities of pseudoephedrine products sold. Explanation: The CMEA was enacted to regulate the over-the-counter sales of pseudoephedrine, a common ingredient in cold medications that can be used to illicitly manufacture methamphetamine. By limiting the quantities sold and imposing record-keeping requirements, the CMEA aims to curb the production of methamphetamine while maintaining access to these medications for legitimate use.

41. Which regulatory body is responsible for enforcing the guidelines for the disposal of hazardous pharmaceutical waste in the United States?
a. Drug Enforcement Administration (DEA)
b. Food and Drug Administration (FDA)
c. Environmental Protection Agency (EPA)
d. Centers for Disease Control and Prevention (CDC)

Answer: c. Environmental Protection Agency (EPA). Explanation: The EPA is responsible for establishing and enforcing guidelines for the disposal of hazardous pharmaceutical waste to protect public health and the environment. These regulations ensure that hazardous waste is managed and disposed of in a manner that minimizes the risk of exposure and contamination.

42. What is the key difference between a medication's expiration date and its beyond-use date (BUD) when repackaging or compounding?
a. The expiration date is set by the manufacturer, while the BUD is determined by the pharmacy.
b. The expiration date applies to prescription medications, while the BUD applies only to over-the-counter products.
c. The expiration date is legally binding, while the BUD is merely a suggestion.
d. The expiration date and BUD are interchangeable terms with no difference.

Answer: a. The expiration date is set by the manufacturer, while the BUD is determined by the pharmacy. Explanation: The expiration date is established by the manufacturer and indicates the date until which the product is expected to remain stable, effective, and safe under specified storage conditions. The BUD is assigned by the pharmacy when repackaging or compounding a medication, based on factors such as the nature of the drug substance, the potential for microbial proliferation, and the container in which it is held, reflecting the time during which the compounded or repackaged medication is expected to remain stable and safe for use.

43. Under the Federal Food, Drug, and Cosmetic Act (FD&C Act), what is the requirement for a new drug before it is marketed in the U.S.?
a. Approval from the American Medical Association (AMA)
b. A confirmed patent from the United States Patent and Trademark Office (USPTO)
c. Approval of a New Drug Application (NDA) by the FDA
d. Endorsement by the National Institutes of Health (NIH)

Answer: c. Approval of a New Drug Application (NDA) by the FDA. Explanation: Before a new drug can be marketed in the U.S., it must go through a rigorous review process culminating in the approval of a New Drug Application (NDA) by the FDA. The NDA includes all relevant data on the drug's safety and effectiveness, manufacturing processes, and proposed labeling, ensuring that the drug meets the required standards for public use.

44. What does the Ryan Haight Online Pharmacy Consumer Protection Act regulate?
a. The sale of homeopathic remedies
b. The operation of online pharmacies and the dispensing of controlled substances online
c. The importation of prescription drugs from Canada
d. The advertising of pharmaceuticals on social media platforms

Answer: b. The operation of online pharmacies and the dispensing of controlled substances online. Explanation: The Ryan Haight Act was enacted to address the growing concerns associated with the online sale and distribution of controlled substances. It establishes specific requirements for online pharmacies, including registration with the DEA, to prevent the illegal distribution of controlled substances and ensure patient safety in the digital age.

45. When documenting the destruction of controlled substances, which DEA form is utilized?
a. DEA Form 41
b. DEA Form 106
c. DEA Form 222
d. DEA Form 224

Answer: a. DEA Form 41. Explanation: DEA Form 41 is used to document the destruction of controlled substances. This form ensures a proper record is maintained for the disposal of these substances, complying with regulatory requirements and safeguarding against diversion and misuse within the pharmaceutical and healthcare industries.

46. Under the Drug Quality and Security Act (DQSA), a compounding pharmacy must register as an outsourcing facility if it intends to:
a. Compound non-patient specific medications.
b. Operate solely within one state.
c. Provide compounded medications to a single prescriber.
d. Compound medications in quantities not exceeding 5% of total prescriptions dispensed.

Answer: a. Compound non-patient specific medications. Explanation: The DQSA allows compounding pharmacies to register as outsourcing facilities to legally compound non-patient specific medications, subject to FDA oversight, reflecting an understanding of federal compounding regulations.

47. A pharmacy technician discovers a significant discrepancy during a controlled substance inventory. According to the DEA's regulations, within what time frame must this discrepancy be reported?
a. Immediately upon discovery.
b. Within 24 hours of discovery.
c. Within 3 business days of discovery.
d. Within 7 days of the end of the month in which it was discovered.

Answer: a. Immediately upon discovery. Explanation: DEA regulations require that significant discrepancies in controlled substances be reported immediately to prevent diversion, emphasizing the importance of regulatory compliance and inventory management in pharmacy practice.

48. When transferring a prescription for a Schedule II controlled substance, what is the most important legal consideration?
a. The transfer must be communicated directly between two licensed pharmacists.
b. The prescription can only be transferred once, regardless of the number of refills.
c. The receiving pharmacy must use a DEA Form 222 for the transfer.
d. The patient's consent must be obtained in writing before the transfer.

Answer: b. The prescription can only be transferred once, regardless of the number of refills. Explanation: Federal law prohibits refills on Schedule II prescriptions and generally does not allow for the transfer of these prescriptions; this highlights the strict regulations surrounding Schedule II medications.

49. Which of the following best describes the requirement for a pharmacy to maintain an accurate and current Formulary of Approved Drugs and Devices according to most state pharmacy laws?
a. It must include all drugs dispensed within the last 5 years.
b. It should be updated whenever a new drug is approved by the FDA.
c. It must only list those drugs that are covered by the major insurance plans.
d. It should include a list of all over-the-counter medications available at the pharmacy.

Answer: b. It should be updated whenever a new drug is approved by the FDA. Explanation: Maintaining an up-to-date formulary ensures that pharmacies dispense only approved medications, aligning with regulatory standards for drug safety and efficacy.

50. In the context of electronic prescribing of controlled substances (EPCS), what is a critical security measure required by the DEA?
a. Two-factor authentication for prescriber logins.
b. Biometric verification for all pharmacy technicians.
c. Encryption of all prescription data stored on pharmacy servers.
d. Annual cybersecurity training for all pharmacy staff.

Answer: a. Two-factor authentication for prescriber logins. Explanation: The DEA requires two-factor authentication for EPCS to enhance security and prevent unauthorized access, reflecting the importance of secure electronic prescription practices.

51. A pharmacy is audited and found to have dispensed a controlled substance based on a prescription that lacked one of the required elements. Which element, if missing, would be considered a violation of the Controlled Substances Act?
a. The patient's address.
b. The prescriber's DEA number.
c. The pharmacy's NPI number.
d. The date the prescription was written.

Answer: b. The prescriber's DEA number. Explanation: A prescriber's DEA number is essential for controlled substance prescriptions to ensure legitimacy and traceability, emphasizing regulatory compliance in dispensing controlled substances.

52. According to the Health Insurance Portability and Accountability Act (HIPAA), which of the following patient information is considered Protected Health Information (PHI)?
a. The patient's medication list.
b. The number of refills remaining on a prescription.
c. The cost of the medication dispensed.
d. The expiration date of the medication.

Answer: a. The patient's medication list. Explanation: Under HIPAA, a patient's medication list is considered PHI because it relates to the individual's health condition and treatment, underscoring the importance of confidentiality in handling patient information.

53. What is the primary purpose of the Poison Prevention Packaging Act (PPPA) as it relates to pharmacy practice?
a. To ensure that all medications are dispensed in child-resistant packaging.
b. To mandate that all controlled substances be double-locked in the pharmacy.
c. To require that pharmacies provide medication disposal services.

d. To establish guidelines for the labeling of hazardous substances.

Answer: a. To ensure that all medications are dispensed in child-resistant packaging. Explanation: The PPPA requires child-resistant packaging for most medications to prevent accidental poisoning in children, highlighting the role of packaging in medication safety.

54. Under the Ryan Haight Online Pharmacy Consumer Protection Act, online pharmacies must:
a. Obtain a special registration with the DEA.
b. Dispense controlled substances exclusively via electronic prescriptions.
c. Conduct a monthly audit of all controlled substances dispensed.
d. Verify the identity of each patient using a government-issued ID.

Answer: a. Obtain a special registration with the DEA. Explanation: The Act requires online pharmacies to register with the DEA to combat the abuse of controlled substances prescribed online, reflecting efforts to ensure safe and lawful online medication dispensing.

55. When dealing with a medication recall, what is the FIRST action a pharmacy should take upon notification?
a. Remove the medication from the shelves and return it to the manufacturer.
b. Notify all patients who have received the medication in the last 12 months.
c. Quarantine the affected medication to prevent further dispensing.
d. Document the recall notification and the pharmacy's response plan.

Answer: c. Quarantine the affected medication to prevent further dispensing. Explanation: The initial step in handling a medication recall is to quarantine the affected product to prevent any further distribution or dispensing, ensuring patient safety and compliance with regulatory guidelines.

56. A physician orders a customized topical ointment containing hydrocortisone 1%, salicylic acid 3%, and pramoxine 1%. The pharmacist asks you to compound this preparation. Which of the following resources would be most helpful for ensuring compatibility and stability?
a. Trissel's Stability of Compounded Formulations
b. Micromedex Solutions
c. The pharmacy's inventory software
d. The original drug package inserts

Answer: a. Trissel's Stability of Compounded Formulations. Explanation: Trissel's is a specialized reference providing information on the compatibility, stability, and beyond-use dating of compounded preparations. It's invaluable when creating custom formulations that lack standard manufacturer information.

57. A technician is preparing a TPN (total parenteral nutrition) admixture. Which of the following is essential to verify before releasing the compounded product?

a. Patient's current blood pressure
b. Final solution volume and weight
c. Expiration dates of all ingredients used
d. Compatibility of the TPN with other IV fluids

Answer: b. Final solution volume and weight. Explanation: Accuracy in volume and weight is paramount in TPNs, as they provide the patient's essential nutrients. Verifying these measurements ensures the patient receives the intended caloric and electrolyte intake.

58. A patient on long-term IV antibiotics at home reports their PICC line dressing has become loose. The home health nurse is unavailable for a replacement. What advice should the pharmacy technician provide?
a. Remove the old dressing and apply a new sterile dressing at home.
b. Leave the loose dressing in place and wait for the home health nurse.
c. Advise the patient to go to the nearest urgent care for dressing replacement.
d. Instruct the patient on how to reinforce the dressing with medical tape.

Answer: c. Advise the patient to go to the nearest urgent care for dressing replacement. Explanation: PICC line dressings require sterile technique to prevent infection risk. Recommending urgent care ensures proper assessment and replacement, minimizing complications for the patient.

59. A technician receives a prescription for clindamycin oral suspension with instructions to "Shake well before using." Which of the following should be calculated to determine the appropriate beyond-use date (BUD)?
a. The date the prescription was written
b. The date the suspension was reconstituted
c. The manufacturer's expiration date for the dry powder
d. The date the prescription is dispensed to the patient

Answer: b. The date the suspension was reconstituted. Explanation: Reconstituted oral suspensions typically have a shorter BUD than the dry powder form. The BUD is calculated from the reconstitution date, not the dispensing or prescription date.

60. A chemotherapy order requires the preparation of multiple syringes of varying doses from a single-dose vial. Which of the following practices is essential to ensure patient safety?
a. Prepare all syringes under a horizontal airflow hood to maximize sterility.
b. Utilize filter needles to prevent glass shards from entering the syringes.
c. Calculate the total volume needed and withdraw it in a single step to reduce waste.
d. Label each syringe with the patient's name, drug, dose, and administration route.

Answer: d. Label each syringe with the patient's name, drug, dose, and administration route. Explanation: Chemotherapy safety mandates meticulous, individual labeling to prevent devastating medication errors. While other options are important, accurate labeling is the most critical step in this scenario.

61. You receive a high-risk sterile compounding order that exceeds your current skill level. The pharmacist offers to supervise you through the process. Which of the following is the most appropriate response?
a. Proceed with the compounding to gain experience.
b. Decline, but offer to observe the pharmacist prepare the medication.
c. Ask a fellow technician if they are comfortable preparing the order.
d. Suggest utilizing a premixed, commercially available product if possible.

Answer: b. Decline, but offer to observe the pharmacist prepare the medication. Explanation: Patient safety and preparation quality take precedence. Declining shows good judgment and a desire to learn, while observing allows you to gain the needed skills for future compounding.

62. A pharmacist compounds a sterile ophthalmic solution and notices small fibers floating in the final product. Which of the following is the most likely cause?
a. The solution was not filtered during preparation.
b. The laminar airflow hood was not cleaned recently.
c. Expired ingredients were used.
d. Incompatible medications were mixed together.

Answer: a. The solution was not filtered during preparation. Explanation: Sterile filtration is essential to remove particulate matter. Fibers in the final solution strongly suggest a missed filtration step.

63. The pharmacy receives an increased volume of orders for IV admixtures. Which of the following would be the most efficient way to improve workflow?
a. Hire additional pharmacy technicians.
b. Batch similar IV preparations together.
c. Require prescribers to submit IV orders electronically.
d. Train technicians on cross-functional tasks.

Answer: b. Batch similar IV preparations together. Explanation: Batching streamlines compounding by allowing technicians to focus on one preparation type at a time, reducing setup time and the potential for errors.

64. When compounding a sterile intravenous (IV) solution, which of the following environmental conditions must be strictly monitored to ensure compliance with USP <797> standards?
a. Room temperature between 20°C and 25°C
b. Relative humidity not exceeding 60%
c. Air changes per hour (ACPH) in the compounding area
d. Lighting intensity of at least 450 lux in the compounding area

Answer: c. Air changes per hour (ACPH) in the compounding area. Explanation: USP <797> emphasizes the importance of adequate air changes per hour (ACPH) in sterile compounding areas to maintain air quality and reduce contamination risk, reflecting principles of controlled environment requirements.

65. In non-sterile compounding, when is the use of a mortar and pestle contraindicated?
a. When combining two liquid medications
b. When triturating a very potent drug
c. When mixing a hydrophilic powder with a hydrophobic base
d. When crushing tablets to create a fine powder

Answer: b. When triturating a very potent drug. Explanation: The use of a mortar and pestle may be contraindicated when triturating very potent drugs due to the risk of cross-contamination and the difficulty in completely removing potent drug residues, aligning with safety principles in compounding.

66. Which component is crucial in a laminar airflow workbench (LAFW) to ensure sterility in sterile compounding?
a. High-efficiency particulate air (HEPA) filter
b. Ultraviolet (UV) light
c. Stainless steel surface
d. Digital airflow meter

Answer: a. High-efficiency particulate air (HEPA) filter. Explanation: The HEPA filter in a LAFW is critical for removing particles from the air, ensuring a sterile environment for compounding, in accordance with USP <797> guidelines on sterile preparation.

67. During the compounding of a sterile medication, a pharmacy technician notices a small tear in their glove. What is the immediate next step according to USP <797> guidelines?
a. Apply a new glove over the torn glove.
b. Disinfect the torn glove with 70% isopropyl alcohol.
c. Remove gloves and perform hand hygiene before re-gloving.
d. Continue compounding if the tear is on the non-dominant hand.

Answer: c. Remove gloves and perform hand hygiene before re-gloving. Explanation: USP <797> mandates immediate removal of compromised personal protective equipment (PPE) and performing hand hygiene before re-gloving to maintain sterility, emphasizing the importance of aseptic technique.

68. What is the primary reason for performing a fingertip test in sterile compounding?
a. To ensure the compounding area is free from contaminants
b. To check the efficacy of the laminar airflow workbench
c. To assess the aseptic technique of compounding personnel
d. To verify the sterility of compounded preparations

Answer: c. To assess the aseptic technique of compounding personnel. Explanation: The fingertip test is used to assess the aseptic technique of individuals involved in sterile compounding by detecting microbial contamination on the fingertips, as part of personnel qualification under USP <797>.

69. In the context of stability and beyond-use dating for non-sterile compounded formulations, which factor is NOT typically considered?
a. The chemical stability of active ingredients
b. The intended use of the compounded preparation
c. The storage conditions of the final product
d. The color of the final product

Answer: d. The color of the final product. Explanation: While the physical appearance can be an indicator of stability, the color of the final product is not a primary factor in determining beyond-use dating, which is more directly influenced by chemical stability, intended use, and storage conditions.

70. When selecting a base for a compounded dermatological cream, which consideration is most critical for ensuring patient safety and therapeutic efficacy?
a. The viscosity of the base
b. The compatibility with the active ingredient
c. The base's expiration date
d. The cost of the base

Answer: b. The compatibility with the active ingredient. Explanation: The compatibility of the base with the active ingredient is crucial to ensure that the active ingredient remains effective and stable, and that the final product is safe for patient use, reflecting principles of formulation science in compounding.

71. For a high-risk sterile compounding procedure, what is the minimum required garb for personnel according to USP <797>?
a. Gowns, gloves, and hair covers
b. Gowns, gloves, hair covers, and shoe covers
c. Gowns, gloves, hair covers, shoe covers, and face masks
d. Gowns, gloves, hair covers, shoe covers, face masks, and sterile goggles

Answer: d. Gowns, gloves, hair covers, shoe covers, face masks, and sterile goggles. Explanation: USP <797> requires comprehensive garbing for high-risk compounding, including gowns, gloves, hair and shoe covers, face masks, and sterile goggles to maintain aseptic conditions and protect the compounded preparations.

72. What is the primary purpose of conducting a risk assessment for non-sterile compounding procedures?
a. To determine the appropriate personal protective equipment (PPE)
b. To identify potential hazards and implement control measures
c. To assess the financial impact of compounding activities

d. To calculate the beyond-use date of compounded preparations

Answer: b. To identify potential hazards and implement control measures. Explanation: Risk assessments in non-sterile compounding are conducted to identify potential chemical, physical, and biological hazards, and to implement control measures to mitigate risks, ensuring the safety and efficacy of compounded preparations.

73. In sterile compounding, what is the significance of using a buffer area (also known as a cleanroom)?
a. To store finished compounded sterile products
b. To provide a controlled environment for the preparation of sterile products
c. To house the pharmacy's inventory of sterile supplies
d. To serve as a changing area for compounding personnel

Answer: b. To provide a controlled environment for the preparation of sterile products. Explanation: The buffer area, or cleanroom, is designed to provide a controlled environment with minimized particle and microbial contamination levels, critical for the aseptic preparation of sterile compounded products, as per USP <797>.

74. A patient picks up two prescriptions: metformin for diabetes and a new antibiotic, amoxicillin-clavulanate. Which of the following counseling points is most important to emphasize to prevent a potential adverse drug reaction?
a. Take both medications with a full glass of water.
b. Metformin can cause stomach upset, so take it with food.
c. The antibiotic may decrease the effectiveness of birth control pills.
d. Report any signs of diarrhea, as this could indicate a serious side effect of the antibiotic.

Answer: d. Report any signs of diarrhea, as this could indicate a serious side effect of the antibiotic. Explanation: While other options are valid counseling points, severe diarrhea could signal C. difficile infection, a potentially life-threatening complication of antibiotic use. Prioritizing immediate reporting of this symptom is crucial for patient safety.

75. A pharmacy technician receives a phone call from a frantic patient who accidentally took twice their usual dose of blood pressure medication. Which of the following actions should the technician take first?
a. Instruct the patient to drink plenty of fluids to counteract low blood pressure.
b. Advise the patient to go to the emergency room immediately.
c. Ask to speak with a family member to gather more information.
d. Calmly obtain the name and strength of the medication, time taken, and the patient's current condition.

Answer: d. Calmly obtain the name and strength of the medication, time taken, and the patient's current condition. Explanation: Before any action, it's crucial to assess the situation. Gathering essential information allows the technician to provide informed guidance or escalate the situation to the pharmacist for further evaluation.

76. A physician prescribes a medication with a known risk of causing severe birth defects. The patient is a 25-year-old female. How should the pharmacy proceed?
a. Fill the prescription as written after verifying the patient's gender.
b. Dispense the medication and provide extensive patient counseling on the risks.
c. Contact the prescriber to confirm the patient is aware of the risks and discuss alternative therapies.
d. Refuse to fill the prescription due to the potential for harm.

Answer: c. Contact the prescriber to confirm the patient is aware of the risks and discuss alternative therapies. Explanation: Pharmacies have an ethical responsibility in dispensing teratogenic medications. Collaboration with the prescriber ensures the patient understands the risks and allows for exploration of safer options, promoting informed consent.

77. A new technician is reconciling an outpatient's medication list with recent hospital discharge orders. The technician notices discrepancies in dosages between the two lists. What is the best course of action?
a. Update the patient's profile based on the hospital discharge orders.

b. Average the two dosages and dispense the medication accordingly.
c. Consult the pharmacist to clarify the discrepancies and contact the prescriber if necessary.

d. Inform the patient about the discrepancies and advise them to follow the hospital instructions.

Answer: c. Consult the pharmacist to clarify the discrepancies and contact the prescriber if necessary. Explanation: Medication reconciliation requires pharmacist oversight. Dosage discrepancies could be intentional or an error, necessitating further investigation before providing potentially incorrect medication to the patient.

78. The pharmacy receives a prescription for warfarin with an INR monitoring frequency of "weekly." Which of the following actions is most appropriate?
a. Fill the prescription with instructions to the patient about weekly INR testing.
b. Contact the prescriber to clarify if INR monitoring is intended to be daily or weekly.
c. Assume the prescriber meant daily INR monitoring, as this is standard practice.
d. Refuse to fill the prescription until a clear INR monitoring frequency is provided.

Answer: b. Contact the prescriber to clarify if INR monitoring is intended to be daily or weekly. Explanation: Ambiguous orders create safety risks. INR monitoring frequency on warfarin therapy can vary, so it's critical to confirm the prescriber's intent before dispensing.

79. A patient taking carbamazepine reports that their grapefruit juice tastes unusually bitter. What key safety concern does this raise?
a. The patient might develop a grapefruit allergy.
b. Grapefruit juice can decrease the effectiveness of carbamazepine.
c. Carbamazepine can increase the risk of photosensitivity (sunburn).
d. Grapefruit juice can increase carbamazepine levels, potentially leading to toxicity.

Answer: d. Grapefruit juice can increase carbamazepine levels, potentially leading to toxicity. Explanation: Grapefruit juice inhibits CYP3A4 metabolism, which can significantly raise carbamazepine levels. Recognizing this interaction is essential to prevent serious side effects.

80. A patient with a penicillin allergy is prescribed cephalexin for a skin infection. Which of the following actions is most appropriate?
a. Fill the prescription as written, cephalexin is safe for those with penicillin allergies.
b. Contact the prescriber to discuss alternative antibiotics due to cross-sensitivity risk.
c. Dispense the cephalexin and provide the patient with an EpiPen in case of a reaction.
d. Advise the patient to monitor closely for signs of an allergic reaction.

Answer: b. Contact the prescriber to discuss alternative antibiotics due to cross-sensitivity risk. Explanation: While not all penicillin-allergic patients react to cephalosporins, there's a potential for cross-reactivity. Choosing a safer antibiotic class minimizes the risk to the patient.

81. In the preparation of intravenous (IV) medications, which of the following is considered the most critical aspect to ensure sterility?
a. Using gloves that are powdered to reduce sweating
b. Swabbing the vial septum with alcohol for 5 seconds before piercing
c. Performing hand hygiene for at least 20 seconds prior to compounding
d. Selecting syringes and needles from the same manufacturer

Answer: c. Performing hand hygiene for at least 20 seconds prior to compounding. Explanation: Hand hygiene is a fundamental aseptic technique to prevent contamination during sterile compounding. Proper hand hygiene significantly reduces the risk of introducing microorganisms into sterile preparations, aligning with USP <797> guidelines.

82. A pharmacy technician is preparing a chemotherapy medication. According to USP <800>, which of the following is an essential requirement for personal protective equipment (PPE)?
a. Double gloving with latex gloves
b. Use of a water-resistant gown
c. A surgical mask for respiratory protection
d. Hairnets and beard covers are optional

Answer: b. Use of a water-resistant gown. Explanation: USP <800> specifies that personnel handling hazardous drugs, such as chemotherapy medications, must wear PPE including a gown that is water and chemical-resistant to protect against spills and splashes, underscoring the importance of safety in handling hazardous substances.

83. When compounding a non-sterile ointment that requires the use of a mortar and pestle, which of the following techniques is crucial to ensure uniformity and potency?

a. Levigation
b. Geometric dilution
c. Fusion
d. Pulverization by intervention

Answer: b. Geometric dilution. Explanation: Geometric dilution is a technique used to ensure that a small amount of a potent substance is evenly distributed throughout a mixture. It involves mixing the potent substance with an equal amount of a diluent and then progressively adding in more diluent in amounts that double each time.

84. For a pharmacy technician working in an anteroom with positive pressure, which of the following tasks is appropriate?
a. Preparing non-hazardous IV solutions
b. Compounding hazardous drugs
c. Storing sterile compounding supplies
d. Performing final checks of compounded sterile products

Answer: c. Storing sterile compounding supplies. Explanation: An anteroom with positive pressure relative to adjacent areas is suitable for storing sterile supplies but not for compounding sterile products, which requires a cleanroom with negative pressure to prevent contamination and ensure safety, especially when not dealing with hazardous drugs.

85. In the process of reconstituting a lyophilized powder for injection, what is the first step a pharmacy technician should take after calculating the required volume of diluent?
a. Inject air into the vial equal to the volume of diluent to be added
b. Swab the vial's rubber stopper with isopropyl alcohol
c. Shake the vial to loosen the powder
d. Verify the expiration date of the diluent

Answer: b. Swab the vial's rubber stopper with isopropyl alcohol. Explanation: Swabbing the vial's rubber stopper with isopropyl alcohol is essential to disinfect the stopper before piercing it with a needle, which is a critical step to maintain sterility before reconstitution.

86. When compounding an ophthalmic solution, which of the following conditions is most critical to prevent microbial contamination?
a. The solution must be isotonic
b. The pH should be adjusted to 7.4
c. Use of a preservative if not used immediately
d. Filtration through a 0.22 μm filter

Answer: d. Filtration through a 0.22 μm filter. Explanation: Filtration through a 0.22 μm filter is essential for removing microbial contaminants from solutions that will be used in the eyes, a critical requirement to ensure the safety and efficacy of ophthalmic preparations.

87. A pharmacy technician is asked to prepare a total parenteral nutrition (TPN) solution. Which of the following components must be added last to minimize the risk of precipitation?
a. Amino acids
b. Dextrose
c. Multivitamins
d. Calcium and phosphate salts

Answer: d. Calcium and phosphate salts. Explanation: Calcium and phosphate salts should be added last and carefully managed in a TPN solution to minimize the risk of precipitation, a critical consideration in ensuring the safety and compatibility of TPN components.

88. Which of the following best describes the purpose of using a laminar airflow workbench (LAFW) in sterile compounding?
a. To remove toxic fumes from volatile compounds
b. To provide a barrier between the compounder and the sterile field
c. To maintain a sterile environment by directing HEPA-filtered air over the work area
d. To dry sterilize equipment and glassware before use

Answer: c. To maintain a sterile environment by directing HEPA-filtered air over the work area. Explanation: A LAFW is designed to maintain a sterile environment by providing unidirectional, HEPA-filtered airflow across the work surface, which prevents contamination of sterile materials.

89. When using an automated compounding device for preparing IV admixtures, which of the following is a critical step for ensuring accuracy and safety?
a. Calibrating the device for each medication added
b. Using the same brand of syringe for all medications
c. Selecting the fastest infusion rate to reduce compounding time
d. Verifying the final product's volume and concentration

Answer: d. Verifying the final product's volume and concentration. Explanation: Verifying the final product's volume and concentration after using an automated compounding device is crucial to ensure that the IV admixture meets the prescribed specifications for patient safety and efficacy.

90. In the context of USP <797>, when compounding sterile preparations, which of the following environmental monitoring methods is essential for ensuring an aseptic compounding environment?
a. Daily air particle counting
b. Weekly fingertip sampling of compounding personnel
c. Biannual certification of the cleanroom and LAFW

d. Monthly surface sampling for microbial contamination

Answer: d. Monthly surface sampling for microbial contamination. Explanation: Monthly surface sampling for microbial contamination is a key component of environmental monitoring under USP <797> to assess the cleanliness of compounding areas and to ensure the maintenance of an aseptic compounding environment.

91. A pharmacy technician receives a medication order for a pediatric patient that seems unusually high. What is the most appropriate initial action?
a. Dispense the medication as prescribed, assuming the prescriber knows best.
b. Contact the prescriber to verify the dose.
c. Reduce the dose to what seems appropriate based on the technician's experience.
d. Consult with a pharmacist to discuss the patient's medication history.

Answer: b. Contact the prescriber to verify the dose. Explanation: In situations where a prescribed dose appears unusually high, especially for vulnerable populations like pediatric patients, the most appropriate and safe action is to verify the dose with the prescriber. This step ensures that any potential prescribing errors are caught and corrected before dispensing, enhancing medication safety.

92. When reviewing a prescription for warfarin, the pharmacy technician notices that the patient is also taking aspirin daily. What is the potential concern with this combination?
a. Decreased efficacy of warfarin
b. Increased risk of bleeding
c. Aspirin will negate the effects of warfarin
d. Warfarin will increase the risk of aspirin-induced asthma

Answer: b. Increased risk of bleeding. Explanation: Both warfarin and aspirin have anticoagulant properties; warfarin as an oral anticoagulant and aspirin as an antiplatelet. When taken together, they can synergistically increase the risk of bleeding. It's crucial for healthcare providers to assess the risk versus benefit in patients who are prescribed this combination.

93. A patient is prescribed a nitroglycerin transdermal patch. What is an important counseling point regarding its application?
a. Apply the patch to the same site each time to maintain efficacy.
b. The patch should be worn continuously, without any breaks.
c. Rotate the application site to prevent skin irritation.
d. Apply the patch only at night to reduce the risk of orthostatic hypotension.

Answer: c. Rotate the application site to prevent skin irritation. Explanation: Rotating the site of application for transdermal patches, like those containing nitroglycerin, is important to prevent skin irritation and ensure the medication's efficacy. Continuous application to the same skin site can lead to local skin reactions and decrease the absorption of the medication.

94. In the context of high-alert medications, what is a recommended strategy to minimize errors?
a. Store high-alert medications next to commonly used medications for easy access.
b. Use tall-man lettering to distinguish look-alike/sound-alike medications.
c. Limit the use of high-alert medications to senior pharmacists only.
d. Avoid labeling high-alert medications to reduce patient anxiety.

Answer: b. Use tall-man lettering to distinguish look-alike/sound-alike medications. Explanation: Tall-man lettering is a strategy used to highlight the differences in look-alike/sound-alike medication names to prevent dispensing errors. It enhances the visual distinction between similar medication names, reducing the risk of medication errors associated with high-alert medications.

95. What is the significance of a "black box warning" on a medication label?
a. It indicates the medication is safe for use in all patient populations.
b. It signifies that the medication should be stored in a secure area.
c. It highlights serious or life-threatening risks associated with the medication.
d. It means the medication is contraindicated in pediatric patients.

Answer: c. It highlights serious or life-threatening risks associated with the medication. Explanation: A black box warning, or boxed warning, is the FDA's most stringent warning for prescription drugs. It signifies that clinical studies have identified serious or life-threatening risks associated with the drug, alerting both prescribers and patients to weigh the benefits against the potential risks.

96. A pharmacy is implementing a bar-code medication administration (BCMA) system. What is the primary benefit of this technology?
a. It eliminates the need for pharmacist verification of prescriptions.
b. It automatically refills medications when stock is low.
c. It reduces the risk of medication errors during administration.
d. It increases the speed of medication dispensing without regard for accuracy.

Answer: c. It reduces the risk of medication errors during administration. Explanation: BCMA technology involves scanning bar codes on patient identification bands and medications before administration, ensuring the correct patient receives the correct medication at the correct dose and time. This system significantly reduces the risk of medication errors at the point of care.

97. When preparing a chemotherapy medication, what is a critical safety measure?
a. Preparing the medication in an open environment to ensure sterility.
b. Using personal protective equipment (PPE) and a biological safety cabinet (BSC).
c. Allowing the medication to sit for 24 hours before use to ensure potency.
d. Shaking the medication vigorously before administration to ensure proper mixing.

Answer: b. Using personal protective equipment (PPE) and a biological safety cabinet (BSC). Explanation: When preparing chemotherapy medications, it's critical to use PPE to protect the pharmacy technician from exposure to hazardous drugs and a BSC to maintain sterility and protect the medication from contamination. This ensures the safety of both the healthcare provider and the patient.

98. For a medication known to have a narrow therapeutic index (NTI), what is the primary concern when monitoring therapy?
a. Ensuring that the patient's insurance covers the medication
b. The medication's flavor and palatability
c. The risk of significant toxicity if the dose is slightly above the therapeutic range
d. The ease of administration of the medication

Answer: c. The risk of significant toxicity if the dose is slightly above the therapeutic range. Explanation: Medications with a narrow therapeutic index have a small margin between therapeutic and toxic doses. Close monitoring is essential to ensure that blood levels remain within the therapeutic range to avoid toxicity while still achieving the desired therapeutic effect.

99. A patient presents a prescription for an oral solution of a medication known for its poor palatability. What can be done to improve patient adherence to this medication?
a. Advising the patient to dilute the medication with water before ingestion
b. Flavoring the medication, if no contraindications exist, to mask the taste
c. Switching the medication to an injectable form without consulting the prescriber
d. Recommending that the patient hold their nose while taking the medication to avoid tasting it

Answer: b. Flavoring the medication, if no contraindications exist, to mask the taste. Explanation: Flavoring medications can significantly improve palatability and patient adherence, especially for oral solutions known for poor taste. This should be done considering any contraindications and in consultation with the prescriber if necessary.

100. A pharmacy receives a prescription for a medication that must be taken on an empty stomach for optimal absorption. Which of the following instructions should be included on the label?
a. "Take this medication with a large meal."
b. "Take this medication with at least 8 ounces of milk."
c. "Take this medication 1 hour before or 2 hours after meals."
d. "Take this medication right before bedtime."

Answer: c. "Take this medication 1 hour before or 2 hours after meals." Explanation: Certain medications require administration on an empty stomach to enhance absorption. Instructing patients to take the medication 1 hour before or 2 hours after meals ensures the stomach is empty, facilitating optimal drug absorption.

101. In managing pharmacy inventory, what is the primary purpose of implementing an automated dispensing system?

a. To eliminate the need for pharmacist verification
b. To reduce medication errors and improve patient safety
c. To increase the pharmacy's revenue by fast-tracking high-cost medications
d. To remove the necessity for manual inventory counts

Answer: b. To reduce medication errors and improve patient safety. Explanation: Automated dispensing systems are primarily implemented to reduce medication errors and improve patient safety by ensuring accurate dispensing, tracking usage, and maintaining inventory levels, aligning with the principles of medication safety and inventory management.

102. When considering the turnover rate of a pharmacy's inventory, which of the following metrics is most directly improved by increasing the turnover rate?
a. Gross margin
b. Carrying costs
c. Revenue per square foot
d. Prescription volume

Answer: b. Carrying costs. Explanation: Increasing the turnover rate reduces carrying costs by minimizing the amount of inventory held, thereby reducing storage, insurance, and potential obsolescence costs, a key principle in efficient inventory management.

103. In the context of a high-cost biologic medication with specific storage requirements, what is the most critical factor for a pharmacy technician to monitor?
a. The reorder level to maintain inventory
b. Temperature and humidity controls
c. The number of generic alternatives available
d. The insurance reimbursement rate

Answer: b. Temperature and humidity controls. Explanation: For high-cost biologic medications, maintaining proper storage conditions, including temperature and humidity, is critical to ensure the medication's efficacy and safety, reflecting the importance of specialized storage requirements in inventory management.

104. A pharmacy is evaluating its inventory management system. Which strategy would best help in identifying slow-moving items that may need to be discontinued?
a. Implementing a first-expired, first-out (FEFO) system
b. Conducting regular ABC analyses
c. Increasing the reorder frequency for all items
d. Reducing prices for overstocked items

Answer: b. Conducting regular ABC analyses. Explanation: ABC analysis categorizes inventory items based on their importance, with "C" items being slow movers. This strategy helps in identifying items that may need to be discontinued, optimizing inventory levels and reducing waste.

105. In managing a pharmacy's inventory, what is the primary goal of employing a just-in-time (JIT) inventory system?
a. To increase the variety of medications stocked
b. To reduce inventory carrying costs by minimizing stock levels
c. To ensure a 100% in-stock rate for all medications
d. To simplify the ordering process

Answer: b. To reduce inventory carrying costs by minimizing stock levels. Explanation: JIT inventory systems aim to reduce carrying costs and minimize stock levels by ordering goods only as they are needed, a principle that enhances efficiency and reduces waste in inventory management.

106. When a pharmacy technician identifies a medication that has been recalled, what is the immediate next step they should take according to best practices?
a. Continue dispensing the medication until a substitute is found
b. Quarantine the medication and notify the pharmacy manager
c. Dispose of the medication immediately
d. Return the medication to the shelf and report the recall to the FDA

Answer: b. Quarantine the medication and notify the pharmacy manager. Explanation: The immediate step is to quarantine the recalled medication to prevent its use and notify the pharmacy manager for further action, ensuring patient safety and compliance with recall procedures.

107. What is the primary consideration when a pharmacy decides to stock a new over-the-counter (OTC) medication?
a. The medication's potential for abuse
b. The shelf space required for the new product
c. The demand and needs of the pharmacy's customer base
d. The number of similar products already available

Answer: c. The demand and needs of the pharmacy's customer base. Explanation: The primary consideration is the demand and needs of the pharmacy's customers, ensuring that the new OTC medication meets their health care requirements and preferences, aligning with customer-centric inventory management.

108. In a scenario where a popular medication is on backorder, what is the most appropriate action for a pharmacy technician to take to manage patient care effectively?
a. Substitute the medication with a similar product without consulting the prescriber
b. Inform patients about the delay and coordinate with prescribers for alternative options
c. Advise patients to skip doses until the medication is back in stock
d. Purchase the medication at a higher cost from a secondary supplier

Answer: b. Inform patients about the delay and coordinate with prescribers for alternative options. Explanation: Communicating with patients about the backorder and collaborating with prescribers for alternatives ensures continuity of care and maintains patient safety, reflecting best practices in inventory management during supply issues.

109. How does the implementation of a perpetual inventory system benefit a pharmacy's inventory management?
a. It eliminates the need for physical inventory counts
b. It provides real-time, accurate inventory levels and tracking
c. It automatically orders medications when stock is low
d. It prioritizes the dispensing of medications with the highest profit margins

Answer: b. It provides real-time, accurate inventory levels and tracking. Explanation: A perpetual inventory system offers real-time inventory tracking, ensuring accurate levels and facilitating efficient management, a cornerstone of modern pharmacy inventory management practices.

110. Considering the principles of inventory management, what is the most effective method for a pharmacy to manage the risk of medication shortages?
a. Limiting the number of suppliers to negotiate better prices
b. Maintaining a higher safety stock level for critical medications
c. Ordering large quantities infrequently to take advantage of bulk discounts
d. Focusing exclusively on generic medications to reduce costs

Answer: b. Maintaining a higher safety stock level for critical medications. Explanation: Keeping a higher safety stock for critical medications mitigates the risk of shortages, ensuring that patient care is not compromised, a key strategy in inventory risk management.

111. The pharmacy receives a recall notice for a specific lot number of metformin due to contamination concerns. Which of the following actions should be prioritized?
a. Immediately quarantine all metformin stock and await further instructions from the FDA.
b. Contact patients who recently filled prescriptions for metformin to notify them of the recall.
c. Verify the lot numbers of current metformin stock and isolate any matching the recall.
d. Submit a claim to the wholesaler for reimbursement of the recalled medication.

Answer: c. Verify the lot numbers of current metformin stock and isolate any matching the recall. Explanation: The first step in a recall is preventing further dispensing of potentially contaminated products. Isolating the affected lots is crucial, followed by contacting affected patients and working with the supplier on returns.

112. A pharmacy technician notices a significant price increase for a commonly used medication when placing an order with the wholesaler. Which of the following is the most likely explanation?
a. The purchase price was entered incorrectly during the last order.

b. The manufacturer has decreased production of the medication.
c. There has been an error in the wholesaler's inventory system.
d. The medication's patent has recently expired, leading to generic competition.

Answer: b. The manufacturer has decreased production of the medication. Explanation: Price increases often signal supply disruptions. Decreased production, raw material shortages, or increased demand can lead to higher prices from the wholesaler.

113. A new medication with a high acquisition cost is added to the pharmacy's formulary. Which of the following inventory strategies would be most appropriate?
a. Order a large quantity to take advantage of bulk discounts.
b. Maintain minimal stock levels and utilize just-in-time ordering.
c. Set a high PAR level to ensure sufficient stock on hand.
d. Add the medication to the pharmacy's auto-reorder list.

Answer: b. Maintain minimal stock levels and utilize just-in-time ordering. Explanation: Expensive medications require careful inventory management. Just-in-time ordering minimizes the financial burden of carrying excess stock while ensuring the medication is available when needed.

114. A medication is listed on the national drug shortage list. The pharmacy's current stock is nearing depletion. Which of the following actions is most appropriate?
a. Place an order with the wholesaler for the usual quantity.
b. Limit dispensing to patients with prescriptions for urgent indications.
c. Contact the prescriber to discuss alternative therapies not affected by the shortage.
d. Increase the price of the medication to reduce demand.

Answer: b. Limit dispensing to patients with prescriptions for urgent indications. Explanation: Drug shortages necessitate rationing available supplies to prioritize the most critical patient needs. Collaborating with prescribers to find alternatives when possible is also important.

115. The pharmacy experiences an unexpected surge in demand for oseltamivir (Tamiflu) due to a flu outbreak. Which of the following would be the most efficient way to replenish stock quickly?
a. Contact the primary wholesaler to place an emergency order.
b. Search online for reputable secondary suppliers.
c. Borrow stock from a nearby chain pharmacy.
d. Refer patients to urgent care clinics for prescriptions.

Answer: a. Contact the primary wholesaler to place an emergency order. Explanation: Established wholesalers are the most reliable source in urgent situations. They often have expedited shipping options for critical medications.

116. A medication is set to expire in two months. The pharmacy has a high quantity on hand, and the wholesaler is not accepting returns. Which of the following is the best course of action?
a. Dispose of the medication according to hazardous waste protocols.
b. Promote the medication to prescribers to increase utilization before expiration.
c. Transfer the excess stock to another pharmacy within the same chain.
d. Donate the medication to a charitable medical organization.

Answer: c. Transfer the excess stock to another pharmacy within the same chain. Explanation: Transferring within the chain helps another pharmacy, reduces waste, and potentially avoids a financial loss. Promoting soon-to-expire meds can be unethical, while donations require specific licensing.

117. A pharmacy's refrigerator storing temperature-sensitive medications malfunctions overnight. Which action should the technician take first?
a. Attempt to repair the refrigerator.
b. Relocate the medications to a temporary, working refrigerator.
c. Document the temperature excursion and monitor medications for stability concerns.
d. Dispose of all the medications that were in the refrigerator.

Answer: b. Relocate the medications to a temporary, working refrigerator. Explanation: Protecting the integrity of the medications is paramount. Immediate relocation to proper storage is crucial, followed by assessing potential damage and documenting the incident.

118. The pharmacy updates its inventory management software. What is a critical task the technician should perform to ensure accurate PAR levels in the new system?
a. Reconcile purchase history and current on-hand quantities.
b. Increase PAR levels for all medications to prevent stock-outs.
c. Delete old inventory records that are no longer relevant.
d. Adjust reorder points based on the new software's recommendations.

Answer: a. Reconcile purchase history and current on-hand quantities. Explanation: Accurate data migration is essential for the new system to function properly. Verifying on-hand counts against records from the old system ensures PAR levels reflect reality.

119. In the context of continuous quality improvement (CQI) in pharmacy practice, which of the following is an essential first step in the Plan-Do-Study-Act (PDSA) cycle?
a. Implementing a new workflow based on team suggestions
b. Identifying areas for improvement based on error reports
c. Comparing the pharmacy's error rate to national benchmarks
d. Training staff on new technologies to reduce dispensing errors

Answer: b. Identifying areas for improvement based on error reports. Explanation: The first step in the PDSA cycle is to plan by identifying areas that need improvement, often informed by analyzing error reports or other quality metrics, setting the stage for targeted interventions in the quality improvement process.

120. When a pharmacy technician discovers a compounding error involving the incorrect weight of an ingredient, what immediate action should be taken?
a. Correct the error and proceed without reporting.
b. Document the error and notify the pharmacist for further action.
c. Dispose of the compounded product without recording the incident.
d. Continue with the preparation if the error is within a 10% variance.

Answer: b. Document the error and notify the pharmacist for further action. Explanation: Documenting the error and informing the pharmacist is crucial for addressing the mistake and preventing similar future occurrences, reflecting the principles of accountability and transparency in pharmacy quality assurance.

121. In ensuring the quality of compounded sterile preparations (CSPs), which environmental monitoring technique is critical?
a. Regular calibration of the compounding balance
b. Daily temperature logs for the compounding area
c. Airborne particle counting in the cleanroom
d. Biannual review of compounding procedures

Answer: c. Airborne particle counting in the cleanroom. Explanation: Airborne particle counting is essential in monitoring the cleanroom environment to ensure it meets the required ISO Class standards for CSPs, a key aspect of maintaining sterility and preventing contamination.

122. What is the primary purpose of utilizing bar-code scanning technology in the medication dispensing process?
a. To expedite the billing process
b. To reduce dispensing errors by verifying medication and dose
c. To track inventory levels in real-time
d. To monitor pharmacist productivity

Answer: b. To reduce dispensing errors by verifying medication and dose. Explanation: Bar-code scanning is primarily used to reduce dispensing errors by ensuring that the correct medication and dose are dispensed, enhancing patient safety and quality of care.

123. In the event of a medication recall, what is the most critical action for a pharmacy to take to maintain quality assurance?
a. Continue dispensing the medication until stock is depleted.
b. Isolate and return the recalled medication as per manufacturer guidelines.
c. Offer discounts on alternative medications to affected patients.
d. Wait for direct instructions from the FDA before taking any action.

Answer: b. Isolate and return the recalled medication as per manufacturer guidelines. Explanation: Isolating and returning the recalled medication promptly is crucial to prevent harm and comply with regulatory and safety standards, reflecting the pharmacy's commitment to quality assurance and patient safety.

124. How does performing a root cause analysis (RCA) after a dispensing error contribute to pharmacy quality assurance?
a. It assigns blame to the individual responsible for the error.
b. It identifies underlying system issues that led to the error.
c. It focuses on punitive measures to prevent future errors.
d. It assesses the financial impact of the error on the pharmacy.

Answer: b. It identifies underlying system issues that led to the error. Explanation: RCA is a systematic process used to identify the fundamental causes of errors, facilitating the development of strategies to prevent recurrence, thus enhancing overall quality and safety in pharmacy practice.

125. In the implementation of a high-alert medication policy, what key factor should be considered to enhance patient safety?
a. Limiting the prescription of high-alert medications to specialists
b. Providing auxiliary labels and patient counseling for high-alert medications
c. Increasing the price of high-alert medications to discourage overuse
d. Requiring a pharmacist's approval for all over-the-counter medication sales

Answer: b. Providing auxiliary labels and patient counseling for high-alert medications. Explanation: Auxiliary labeling and thorough patient counseling for high-alert medications are crucial strategies to mitigate the risks associated with these drugs, emphasizing the role of education and communication in patient safety.

126. What role does a medication safety officer (MSO) play in a pharmacy's quality assurance program?
a. Solely responsible for reporting errors to regulatory agencies
b. Coordinates initiatives to minimize medication errors and enhance patient safety
c. Focuses exclusively on the financial aspects of medication errors
d. Implements punitive measures for staff involved in medication errors

Answer: b. Coordinates initiatives to minimize medication errors and enhance patient safety. Explanation: An MSO coordinates efforts to reduce medication errors and improve safety, working collaboratively with pharmacy staff to implement evidence-based practices and safety initiatives, underscoring a proactive approach to quality assurance.

127. In the development of standard operating procedures (SOPs) for a new pharmacy service, what is a crucial consideration to ensure quality and consistency?
a. The SOPs should be complex to cover all possible scenarios.

b. The SOPs should be reviewed and updated only when an error occurs.

c. The SOPs should be accessible and easily understood by all staff members.

d. The SOPs should be developed by the pharmacy manager exclusively.

Answer: c. The SOPs should be accessible and easily understood by all staff members. Explanation: Developing clear, concise, and accessible SOPs ensures that all staff members can consistently apply best practices, a fundamental aspect of maintaining quality and consistency in pharmacy services.

128. How does the implementation of a continuous quality improvement (CQI) program impact a pharmacy's operations?

a. It focuses solely on meeting minimum regulatory standards.

b. It fosters a culture of safety and encourages reporting of errors and near misses.

c. It eliminates the need for periodic quality audits and assessments.

d. It prioritizes cost-saving measures over patient safety initiatives.

Answer: b. It fosters a culture of safety and encourages reporting of errors and near misses. Explanation: A CQI program promotes a safety culture where staff are encouraged to report errors and near misses without fear of retribution, facilitating ongoing learning and improvement in pharmacy operations and patient care.

129. A patient reports receiving tablets of the wrong color in their last refill of lisinopril. The technician investigates and confirms the patient's previous refills were the correct medication. What type of error does this most likely represent?

a. Wrong drug dispensed due to a look-alike mix-up

b. Wrong dosage strength mistakenly dispensed

c. Manufacturing error resulting in incorrect product

d. Expired medication was accidentally dispensed

Answer: c. Manufacturing error resulting in incorrect product. Explanation: While other errors are possible, a consistent change in tablet appearance for a regularly filled medication strongly suggests a problem upstream at the manufacturing level.

130. A pharmacy technician receives a prescription for amoxicillin oral suspension with instructions that don't specify a volume. After contacting the prescriber, it's determined the intended dose is 500mg twice a day. Which of the following actions demonstrates good quality assurance practices?

a. Calculate the volume based on the standard concentration and dispense the medication.

b. Ask another technician to double-check the calculated volume before dispensing.

c. Request the prescriber to send a new prescription with the complete dosing instructions.

d. Inform the patient that the prescription cannot be filled as written.

Answer: b. Ask another technician to double-check the calculated volume before dispensing. Explanation: Independent double-checks are a cornerstone of quality assurance, especially for calculations. While contacting the prescriber is sometimes necessary, it shouldn't replace the internal safety check.

131. During a routine controlled substance inventory, the pharmacy discovers a discrepancy in the on-hand count for oxycodone tablets. What is the first step in addressing this issue?
a. Recount the medication and carefully review recent dispensing records.
b. Notify the DEA and local law enforcement of the potential diversion.
c. Implement new security measures for handling controlled substances.
d. Discipline the staff members who were working when the discrepancy likely occurred.

Answer: a. Recount the medication and carefully review recent dispensing records. Explanation: Initial investigation is crucial before escalating the issue. Discrepancies can stem from simple counting errors or documentation mistakes, and a thorough review might uncover the cause.

132. A technician notices a medication vial labeled with both a brand and generic name, but only the generic name is circled. What potential quality issue should be investigated?
a. The wrong medication might be in the vial.
b. The vial might be expired or counterfeit.
c. The medication might have been recalled.
d. The patient might be allergic to the brand-name product.

Answer: a. The wrong medication might be in the vial. Explanation: Mismatched labeling raises concerns about the vial's contents. This could be a repackaging error or indicate a returned medication was placed in the wrong vial, necessitating further investigation.

133. A technician discovers a patient's medication profile lists them as being allergic to penicillin, yet they recently filled a prescription for amoxicillin without incident. What is the most appropriate course of action?
a. Delete the penicillin allergy, as it was likely documented in error.
b. Flag the patient's profile and notify the pharmacist of the potential discrepancy.
c. Advise the patient to avoid all penicillin-class antibiotics in the future.
d. Contact the patient to confirm if they experienced a reaction to amoxicillin.

Answer: b. Flag the patient's profile and notify the pharmacist of the potential discrepancy. Explanation: Allergies require pharmacist assessment. There could be a documentation error, a cross-sensitivity that wasn't considered, or the patient may no longer be allergic.

134. The FDA issues a Class I recall for a specific lot of prefilled heparin syringes due to an increased risk of serious adverse events. Which of the following actions should the pharmacy prioritize?
a. Immediately remove all prefilled heparin syringes from stock.
b. Cease dispensing prefilled heparin syringes and compound them in-house if needed.
c. Notify the wholesaler to arrange for a return and credit.

d. Identify patients who received the affected lot and contact them immediately.

Answer: d. Identify patients who received the affected lot and contact them immediately. Explanation: Patient safety is paramount in Class I recalls. Preventing further harm by notifying affected patients takes precedence over other actions.

135. A technician reviews an error report describing a patient who received a prescription labeled for TID (three times daily) instead of the intended daily dosing. Which root cause analysis tool would be most helpful in preventing similar errors?
a. Fishbone diagram (Ishikawa Diagram)
b. The 5 Whys
c. Failure Mode and Effects Analysis (FMEA)
d. Pareto chart

Answer: a. Fishbone diagram (Ishikawa Diagram). Explanation: Fishbone diagrams help visualize contributing factors to errors, such as confusing abbreviations (TID vs. daily), distractions during order entry, or unclear prescriptions.

136. A pharmacy implements a new barcode scanning system at dispensing. What key metric should be closely monitored to evaluate the system's impact on medication safety?
a. Average prescription fill times
b. Dispensing error rates
c. Inventory turnover ratio
d. Patient satisfaction scores

Answer: b. Dispensing error rates. Explanation: Barcode scanning is directly intended to reduce dispensing errors. Tracking error rates before and after implementation provides the most relevant data about the system's effectiveness.

137. In the process of continuous quality improvement (CQI) in a pharmacy setting, which step is crucial after identifying a medication error?
a. Assigning blame to the individual responsible for the error
b. Immediately implementing new policies to prevent future errors
c. Analyzing the root cause of the error
d. Reporting the individual to the state board of pharmacy

Answer: c. Analyzing the root cause of the error. Explanation: A fundamental principle of CQI is understanding the underlying reasons for errors to prevent future occurrences. Root cause analysis focuses on systems and processes, not individual fault, to identify where changes can be made to improve quality and safety.

138. When a pharmacy technician discovers a discrepancy during inventory management, what is the first step they should take according to quality assurance protocols?
a. Adjust the inventory records to match the physical count
b. Investigate the discrepancy to determine its cause
c. Report the discrepancy to the pharmacy manager
d. Write off the discrepancy as shrinkage without further investigation

Answer: b. Investigate the discrepancy to determine its cause. Explanation: Quality assurance emphasizes accurate and reliable inventory management. Investigating discrepancies helps in identifying potential errors or issues in the inventory process, leading to corrective actions that ensure accuracy and accountability.

139. A patient returns a medication due to a perceived adverse reaction. What action aligns with best practices in pharmacy quality assurance?
a. Reselling the returned medication to avoid financial loss
b. Documenting the incident and reporting it to the medication safety committee
c. Advising the patient to discuss the reaction with their insurance company
d. Ignoring the incident as adverse reactions are the responsibility of the prescriber

Answer: b. Documenting the incident and reporting it to the medication safety committee. Explanation: Documenting and reviewing adverse reactions are integral to quality assurance. This process helps in identifying potential medication-related issues, enhancing patient safety, and improving pharmacy practices through systemic review and action.

140. In the context of USP <797> standards, what is the primary focus for ensuring quality in the preparation of compounded sterile products (CSPs)?
a. Maximizing production speed to ensure efficiency
b. Ensuring CSPs are aesthetically pleasing to patients
c. Maintaining an aseptic environment to prevent microbial contamination
d. Using the least expensive compounding materials to reduce costs

Answer: c. Maintaining an aseptic environment to prevent microbial contamination. Explanation: USP <797> provides guidelines to ensure the sterility of CSPs, emphasizing the importance of an aseptic compounding environment to prevent contamination, which is critical for patient safety and the efficacy of the compounded medications.

141. During a quality assurance review, it's noted that a specific medication has a higher-than-normal dispensing error rate. What is an effective strategy to address this issue?
a. Increasing the workload of pharmacy staff to improve focus
b. Implementing additional training and education on the medication for staff
c. Discontinuing the sale of the medication to eliminate errors
d. Encouraging staff not to report errors to reduce documented error rates

Answer: b. Implementing additional training and education on the medication for staff. Explanation: Education and training are key components of quality assurance, addressing specific errors by increasing staff competence and awareness, thus reducing the likelihood of repeat errors and enhancing overall medication safety.

142. What role does the use of bar-code scanning technology play in a pharmacy's quality assurance program?
a. It eliminates the need for pharmacists to review prescriptions
b. It reduces the reliance on electronic health records for medication verification
c. It enhances the accuracy of medication dispensing and administration
d. It increases the speed of dispensing at the cost of accuracy

Answer: c. It enhances the accuracy of medication dispensing and administration. Explanation: Bar-code scanning is a tool that supports quality assurance by verifying that the correct medication is selected for dispensing, thereby reducing the risk of medication errors and improving patient safety.

143. When conducting a failure mode and effects analysis (FMEA) in a pharmacy, what is the primary objective?
a. To identify all employees who have made errors in the past year
b. To retrospectively analyze medication errors that have already occurred
c. To proactively assess processes for potential failures and their impact
d. To focus solely on financial losses associated with medication errors

Answer: c. To proactively assess processes for potential failures and their impact. Explanation: FMEA is a systematic, proactive method for evaluating a process to identify where and how it might fail and assessing the relative impact of different failures, with the goal of identifying the parts of the process that are most in need of change.

144. In handling a medication recall, what is the first action a pharmacy should take to ensure quality assurance?
a. Continuing to dispense the medication until stocks are depleted
b. Notifying all patients who have received the medication in the past year
c. Removing the recalled medication from inventory and segregating it
d. Waiting for instructions from the medication manufacturer before taking action

Answer: c. Removing the recalled medication from inventory and segregating it. Explanation: The initial step in managing a medication recall involves promptly removing the affected medication from the pharmacy inventory to prevent further dispensing, followed by segregation to ensure it is not inadvertently used or dispensed.

145. How does implementing a continuous medication monitoring system contribute to a pharmacy's quality assurance efforts?
a. By reducing the need for pharmacist intervention in medication therapy management
b. By providing real-time data on medication efficacy and safety for each patient
c. By automatically dispensing all medications, eliminating human error
d. By solely focusing on reducing the pharmacy's liability in medication errors

Answer: b. By providing real-time data on medication efficacy and safety for each patient. Explanation: Continuous medication monitoring systems enhance quality assurance by offering ongoing assessment of medication therapy's effectiveness and safety, allowing for timely interventions and adjustments to optimize patient outcomes.

146. In the development of a quality assurance program for a compounding pharmacy, what is a critical component to ensure the accuracy and safety of compounded medications?
a. Limiting compoundings to only the most experienced pharmacists
b. Basing all compoundings on historical formulas without customization
c. Regular testing of compounded preparations for potency and purity
d. Focusing primarily on the aesthetic appearance of the final compounded product

Answer: c. Regular testing of compounded preparations for potency and purity. Explanation: Regular testing of compounded medications for potency and purity is essential to ensure they meet the required standards for safety and efficacy, addressing the inherent risks associated with compounding and fulfilling the pharmacy's commitment to quality assurance.

147. The pharmacy receives a prescription for lamotrigine 100mg #60 with instructions "Take 1/2 tablet twice daily." Which of the following actions is most appropriate?
a. Dispense the medication as written.
b. Change the quantity to #30 to match the intended supply.
c. Contact the prescriber to clarify the dosing instructions.
d. Advise the patient to cut the tablets in half before each dose.

Answer: c. Contact the prescriber to clarify the dosing instructions. Explanation: The quantity and instructions create a discrepancy. The prescriber needs to confirm whether 60 tablets were intended as a two-month supply or there's an error in the dosing instructions.

148. A technician receives a verbal prescription over the phone for zolpidem. Which of the following pieces of information is NOT essential to document before processing the order?
a. Prescriber's DEA number
b. Patient's home address
c. Date the prescription was called in
d. Pharmacy technician's initials

Answer: b. Patient's home address. Explanation: While the address might be needed for delivery, it's not immediately required for processing the controlled substance prescription. The other options are mandatory for a valid verbal order.

149. A new patient presents with a prescription for levothyroxine 0.125 mg daily. The technician notices the patient's profile indicates they are 75 years old. What is the most appropriate next step?
a. Fill the prescription as written, as levothyroxine is usually well-tolerated.

b. Double-check the dose and contact the prescriber if it seems unusually high for an elderly patient.
c. Inform the patient that levothyroxine doses are usually in micrograms (mcg), not milligrams (mg).
d. Suggest the patient split the tablets to reduce the starting dose.

Answer: b. Double-check the dose and contact the prescriber if it seems unusually high for an elderly patient.
Explanation: Elderly patients often require lower starting doses of levothyroxine. While there might be a valid reason for the high dose, a safety-conscious technician would verify this with the prescriber.

150. A patient with a new insurance plan brings in a prescription, but the pharmacy's system doesn't recognize their insurance ID number. Which of the following is the best way to proceed?
a. Inform the patient the medication is not covered by their insurance.
b. Ask the patient to obtain a correct insurance card from their provider.
c. Submit a test claim electronically to verify coverage.
d. Call the patient's insurance company to verify eligibility and benefits.

Answer: d. Call the patient's insurance company to verify eligibility and benefits. Explanation: Insurance systems can sometimes lag behind. Contacting the insurer directly is the fastest way to confirm the patient's coverage and troubleshoot any ID number issues.

151. A hard-copy prescription for insulin glargine pens has no refills indicated. The patient requests a 90-day supply. What is the most appropriate course of action?
a. Dispense the 90-day supply as maintenance medications can often be refilled.
b. Provide a one-time emergency supply and advise the patient to obtain a new prescription.
c. Contact the prescriber to request authorization for refills.
d. Refuse to fill the prescription due to the lack of refills.

Answer: c. Contact the prescriber to request authorization for refills. Explanation: Insulin prescriptions often require specific refill authorization due to safety and cost concerns. Collaborating with the prescriber is necessary to ensure the patient receives the needed medication.

152. A prescriber's office faxes a prescription with complex compounding instructions. The technician has difficulty deciphering the prescriber's handwriting. Which of the following is the safest course of action?
a. Attempt to interpret the instructions to the best of your ability.
b. Ask a more experienced technician to try to decipher the prescription.
c. Contact the prescriber's office for verbal clarification of the instructions.
d. Inform the patient that the prescription cannot be filled as written.

Answer: c. Contact the prescriber's office for verbal clarification of the instructions. Explanation: Patient safety is paramount. Any ambiguity in compounding instructions, especially for complex preparations, necessitates direct communication with the prescriber to ensure accuracy.

153. A patient requests a refill of their losartan prescription. Their last refill was one week ago. Which of the following actions is most appropriate?
a. Override the refill-too-soon warning and dispense the medication.
b. Provide the refill and offer counseling on the importance of medication adherence.
c. Investigate the early refill request and contact the prescriber if necessary.
d. Advise the patient about the pharmacy's policy on early refills.

Answer: c. Investigate the early refill request and contact the prescriber if necessary. Explanation: Early refills can signal medication misuse, a lost prescription, or a change in therapy. Investigation is warranted for patient safety, potentially involving collaboration with the prescriber.

154. A patient on warfarin reports they will be traveling internationally for an extended period. Which of the following is an important consideration for the pharmacy technician?
a. Adjust the warfarin dose in anticipation of dietary changes while traveling.
b. Provide the patient with a sufficient supply of medication for their trip.
c. Counsel the patient on the importance of consistent INR monitoring while abroad.
d. Instruct the patient to avoid foods high in vitamin K while traveling.

Answer: c. Counsel the patient on the importance of consistent INR monitoring while abroad. Explanation: Travel can disrupt warfarin therapy due to time zone changes, dietary variations, and access to INR monitoring. Emphasizing the need for continued monitoring is crucial for the patient's safety.

155. In processing a prescription for a pediatric patient, the pharmacy technician notices that the prescribed dosage of amoxicillin exceeds typical pediatric dosing guidelines. What is the most appropriate action for the technician to take?
a. Adjust the dosage to fit within the standard pediatric guidelines.
b. Contact the prescriber to verify the intended dosage.
c. Dispense the medication as prescribed without consultation.
d. Advise the parent to adjust the dose at home.

Answer: b. Contact the prescriber to verify the intended dosage. Explanation: Contacting the prescriber to verify the dosage is crucial when discrepancies or potential errors are identified, especially in pediatric patients, to ensure safety and efficacy, aligning with the principle of verification in order entry and processing.

156. A prescription for a controlled substance is presented with no DEA number on the prescription. What should the pharmacy technician do next?
a. Dispense the medication and document the omission.
b. Refuse to fill the prescription until a DEA number is provided.
c. Call the prescriber to obtain the DEA number.
d. Fill the prescription and obtain the DEA number at the next refill.

Answer: c. Call the prescriber to obtain the DEA number. Explanation: Obtaining the prescriber's DEA number is necessary for controlled substance prescriptions to ensure compliance with legal requirements, highlighting the importance of complete and accurate prescription information in order entry.

157. When entering a new prescription into the pharmacy management system, what information is essential to ensure accurate processing?
a. The prescriber's favorite color
b. The patient's insurance member ID
c. The pharmacy's stock levels
d. The technician's initials

Answer: b. The patient's insurance member ID. Explanation: The patient's insurance member ID is crucial for billing and ensuring coverage of the prescribed medication, reflecting the importance of accurate patient and insurance information in prescription processing.

158. A patient presents a prescription for a high-risk medication that requires enrollment in a Risk Evaluation and Mitigation Strategy (REMS) program. What is the technician's responsibility in this scenario?
a. Enroll the patient in the REMS program themselves.
b. Verify that the prescriber and patient are enrolled in the REMS program.
c. Ignore the REMS requirement as it is the prescriber's responsibility.
d. Advise the patient to discuss the REMS program with their doctor.

Answer: b. Verify that the prescriber and patient are enrolled in the REMS program. Explanation: Verifying enrollment in REMS for both prescriber and patient is essential for dispensing high-risk medications, ensuring patient safety and compliance with regulatory requirements.

159. A prescription is received for a medication with a known significant drug interaction with another medication the patient is currently taking. What should the pharmacy technician do upon discovery of this interaction?
a. Proceed with dispensing both medications without intervention.
b. Remove the conflicting medication from the patient's profile.
c. Alert the pharmacist to the potential drug interaction for further review.
d. Contact the prescriber to change the medication without consulting the pharmacist.

Answer: c. Alert the pharmacist to the potential drug interaction for further review. Explanation: Alerting the pharmacist allows for professional assessment and appropriate intervention, such as consulting the prescriber or counseling the patient, emphasizing the role of the pharmacy team in managing drug interactions.

160. In processing a prescription, the pharmacy technician notices that the prescribed drug is not covered by the patient's insurance but a therapeutically equivalent alternative is. What is the next step?
a. Dispense the original medication and inform the patient of the higher cost.
b. Substitute the medication with the covered alternative without notifying the prescriber.

c. Contact the prescriber to discuss the insurance-preferred alternative.
d. Advise the patient to pay out-of-pocket for the prescribed medication.

Answer: c. Contact the prescriber to discuss the insurance-preferred alternative. Explanation: Consulting with the prescriber about covered alternatives ensures that the patient receives an effective treatment that is also covered by their insurance, maintaining the balance between clinical efficacy and cost-effectiveness.

161. When receiving a medication order for a patient with a known allergy to penicillin, the prescribed medication is a cephalosporin. What action should the pharmacy technician take?
a. Dispense the medication as cephalosporins are not related to penicillin.
b. Substitute the cephalosporin with another antibiotic class without consultation.
c. Note the allergy but proceed with dispensing as the risk is minimal.
d. Notify the pharmacist for a clinical review of the potential cross-reactivity.

Answer: d. Notify the pharmacist for a clinical review of the potential cross-reactivity. Explanation: Notifying the pharmacist allows for a clinical assessment of the potential cross-reactivity risk between penicillins and cephalosporins, ensuring patient safety given the potential for allergic reactions.

162. A patient's electronic health record indicates that they are lactose intolerant. A new prescription entered contains lactose as an inactive ingredient. What should be the technician's course of action?
a. Ignore the intolerance as it pertains to inactive ingredients.
b. Advise the patient to take the medication with food to reduce intolerance effects.
c. Notify the pharmacist to assess the relevance of the lactose content in the medication.
d. Automatically substitute with a lactose-free alternative.

Answer: c. Notify the pharmacist to assess the relevance of the lactose content in the medication. Explanation: Notifying the pharmacist allows for a professional determination of whether the lactose content poses a risk to the patient and if an alternative formulation or medication is necessary.

163. In processing orders for a patient admitted to the hospital, the pharmacy technician notices two orders for blood pressure medications that belong to the same drug class. What is the most appropriate action?
a. Fill both orders as physicians often prescribe multiple medications for better control.
b. Contact the nursing staff to clarify the orders before proceeding.
c. Alert the pharmacist to the potential for therapeutic duplication.
d. Cancel the first medication order in favor of the more recent one.

Answer: c. Alert the pharmacist to the potential for therapeutic duplication. Explanation: Alerting the pharmacist to potential therapeutic duplication allows for appropriate intervention, such as clarifying with the prescriber, to ensure optimal and safe patient care.

164. A pharmacy technician is entering a new prescription and notices that the patient's profile lists an expired medication allergy. What should the technician do?
a. Remove the allergy from the profile as it is no longer valid.
b. Update the allergy status without consulting the patient.
c. Confirm with the patient or their representative if the allergy is still relevant.
d. Ignore the allergy for the purpose of the new prescription.

Answer: c. Confirm with the patient or their representative if the allergy is still relevant. Explanation: Confirming the current relevance of a listed allergy with the patient ensures the accuracy of patient records and prevents potential adverse reactions, highlighting the importance of up-to-date and accurate patient information in order entry and processing.

165. A prescription for amoxicillin suspension is received with the instruction "5 mL PO bid x 10 days." The available stock solution is 250 mg/5 mL. How many milliliters should be dispensed to fulfill the prescription?
a. 50 mL
b. 100 mL
c. 150 mL
d. 200 mL

Answer: b. 100 mL. Explanation: The prescription requires 5 mL twice daily for 10 days. Calculating the total volume for 10 days: 5 mL/dose × 2 doses/day × 10 days = 100 mL. Therefore, 100 mL of the amoxicillin suspension should be dispensed to fulfill the 10-day course.

166. When processing an electronic prescription for a controlled substance, what is an essential verification step to ensure its validity?
a. Confirming the medication is covered by the patient's insurance
b. Verifying the prescriber's DEA registration and digital certificate
c. Checking the patient's medication history for allergies
d. Ensuring the prescription includes a patient's email address

Answer: b. Verifying the prescriber's DEA registration and digital certificate. Explanation: For electronic prescriptions of controlled substances, it's crucial to verify the prescriber's DEA registration to ensure they are authorized to prescribe controlled substances, and the digital certificate confirms the prescription's integrity and security.

167. A patient presents a prescription that reads "ibuprofen 400 mg, take 1 tablet by mouth three times a day as needed for pain." Which auxiliary label should be affixed to the medication container?
a. "Take with food or milk"
b. "Shake well before use"
c. "Refrigerate after opening"
d. "For external use only"

Answer: a. "Take with food or milk." Explanation: Ibuprofen can cause gastrointestinal irritation. Advising the patient to take the medication with food or milk can help minimize this risk, making it a crucial counseling point and auxiliary label recommendation.

168. During the order entry process, a technician notices that a patient is prescribed warfarin and is also buying over-the-counter (OTC) aspirin. What is the most appropriate action?
a. Proceed with the order without any intervention
b. Recommend a different OTC pain reliever that does not interact with warfarin
c. Inform the pharmacist for a potential drug-drug interaction review
d. Advise the patient to stop taking warfarin while taking OTC aspirin

Answer: c. Inform the pharmacist for a potential drug-drug interaction review. Explanation: Warfarin and aspirin both have anticoagulant effects, and their concomitant use can significantly increase the risk of bleeding. The pharmacist should review this potential interaction and provide appropriate counseling or contact the prescriber if necessary.

169. A pharmacy technician is entering a new prescription for a liquid medication. The sig reads "15 mL PO q4h prn for cough." How should this instruction be translated for the patient label?
a. "Take 15 mL by mouth every 4 hours as needed for cough"
b. "Inject 15 mL into the muscle every 4 hours for cough relief"
c. "Apply 15 mL topically every 4 hours as needed for pain"
d. "Dissolve 15 mL in water and drink every 4 hours for fever"

Answer: a. "Take 15 mL by mouth every 4 hours as needed for cough." Explanation: The sig translation maintains the original prescription's intent, providing clear patient instructions. PO indicates oral administration, q4h signifies every 4 hours, and prn indicates as needed, specifically for cough in this case.

170. A prescription is received for a topical cream with the sig: "Apply to the affected area bid." The patient expresses uncertainty about what "bid" means. How should the pharmacy technician clarify this instruction?
a. "Bid means twice a day, so apply the cream once in the morning and once at night."
b. "Bid means before meals, so apply the cream before breakfast and dinner."
c. "Bid stands for 'as needed,' so use the cream whenever you feel discomfort."
d. "Bid means every other day, so apply the cream every two days."

Answer: a. "Bid means twice a day, so apply the cream once in the morning and once at night." Explanation: "Bid" is an abbreviation for "bis in die," which is Latin for "twice a day." The clarification provides the patient with a clear understanding of how frequently to apply the medication.

171. A prescription reads: "Prednisone 10 mg, take 2 tablets daily for 5 days, then 1 tablet daily for 5 days." How many tablets should be dispensed in total?
a. 10 tablets
b. 15 tablets

c. 20 tablets
d. 25 tablets

Answer: b. 15 tablets. Explanation: The prescription requires 2 tablets daily for the first 5 days (2 tablets/day × 5 days = 10 tablets) and then 1 tablet daily for the next 5 days (1 tablet/day × 5 days = 5 tablets), totaling 15 tablets.

172. When inputting a prescription for insulin into the pharmacy management system, what is an important detail to ensure accurate dispensing?
a. The patient's shoe size
b. The insulin concentration (units/mL)
c. The color of the insulin vial
d. The prescriber's office hours

Answer: b. The insulin concentration (units/mL). Explanation: Insulin concentration is critical for ensuring the patient receives the correct dosage. Insulin is available in various concentrations, and inputting this detail accurately helps prevent dosing errors, which can have serious consequences.

173. A prescription is received for a compound that requires mixing two solutions in a specific ratio. The sig says "Mix 1 part Solution A with 3 parts Solution B." If the final volume needed is 120 mL, how much of Solution A is required?
a. 30 mL
b. 40 mL
c. 90 mL
d. 60 mL

Answer: a. 30 mL. Explanation: The final mixture consists of 4 parts in total (1 part Solution A + 3 parts Solution B = 4 parts). For a final volume of 120 mL, each part is 120 mL ÷ 4 = 30 mL. Therefore, 30 mL of Solution A is required.

174. A technician receives a prescription for "Zolpidem 10 mg at hs." The patient asks for clarification on when to take the medication. What should the technician say?
a. "Take 10 mg of Zolpidem with food."
b. "Take 10 mg of Zolpidem in the morning."
c. "Take 10 mg of Zolpidem at bedtime."
d. "Take 10 mg of Zolpidem every hour as needed."

Answer: c. "Take 10 mg of Zolpidem at bedtime." Explanation: "Hs" is an abbreviation for "hora somni," which means "at bedtime" in Latin. The instruction is advising the patient to take the medication at bedtime, which is typical for Zolpidem, a medication used to treat insomnia.

175. A physician prescribes 0.25 g of a medication. The available tablets are 125 mg each. How many tablets should be administered?

a. 1 tablet
b. 2 tablets
c. 3 tablets
d. 4 tablets

Answer: b. 2 tablets. Explanation: 0.25 g equals 250 mg (since 1 g = 1000 mg). Each tablet is 125 mg, so 250 mg / 125 mg per tablet = 2 tablets. The patient should be administered 2 tablets to meet the prescribed dose.

176. A prescription calls for a 2% w/v solution of medication to be prepared. How many grams of medication are needed to prepare 500 mL of this solution?
a. 5 grams
b. 10 grams
c. 15 grams
d. 20 grams

Answer: b. 10 grams. Explanation: A 2% w/v solution means 2 grams of medication per 100 mL of solution. To prepare 500 mL, the calculation is (2 g/100 mL) × 500 mL = 10 grams. Therefore, 10 grams of medication are needed.

177. A patient is prescribed 75 mcg of levothyroxine daily. The pharmacy has 25 mcg tablets in stock. How many tablets should be given to the patient each day?
a. 1 tablet
b. 2 tablets
c. 3 tablets
d. 4 tablets

Answer: c. 3 tablets. Explanation: The patient needs 75 mcg of the medication daily, and each tablet contains 25 mcg. Therefore, 75 mcg / 25 mcg per tablet = 3 tablets. The patient should take 3 tablets daily to meet the prescribed dose.

178. If a patient requires 0.5 L of saline solution and the pharmacy stocks saline in 250 mL bottles, how many bottles are needed to fulfill the prescription?
a. 1 bottle
b. 2 bottles
c. 3 bottles
d. 4 bottles

Answer: b. 2 bottles. Explanation: 0.5 L is equivalent to 500 mL (since 1 L = 1000 mL). Each bottle contains 250 mL, so 500 mL / 250 mL per bottle = 2 bottles. The patient needs 2 bottles of saline solution.

179. A medication is prescribed at a dose of 1.2 g. The medication is available in 400 mg capsules. How many capsules are required for each dose?

a. 2 capsules
b. 3 capsules
c. 4 capsules
d. 5 capsules

Answer: b. 3 capsules. Explanation: 1.2 g equals 1200 mg (since 1 g = 1000 mg). Each capsule is 400 mg, so 1200 mg / 400 mg per capsule = 3 capsules. The patient should take 3 capsules to achieve the prescribed dose.

180. A compounding recipe requires 15% of the active ingredient in a 200 g ointment. How many grams of the active ingredient are needed?
a. 15 grams
b. 20 grams
c. 30 grams
d. 40 grams

Answer: c. 30 grams. Explanation: 15% of 200 g is calculated as (15/100) × 200 g = 30 grams. Therefore, 30 grams of the active ingredient are needed to compound the ointment.

181. A syrup contains 120 mg of medication per 5 mL. How many mg of medication are in 30 mL of this syrup?
a. 240 mg
b. 480 mg
c. 720 mg
d. 960 mg

Answer: c. 720 mg. Explanation: If 5 mL contains 120 mg, then 30 mL (which is 6 times 5 mL) will contain 6 × 120 mg = 720 mg of the medication.

182. To prepare a 250 mL solution with a concentration of 40 mg/mL, how much total medication is required?
a. 5,000 mg
b. 6,000 mg
c. 10,000 mg
d. 12,000 mg

Answer: c. 10,000 mg. Explanation: The total amount of medication needed is the volume of the solution multiplied by the desired concentration: 250 mL × 40 mg/mL = 10,000 mg.

183. A patient needs an IV infusion of 0.9% NaCl at a rate of 50 mL/hour. If the infusion bag contains 1 L of the solution, how many hours will the bag last?
a. 10 hours
b. 20 hours

c. 30 hours

d. 40 hours

Answer: b. 20 hours. Explanation: 1 L is equivalent to 1000 mL. If the infusion rate is 50 mL/hour, the bag will last for 1000 mL / 50 mL/hour = 20 hours.

184. A prescription reads "Administer 0.8 g of medication stat." The stock solution is 400 mg/2 mL. How many mL of this solution are required to administer the prescribed dose?

a. 2 mL

b. 4 mL

c. 6 mL

d. 8 mL

Answer: b. 4 mL. Explanation: 0.8 g is equivalent to 800 mg. The stock solution provides 400 mg per 2 mL, so for 800 mg, the volume needed is (800 mg / 400 mg) × 2 mL = 4 mL.

185. A child weighing 22 lb is prescribed a drug at a dose of 15 mg/kg/day in divided doses every 8 hours. What will be the dose in mg for each administration?

a. 45 mg

b. 55 mg

c. 65 mg

d. 75 mg

Answer: d. 75 mg. Explanation: First, convert the child's weight to kg by dividing by 2.2 (22 lb / 2.2 = 10 kg). The total daily dose is 15 mg/kg/day × 10 kg = 150 mg/day. Since the dose is divided every 8 hours, each dose will be 150 mg/day ÷ 3 = 50 mg. This question tests the application of pediatric dosing principles, which are critical for safe and effective medication administration in children.

186. If a medication's half-life is 8 hours, how much of a 160 mg dose remains in the body after 24 hours?

a. 20 mg

b. 40 mg

c. 60 mg

d. 80 mg

Answer: a. 20 mg. Explanation: After one half-life (8 hours), 80 mg would remain (half of 160 mg). After a second half-life (16 hours total), 40 mg would remain. After a third half-life (24 hours total), 20 mg would remain. Understanding half-life is crucial for calculating drug levels and ensuring therapeutic effectiveness.

187. A topical cream is prescribed at 0.05% strength, but only a 0.1% cream is available. How many grams of the 0.1% cream should be mixed with how many grams of a cream base to prepare 30 g of the 0.05% cream?
a. 15 g of 0.1% cream and 15 g of base
b. 20 g of 0.1% cream and 10 g of base
c. 25 g of 0.1% cream and 5 g of base
d. 30 g of 0.1% cream and 0 g of base

Answer: a. 15 g of 0.1% cream and 15 g of base. Explanation: To achieve a 0.05% strength from a 0.1% cream, you need an equal dilution with the base. Mixing 15 g of 0.1% cream with 15 g of base yields 30 g of a 0.05% cream, applying the principle of dilution in compounding.

188. A medication is ordered to infuse at 50 mg/hr using an IV solution containing 800 mg of medication in 500 mL of fluid. At what rate in mL/hr should the IV pump be set?
a. 15 mL/hr
b. 20 mL/hr
c. 25 mL/hr
d. 31.25 mL/hr

Answer: d. 31.25 mL/hr. Explanation: To find the infusion rate, calculate the concentration of the solution (800 mg in 500 mL = 1.6 mg/mL) and then divide the ordered dose rate by the concentration (50 mg/hr ÷ 1.6 mg/mL = 31.25 mL/hr). This calculation is vital for ensuring accurate IV medication administration.

189. A prescription calls for erythromycin 400 mg/5 mL, and the patient needs to take 800 mg every 8 hours for 10 days. How many mL of erythromycin should be dispensed to fulfill this prescription?
a. 150 mL
b. 300 mL
c. 450 mL
d. 600 mL

Answer: b. 300 mL. Explanation: The patient requires 800 mg per dose, which corresponds to 10 mL per dose (800 mg × 5 mL/400 mg). Over 10 days at 3 doses per day, the total volume required is 10 mL/dose × 3 doses/day × 10 days = 300 mL. This question assesses the ability to calculate total medication volume needed over a specified treatment duration.

190. For an IV bolus, a drug is prescribed at 2 mg/kg for a patient weighing 70 kg. The drug is supplied in vials of 10 mg/mL. How many mL should be administered?
a. 7 mL
b. 14 mL
c. 21 mL
d. 28 mL

Answer: b. 14 mL. Explanation: The patient's total dose is 2 mg/kg × 70 kg = 140 mg. At a concentration of 10 mg/mL, 140 mg ÷ 10 mg/mL = 14 mL. This calculation is fundamental in ensuring accurate dosing for IV medications.

191. A 2% w/v solution is ordered to be diluted to a 0.5% w/v solution. If you start with 100 mL of the 2% solution, how much diluent must be added?
a. 100 mL
b. 200 mL
c. 300 mL
d. 400 mL

Answer: c. 300 mL. Explanation: To dilute a 2% solution to 0.5%, you need a 1:3 dilution (2% ÷ 0.5% = 4, and 1 part solution to 3 parts diluent makes 4 parts total). For 100 mL of the original solution, 300 mL of diluent is needed to achieve the desired concentration, illustrating the principle of dilution factor in compounding.

192. An order for an infusion requires a final concentration of 0.9 mg/mL in a total volume of 250 mL. The medication comes in a concentration of 1.8 mg/mL. How many mL of the original medication and diluent are needed?
a. 125 mL of medication and 125 mL of diluent
b. 100 mL of medication and 150 mL of diluent
c. 150 mL of medication and 100 mL of diluent
d. 112.5 mL of medication and 137.5 mL of diluent

Answer: a. 125 mL of medication and 125 mL of diluent. Explanation: To achieve a final concentration of 0.9 mg/mL from a 1.8 mg/mL solution, a 1:1 dilution is needed (1.8 mg/mL ÷ 0.9 mg/mL = 2, and 1 part medication to 1 part diluent makes 2 parts total). Therefore, 125 mL of medication is mixed with 125 mL of diluent to maintain the desired concentration in a 250 mL total volume, applying the concept of dilution in IV compounding.

193. When calculating the BSA for a chemotherapeutic regimen using the Boyd formula, which factor is unique to this method compared to Mosteller or DuBois formulas?
a. Inclusion of the patient's age
b. Use of body weight only
c. Incorporation of body weight and height
d. Adjustment for body mass index (BMI)

Answer: a. Inclusion of the patient's age. Explanation: The Boyd formula is unique in that it can include age as a factor in some variations, unlike the Mosteller or DuBois formulas, which rely solely on height and weight. This can be particularly relevant for pediatric oncology.

194. Using the Fujimoto formula for BSA calculation, how does the inclusion of body weight and height compare to the Mosteller formula in terms of complexity and accuracy for chemotherapy dosing?
a. More complex and less accurate
b. More complex and more accurate
c. Less complex and less accurate

d. Less complex and more accurate

Answer: b. More complex and more accurate. Explanation: The Fujimoto formula is considered more complex because it involves more detailed calculations, including constants and exponents, but it is believed to provide more accurate BSA estimations, which is crucial for precise chemotherapy dosing.

195. Which class of medications is primarily used to prevent blood clots by inhibiting platelet aggregation?
a. Beta-blockers
b. Anticoagulants
c. Antiplatelet agents
d. ACE inhibitors

Answer: c. Antiplatelet agents. Explanation: Antiplatelet agents, such as aspirin and clopidogrel, work by preventing platelets from clumping together, which is a crucial step in the formation of blood clots. This mechanism is distinct from anticoagulants, which act on the clotting cascade.

196. What is the mechanism of action of HMG-CoA reductase inhibitors, commonly known as statins, in reducing cholesterol levels?
a. Increasing the excretion of bile acids
b. Inhibiting the synthesis of cholesterol in the liver
c. Blocking the absorption of cholesterol in the intestine
d. Activating lipoprotein lipase in adipose tissue

Answer: b. Inhibiting the synthesis of cholesterol in the liver. Explanation: Statins inhibit the enzyme HMG-CoA reductase, which is a key enzyme in the hepatic synthesis of cholesterol. This results in reduced cholesterol levels in the liver, prompting an increase in the uptake of LDL from the blood, thereby lowering blood cholesterol levels.

197. Which drug class is primarily used in the treatment of Parkinson's disease by mimicking the action of dopamine in the brain?
a. Monoamine oxidase inhibitors (MAOIs)
b. Dopamine agonists
c. Cholinesterase inhibitors
d. NMDA receptor antagonists

Answer: b. Dopamine agonists. Explanation: Dopamine agonists act by directly stimulating dopamine receptors in the brain, compensating for the decreased production of dopamine in patients with Parkinson's disease, which is crucial for controlling movement and coordination.

198. In the management of asthma, which class of drugs works by relaxing bronchial smooth muscle to open airways?
a. Corticosteroids

b. Leukotriene modifiers
c. Beta-agonists
d. Anticholinergics

Answer: c. Beta-agonists. Explanation: Beta-agonists, such as albuterol, work by stimulating beta-2 adrenergic receptors on bronchial smooth muscle, leading to muscle relaxation and bronchodilation, which helps to relieve asthma symptoms like wheezing and shortness of breath.

199. What is the primary action of angiotensin-converting enzyme (ACE) inhibitors in the treatment of hypertension?
a. Dilating blood vessels by blocking calcium channels
b. Increasing the excretion of sodium and water by the kidneys
c. Reducing the conversion of angiotensin I to angiotensin II
d. Inhibiting the sympathetic nervous system

Answer: c. Reducing the conversion of angiotensin I to angiotensin II. Explanation: ACE inhibitors, such as lisinopril, work by inhibiting the enzyme responsible for converting angiotensin I to angiotensin II, a potent vasoconstrictor. This leads to vasodilation and a reduction in blood pressure.

200. Which class of antibiotics works by inhibiting bacterial protein synthesis by binding to the 30S ribosomal subunit?
a. Penicillins
b. Tetracyclines
c. Fluoroquinolones
d. Sulfonamides

Answer: b. Tetracyclines. Explanation: Tetracyclines, such as doxycycline, bind to the 30S ribosomal subunit of bacteria, preventing the attachment of tRNA to the ribosome and thereby inhibiting protein synthesis, which is essential for bacterial growth and replication.

201. For a patient with type 2 diabetes, which class of medications works by increasing insulin sensitivity in peripheral tissues?
a. Sulfonylureas
b. DPP-4 inhibitors
c. Thiazolidinediones
d. Meglitinides

Answer: c. Thiazolidinediones. Explanation: Thiazolidinediones, such as pioglitazone, enhance insulin sensitivity in adipose tissue, skeletal muscle, and the liver, improving glucose uptake and utilization, which is crucial in the management of type 2 diabetes.

202. In the treatment of major depressive disorder, which class of drugs increases the levels of serotonin and norepinephrine in the brain?
a. Selective serotonin reuptake inhibitors (SSRIs)
b. Serotonin-norepinephrine reuptake inhibitors (SNRIs)
c. Atypical antipsychotics
d. Tricyclic antidepressants (TCAs)

Answer: b. Serotonin-norepinephrine reuptake inhibitors (SNRIs). Explanation: SNRIs, such as venlafaxine, work by inhibiting the reuptake of both serotonin and norepinephrine in the brain, enhancing the neurotransmission of these mood-regulating chemicals.

203. What is the mechanism of action of proton pump inhibitors (PPIs) in the treatment of gastroesophageal reflux disease (GERD)?
a. Neutralizing stomach acid
b. Blocking histamine H2 receptors on parietal cells
c. Inhibiting the proton pump in gastric parietal cells
d. Coating the esophageal lining to protect against acid

Answer: c. Inhibiting the proton pump in gastric parietal cells. Explanation: PPIs, such as omeprazole, irreversibly inhibit the H+/K+ ATPase enzyme (proton pump) in stomach parietal cells, effectively reducing the production of gastric acid, which is a key factor in managing GERD symptoms.

204. Which class of antineoplastic agents works by cross-linking DNA, thereby inhibiting DNA replication and transcription in cancer cells?
a. Antimetabolites
b. Alkylating agents
c. Tyrosine kinase inhibitors
d. Topoisomerase inhibitors

Answer: b. Alkylating agents. Explanation: Alkylating agents, such as cyclophosphamide, introduce alkyl groups into DNA strands, leading to cross-linking and breaks in the DNA. This interferes with DNA replication and transcription, ultimately inhibiting cancer cell growth.

205. A patient is prescribed an IV infusion of 1,000 mL normal saline over 8 hours. What is the required flow rate in mL/hour?
a. 100 mL/hour
b. 125 mL/hour
c. 150 mL/hour
d. 200 mL/hour

Answer: b. 125 mL/hour. Explanation: To find the flow rate in mL/hour, divide the total volume of the IV fluid (1,000 mL) by the total infusion time (8 hours). 1,000 mL / 8 hours = 125 mL/hour. This flow rate ensures the prescribed volume is administered within the specified time frame.

206. An IV drip set with a drop factor of 15 gtt/mL is used for a 500 mL IV bag to be administered over 4 hours. What is the required flow rate in drops per minute (gtt/min)?
a. 15 gtt/min
b. 31.25 gtt/min
c. 62.5 gtt/min
d. 125 gtt/min

Answer: b. 31.25 gtt/min. Explanation: First, calculate the flow rate in mL/hour: 500 mL / 4 hours = 125 mL/hour. Then, convert mL/hour to gtt/min using the drop factor: (125 mL/hour × 15 gtt/mL) / 60 minutes/hour = 31.25 gtt/min. This ensures the IV is administered at the correct rate according to the drop factor.

207. A patient requires a medication infusion of 250 mL to be administered over 30 minutes. The IV tubing being used has a drop factor of 20 gtt/mL. What should the drip rate be set at in gtt/min?
a. 100 gtt/min
b. 167 gtt/min
c. 250 gtt/min
d. 500 gtt/min

Answer: b. 167 gtt/min. Explanation: Calculate the flow rate in mL/min first: 250 mL / 30 min = 8.33 mL/min. Then, use the drop factor to find gtt/min: 8.33 mL/min × 20 gtt/mL = 166.6, rounded to 167 gtt/min. This calculation ensures the medication is infused at the correct rate for the prescribed duration.

208. An IV antibiotic is to be given over 1.5 hours. The total volume of the IV fluid is 200 mL. What is the flow rate in mL/hour?
a. 100 mL/hour
b. 133.33 mL/hour
c. 150 mL/hour
d. 200 mL/hour

Answer: b. 133.33 mL/hour. Explanation: The flow rate is calculated by dividing the total volume by the total time in hours: 200 mL / 1.5 hours = 133.33 mL/hour. This flow rate ensures the entire volume of the antibiotic is administered within the prescribed time.

209. A chemotherapy drug is to be infused over 2 hours using an IV set with a drop factor of 10 gtt/mL. The total volume for infusion is 400 mL. What is the drip rate in gtt/min?
a. 20 gtt/min
b. 33.33 gtt/min
c. 40 gtt/min

d. 50 gtt/min

Answer: b. 33.33 gtt/min. Explanation: First, find the flow rate in mL/min: 400 mL / 120 min = 3.33 mL/min. Then, calculate the drip rate using the drop factor: 3.33 mL/min × 10 gtt/mL = 33.33 gtt/min. This sets the correct rate for the chemotherapy infusion.

210. For an IV infusion of 0.9% NaCl, 1,500 mL is to be administered over 12 hours. What is the infusion rate in mL/hour?
a. 100 mL/hour
b. 125 mL/hour
c. 150 mL/hour
d. 175 mL/hour

Answer: b. 125 mL/hour. Explanation: The infusion rate is calculated by dividing the total volume by the total infusion time: 1,500 mL / 12 hours = 125 mL/hour. This rate ensures the saline solution is administered over the intended duration.

211. An IV fluid order requires 850 mL of D5W to be infused over a 10-hour period. Using an IV administration set with a drop factor of 60 gtt/mL, what would be the appropriate flow rate in gtt/min?
a. 8.5 gtt/min
b. 42.5 gtt/min
c. 85 gtt/min
d. 170 gtt/min

Answer: a. 8.5 gtt/min. Explanation: First, determine the flow rate in mL/hour: 850 mL / 10 hours = 85 mL/hour. Then, convert this to gtt/min using the drop factor: (85 mL/hour × 60 gtt/mL) / 60 min/hour = 85 gtt/min. However, since the drop factor seems unusually high for standard IV sets, there might be a typo, and the drop factor could be more commonly 10 or 15 gtt/mL, which would significantly change the answer. Please verify the drop factor for accurate calculations.

212. A pediatric patient is ordered a continuous IV infusion at a rate of 25 mL/hour. If the drop factor of the available IV tubing is 20 gtt/mL, what will be the drip rate in gtt/min?
a. 8.33 gtt/min
b. 10 gtt/min
c. 12.5 gtt/min
d. 15 gtt/min

Answer: a. 8.33 gtt/min. Explanation: To find the drip rate in gtt/min, use the formula: (mL/hour × drop factor) / 60. So, (25 mL/hour × 20 gtt/mL) / 60 min/hour = 8.33 gtt/min. This ensures the pediatric patient receives the IV infusion at the prescribed rate.

213. An emergency department orders an IV bolus of 100 mL to be given over 15 minutes. What is the required infusion rate in mL/hour?
a. 200 mL/hour
b. 300 mL/hour
c. 400 mL/hour
d. 600 mL/hour

Answer: c. 400 mL/hour. Explanation: Convert the infusion time to hours (15 minutes = 0.25 hours) and then calculate the rate: 100 mL / 0.25 hours = 400 mL/hour. This rate ensures the bolus is delivered over the intended short duration.

214. If a patient's IV order specifies an infusion of 750 mL to be completed over a 6-hour period and the IV tubing delivers 15 gtt/mL, what is the correct flow rate in gtt/min?
a. 15 gtt/min
b. 18.75 gtt/min
c. 31.25 gtt/min
d. 37.5 gtt/min

Answer: b. 18.75 gtt/min. Explanation: First, find the hourly rate: 750 mL / 6 hours = 125 mL/hour. Then, convert to gtt/min: (125 mL/hour × 15 gtt/mL) / 60 min/hour = 31.25 gtt/min. The correct flow rate to deliver the prescribed volume over 6 hours using the given IV tubing is 31.25 gtt/min.

215. What is the primary mechanism by which ACE inhibitors lower blood pressure?
a. They block the conversion of angiotensin I to angiotensin II, reducing vasoconstriction.
b. They block beta-adrenergic receptors, decreasing heart rate and cardiac output.
c. They inhibit calcium ions from entering cardiac and smooth muscle cells, causing vasodilation.
d. They promote sodium and water excretion, reducing plasma volume.

Answer: a. They block the conversion of angiotensin I to angiotensin II, reducing vasoconstriction. Explanation: ACE inhibitors impede the angiotensin-converting enzyme, crucial in the renin-angiotensin system, which converts angiotensin I to angiotensin II. Angiotensin II is a potent vasoconstrictor; thus, its inhibition leads to decreased blood pressure.

216. Angiotensin Receptor Blockers (ARBs) are preferred over ACE inhibitors in patients with which of the following conditions?
a. Diabetes mellitus
b. Chronic kidney disease
c. Cough induced by ACE inhibitors
d. High renin hypertension

Answer: c. Cough induced by ACE inhibitors. Explanation: ARBs are often chosen for patients who develop a persistent cough as a side effect of ACE inhibitors because they provide similar blood pressure-lowering effects without inhibiting the breakdown of bradykinin, which is thought to contribute to the cough associated with ACE inhibitors.

217. Which class of antihypertensive drugs is most associated with the side effect of ankle edema?
a. Beta-blockers
b. Calcium channel blockers
c. Diuretics
d. ARBs

Answer: b. Calcium channel blockers. Explanation: Calcium channel blockers, particularly the dihydropyridine class (e.g., amlodipine), can cause peripheral edema, including ankle edema, as a side effect due to their vasodilatory action on peripheral arterioles, leading to fluid accumulation in the extremities.

218. In treating hypertension, beta-blockers not only reduce heart rate but also:
a. Decrease renin secretion from the kidneys.
b. Increase the reabsorption of sodium in the kidneys.
c. Directly dilate peripheral arteries.
d. Block angiotensin II receptors in vascular smooth muscle.

Answer: a. Decrease renin secretion from the kidneys. Explanation: Beta-blockers diminish heart rate and myocardial contractility, leading to reduced cardiac output. Additionally, they inhibit renin release from the kidneys, a significant component of the renin-angiotensin-aldosterone system, thereby contributing to their antihypertensive effect.

219. For a patient with asthma and hypertension, which class of antihypertensive medication should generally be avoided?
a. ACE inhibitors
b. ARBs
c. Beta-blockers
d. Calcium channel blockers

Answer: c. Beta-blockers. Explanation: Beta-blockers can exacerbate asthma symptoms by causing bronchoconstriction due to blockade of beta-2 adrenergic receptors in the lungs. Therefore, they are generally not recommended for patients with reactive airway diseases like asthma.

220. Which type of diuretic is most effective for potent diuresis and is commonly used in conditions like pulmonary edema?
a. Thiazides
b. Loop diuretics
c. Potassium-sparing diuretics
d. Osmotic diuretics

Answer: b. Loop diuretics. Explanation: Loop diuretics, such as furosemide, are the most potent diuretics and are often used in acute settings such as pulmonary edema and heart failure to quickly reduce fluid overload by inhibiting sodium and chloride reabsorption in the loop of Henle.

221. A patient on antihypertensive therapy with a calcium channel blocker reports experiencing gingival hyperplasia. Which drug is most likely responsible for this side effect?
a. Amlodipine
b. Verapamil
c. Losartan
d. Metoprolol

Answer: b. Verapamil. Explanation: Gingival hyperplasia is a known side effect of some calcium channel blockers, with verapamil having a higher association with this condition. It involves overgrowth of gum tissue and can occur as a response to certain medications.

222. In the context of diuretic therapy for hypertension, what is a common electrolyte disturbance associated with thiazide diuretics?
a. Hyperkalemia
b. Hyponatremia
c. Hypercalcemia
d. Hypomagnesemia

Answer: b. Hyponatremia. Explanation: Thiazide diuretics can lead to hyponatremia, a condition characterized by low sodium levels in the blood. This occurs due to increased sodium excretion facilitated by thiazides, which can also lead to hypokalemia (low potassium levels).

223. When considering the use of ARBs in hypertensive patients, what is a key advantage they have over ACE inhibitors?
a. They are more effective in lowering blood pressure.
b. They do not cause hyperkalemia.
c. They do not lead to a dry cough as a side effect.
d. They improve insulin sensitivity.

Answer: c. They do not lead to a dry cough as a side effect. Explanation: ARBs do not inhibit the enzyme ACE and therefore do not increase bradykinin levels in the lungs, which is associated with the dry cough seen in patients taking ACE inhibitors. This makes ARBs a preferred choice for patients who develop a cough from ACE inhibitors.

224. Considering drug interactions, which antihypertensive class should be used cautiously with nonsteroidal anti-inflammatory drugs (NSAIDs) due to the risk of reduced antihypertensive effect?
a. Beta-blockers

b. Diuretics
c. Calcium channel blockers
d. ACE inhibitors

Answer: d. ACE inhibitors. Explanation: NSAIDs can reduce the antihypertensive effect of ACE inhibitors by inhibiting prostaglandin synthesis, which is involved in the vasodilatory action of ACE inhibitors. This interaction can potentially diminish the blood pressure-lowering effects of ACE inhibitors.

225. Which mechanism of action is primarily associated with penicillins?
a. Inhibition of DNA gyrase
b. Disruption of bacterial cell wall synthesis
c. Inhibition of protein synthesis at the 50S ribosomal subunit
d. Disruption of folate synthesis

Answer: b. Disruption of bacterial cell wall synthesis. Explanation: Penicillins exert their bactericidal effect by inhibiting the synthesis of peptidoglycan, a key component of the bacterial cell wall. This action weakens the cell wall, leading to osmotic instability and ultimately the lysis and death of the bacteria.

226. A patient allergic to penicillin is at increased risk of cross-reactivity with which class of antibiotics?
a. Macrolides
b. Aminoglycosides
c. Cephalosporins
d. Tetracyclines

Answer: c. Cephalosporins. Explanation: Patients with a penicillin allergy may have a cross-reactivity risk with cephalosporins due to structural similarities in the beta-lactam ring, although this risk is lower with later generations of cephalosporins.

227. Which antibiotic is known for its efficacy against atypical pathogens and is commonly used for community-acquired pneumonia?
a. Ciprofloxacin
b. Vancomycin
c. Azithromycin
d. Meropenem

Answer: c. Azithromycin. Explanation: Azithromycin, a macrolide antibiotic, is effective against a wide range of pathogens, including atypical bacteria such as Mycoplasma pneumoniae and Chlamydophila pneumoniae, making it a common choice for the treatment of community-acquired pneumonia.

228. Fluoroquinolones, such as ciprofloxacin, carry a boxed warning for the increased risk of:

a. Hepatotoxicity
b. Tendon rupture
c. Hemolytic anemia
d. Stevens-Johnson syndrome

Answer: b. Tendon rupture. Explanation: Fluoroquinolones carry a boxed warning from the FDA for an increased risk of tendonitis and tendon rupture, which can occur during or after treatment with these medications. This risk is particularly noted in older adults, patients with kidney, heart, or lung transplants, and those concomitantly using corticosteroids.

229. Which cephalosporin is commonly used for surgical prophylaxis due to its efficacy against skin flora?
a. Ceftriaxone
b. Cephalexin
c. Cefazolin
d. Ceftaroline

Answer: c. Cefazolin. Explanation: Cefazolin, a first-generation cephalosporin, is frequently used for surgical prophylaxis, especially in procedures involving incisions through the skin, due to its effective coverage against gram-positive cocci, including staphylococci and streptococci, which are part of the normal skin flora.

230. A patient diagnosed with acute otitis media should be cautious with which antibiotic due to its ototoxic potential?
a. Amoxicillin
b. Gentamicin
c. Levofloxacin
d. Clarithromycin

Answer: b. Gentamicin. Explanation: Gentamicin, an aminoglycoside antibiotic, carries a risk of ototoxicity, which can lead to hearing loss or balance issues. While not a first-line treatment for acute otitis media, its ototoxic potential warrants caution in scenarios where its use might be considered.

231. For a patient with a severe pseudomonal infection, which fluoroquinolone is preferred due to its enhanced activity against Pseudomonas aeruginosa?
a. Levofloxacin
b. Moxifloxacin
c. Norfloxacin
d. Ciprofloxacin

Answer: d. Ciprofloxacin. Explanation: Ciprofloxacin has significant activity against Pseudomonas aeruginosa, making it a preferred choice in treating severe infections caused by this pathogen, such as hospital-acquired pneumonia or complicated urinary tract infections.

232. In treating streptococcal pharyngitis, which antibiotic is considered a first-line therapy due to its narrow spectrum and efficacy?
a. Clindamycin
b. Erythromycin
c. Penicillin V
d. Doxycycline

Answer: c. Penicillin V. Explanation: Penicillin V is the first-line therapy for streptococcal pharyngitis due to its narrow spectrum, which minimizes disruption of normal flora, and its effectiveness against Streptococcus pyogenes, the bacterium responsible for the infection.

233. A healthcare provider should be cautious prescribing macrolides to patients with which condition due to potential cardiac side effects?
a. Diabetes mellitus
b. Glaucoma
c. Long QT syndrome
d. Hypothyroidism

Answer: c. Long QT syndrome. Explanation: Macrolides, such as erythromycin and azithromycin, can prolong the QT interval on an electrocardiogram, posing a risk of developing torsades de pointes, particularly in patients with a history of Long QT syndrome or other cardiac conditions predisposing them to arrhythmias.

234. For outpatient management of a mild non-purulent skin infection, which class of antibiotics is typically recommended?
a. Glycopeptides
b. Penicillins
c. Sulfonamides
d. Carbapenems

Answer: b. Penicillins. Explanation: Penicillins, such as dicloxacillin or amoxicillin/clavulanate, are often recommended for outpatient management of mild non-purulent skin infections like cellulitis, which are commonly caused by streptococci and are effectively treated with this class of antibiotics.

235. A patient on warfarin therapy is scheduled for surgery in two weeks. Which medication might be prescribed to reverse the effects of warfarin prior to surgery?
a. Protamine sulfate
b. Vitamin K
c. Idarucizumab
d. Andexanet alfa

Answer: b. Vitamin K. Explanation: Vitamin K is used to reverse the anticoagulant effects of warfarin, especially in preparation for surgery, to reduce the risk of bleeding. While protamine sulfate reverses heparin, idarucizumab is specific for dabigatran, and andexanet alfa is used for factor Xa inhibitors.

236. A patient presents with acute deep vein thrombosis (DVT). Which anticoagulant is most likely to be initiated for immediate anticoagulation?
a. Warfarin
b. Dabigatran
c. Heparin
d. Apixaban

Answer: c. Heparin. Explanation: Heparin is often used for immediate anticoagulation due to its rapid onset of action, making it ideal for acute conditions like DVT. Warfarin takes several days to reach therapeutic levels, while dabigatran and apixaban are direct oral anticoagulants (DOACs) with specific indications.

237. A patient on dabigatran requires urgent reversal due to a bleeding complication. Which agent is specifically indicated for this purpose?
a. Vitamin K
b. Protamine sulfate
c. Idarucizumab
d. Andexanet alfa

Answer: c. Idarucizumab. Explanation: Idarucizumab is a monoclonal antibody specifically designed to reverse the anticoagulant effects of dabigatran. Vitamin K is for warfarin, protamine sulfate for heparin, and andexanet alfa for factor Xa inhibitors, not dabigatran.

238. For a patient receiving enoxaparin who develops heparin-induced thrombocytopenia (HIT), what is the most appropriate next step in management?
a. Switch to unfractionated heparin.
b. Initiate treatment with warfarin.
c. Discontinue all heparin products and start a direct thrombin inhibitor.
d. Increase the dose of enoxaparin to overcome the resistance.

Answer: c. Discontinue all heparin products and start a direct thrombin inhibitor. Explanation: In cases of HIT, all forms of heparin must be discontinued to prevent further platelet activation, and an alternative anticoagulant such as a direct thrombin inhibitor (e.g., argatroban) should be initiated.

239. When transitioning a patient from IV heparin to oral warfarin therapy, what is a key consideration to ensure therapeutic anticoagulation?
a. Discontinue heparin as soon as the first warfarin dose is administered.
b. Overlap heparin and warfarin therapy until the INR is within the target range.

c. Start warfarin with a loading dose to rapidly achieve therapeutic levels.

d. Use protamine sulfate to bridge the transition between heparin and warfarin.

Answer: b. Overlap heparin and warfarin therapy until the INR is within the target range. Explanation: Overlapping heparin and warfarin therapy is necessary because warfarin requires several days to deplete existing clotting factors and achieve therapeutic anticoagulation, as indicated by an INR within the target range.

240. A patient on rivaroxaban experiences a major bleed. What is the most appropriate reversal agent to administer?

a. Vitamin K

b. Protamine sulfate

c. Idarucizumab

d. Andexanet alfa

Answer: d. Andexanet alfa. Explanation: Andexanet alfa is a reversal agent specifically designed to counteract the anticoagulant effects of factor Xa inhibitors like rivaroxaban in the event of a major bleed.

241. In managing a patient on long-term anticoagulation with warfarin, which dietary advice is most pertinent to ensure stable INR levels?

a. Increase intake of green leafy vegetables.

b. Maintain consistent vitamin K intake in the diet.

c. Avoid foods high in vitamin D.

d. Consume grapefruit juice daily to enhance warfarin's effect.

Answer: b. Maintain consistent vitamin K intake in the diet. Explanation: Vitamin K can antagonize the effect of warfarin, affecting INR levels. Patients are advised to maintain a consistent intake of vitamin K to avoid fluctuations in their INR.

242. For a patient requiring rapid reversal of unfractionated heparin in an emergency, which agent should be administered?

a. Vitamin K

b. Protamine sulfate

c. Idarucizumab

d. Andexanet alfa

Answer: b. Protamine sulfate. Explanation: Protamine sulfate is the reversal agent for heparin, effectively neutralizing its anticoagulant effects rapidly, which is crucial in emergency situations where reversal of heparin's effect is necessary.

243. A patient with a mechanical heart valve is on anticoagulation therapy. Which medication is most commonly prescribed for long-term management in this scenario?

a. Heparin
b. Enoxaparin
c. Warfarin
d. Rivaroxaban

Answer: c. Warfarin. Explanation: Warfarin is commonly used for long-term anticoagulation in patients with mechanical heart valves due to its proven efficacy in this population, while DOACs like rivaroxaban are generally not recommended for these patients.

244. In monitoring a patient on low molecular weight heparin (LMWH), such as enoxaparin, what laboratory test is routinely assessed?
a. Prothrombin time (PT)
b. Activated partial thromboplastin time (aPTT)
c. Anti-factor Xa levels
d. Complete blood count (CBC) only

Answer: c. Anti-factor Xa levels. Explanation: Anti-factor Xa levels are specifically used to monitor the anticoagulant effect of LMWHs like enoxaparin, providing a direct measure of the inhibition of factor Xa, which is central to their mechanism of action.

245. Which insulin type has the fastest onset of action and is often used at meal times to control postprandial blood glucose levels?
a. Rapid-acting insulin
b. Short-acting insulin
c. Intermediate-acting insulin
d. Long-acting insulin

Answer: a. Rapid-acting insulin. Explanation: Rapid-acting insulins, such as insulin lispro, aspart, and glulisine, have the fastest onset of action, typically within 15 minutes, making them ideal for controlling spikes in blood glucose levels immediately after meals.

246. A patient with type 2 diabetes is prescribed metformin. What is the primary mechanism of action of this medication?
a. Increases insulin secretion from the pancreas
b. Decreases hepatic glucose production
c. Delays intestinal absorption of glucose
d. Enhances sensitivity of peripheral tissues to insulin

Answer: b. Decreases hepatic glucose production. Explanation: Metformin primarily works by inhibiting gluconeogenesis in the liver, thereby reducing hepatic glucose production. It may also enhance insulin sensitivity in peripheral tissues, but its primary action is on the liver.

247. Which of the following insulin types is most likely to be administered once daily to maintain basal insulin levels?
a. Rapid-acting insulin
b. Short-acting insulin
c. Intermediate-acting insulin
d. Long-acting insulin

Answer: d. Long-acting insulin. Explanation: Long-acting insulins, such as insulin glargine and detemir, have a prolonged duration of action with no pronounced peak, making them suitable for maintaining basal insulin levels over 24 hours with once-daily dosing.

248. A patient on insulin therapy experiences hypoglycemia in the late afternoon. Their current regimen includes NPH insulin in the morning. What might be the cause of the hypoglycemia?
a. Rapid-acting insulin peaking
b. Short-acting insulin peaking
c. Intermediate-acting insulin peaking
d. Long-acting insulin peaking

Answer: c. Intermediate-acting insulin peaking. Explanation: NPH insulin, an intermediate-acting insulin, typically has a peak action 4 to 12 hours after administration. Morning dosing could lead to a peak and potential hypoglycemia in the late afternoon.

249. For a patient with type 2 diabetes, which oral antidiabetic agent acts by increasing insulin sensitivity in muscle and adipose tissue?
a. Sulfonylureas
b. Meglitinides
c. Thiazolidinediones
d. DPP-4 inhibitors

Answer: c. Thiazolidinediones. Explanation: Thiazolidinediones, such as pioglitazone and rosiglitazone, improve insulin sensitivity in peripheral tissues, particularly muscle and fat, making them effective in lowering blood glucose levels in type 2 diabetes.

250. What is the primary action of sulfonylureas in the treatment of type 2 diabetes?
a. Stimulate the pancreas to produce more insulin
b. Block the absorption of carbohydrates from the intestine
c. Increase the excretion of glucose in the urine
d. Inhibit the breakdown of incretins

Answer: a. Stimulate the pancreas to produce more insulin. Explanation: Sulfonylureas, such as glipizide and glyburide, work by stimulating beta cells in the pancreas to release more insulin, thereby lowering blood glucose levels.

251. A diabetes patient is prescribed a medication that mimics incretin hormones, enhancing glucose-dependent insulin secretion. Which class of medication does this describe?
a. GLP-1 receptor agonists
b. SGLT2 inhibitors
c. Alpha-glucosidase inhibitors
d. Amylin analogs

Answer: a. GLP-1 receptor agonists. Explanation: GLP-1 receptor agonists, such as exenatide and liraglutide, mimic the action of incretin hormones, which increase insulin secretion in a glucose-dependent manner, enhancing glycemic control without significantly increasing the risk of hypoglycemia.

252. Which class of oral antidiabetic drugs works by inhibiting the renal reabsorption of glucose, leading to increased glucose excretion in the urine?
a. Sulfonylureas
b. SGLT2 inhibitors
c. DPP-4 inhibitors
d. Thiazolidinediones

Answer: b. SGLT2 inhibitors. Explanation: SGLT2 inhibitors, such as canagliflozin and dapagliflozin, reduce blood glucose levels by blocking the reabsorption of glucose in the kidneys, resulting in increased excretion of glucose in the urine.

253. In the management of diabetes, which drug class slows the digestion and absorption of carbohydrates in the small intestine?
a. Alpha-glucosidase inhibitors
b. Bile acid sequestrants
c. Dopamine-2 agonists
d. Beta-blockers

Answer: a. Alpha-glucosidase inhibitors. Explanation: Alpha-glucosidase inhibitors, such as acarbose and miglitol, slow down the digestion and absorption of carbohydrates in the small intestine, leading to a reduction in postprandial blood glucose levels.

254. A patient with type 1 diabetes is adjusting their insulin regimen for exercise. Which insulin adjustment is most appropriate to prevent exercise-induced hypoglycemia?
a. Increase rapid-acting insulin before exercise
b. Decrease rapid-acting insulin before exercise
c. Increase long-acting insulin on exercise days

d. Decrease intermediate-acting insulin after exercise

Answer: b. Decrease rapid-acting insulin before exercise. Explanation: Decreasing rapid-acting insulin before exercise can help prevent hypoglycemia induced by increased glucose uptake by muscles during physical activity. Adjusting insulin doses for exercise is crucial in diabetes management to maintain glycemic control while avoiding hypoglycemia.

255. What is the primary action of short-acting beta-agonists (SABAs) in the treatment of asthma?
a. Reduce inflammation in the airways
b. Prevent the release of inflammatory mediators
c. Provide quick relief from bronchoconstriction
d. Repair damaged airway epithelium

Answer: c. Provide quick relief from bronchoconstriction. Explanation: SABAs, such as albuterol, act quickly to relax bronchial smooth muscle, providing rapid relief from symptoms of bronchoconstriction in asthma attacks. They are often referred to as "rescue" inhalers due to their fast-acting nature.

256. A patient is instructed to use a spacer with their metered-dose inhaler (MDI) to help manage their asthma. What is the primary benefit of using a spacer?
a. It increases the speed of medication delivery.
b. It decreases the need for hand-breath coordination.
c. It reduces the risk of oral thrush.
d. It enhances the absorption of medication in the lungs.

Answer: b. It decreases the need for hand-breath coordination. Explanation: A spacer attached to an MDI decreases the need for precise hand-breath coordination, allowing more medication to reach the lungs and less to deposit in the mouth and throat, which can also indirectly reduce the risk of oral thrush.

257. Inhaled corticosteroids are a cornerstone in the long-term management of asthma. What is their primary mechanism of action?
a. Immediate relaxation of bronchial smooth muscle
b. Long-term reduction of airway inflammation
c. Quick reversal of bronchospasm
d. Immediate increase in airway diameter

Answer: b. Long-term reduction of airway inflammation. Explanation: Inhaled corticosteroids work by reducing inflammation in the airways, decreasing the frequency and severity of asthma symptoms and exacerbations over time. They are considered controllers, not relievers.

258. What distinguishes long-acting beta-agonists (LABAs) from short-acting beta-agonists (SABAs) in asthma management?
a. LABAs provide immediate relief of asthma symptoms.
b. LABAs are used for quick relief during an asthma attack.
c. LABAs are used in combination with inhaled corticosteroids for long-term control.
d. SABAs are effective in controlling chronic inflammation.

Answer: c. LABAs are used in combination with inhaled corticosteroids for long-term control. Explanation: LABAs, such as salmeterol and formoterol, are used for long-term control of asthma in combination with inhaled corticosteroids. They are not intended for immediate relief of symptoms.

259. A patient using a dry powder inhaler (DPI) for asthma control should be instructed to:
a. Slowly inhale the medication over 5-10 seconds.
b. Use a spacer to ensure medication delivery.
c. Breathe in quickly and deeply to ensure the medication reaches the lungs.
d. Shake the inhaler vigorously before use.

Answer: c. Breathe in quickly and deeply to ensure the medication reaches the lungs. Explanation: DPIs require a quick and deep inhalation to deliver the powdered medication effectively to the lungs. Unlike MDIs, spacers are not used with DPIs, and shaking is not necessary.

260. Anticholinergics such as ipratropium are used in COPD management. What is their mechanism of action?
a. They stimulate the sympathetic nervous system to dilate the airways.
b. They inhibit the parasympathetic nervous system to relax airway smooth muscles.
c. They block the inflammatory response in the airways.
d. They increase the clearance of mucus in the airways.

Answer: b. They inhibit the parasympathetic nervous system to relax airway smooth muscles. Explanation: Anticholinergics work by blocking the action of the neurotransmitter acetylcholine in the parasympathetic nervous system, leading to relaxation of airway smooth muscles and dilation of the airways.

261. For a patient with both asthma and chronic obstructive pulmonary disease (COPD), why might a combination inhaler containing both a corticosteroid and a LABA be prescribed?
a. To provide immediate relief of bronchospasm
b. To reduce systemic steroid exposure
c. To address airway inflammation and improve airflow over time
d. To decrease the frequency of inhaler use

Answer: c. To address airway inflammation and improve airflow over time. Explanation: A combination inhaler with a corticosteroid and a LABA addresses the chronic inflammation associated with asthma and the need for long-term bronchodilation in COPD, improving symptom control and lung function over time.

262. A patient with persistent nocturnal asthma symptoms might benefit most from which type of medication adjustment?
a. Increasing the dose of their SABA inhaler at bedtime
b. Adding a long-acting muscarinic antagonist (LAMA) to their regimen
c. Using a long-acting beta-agonist (LABA) in combination with an inhaled corticosteroid
d. Switching from an inhaled corticosteroid to an oral corticosteroid

Answer: c. Using a long-acting beta-agonist (LABA) in combination with an inhaled corticosteroid. Explanation: Adding a LABA to an inhaled corticosteroid regimen can provide improved control of asthma symptoms, including nocturnal symptoms, by providing sustained bronchodilation and anti-inflammatory effects.

263. A patient on a LABA for COPD reports increased palpitations and nervousness. What is a possible explanation for these side effects?
a. LABAs can stimulate beta-2 adrenergic receptors, leading to cardiovascular effects.
b. Inhaled corticosteroids in combination products may cause systemic side effects.
c. Anticholinergic components may lead to sympathetic nervous system activation.
d. The patient may be incorrectly using their DPI, leading to excessive dosing.

Answer: a. LABAs can stimulate beta-2 adrenergic receptors, leading to cardiovascular effects. Explanation: While LABAs primarily act on the lungs, they can also stimulate beta-2 adrenergic receptors in the heart, potentially leading to side effects like palpitations and nervousness due to increased heart rate.

264. In instructing a patient on the use of a nebulizer for bronchodilator therapy, what key point should be emphasized to ensure effective treatment?
a. The medication must be inhaled rapidly to maximize effect.
b. A spacer should be used with the nebulizer for better drug delivery.
c. The patient should breathe normally and deeply through the mouthpiece or mask.
d. The nebulizer should be used only in emergency situations for immediate relief.

Answer: c. The patient should breathe normally and deeply through the mouthpiece or mask. Explanation: Effective nebulizer treatment requires the patient to breathe normally and deeply through the mouthpiece or mask to ensure the medication is adequately deposited in the lungs.

265. What is the primary mechanism of action of SSRIs in the treatment of depression?
a. Blockade of dopamine receptors
b. Inhibition of serotonin reuptake
c. Enhancement of GABA activity
d. Inhibition of norepinephrine reuptake

Answer: b. Inhibition of serotonin reuptake. Explanation: SSRIs (Selective Serotonin Reuptake Inhibitors) work by inhibiting the reuptake of serotonin in the brain, increasing the availability of serotonin in the synaptic cleft, and enhancing neurotransmission, which is thought to improve mood and reduce symptoms of depression.

266. Which of the following side effects is commonly associated with the use of atypical antipsychotics?
a. Urinary retention
b. Metabolic syndrome
c. Acute renal failure
d. Hypothyroidism

Answer: b. Metabolic syndrome. Explanation: Atypical antipsychotics are known to be associated with metabolic side effects, including weight gain, dyslipidemia, and increased risk of diabetes, collectively referred to as metabolic syndrome, which requires monitoring and management in patients undergoing treatment.

267. A patient on an SSRI reports experiencing sexual dysfunction. Which class of antidepressants is known to have a lower incidence of sexual side effects and might be considered as an alternative?
a. Tricyclic antidepressants (TCAs)
b. Monoamine oxidase inhibitors (MAOIs)
c. Serotonin-Norepinephrine Reuptake Inhibitors (SNRIs)
d. Norepinephrine-Dopamine Reuptake Inhibitors (NDRIs)

Answer: d. Norepinephrine-Dopamine Reuptake Inhibitors (NDRIs). Explanation: NDRIs, such as bupropion, are known to have a lower incidence of sexual side effects compared to SSRIs and might be considered as an alternative for patients experiencing this issue.

268. When switching a patient from a benzodiazepine to buspirone for the treatment of anxiety, what is an important consideration?
a. Buspirone requires several weeks to achieve its full effect.
b. Buspirone can be used as a prn (as needed) medication for acute anxiety.
c. Buspirone increases the risk of dependency compared to benzodiazepines.
d. Buspirone's efficacy is enhanced when taken with alcohol.

Answer: a. Buspirone requires several weeks to achieve its full effect. Explanation: Unlike benzodiazepines, which have an immediate effect, buspirone does not provide rapid relief of anxiety symptoms. It may take several weeks to achieve its full therapeutic effect, making it less suitable for prn use.

269. A patient with bipolar disorder is experiencing a manic episode. Which class of medication is typically used to stabilize mood in this condition?
a. SSRIs
b. Benzodiazepines
c. Antipsychotics
d. Stimulants

Answer: c. Antipsychotics. Explanation: Antipsychotics, particularly atypical antipsychotics, are commonly used to manage manic episodes in patients with bipolar disorder due to their ability to stabilize mood and reduce manic symptoms.

270. For a patient with generalized anxiety disorder (GAD) not responding well to SSRIs, which class of medication might be added as an adjunct treatment?
a. Beta-blockers
b. Anticholinergics
c. Corticosteroids
d. SNRIs

Answer: d. SNRIs. Explanation: SNRIs (Serotonin-Norepinephrine Reuptake Inhibitors) can be effective in treating GAD, particularly in patients who do not respond adequately to SSRIs. They work by increasing the levels of both serotonin and norepinephrine neurotransmitters in the brain.

271. What is a significant risk associated with the long-term use of benzodiazepines for anxiety?
a. Bradykinesia
b. Dependency and withdrawal symptoms
c. Neuroleptic malignant syndrome
d. Extrapyramidal symptoms

Answer: b. Dependency and withdrawal symptoms. Explanation: Long-term use of benzodiazepines can lead to physical dependency and the potential for withdrawal symptoms upon discontinuation, making it important to use these medications judiciously and consider tapering strategies when stopping treatment.

272. A patient with depression and chronic pain might benefit most from which class of antidepressants, given their dual efficacy?
a. SSRIs
b. SNRIs
c. TCAs
d. MAOIs

Answer: b. SNRIs. Explanation: SNRIs, such as duloxetine, have been shown to be effective in treating both depression and chronic pain conditions, such as neuropathic pain and fibromyalgia, making them a suitable option for patients with both conditions.

273. When initiating a patient on clozapine for treatment-resistant schizophrenia, what is a critical safety monitoring requirement?
a. Regular liver function tests

b. Weekly white blood cell counts
c. Monthly thyroid function tests
d. Biannual echocardiograms

Answer: b. Weekly white blood cell counts. Explanation: Clozapine can cause agranulocytosis, a potentially life-threatening decrease in white blood cells. Therefore, regular monitoring of white blood cell counts, especially during the first few months of treatment, is essential for early detection and management.

274. In the management of acute psychotic episodes in schizophrenia, which medication type is preferred for rapid symptom control?
a. Oral atypical antipsychotics
b. Injectable long-acting antipsychotics
c. Intramuscular (IM) fast-acting antipsychotics
d. Oral SSRIs

Answer: c. Intramuscular (IM) fast-acting antipsychotics. Explanation: IM fast-acting antipsychotics, such as haloperidol or olanzapine IM formulations, are often used for rapid control of acute psychotic symptoms due to their quick onset of action compared to oral formulations.

275. What pharmacokinetic parameter best describes the body's elimination of a drug via metabolism and excretion?
a. Absorption
b. Distribution
c. Clearance
d. Bioavailability

Answer: c. Clearance. Explanation: Clearance refers to the volume of plasma from which a substance is completely removed per unit time and is a key pharmacokinetic parameter that encompasses both metabolism and excretion processes in drug elimination.

276. Which pharmacodynamic principle explains the increased response to a drug until a certain point, beyond which no further increase in effect is achieved?
a. Potency
b. Efficacy
c. Ceiling effect
d. Therapeutic index

Answer: c. Ceiling effect. Explanation: The ceiling effect occurs when a drug reaches a point where increasing the dose does not increase the therapeutic response. This principle is important in understanding the maximal efficacy of a drug and avoiding unnecessary dose escalation.

277. In the context of drug distribution, what role does protein binding play?
a. It increases the rate of drug absorption.
b. It decreases the drug's half-life.
c. It determines the drug's volume of distribution.
d. It limits the amount of free drug available for activity.

Answer: d. It limits the amount of free drug available for activity. Explanation: Protein binding in the bloodstream restricts the amount of free (unbound) drug that is available to exert a pharmacological effect, as only the unbound fraction can diffuse across cell membranes and reach the site of action.

278. What is the significance of the first-pass effect in drug metabolism?
a. It refers to the rapid absorption of drugs administered intravenously.
b. It describes the initial concentration peak of a drug after oral administration.
c. It involves the reduction of drug concentration before it reaches systemic circulation.
d. It signifies the enhancement of drug effects by liver enzymes.

Answer: c. It involves the reduction of drug concentration before it reaches systemic circulation. Explanation: The first-pass effect occurs when an orally administered drug is metabolized at a significant rate by the liver before it reaches the systemic circulation, reducing the amount of active drug available and potentially necessitating higher oral doses.

279. How does a drug with a narrow therapeutic index impact clinical management?
a. It allows for a wide range of safe dosages.
b. It requires close monitoring of drug levels to avoid toxicity.
c. It is less likely to interact with other medications.
d. It ensures a rapid onset of action.

Answer: b. It requires close monitoring of drug levels to avoid toxicity. Explanation: A narrow therapeutic index indicates a small margin between therapeutic and toxic doses, necessitating careful monitoring of drug levels in the blood to ensure safety and efficacy.

280. In pharmacokinetics, what does the term "bioavailability" refer to?
a. The rate at which a drug is absorbed and becomes available at the site of action
b. The total volume of distribution of a drug throughout the body
c. The percentage of an administered dose that reaches the systemic circulation
d. The time it takes for half of the drug to be eliminated from the body

Answer: c. The percentage of an administered dose that reaches the systemic circulation. Explanation: Bioavailability is defined as the fraction of an administered dose of unchanged drug that reaches the systemic circulation, a key factor in determining the dose needed to achieve a therapeutic effect, especially for drugs administered via non-intravenous routes.

281. Which term best describes the phenomenon where repeated administration of a drug results in a diminished effect, or increasingly larger doses are required to produce the same effect?
a. Potentiation
b. Synergism
c. Tachyphylaxis
d. Antagonism

Answer: c. Tachyphylaxis. Explanation: Tachyphylaxis refers to a rapid decrease in the response to a drug after repeated doses over a short period, necessitating an increase in dosage to achieve the desired pharmacological effect.

282. What factor primarily influences the volume of distribution (Vd) of a drug?
a. The rate of renal excretion
b. The degree of ionization of the drug
c. The extent of drug binding to plasma proteins and tissues
d. The pH of the gastrointestinal tract

Answer: c. The extent of drug binding to plasma proteins and tissues. Explanation: The volume of distribution is influenced by how extensively a drug binds to plasma proteins and tissues. Drugs with high tissue binding have a larger Vd, indicating wider distribution throughout the body, beyond the vascular compartment.

283. In the case of drug-drug interactions, what is the effect of enzyme induction on the metabolism of a concurrently administered drug?
a. It increases the metabolism, potentially reducing the efficacy of the affected drug.
b. It decreases the metabolism, leading to possible accumulation and toxicity.
c. It enhances the absorption, increasing the bioavailability of the affected drug.
d. It inhibits renal excretion, prolonging the half-life of the affected drug.

Answer: a. It increases the metabolism, potentially reducing the efficacy of the affected drug. Explanation: Enzyme induction speeds up drug metabolism, which can lead to decreased plasma levels of the affected drug, potentially reducing its therapeutic effectiveness.

284. Which pharmacodynamic property is best described as the capacity of a drug to elicit a maximal response?
a. Affinity
b. Efficacy
c. Potency
d. Selectivity

Answer: b. Efficacy. Explanation: Efficacy refers to the intrinsic ability of a drug to produce a maximum effect, regardless of dose. A drug with high efficacy can elicit its maximum response even if its potency, or the dose required to achieve a certain effect, is low.

285. Which factor primarily affects the absorption of orally administered medications?
a. The pH of the stomach and the presence of food
b. The patient's age and gender
c. The time of day the medication is administered
d. The color and size of the tablet or capsule

Answer: a. The pH of the stomach and the presence of food. Explanation: The absorption of orally administered medications is significantly influenced by the stomach's pH and whether the medication is taken with or without food. Some medications are better absorbed in an acidic environment, while others may require or need to avoid concomitant food intake to enhance or reduce absorption.

286. How does the first-pass effect influence the bioavailability of a drug?
a. It increases the drug concentration in the bloodstream.
b. It decreases the drug concentration before it reaches systemic circulation.
c. It enhances the speed of drug distribution to the target tissues.
d. It reduces the metabolism of the drug in the liver.

Answer: b. It decreases the drug concentration before it reaches systemic circulation. Explanation: The first-pass effect refers to the metabolism of a drug in the liver before it reaches systemic circulation, often resulting in a significant reduction in the amount of active drug available, thereby decreasing its bioavailability.

287. Which protein is primarily responsible for the distribution of drugs within the plasma?
a. Hemoglobin
b. Albumin
c. Collagen
d. Myoglobin

Answer: b. Albumin. Explanation: Albumin, a protein in the blood plasma, plays a crucial role in the distribution of many drugs. It acts as a carrier and can bind to various drugs, affecting their distribution and availability to target tissues.

288. In the context of drug metabolism, what is the significance of the cytochrome P450 enzymes?
a. They are involved in the renal excretion of drugs.
b. They catalyze the phase I metabolic reactions in the liver.
c. They decrease the solubility of drugs in water.
d. They are primarily found in the brain and affect neurotransmitter reuptake.

Answer: b. They catalyze the phase I metabolic reactions in the liver. Explanation: The cytochrome P450 enzyme system is a collection of enzymes in the liver that play a key role in the phase I metabolism of drugs, involving reactions such as oxidation, reduction, and hydrolysis, which often prepare drugs for further metabolism or excretion.

289. What role does glomerular filtration play in drug excretion?
a. It is the primary mechanism for excreting lipid-soluble drugs.
b. It involves the active secretion of drugs into the bile.
c. It filters drugs out of the blood into the urine in the kidneys.
d. It is responsible for metabolizing drugs into inactive compounds.

Answer: c. It filters drugs out of the blood into the urine in the kidneys. Explanation: Glomerular filtration is a process in the kidneys where blood is filtered through the glomeruli, allowing for the excretion of water-soluble substances, including drugs and their metabolites, into the urine.

290. How does protein binding affect drug distribution within the body?
a. Drugs bound to plasma proteins are more rapidly excreted by the kidneys.
b. Only the free, unbound portion of a drug is pharmacologically active.
c. Protein binding increases the lipid solubility of drugs.
d. All bound drugs are immediately available for therapeutic action.

Answer: b. Only the free, unbound portion of a drug is pharmacologically active. Explanation: The pharmacological activity of a drug is determined by its free, unbound fraction in the plasma. Drugs that are bound to plasma proteins, such as albumin, are not available to interact with target receptors until they are released or displaced from the protein.

291. What factor primarily influences the rate of drug excretion through the kidneys?
a. The patient's hair color
b. The drug's lipid solubility
c. The pH of the urine
d. The ambient temperature

Answer: c. The pH of the urine. Explanation: The pH of the urine can significantly influence the rate of renal excretion of drugs. The ionization state of a drug can be affected by the urine's pH, with acidic drugs being more rapidly excreted in alkaline urine and vice versa, due to the ion trapping phenomenon.

292. Why is the blood-brain barrier (BBB) significant in pharmacokinetics?
a. It prevents all drugs from entering the brain.
b. It selectively allows lipid-soluble drugs to cross into the central nervous system.
c. It actively transports all drugs out of the brain.
d. It increases the metabolism of drugs within the brain.

Answer: b. It selectively allows lipid-soluble drugs to cross into the central nervous system. Explanation: The BBB is a selective barrier that only allows certain substances to pass from the bloodstream into the brain. Lipid-soluble drugs can cross the BBB more readily than water-soluble drugs, affecting their distribution and therapeutic effects within the central nervous system.

293. In the phase II drug metabolism, what is the primary process that occurs?
a. Oxidation
b. Conjugation
c. Hydrolysis
d. Reduction

Answer: b. Conjugation. Explanation: Phase II drug metabolism involves conjugation reactions where the drug or its phase I metabolites are coupled with an endogenous substrate (such as glucuronic acid, sulfuric acid, or amino acids), making them more water-soluble and easier to excrete.

294. What is the impact of renal failure on drug excretion?
a. It increases the rate of drug excretion.
b. It has no effect on drug excretion.
c. It decreases the rate of drug excretion, potentially leading to drug accumulation.
d. It changes the primary excretion route from renal to hepatic.

Answer: c. It decreases the rate of drug excretion, potentially leading to drug accumulation. Explanation: Renal failure can significantly impair the kidneys' ability to excrete drugs and their metabolites, leading to decreased drug clearance and the potential for drug accumulation and toxicity. Dosage adjustments are often required in patients with impaired renal function.

295. Which route of administration is known to provide 100% bioavailability of a drug?
a. Oral
b. Intravenous (IV)
c. Subcutaneous (SC)
d. Intramuscular (IM)

Answer: b. Intravenous (IV). Explanation: Intravenous administration bypasses the absorption phase, directly entering the systemic circulation, which results in 100% bioavailability, ensuring the entire dose reaches the site of action without any loss.

296. How does the first-pass effect primarily affect drugs administered orally?
a. Increases the rate of absorption
b. Reduces bioavailability by hepatic metabolism
c. Enhances the effect of the drug

177

d. Prolongs the duration of action

Answer: b. Reduces bioavailability by hepatic metabolism. Explanation: The first-pass effect refers to the metabolism of a drug within the liver after oral absorption and before it reaches systemic circulation, significantly reducing its bioavailability due to chemical alteration or breakdown.

297. For a medication that undergoes extensive first-pass metabolism, which alternative route of administration could bypass this effect and increase bioavailability?
a. Oral
b. Rectal
c. Transdermal
d. Inhalation

Answer: c. Transdermal. Explanation: Transdermal administration allows the drug to be absorbed through the skin directly into the systemic circulation, effectively bypassing the liver and the first-pass metabolism, thereby enhancing bioavailability.

298. Which factor most significantly impacts the bioavailability of a drug administered intramuscularly (IM)?
a. Skin thickness at the site of administration
b. Blood flow to the muscle tissue
c. The pH of the drug solution
d. The presence of food in the stomach

Answer: b. Blood flow to the muscle tissue. Explanation: Blood flow to the muscle tissue is a critical factor for IM administration as it determines the rate at which the drug is absorbed into the systemic circulation, influencing its bioavailability and onset of action.

299. Why might sublingual administration be preferred for certain drugs over oral administration?
a. Faster onset of action due to rapid absorption
b. Avoidance of the acidic environment of the stomach
c. Higher patient compliance due to ease of administration
d. Both A and B

Answer: d. Both A and B. Explanation: Sublingual administration allows drugs to be absorbed directly into the bloodstream through the tissues under the tongue, providing a faster onset of action and avoiding the acidic environment of the stomach, which can degrade certain medications.

300. In comparing bioavailability, why might a drug delivered via a transdermal patch have a slower onset of action than the same drug administered IV?
a. The patch allows for controlled, slow release of the drug into the bloodstream.

b. The adhesive on the patch can delay drug absorption.
c. Skin acts as a natural barrier to drug absorption.
d. Both A and C

Answer: d. Both A and C. Explanation: Transdermal patches provide controlled, slow release of the drug, and the skin acts as a barrier to absorption, contributing to a slower onset of action compared to the immediate effect seen with IV administration.

301. What is the primary advantage of inhalation administration for respiratory drugs?
a. Avoidance of systemic side effects
b. Immediate onset of action
c. Convenience and ease of use
d. All of the above

Answer: d. All of the above. Explanation: Inhalation administration delivers the drug directly to the site of action in the lungs, providing an immediate onset of action and minimizing systemic absorption, which reduces the potential for systemic side effects.

302. For a medication with low oral bioavailability due to poor absorption, which formulation strategy might improve its bioavailability?
a. Enteric coating
b. Liposomal encapsulation
c. Subcutaneous injection form
d. Immediate-release tablet

Answer: b. Liposomal encapsulation. Explanation: Liposomal encapsulation can enhance the absorption of drugs with poor oral bioavailability by facilitating drug transport across cellular membranes, protecting the drug from degradation in the gastrointestinal tract.

303. In the case of prodrugs, how is bioavailability affected by the conversion process in the body?
a. Bioavailability is decreased as the active drug is metabolized.
b. Bioavailability is increased as the prodrug is converted to its active form.
c. Bioavailability remains unchanged as prodrugs are inactive.
d. Bioavailability is unpredictable and varies widely between individuals.

Answer: b. Bioavailability is increased as the prodrug is converted to its active form. Explanation: Prodrugs are designed to be pharmacologically inactive until metabolized into their active form in the body, often enhancing the bioavailability of drugs that are otherwise poorly absorbed or rapidly metabolized.

304. Considering rectal administration, what factor can influence the bioavailability of a drug administered via this route?
a. The presence of hemorrhoids
b. The viscosity of the drug formulation
c. The length of time the drug remains in the rectum
d. All of the above

Answer: d. All of the above. Explanation: The bioavailability of drugs administered rectally can be influenced by various factors, including local conditions like hemorrhoids, the formulation's viscosity affecting retention and absorption, and the duration the drug remains in contact with rectal mucosa.

305. If a medication has a half-life of 4 hours, how much of the original dose remains in the body after 12 hours?
a. 12.5%
b. 25%
c. 50%
d. 75%

Answer: a. 12.5%. Explanation: After one half-life (4 hours), 50% of the drug remains. After two half-lives (8 hours), 25% remains. After three half-lives (12 hours), 12.5% of the original dose remains in the body, demonstrating the exponential decay characteristic of drug elimination.

306. A patient is prescribed a drug with a half-life of 8 hours. How long will it take for the drug to reach steady state concentration if taken consistently?
a. 8 hours
b. 16 hours
c. 32 hours
d. 40 hours

Answer: d. 40 hours. Explanation: The steady-state concentration of a drug is typically achieved after approximately 4 to 5 half-lives. For a drug with an 8-hour half-life, it would take about 32 to 40 hours (4-5 half-lives) to reach steady-state concentration, ensuring a consistent therapeutic level.

307. For a drug administered every 6 hours with a half-life of 24 hours, what is the impact on dosing strategy?
a. The dosing frequency is too high, risking accumulation.
b. The dosing frequency is appropriate for maintaining therapeutic levels.
c. The dosing interval should be shortened to maintain efficacy.
d. The half-life indicates the need for once-daily dosing.

Answer: a. The dosing frequency is too high, risking accumulation. Explanation: With a half-life of 24 hours, the drug is eliminated slowly, and administering it every 6 hours could lead to accumulation and potentially toxicity. The dosing strategy might need adjustment to prevent this, possibly by extending the dosing interval.

308. A medication with a half-life of 3 days is started on day 1. Assuming no dose adjustments, on what day will the drug likely reach its steady state?
a. Day 3
b. Day 6
c. Day 12 to 15
d. Day 18

Answer: c. Day 12 to 15. Explanation: Steady state is typically reached after 4 to 5 half-lives. For a drug with a 3-day half-life, this would be between 12 (4 half-lives) and 15 days (5 half-lives), allowing for consistent drug levels and effects.

309. A patient on a medication with a half-life of 10 hours misses a dose at the 20-hour mark. What advice should be given regarding the next dose?
a. Take the missed dose immediately, then continue as scheduled.
b. Skip the missed dose and wait until the next scheduled dose.
c. Double the next dose to compensate for the missed dose.
d. Take half of the next dose to avoid potential toxicity.

Answer: b. Skip the missed dose and wait until the next scheduled dose. Explanation: After 20 hours (2 half-lives), there's still a significant amount of the drug in the body. Taking the missed dose immediately could lead to increased concentration and potential side effects. Skipping the missed dose and continuing with the next scheduled dose is usually safer.

310. For a drug with a half-life of 6 hours, administered every 6 hours, what fraction of the dose remains after 24 hours?
a. 1/16
b. 1/8
c. 1/4
d. 1/2

Answer: b. 1/8. Explanation: After 24 hours (4 half-lives), the drug concentration would be reduced by half 4 times. So, $1/2^4 = 1/16$ of the dose taken at the 0-hour mark remains, but considering consistent dosing every 6 hours, the overall remaining amount from all doses combined would be higher, approximately 1/8 when considering accumulation and elimination processes.

311. When considering a drug with a very long half-life, what is a potential risk in elderly patients?
a. Rapid clearance leading to subtherapeutic levels
b. Decreased absorption affecting drug efficacy
c. Accumulation leading to increased risk of side effects
d. Immediate hypersensitivity reactions due to rapid onset

Answer: c. Accumulation leading to increased risk of side effects. Explanation: Elderly patients often have reduced renal and hepatic function, leading to slower drug clearance. A drug with a long half-life may accumulate to toxic levels more easily in this population, increasing the risk of adverse effects.

312. How does liver impairment affect the half-life of drugs primarily metabolized by the liver?
a. Decreases the half-life, leading to increased clearance
b. Increases the half-life, leading to potential drug accumulation
c. Has no significant effect on the half-life
d. Shortens the half-life, requiring higher doses for efficacy

Answer: b. Increases the half-life, leading to potential drug accumulation. Explanation: Liver impairment can reduce the metabolic capacity of the liver, leading to a longer half-life for drugs metabolized primarily by this organ. This can result in drug accumulation and increased risk of toxicity, necessitating dose adjustments.

313. In adjusting doses for a medication with a short half-life, what is a key consideration to avoid breakthrough symptoms?
a. Increasing the dose while maintaining the same dosing interval
b. Decreasing the dosing interval to maintain therapeutic levels
c. Switching to a medication with a longer half-life
d. Administering the medication only when symptoms appear

Answer: b. Decreasing the dosing interval to maintain therapeutic levels. Explanation: For drugs with short half-lives, decreasing the dosing interval can help maintain therapeutic levels and prevent the re-emergence of symptoms between doses, ensuring consistent symptom management.

314. What is the significance of a drug's half-life in determining its suitability for once-daily dosing?
a. A short half-life (<12 hours) generally indicates suitability for once-daily dosing.
b. A long half-life (>24 hours) makes a drug a good candidate for once-daily dosing.
c. Half-life has no impact on dosing frequency decisions.
d. Only drugs with half-lives between 1-2 hours are suitable for once-daily dosing.

Answer: b. A long half-life (>24 hours) makes a drug a good candidate for once-daily dosing. Explanation: Drugs with longer half-lives remain in the body for extended periods, allowing for sustained therapeutic effects with once-daily dosing. This improves patient compliance by simplifying the dosing regimen.

315. What classifies a drug as an agonist in pharmacological terms?
a. It blocks the normal action of a receptor.
b. It mimics the action of the body's own chemical messengers.
c. It inhibits the production of enzymes necessary for neurotransmitter synthesis.
d. It enhances the body's immune response to foreign substances.

Answer: b. It mimics the action of the body's own chemical messengers. Explanation: Agonists bind to and activate specific receptors, mimicking the effects of the body's natural neurotransmitters or hormones, thus inducing a biological response.

316. How do antagonists differ from agonists in their mechanism of action at the receptor level?
a. Antagonists bind to receptors and activate them, while agonists do not.
b. Antagonists increase the natural turnover of neurotransmitters.
c. Antagonists bind to receptors without activating them, preventing agonists from binding.
d. Antagonists enhance the effects of natural neurotransmitters.

Answer: c. Antagonists bind to receptors without activating them, preventing agonists from binding. Explanation: Antagonists prevent the action of agonists by occupying the binding sites on receptors without causing activation, effectively blocking the receptor's natural ligand or agonist from inducing a response.

317. In the context of opioid medications, how does naloxone function in relation to opioid receptors?
a. As a full agonist, increasing the analgesic effect
b. As a partial agonist, providing moderate pain relief
c. As a competitive antagonist, reversing the effects of opioids
d. As a non-competitive antagonist, permanently inactivating the receptor

Answer: c. As a competitive antagonist, reversing the effects of opioids. Explanation: Naloxone is a competitive opioid receptor antagonist that reverses the effects of opioid agonists, such as morphine, by displacing them from the receptors, which is crucial in treating opioid overdoses.

318. Which type of drug would be used to reduce hypertension by blocking beta-adrenergic receptors?
a. Beta-agonist
b. Beta-blocker
c. Alpha-agonist
d. Calcium channel agonist

Answer: b. Beta-blocker. Explanation: Beta-blockers, or beta-adrenergic antagonists, reduce blood pressure by blocking the effects of adrenaline on the body's beta receptors, which decreases heart rate and force of contraction, leading to lower blood pressure.

319. What is the primary action of an angiotensin receptor blocker (ARB) in treating hypertension?
a. It mimics angiotensin II, increasing blood pressure.
b. It blocks angiotensin II receptors, preventing vasoconstriction.
c. It acts as an agonist to angiotensin-converting enzyme (ACE).
d. It enhances the release of aldosterone, increasing sodium reabsorption.

Answer: b. It blocks angiotensin II receptors, preventing vasoconstriction. Explanation: ARBs function as antagonists at angiotensin II receptors, inhibiting the effects of angiotensin II, a potent vasoconstrictor, thereby lowering blood pressure.

320. In asthma management, how do inhaled corticosteroids function at the cellular level?
a. By mimicking the action of adrenergic agonists to dilate airways
b. By acting as antagonists to inflammatory mediators
c. By blocking muscarinic receptors to prevent bronchoconstriction
d. By activating glucocorticoid receptors, reducing inflammation

Answer: d. By activating glucocorticoid receptors, reducing inflammation. Explanation: Inhaled corticosteroids act as agonists at glucocorticoid receptors, leading to the activation of anti-inflammatory pathways and suppression of inflammatory gene expression, thereby reducing airway inflammation in asthma.

321. What characterizes a partial agonist's action when compared to a full agonist?
a. It causes a maximum physiological response that full agonists cannot achieve.
b. It binds to receptors but does not produce any physiological response.
c. It produces a lesser physiological response than a full agonist at the same receptor.
d. It acts as an antagonist in the presence of a full agonist.

Answer: c. It produces a lesser physiological response than a full agonist at the same receptor. Explanation: Partial agonists bind to and partially stimulate receptors, producing a submaximal response compared to full agonists, which can elicit a full response from the receptor system.

322. How do muscarinic receptor antagonists, such as atropine, affect the parasympathetic nervous system?
a. By mimicking acetylcholine and stimulating the parasympathetic system
b. By inhibiting acetylcholinesterase, increasing acetylcholine levels
c. By blocking acetylcholine receptors, inhibiting parasympathetic actions
d. By facilitating the release of norepinephrine, enhancing sympathetic activity

Answer: c. By blocking acetylcholine receptors, inhibiting parasympathetic actions. Explanation: Muscarinic antagonists like atropine block acetylcholine receptors, particularly in the parasympathetic nervous system, reducing parasympathetic activity such as salivation, bronchial secretions, and heart rate.

323. Considering the treatment of Parkinson's disease, why are dopamine agonists used?
a. To block the excessive action of acetylcholine in the striatum
b. To enhance the reuptake of dopamine in the synapse
c. To mimic dopamine and stimulate dopamine receptors in the brain
d. To inhibit monoamine oxidase B, increasing dopamine availability

Answer: c. To mimic dopamine and stimulate dopamine receptors in the brain. Explanation: In Parkinson's disease, dopamine levels are decreased. Dopamine agonists act by directly stimulating dopamine receptors in the brain, compensating for the lack of endogenous dopamine and alleviating symptoms such as bradykinesia and rigidity.

324. Which of the following medications increases the risk of bleeding when taken with warfarin?
a. Acetaminophen
b. Furosemide
c. Levothyroxine
d. Metformin

Answer: a. Acetaminophen. Explanation: Acetaminophen (Tylenol), especially when used in high doses or for prolonged periods, can increase the risk of bleeding in patients taking warfarin by interfering with the clotting mechanism. This interaction necessitates careful monitoring of INR levels in patients taking both medications.

325. A patient is taking simvastatin for hyperlipidemia. Which medication should be used cautiously due to the increased risk of myopathy?
a. Amlodipine
b. Fluconazole
c. Lisinopril
d. Metoprolol

Answer: b. Fluconazole. Explanation: Fluconazole, a potent inhibitor of the CYP3A4 enzyme, can increase the plasma concentration of simvastatin, thereby increasing the risk of myopathy and rhabdomyolysis. Patients should be monitored for signs and symptoms of muscle pain, tenderness, or weakness, especially if taking high doses of simvastatin.

326. Combining a phosphodiesterase type 5 inhibitor (such as sildenafil) with which of the following medications could lead to a significant drop in blood pressure?
a. Alendronate
b. Nitroglycerin
c. Omeprazole
d. Prednisone

Answer: b. Nitroglycerin. Explanation: Phosphodiesterase type 5 inhibitors, used for erectile dysfunction, can cause vasodilation and lower blood pressure. When combined with nitroglycerin, a nitrate also causing vasodilation, there is a significant risk for hypotension, warranting caution with this combination.

327. A patient on lithium therapy for bipolar disorder is prescribed ibuprofen for pain. What is the potential concern with this drug combination?

a. Decreased effectiveness of lithium
b. Increased risk of lithium toxicity
c. Reduced anti-inflammatory effects of ibuprofen
d. Enhanced sedative effect of ibuprofen

Answer: b. Increased risk of lithium toxicity. Explanation: Nonsteroidal anti-inflammatory drugs (NSAIDs) like ibuprofen can reduce renal clearance of lithium, leading to increased lithium levels and potential toxicity. Patients should be closely monitored for signs of lithium toxicity when NSAIDs are initiated.

328. Which antibiotic should be used with caution in patients taking methotrexate due to the risk of increased methotrexate toxicity?
a. Azithromycin
b. Cephalexin
c. Trimethoprim/sulfamethoxazole
d. Doxycycline

Answer: c. Trimethoprim/sulfamethoxazole. Explanation: Trimethoprim/sulfamethoxazole can inhibit the renal tubular secretion of methotrexate, leading to increased levels of methotrexate and the risk of toxicity. This combination requires careful monitoring, especially in patients with renal impairment or those taking high doses of methotrexate.

329. A patient taking a calcium channel blocker for hypertension is prescribed clarithromycin for a respiratory infection. What is the primary concern with this combination?
a. Reduced effectiveness of the calcium channel blocker
b. Increased risk of hypotension
c. Decreased antibiotic effectiveness
d. Induction of antibiotic resistance

Answer: b. Increased risk of hypotension. Explanation: Clarithromycin, a potent inhibitor of the CYP3A4 enzyme, can increase the levels of certain calcium channel blockers, enhancing their hypotensive effects and potentially leading to severe hypotension.

330. When a patient taking theophylline for asthma is prescribed ciprofloxacin for an infection, what is a potential risk?
a. Theophylline clearance may increase, reducing its efficacy.
b. Theophylline levels may rise, increasing the risk of toxicity.
c. Ciprofloxacin may become less effective.
d. Increased risk of ciprofloxacin-induced tendon rupture.

Answer: b. Theophylline levels may rise, increasing the risk of toxicity. Explanation: Ciprofloxacin can inhibit the metabolism of theophylline, leading to increased plasma concentrations and the risk of theophylline toxicity. Monitoring theophylline levels and adjusting the dose may be necessary.

331. A patient on digoxin for heart failure is prescribed erythromycin for an infection. What is the primary concern with this drug combination?
a. Reduced efficacy of digoxin
b. Increased risk of digoxin toxicity
c. Erythromycin may cause rapid heart rate
d. Decreased absorption of erythromycin

Answer: b. Increased risk of digoxin toxicity. Explanation: Erythromycin can inhibit P-glycoprotein, a transporter protein that pumps digoxin out of cells, leading to increased digoxin levels and potential toxicity. Patients should be monitored for signs of digoxin toxicity.

332. Combining an ACE inhibitor with which of the following medications can increase the risk of hyperkalemia?
a. Calcium channel blockers
b. Spironolactone
c. Beta-blockers
d. H2 antagonists

Answer: b. Spironolactone. Explanation: Spironolactone, a potassium-sparing diuretic, can increase potassium levels. When combined with an ACE inhibitor, which can also raise potassium levels, there is an increased risk of hyperkalemia, requiring careful monitoring of serum potassium levels.

333. A patient on anticoagulant therapy with warfarin has been prescribed amiodarone for arrhythmia. What is a necessary precaution with this combination?
a. Increase the dose of warfarin to maintain INR.
b. Monitor for signs of warfarin underdosing.
c. Adjust the warfarin dose based on INR monitoring.
d. Discontinue warfarin therapy due to interaction risk.

Answer: c. Adjust the warfarin dose based on INR monitoring. Explanation: Amiodarone can inhibit the metabolism of warfarin, leading to increased warfarin levels and an enhanced anticoagulant effect. Close monitoring of INR and adjustment of the warfarin dose are essential to prevent bleeding complications.

334. Which of the following is a known potent inducer of CYP3A4, potentially decreasing the plasma concentrations of drugs metabolized by this enzyme?
a. Grapefruit juice
b. Ketoconazole
c. Rifampin
d. Omeprazole

Answer: c. Rifampin. Explanation: Rifampin is a potent inducer of CYP3A4 and can significantly decrease the plasma concentrations of drugs metabolized by this enzyme, potentially reducing their efficacy. This is important in managing drug interactions, especially in multi-drug regimens.

335. A patient taking warfarin should be advised to monitor their intake of which substance known to inhibit CYP2C9, potentially increasing the risk of bleeding?
a. Cranberry juice
b. Green leafy vegetables
c. St. John's Wort
d. Grapefruit juice

Answer: a. Cranberry juice. Explanation: Cranberry juice has been reported to inhibit CYP2C9, the enzyme responsible for the metabolism of warfarin. This inhibition can lead to increased warfarin levels and an elevated risk of bleeding, necessitating close monitoring of INR levels in patients.

336. Which medication, when co-administered with a CYP1A2 substrate, may lead to increased plasma levels of the substrate due to enzyme inhibition?
a. Fluvoxamine
b. Rifampin
c. Phenytoin
d. Carbamazepine

Answer: a. Fluvoxamine. Explanation: Fluvoxamine is a known inhibitor of CYP1A2 and can increase the plasma concentrations of drugs metabolized by CYP1A2, such as certain antipsychotics and antidepressants. This may necessitate dose adjustments to avoid toxicity.

337. In the context of CYP450 interactions, what is the potential effect of smoking tobacco on the metabolism of medications?
a. It may inhibit CYP enzymes, leading to increased drug levels.
b. It may induce certain CYP enzymes, leading to decreased drug levels.
c. It has no significant effect on CYP enzyme activity.
d. It selectively inhibits only CYP3A4, with no effect on other enzymes.

Answer: b. It may induce certain CYP enzymes, leading to decreased drug levels. Explanation: Smoking tobacco is known to induce CYP1A2 activity, which can lead to increased metabolism of drugs processed by this enzyme, potentially reducing their therapeutic effect.

338. Which antibiotic is known to be a strong inhibitor of CYP3A4, requiring careful consideration when prescribing with medications metabolized by this enzyme?

a. Amoxicillin
b. Ciprofloxacin
c. Clarithromycin
d. Doxycycline

Answer: c. Clarithromycin. Explanation: Clarithromycin is a strong inhibitor of CYP3A4 and can significantly increase the plasma concentrations of drugs metabolized by this enzyme, such as certain statins, leading to an increased risk of adverse effects.

339. A patient on long-term therapy with a medication metabolized by CYP2D6 could have altered drug metabolism if they also consume significant amounts of:
a. Red wine
b. Black pepper
c. Green tea
d. Grapefruit juice

Answer: c. Green tea. Explanation: Green tea contains compounds that can inhibit CYP2D6, potentially affecting the metabolism of drugs processed by this enzyme and altering their efficacy and toxicity profile.

340. Considering the role of CYP450 enzymes in drug metabolism, what is the primary concern with the concomitant use of a CYP3A4 substrate and a potent CYP3A4 inducer?
a. The substrate's therapeutic effect may be diminished.
b. The inducer's toxicity may be significantly increased.
c. The risk of allergic reactions may be heightened.
d. The substrate's elimination half-life may be significantly prolonged.

Answer: a. The substrate's therapeutic effect may be diminished. Explanation: A potent CYP3A4 inducer can increase the metabolism of a CYP3A4 substrate, potentially reducing its plasma concentration and therapeutic effect, necessitating dose adjustments or alternative therapies.

341. Which CYP enzyme is primarily involved in the metabolism of most opioid medications, and its inhibition could lead to increased opioid effects?
a. CYP2C19
b. CYP2C9
c. CYP2D6
d. CYP3A4

Answer: c. CYP2D6. Explanation: CYP2D6 plays a significant role in the metabolism of many opioid drugs. Inhibition of CYP2D6 can reduce the metabolic clearance of these opioids, potentially leading to increased drug effects and risk of toxicity.

342. When considering the prescription of a new medication, which patient factor could influence the activity of CYP450 enzymes and thus drug metabolism?
a. Age
b. Height
c. Hair color
d. Shoe size

Answer: a. Age. Explanation: Age can significantly affect the activity of CYP450 enzymes, with both very young and elderly patients often having reduced enzyme activity. This can influence drug metabolism, necessitating adjustments in drug dosing.

343. A patient with a history of chronic alcohol use may require dose adjustments for medications metabolized by:
a. CYP2E1
b. CYP2A6
c. CYP1A1
d. CYP3A5

Answer: a. CYP2E1. Explanation: Chronic alcohol use induces CYP2E1, which can lead to increased metabolism of drugs processed by this enzyme, potentially reducing their effectiveness and necessitating careful monitoring and possible dose adjustments.

344. How does concurrent use of certain antibiotics, like ciprofloxacin, affect warfarin therapy?
a. It decreases warfarin's anticoagulant effect by inducing hepatic enzymes.
b. It increases the risk of bleeding by potentiating warfarin's anticoagulant effect.
c. It has no significant impact on warfarin's pharmacokinetics or pharmacodynamics.
d. It enhances warfarin metabolism, necessitating a higher dose of warfarin.

Answer: b. It increases the risk of bleeding by potentiating warfarin's anticoagulant effect. Explanation: Certain antibiotics, such as ciprofloxacin, can potentiate the effect of warfarin by inhibiting the metabolism of warfarin or by disrupting vitamin K-producing gut flora, increasing the risk of bleeding. Close monitoring of INR levels is recommended when these drugs are used concurrently.

345. What is the primary concern when a patient taking a statin consumes grapefruit or grapefruit juice?
a. Grapefruit decreases the efficacy of statins, leading to higher cholesterol levels.
b. Grapefruit can lead to an increased risk of myopathy or rhabdomyolysis by increasing statin levels.
c. Grapefruit enhances the excretion of statins, reducing their half-life.
d. Grapefruit induces the metabolism of statins, necessitating an increased dose.

Answer: b. Grapefruit can lead to an increased risk of myopathy or rhabdomyolysis by increasing statin levels. Explanation: Compounds in grapefruit inhibit the CYP3A4 enzyme, which is involved in the metabolism of many statins. This inhibition can lead to increased plasma concentrations of the statin, heightening the risk of side effects such as myopathy or rhabdomyolysis.

346. When SSRIs are taken with NSAIDs, what potential risk is increased?
a. Reduced efficacy of SSRIs leading to worsening depression
b. Increased risk of gastrointestinal bleeding
c. Heightened risk of renal failure
d. Diminished analgesic effect of NSAIDs

Answer: b. Increased risk of gastrointestinal bleeding. Explanation: The concomitant use of SSRIs and NSAIDs is associated with an increased risk of gastrointestinal bleeding. SSRIs inhibit the reuptake of serotonin in platelets, impairing platelet aggregation, and NSAIDs affect the gastrointestinal mucosa and platelet function, compounding the risk.

347. How does the combination of potassium-sparing diuretics with ACE inhibitors affect potassium levels?
a. It may lead to hypokalemia due to increased potassium excretion.
b. It has no significant impact on potassium levels.
c. It may cause hyperkalemia due to reduced potassium excretion.
d. It enhances the antihypertensive effect without affecting potassium levels.

Answer: c. It may cause hyperkalemia due to reduced potassium excretion. Explanation: Both potassium-sparing diuretics and ACE inhibitors can lead to increased potassium levels by reducing its excretion. When used together, they can synergistically increase the risk of hyperkalemia, necessitating careful monitoring of potassium levels.

348. What effect does St. John's Wort have on oral contraceptives?
a. It enhances the efficacy of oral contraceptives, increasing their contraceptive effect.
b. It has no interaction with oral contraceptives.
c. It may reduce the effectiveness of oral contraceptives, increasing the risk of unintended pregnancy.
d. It increases the risk of estrogen-related side effects, such as thrombosis.

Answer: c. It may reduce the effectiveness of oral contraceptives, increasing the risk of unintended pregnancy. Explanation: St. John's Wort induces the activity of the CYP3A4 enzyme, which can increase the metabolism of oral contraceptives, potentially reducing their effectiveness and increasing the risk of unintended pregnancy.

349. What is the concern with co-administration of digoxin and loop diuretics?
a. Increased risk of ototoxicity
b. Reduced efficacy of digoxin due to electrolyte imbalance
c. Elevated risk of digoxin toxicity due to potential hypokalemia
d. Decreased diuretic effect of loop diuretics

Answer: c. Elevated risk of digoxin toxicity due to potential hypokalemia. Explanation: Loop diuretics can lead to hypokalemia, which increases the sensitivity of the heart to digoxin and can elevate the risk of digoxin toxicity. Monitoring electrolyte levels and adjusting doses as necessary is important when these medications are used together.

350. How does concurrent use of MAO inhibitors with sympathomimetic drugs (like pseudoephedrine) affect the patient?
a. It may lead to a hypertensive crisis due to increased levels of neurotransmitters.
b. It significantly reduces blood pressure, increasing the risk of syncope.
c. It diminishes the effectiveness of MAO inhibitors in treating depression.
d. It has a calming effect, reducing anxiety and hypertension.

Answer: a. It may lead to a hypertensive crisis due to increased levels of neurotransmitters. Explanation: MAO inhibitors prevent the breakdown of monoamine neurotransmitters. When combined with sympathomimetic drugs, which increase levels of these neurotransmitters, there can be a significant and dangerous increase in blood pressure, leading to a hypertensive crisis.

351. What is the primary risk when combining theophylline, a bronchodilator, with fluoroquinolone antibiotics?
a. Reduced bronchodilation leading to worsening asthma or COPD symptoms
b. Increased risk of tendon rupture
c. Elevated theophylline levels, increasing the risk of theophylline toxicity
d. Decreased effectiveness of fluoroquinolones in treating infections

Answer: c. Elevated theophylline levels, increasing the risk of theophylline toxicity. Explanation: Fluoroquinolones can inhibit the metabolism of theophylline, leading to increased plasma concentrations of theophylline, which can heighten the risk of adverse effects such as nausea, vomiting, seizures, and arrhythmias.

352. When utilizing Micromedex to check for drug interactions, which feature allows for the analysis of multiple drug interactions simultaneously?
a. Drug Identifier
b. IV Compatibility
c. Drug Interactions Checker
d. Trissel's 2 Clinical Pharmaceutics Database

Answer: c. Drug Interactions Checker. Explanation: The Drug Interactions Checker in Micromedex is specifically designed to analyze potential interactions between multiple medications, providing detailed information on the nature, severity, and clinical significance of each identified interaction, aiding healthcare professionals in making informed decisions about patient care.

353. In Lexicomp, where would you find detailed information on the management of specific drug interactions?
a. Drug I.D.
b. Interaction Analysis

c. Drug Comparison
d. Lexi-CALC

Answer: b. Interaction Analysis. Explanation: The Interaction Analysis tool in Lexicomp provides not only a list of potential drug-drug interactions but also detailed management recommendations for each identified interaction, assisting clinicians in mitigating risks associated with concomitant drug therapies.

354. Which resource within Micromedex can be utilized to determine the compatibility of drugs with various infusion solutions?
a. RED BOOK
b. CareNotes
c. IV Compatibility
d. ToxED

Answer: c. IV Compatibility. Explanation: The IV Compatibility tool in Micromedex is a specialized resource designed to provide information on the physical and chemical compatibility of drugs with various infusion solutions, which is crucial for the safe preparation and administration of IV medications.

355. When searching for adverse drug reactions in Lexicomp, which section provides comprehensive information including incidence rates and risk factors?
a. Drug Monographs
b. Adverse Reactions
c. Pharmacogenomics
d. Pregnancy & Lactation

Answer: b. Adverse Reactions. Explanation: The Adverse Reactions section within a drug monograph in Lexicomp provides extensive details on potential adverse effects associated with a medication, including incidence rates and predisposing risk factors, enabling healthcare providers to better assess and communicate risks to patients.

356. For identifying the therapeutic class of a medication and its potential alternatives within the same class, which Lexicomp feature is most appropriate?
a. Drug I.D.
b. Drug Comparison
c. Pharmacogenomics
d. Indexes

Answer: b. Drug Comparison. Explanation: The Drug Comparison tool in Lexicomp allows healthcare professionals to compare medications within the same therapeutic class, providing an easy way to identify potential alternatives based on efficacy, safety, and formulary status.

357. In Micromedex, which resource provides evidence-based clinical decision support and recommendations for medication therapy management?
a. DrugDex
b. Martindale
c. Neofax
d. CareNotes

Answer: a. DrugDex. Explanation: DrugDex in Micromedex offers comprehensive, evidence-based clinical decision support, including in-depth drug information, dosing recommendations, and therapeutic management guidelines, supporting informed and effective medication therapy decisions.

358. When using Lexicomp to review a medication's pharmacokinetics, which subsection would detail the drug's absorption, distribution, metabolism, and excretion?
a. Dosage & Administration
b. Pharmacology
c. Warnings & Precautions
d. Use in Specific Populations

Answer: b. Pharmacology. Explanation: The Pharmacology section of a Lexicomp drug monograph provides detailed information on a drug's pharmacokinetics, including absorption, distribution, metabolism, and excretion (ADME), essential for understanding how the drug behaves in the body.

359. For a healthcare professional looking to understand the impact of genetic variations on drug response, which Micromedex resource would be most helpful?
a. DrugDex
b. ToxED
c. Pharmacogenomics
d. AltMedDex

Answer: c. Pharmacogenomics. Explanation: The Pharmacogenomics resource in Micromedex provides information on how genetic variations affect individual responses to drugs, including efficacy and risk of adverse effects, aiding in the personalization of drug therapy.

360. In the context of patient education, which Lexicomp feature offers customizable patient handouts that explain medication use, side effects, and precautions?
a. Patient Education
b. CareNotes
c. Lexi-Comp ONLINE for Oral Surgery
d. VisualDx

Answer: a. Patient Education. Explanation: The Patient Education feature in Lexicomp provides healthcare professionals with customizable handouts designed to educate patients about their medications, including how to take them, potential side effects, and necessary precautions, enhancing patient understanding and adherence.

361. If a pharmacist needs to check for a drug's formulary status and pricing information, which Micromedex tool would provide this data?
a. RED BOOK
b. DrugDex
c. Neofax
d. CareNotes

Answer: a. RED BOOK. Explanation: RED BOOK in Micromedex is a comprehensive resource that provides the latest pricing information, formulary status, and product availability for prescription and over-the-counter drugs, aiding pharmacists in making cost-effective and formulary-compliant medication choices.

362. Which federal law established the requirement for child-resistant packaging for prescription medications?
a. The Controlled Substances Act (1970)
b. The Poison Prevention Packaging Act (1970)
c. The Durham-Humphrey Amendment (1951)
d. The Kefauver-Harris Amendment (1962)

Answer: b. The Poison Prevention Packaging Act (1970). Explanation: The Poison Prevention Packaging Act of 1970 requires the use of child-resistant packaging for prescription drugs, over-the-counter (OTC) medications, household chemicals, and other hazardous materials to prevent poisoning in children.

363. Under which federal law are medications classified into schedules based on their potential for abuse?
a. The Federal Food, Drug, and Cosmetic Act (1938)
b. The Controlled Substances Act (1970)
c. The Harrison Narcotic Act (1914)
d. The Drug Addiction Treatment Act (2000)

Answer: b. The Controlled Substances Act (1970). Explanation: The Controlled Substances Act of 1970 established the scheduling of drugs, substances, and certain chemicals used to make drugs according to their potential for abuse, medical use, and dependence liability. Drugs are classified into five schedules (I-V) with varying qualifications for each.

364. What is the primary purpose of the Drug Quality and Security Act (DQSA) of 2013?
a. To combat antibiotic resistance
b. To regulate electronic prescribing
c. To provide more stringent guidelines for compound pharmacies
d. To restrict the use of controlled substances in research

Answer: c. To provide more stringent guidelines for compound pharmacies. Explanation: The Drug Quality and Security Act of 2013 outlines critical steps to build an electronic, interoperable system to identify and trace certain prescription drugs as they are distributed within the United States, and establishes more stringent guidelines for compounding pharmacies to ensure medication safety and quality.

365. Which federal law requires pharmacists to offer counseling to Medicaid patients regarding medications?
a. The Omnibus Budget Reconciliation Act (OBRA) of 1990
b. The Medicare Prescription Drug, Improvement, and Modernization Act of 2003
c. The Affordable Care Act (2010)
d. The Health Insurance Portability and Accountability Act (HIPAA) of 1996

Answer: a. The Omnibus Budget Reconciliation Act (OBRA) of 1990. Explanation: OBRA-90 requires pharmacists to offer counseling to Medicaid patients on all new prescriptions, discussing topics such as the name and description of the medication, dosage form, dose, route of administration, and any special directions and precautions for prepared medications.

366. What was a significant contribution of the Durham-Humphrey Amendment of 1951 to pharmacy practice?
a. It established the Food and Drug Administration (FDA).
b. It distinguished between drugs that can be sold with or without a prescription.
c. It mandated the safety testing of drugs.
d. It required drug manufacturers to prove the efficacy of their drugs.

Answer: b. It distinguished between drugs that can be sold with or without a prescription. Explanation: The Durham-Humphrey Amendment to the Federal Food, Drug, and Cosmetic Act of 1938 created a distinction between "over-the-counter" (OTC) and prescription drugs. It also authorized verbal prescription orders and refills to be called into the pharmacy.

367. Which law introduced the concept of "deemed status" for pharmacies participating in Medicare and Medicaid?
a. The Anabolic Steroid Control Act of 1990
b. The Medicare Prescription Drug, Improvement, and Modernization Act of 2003
c. The Omnibus Budget Reconciliation Act (OBRA) of 1987
d. The Drug Supply Chain Security Act (DSCSA) of 2013

Answer: c. The Omnibus Budget Reconciliation Act (OBRA) of 1987. Explanation: OBRA-87 introduced "deemed status," which allows pharmacies to participate in Medicare and Medicaid if they are accredited by a recognized organization, thereby meeting certain federal standards for quality and safety.

368. The Ryan Haight Online Pharmacy Consumer Protection Act of 2008 was enacted in response to:
a. The opioid epidemic
b. The proliferation of internet pharmacies dispensing controlled substances without legitimate prescriptions
c. The need for electronic prescribing standards

d. The increase in counterfeit drugs

Answer: b. The proliferation of internet pharmacies dispensing controlled substances without legitimate prescriptions. Explanation: The Ryan Haight Act addresses issues related to the online sale and distribution of controlled substances by making it illegal to deliver, distribute, or dispense a controlled substance over the internet without a valid prescription.

369. What did the Kefauver-Harris Amendment of 1962 require drug manufacturers to provide for the first time?
a. Proof of drug efficacy
b. Disclosure of side effects
c. Drug samples to physicians
d. A list of active ingredients

Answer: a. Proof of drug efficacy. Explanation: The Kefauver-Harris Amendment required drug manufacturers to provide proof of the effectiveness and safety of their drugs before approval. This law was enacted in response to the thalidomide tragedy, where the drug caused thousands of birth defects.

370. The Combat Methamphetamine Epidemic Act (CMEA) of 2005 was included in which larger legislative act?
a. The USA PATRIOT Act
b. The Affordable Care Act
c. The Controlled Substances Act
d. The Drug Quality and Security Act

Answer: a. The USA PATRIOT Act. Explanation: The CMEA, which is part of the USA PATRIOT Act, regulates the over-the-counter sale of ephedrine, pseudoephedrine, and phenylpropanolamine products to prevent the illicit production of methamphetamine. It imposes restrictions on sales amounts, packaging, and record-keeping for transactions involving these substances.

371. Under the Anabolic Steroid Control Act of 1990, anabolic steroids were classified under which schedule of controlled substances?
a. Schedule I
b. Schedule II
c. Schedule III
d. Schedule IV

Answer: c. Schedule III. Explanation: The Anabolic Steroid Control Act of 1990 classified anabolic steroids as Schedule III controlled substances, placing restrictions on their manufacture, distribution, and use due to their potential for abuse and health risks.

372. Under HIPAA, what constitutes Protected Health Information (PHI)?

a. Any information in a medical record created by healthcare providers that can be used to identify an individual
b. Only the treatment information that is shared with insurance companies
c. Information about health status that is shared within public forums
d. Medical information that patients share with their family and friends

Answer: a. Any information in a medical record created by healthcare providers that can be used to identify an individual. Explanation: Protected Health Information (PHI) under HIPAA includes any part of a patient's medical record or payment history that can be used to identify the individual. It encompasses a wide range of identifiers, not just the medical treatment information.

373. When can a pharmacy share PHI without patient consent under HIPAA?
a. For marketing purposes to promote new pharmacy services
b. When discussing a patient's condition with a family member over the phone
c. For public health activities, such as reporting adverse reactions to medications
d. Posting about a patient's unique case on social media for educational purposes

Answer: c. For public health activities, such as reporting adverse reactions to medications. Explanation: HIPAA allows certain disclosures without patient consent for public health purposes. This includes reporting diseases, injuries, and adverse reactions to medications to government authorities charged with tracking public health issues.

374. What is the minimum necessary standard under HIPAA?
a. Only the minimum amount of PHI needed to accomplish the intended purpose should be disclosed.
b. All health information must be shared with at least a minimum number of healthcare providers.
c. Patients must provide a minimum level of personal information to receive healthcare services.
d. Healthcare providers must document a minimum amount of PHI in medical records.

Answer: a. Only the minimum amount of PHI needed to accomplish the intended purpose should be disclosed. Explanation: The minimum necessary standard requires that healthcare providers and others covered by HIPAA make reasonable efforts to ensure that access to PHI is limited to the minimum necessary to accomplish the intended purpose of the use, disclosure, or request.

375. What are the penalties for non-compliance with HIPAA regulations?
a. Mandatory public service in healthcare facilities
b. Fines ranging from $100 to $1.5 million per violation category, per year
c. Automatic revocation of medical licenses for all involved healthcare providers
d. A fixed penalty of $500 per incident, regardless of the violation severity

Answer: b. Fines ranging from $100 to $1.5 million per violation category, per year. Explanation: HIPAA violations can result in substantial fines for healthcare entities, ranging from $100 to $1.5 million per violation category, per year, depending on the nature of the violation and the perceived level of negligence.

376. How does HIPAA address the use of electronic PHI (e-PHI)?
a. e-PHI is not covered under HIPAA.
b. Requires the implementation of administrative, physical, and technical safeguards to ensure the confidentiality, integrity, and security of e-PHI.
c. Allows unrestricted sharing of e-PHI within the same healthcare system.
d. Mandates that all e-PHI be converted to paper records to ensure security.

Answer: b. Requires the implementation of administrative, physical, and technical safeguards to ensure the confidentiality, integrity, and security of e-PHI. Explanation: HIPAA's Security Rule specifically addresses electronic PHI, requiring covered entities to implement a series of administrative, physical, and technical safeguards to protect e-PHI.

377. In what situation is a pharmacy allowed to use PHI for marketing under HIPAA?
a. When selling PHI to third-party marketers without patient consent
b. For face-to-face communications with the patient about products or services
c. For sending mass emails to patients about a new drug without their prior authorization
d. Using patient information to create targeted social media ads

Answer: b. For face-to-face communications with the patient about products or services. Explanation: HIPAA allows pharmacies to use PHI for face-to-face marketing communications with the patient about health-related products or services. Other forms of marketing typically require patient authorization.

378. What does the Notice of Privacy Practices (NPP) under HIPAA require?
a. Patients must acknowledge that they practice privacy in their health discussions.
b. Healthcare providers to inform patients about their privacy rights and how their PHI is used.
c. All patients to sign a waiver allowing unlimited use of their PHI.
d. Pharmacies to post a list of all individuals who have viewed a patient's PHI.

Answer: b. Healthcare providers to inform patients about their privacy rights and how their PHI is used. Explanation: The Notice of Privacy Practices is a document that HIPAA-covered entities must provide to patients, explaining how their PHI may be used and disclosed, and detailing the patient's rights with respect to their health information.

379. How does HIPAA impact the way pharmacies handle medication errors involving PHI?
a. Medication errors are exempt from HIPAA regulations.
b. Pharmacies must report all medication errors to HHS, regardless of PHI involvement.
c. Pharmacies need to manage the error internally while protecting the involved PHI according to HIPAA guidelines.
d. Any medication error involving PHI must be disclosed publicly to ensure transparency.

Answer: c. Pharmacies need to manage the error internally while protecting the involved PHI according to HIPAA guidelines. Explanation: When handling medication errors, pharmacies must conduct internal investigations and take corrective actions while ensuring that any PHI involved is protected according to HIPAA's privacy and security rules.

380. Under HIPAA, when might a pharmacy disclose PHI to law enforcement without patient consent?
a. At the request of any police officer for any reason
b. In response to a court order, subpoena, or other lawful process
c. Whenever a pharmacist deems it necessary for public safety
d. For any minor violation reported by other patients or staff

Answer: b. In response to a court order, subpoena, or other lawful process. Explanation: HIPAA permits the disclosure of PHI to law enforcement officials in response to a court order, subpoena, summons, warrant, or similar legal process, without patient consent.

381. What is required under HIPAA for electronic transactions involving PHI?
a. Use of encrypted emails for all communications containing PHI
b. Adoption of standardized formats for electronic transactions, such as billing and fund transfers
c. Personal phone calls to confirm all electronic transactions involving PHI
d. Mandatory paper trails for all electronic transactions to ensure compliance

Answer: b. Adoption of standardized formats for electronic transactions, such as billing and fund transfers. Explanation: HIPAA's Transactions and Code Sets Rule requires the use of standardized formats for electronic transactions to ensure the confidentiality and security of PHI during electronic exchanges related to billing, fund transfers, and other healthcare-related transactions.

382. What is the primary goal of the Poison Prevention Packaging Act (PPPA)?
a. To ensure all medications are packaged in child-resistant containers
b. To reduce the risk of poisoning in children under the age of 5
c. To mandate the use of tamper-evident packaging for all over-the-counter medications
d. To standardize the packaging sizes for all household chemicals

Answer: b. To reduce the risk of poisoning in children under the age of 5. Explanation: The PPPA was enacted to reduce the risk of poisoning in children by requiring that certain household substances and medications be packaged in child-resistant containers, specifically aimed at protecting children under the age of 5 from accidental poisoning.

383. Which of the following substances is NOT required to have child-resistant packaging according to the PPPA?
a. Aspirin tablets
b. Ethylene glycol-based antifreeze
c. Prescription medications
d. Dietary supplements with iron

Answer: b. Ethylene glycol-based antifreeze. Explanation: While the PPPA mandates child-resistant packaging for many potentially hazardous household substances and medications, ethylene glycol-based antifreeze is not covered under the act's requirements for child-resistant packaging. However, antifreeze products are often voluntarily equipped with safety features due to their toxicity.

384. Under the PPPA, in what scenario can a non-child-resistant package be dispensed by a pharmacy?
a. When the medication is intended for elderly patients only
b. If the patient or physician specifically requests one for convenience
c. For all over-the-counter (OTC) medications to ensure easy access
d. When the medication is in a liquid form

Answer: b. If the patient or physician specifically requests one for convenience. Explanation: The PPPA allows for the dispensing of medications in non-child-resistant packaging if there is a specific request from the patient or the prescriber. This provision is intended to accommodate those who may have difficulty using child-resistant containers, such as some elderly patients.

385. Which type of medication is exempt from the PPPA's child-resistant packaging requirements?
a. Sublingual nitroglycerin tablets
b. Oral contraceptives in dispenser packs
c. All antibiotics
d. Topical steroids

Answer: a. Sublingual nitroglycerin tablets. Explanation: Sublingual nitroglycerin tablets, used for angina, are exempt from the PPPA's child-resistant packaging requirements due to the need for patients to access them quickly in an emergency situation. Certain other medications may also be exempt when rapid access is crucial for treatment effectiveness.

386. How does the PPPA define a "child-resistant" package?
a. A package that cannot be opened by any child under the age of 5
b. A package that at least 85% of children under 5 cannot open within 5 minutes, but that 90% of adults can open
c. A package that only adults can open with the use of a tool
d. A package that automatically relocks after use

Answer: b. A package that at least 85% of children under 5 cannot open within 5 minutes, but that 90% of adults can open. Explanation: The PPPA defines a "child-resistant" package as one that the majority of children under 5 years old cannot open within a reasonable amount of time, but that can be opened by adults, balancing safety with accessibility for those who need the medication.

387. What is the procedure for testing the effectiveness of child-resistant packaging according to the PPPA guidelines?
a. Testing with a group of adults aged 50-70 to ensure they can open and properly re-secure the package

b. Consumer surveys to gather feedback on the packaging's ease of use and safety

c. Testing with a panel of children aged 3-4 to assess their ability to open the package within a specified time

d. Laboratory analysis to measure the force required to open the packaging

Answer: c. Testing with a panel of children aged 3-4 to assess their ability to open the package within a specified time. Explanation: The effectiveness of child-resistant packaging under the PPPA is tested by having a panel of children aged 3-4 attempt to open the package. The package is considered child-resistant if the majority of the panel cannot open it within a specified time frame.

388. In what situation might a pharmacy provide a medication in a non-child-resistant container despite PPPA regulations?

a. When the medication is a generic brand

b. For all refill prescriptions automatically

c. Upon specific request by the patient for a single prescription fill

d. If the medication is deemed not hazardous

Answer: c. Upon specific request by the patient for a single prescription fill. Explanation: Pharmacies can dispense medications in non-child-resistant containers if there is a specific request by the patient or prescriber, typically for a single prescription fill. This exception accommodates individuals who may have difficulty with child-resistant containers.

389. Which of the following is a requirement for manufacturers under the PPPA?

a. All medications must be packaged in blister packs.

b. Packaging must include a pictogram explaining how to open and close the container.

c. Each batch of child-resistant packaging must be retested every 5 years.

d. They must submit samples of their packaging for testing and approval before market release.

Answer: d. They must submit samples of their packaging for testing and approval before market release. Explanation: Manufacturers are required to submit samples of their child-resistant packaging for testing and approval to ensure compliance with PPPA standards before the products can be released to the market.

390. How are over-the-counter (OTC) medications regulated under the PPPA?

a. All OTC medications are exempt from the PPPA.

b. Only OTC medications deemed "low risk" are exempt from the PPPA.

c. OTC medications must use child-resistant packaging unless specifically exempted.

d. OTC medications are not regulated by the PPPA but by individual state laws.

Answer: c. OTC medications must use child-resistant packaging unless specifically exempted. Explanation: The PPPA requires that OTC medications be packaged in child-resistant containers to prevent child poisoning, with specific exemptions granted for certain products based on risk assessment and the need for accessibility.

391. What is the primary goal of the Drug Supply Chain Security Act (DSCSA)?
a. To reduce the cost of prescription medications across the supply chain
b. To enable the tracking and tracing of prescription medications at each point in the supply chain
c. To eliminate the need for electronic health records in pharmacies
d. To standardize the packaging of all prescription medications

Answer: b. To enable the tracking and tracing of prescription medications at each point in the supply chain.
Explanation: The DSCSA aims to enhance the security of the pharmaceutical supply chain through requirements for tracking and tracing prescription medications, ensuring that drugs are legitimate and safe for patients.

392. By when are dispensers, including pharmacies, required to only engage in transactions with products that have product identifiers according to the DSCSA?
a. Immediately upon the enactment of the DSCSA
b. By 2020
c. By 2023
d. By 2025

Answer: c. By 2023. Explanation: The DSCSA outlines a phased approach to implementing its requirements, with full compliance for product identifiers on individual prescription drug packages expected by November 2023, enhancing the ability to track and trace products through the supply chain.

393. What information must be provided by the seller to the purchaser in a transaction involving prescription drugs under the DSCSA?
a. Transaction history, transaction statement, and transaction information
b. The seller's annual financial report
c. A list of all ingredients in the drug
d. The personal information of the drug manufacturer's CEO

Answer: a. Transaction history, transaction statement, and transaction information. Explanation: The DSCSA requires the exchange of three key pieces of documentation in drug transactions: transaction history (a paper or electronic statement of the drug's transaction history), transaction information (details about the product, including strength, dosage form, and container size), and a transaction statement (an attestation by the seller about the legitimacy of the product).

394. How does the DSCSA affect the verification of returned products before they can be redistributed?
a. Returned products no longer need verification and can be immediately redistributed.
b. Only products returned within 30 days require verification.
c. Products that have been opened or used can be redistributed without verification.
d. Verification of the product identifier, including the serial number, is required before redistribution.

Answer: d. Verification of the product identifier, including the serial number, is required before redistribution. Explanation: Under the DSCSA, returned products that are intended to be redistributed must have their product identifiers, including the serial number, verified to ensure they are legitimate and safe for redistribution.

395. What role do Authorized Trading Partners (ATPs) play in the DSCSA?
a. ATPs are responsible for setting drug prices within the supply chain.
b. ATPs include manufacturers, wholesalers, dispensers, and repackagers who are authorized to engage in transactions involving prescription drugs.
c. ATPs are independent auditors who ensure compliance with DSCSA regulations.
d. ATPs are government agencies tasked with enforcing DSCSA rules.

Answer: b. ATPs include manufacturers, wholesalers, dispensers, and repackagers who are authorized to engage in transactions involving prescription drugs. Explanation: Authorized Trading Partners under the DSCSA are entities that are authorized by law, such as manufacturers, wholesale distributors, dispensers, and repackagers, to engage in transactions involving prescription drugs, ensuring a secure supply chain.

396. Under the DSCSA, what are the requirements for a pharmacy when receiving a suspect product?
a. The pharmacy must immediately return the product to the supplier without any documentation.
b. The pharmacy is required to quarantine and investigate the suspect product to determine its legitimacy.
c. Suspect products can be dispensed as long as they are sold at a discount.
d. Pharmacies must destroy suspect products immediately upon receipt.

Answer: b. The pharmacy is required to quarantine and investigate the suspect product to determine its legitimacy. Explanation: If a pharmacy receives a suspect product, the DSCSA requires that the product be quarantined. The pharmacy must then perform an investigation to verify the product's legitimacy before it can be dispensed or further distributed.

397. How does the DSCSA define a "suspect product"?
a. Any product with a price lower than the market average
b. A product that is potentially counterfeit, diverted, or stolen
c. A product that has been returned by a customer
d. Any generic medication

Answer: b. A product that is potentially counterfeit, diverted, or stolen. Explanation: The DSCSA defines a suspect product as one that may potentially be counterfeit, diverted, stolen, intentionally adulterated, or otherwise unfit for distribution, requiring further investigation to ensure its integrity.

398. What is the significance of the "interoperable electronic system" to be established by 2023 under the DSCSA?
a. It will replace all paper-based tracking with a fully automated drug dispensing system.
b. It aims to facilitate the electronic exchange of transaction information, history, and statements across the pharmaceutical supply chain.
c. It will allow patients to self-verify the authenticity of their medications.

d. It is intended to automate the payment process for prescription medications.

Answer: b. It aims to facilitate the electronic exchange of transaction information, history, and statements across the pharmaceutical supply chain. Explanation: The DSCSA mandates the creation of an interoperable electronic system by 2023 to enhance the security and efficiency of the pharmaceutical supply chain by enabling the electronic tracing of product movement, thereby improving the ability to detect and respond to counterfeit or dangerous products.

399. In the event of a drug recall, how does the DSCSA aid in the process?
a. It requires all drugs to be recalled at least once a year as a test.
b. It limits recalls to drugs manufactured within the last five years.
c. It allows for the efficient identification and removal of affected products from the supply chain.
d. The DSCSA does not cover drug recalls.

Answer: c. It allows for the efficient identification and removal of affected products from the supply chain.
Explanation: The DSCSA enhances the ability to trace drugs through the supply chain, making it easier to identify and remove affected products in the event of a recall, thereby protecting patients from potentially harmful medications.

400. What is required for the serialization of prescription drugs under the DSCSA?
a. All prescription drugs must have a unique serial number on each individual pill or capsule.
b. Prescription drugs must have a unique identifier on the package or container, including a serial number.
c. Serialization is only required for over-the-counter medications.
d. Serialization of prescription drugs is recommended but not required by the DSCSA.

Answer: b. Prescription drugs must have a unique identifier on the package or container, including a serial number.
Explanation: The DSCSA requires that prescription drug packages and cases include a unique product identifier, typically in the form of a serial number, to enhance traceability throughout the supply chain and improve the detection and removal of counterfeit or dangerous drugs.

401. In accordance with state regulations, what is the maximum allowable quantity for a Schedule II controlled substance prescription for acute pain in many states?
a. 3-day supply
b. 7-day supply
c. 14-day supply
d. 30-day supply

Answer: b. 7-day supply. Explanation: Many states have implemented regulations limiting the prescription of Schedule II controlled substances for acute pain to a 7-day supply to combat the opioid crisis. These regulations aim to reduce the risk of addiction and overdose while still providing necessary pain management.

402. Which state board regulation typically requires pharmacists to complete continuing education (CE) credits within a specified renewal period?
a. Pharmacy Practice Act
b. Controlled Substances Act
c. Drug Enforcement Administration regulations
d. Food and Drug Administration guidelines

Answer: a. Pharmacy Practice Act. Explanation: The Pharmacy Practice Act, regulated by state boards of pharmacy, often includes requirements for pharmacists to complete continuing education (CE) credits within a specified renewal period to maintain licensure, ensuring pharmacists stay current with evolving standards of care and pharmacy practice.

403. Under state regulations, who is generally authorized to receive and process verbal prescription orders for non-controlled substances?
a. Only the pharmacist
b. Pharmacy technicians under supervision
c. Any pharmacy staff member
d. Externs or pharmacy interns under direct supervision

Answer: d. Externs or pharmacy interns under direct supervision. Explanation: State regulations often allow externs or pharmacy interns to receive and process verbal prescription orders for non-controlled substances under the direct supervision of a licensed pharmacist, enhancing their practical training while maintaining patient safety.

404. What state regulatory requirement is commonly associated with the establishment of a pharmacist-to-technician ratio in the pharmacy setting?
a. Quality assurance protocols
b. Medication error reduction plans
c. Workforce staffing standards
d. Drug diversion prevention programs

Answer: c. Workforce staffing standards. Explanation: State regulations often specify a maximum pharmacist-to-technician ratio to ensure adequate supervision and maintain the quality of pharmacy services, falling under workforce staffing standards to balance operational efficiency with patient safety.

405. In the context of pharmacy compounding, which regulatory authority's guidelines do state boards often adopt or reference to ensure compounding practices meet quality standards?
a. United States Pharmacopeia (USP)
b. American Pharmacists Association (APhA)
c. National Association of Boards of Pharmacy (NABP)
d. Centers for Disease Control and Prevention (CDC)

Answer: a. United States Pharmacopeia (USP). Explanation: State boards frequently adopt or reference United States Pharmacopeia (USP) guidelines, particularly USP <795> for non-sterile compounding and USP <797> for sterile compounding, to ensure that compounding practices meet nationally recognized quality standards.

406. Which type of pharmacy permit might a state board require for pharmacies engaging in the practice of compounding sterile preparations?
a. Community pharmacy permit
b. Institutional pharmacy permit
c. Sterile compounding pharmacy permit
d. Mail-order pharmacy permit

Answer: c. Sterile compounding pharmacy permit. Explanation: Pharmacies that engage in the compounding of sterile preparations may be required by state boards to obtain a specific sterile compounding pharmacy permit, ensuring they have the necessary facilities, equipment, and procedures to safely compound sterile medications.

407. Regarding the sale of pseudoephedrine-containing products, state laws commonly require pharmacies to:
a. Limit quantities per transaction
b. Sell without any restrictions
c. Provide only with a prescription
d. Report all sales to a state database

Answer: a. Limit quantities per transaction. Explanation: State laws commonly restrict the sale of pseudoephedrine-containing products by limiting the quantities that can be purchased in a single transaction to prevent misuse and diversion for the illegal manufacture of methamphetamine.

408. When a pharmacy dispenses a controlled substance, state regulations typically mandate that the prescription record must include:
a. The patient's diagnosis code
b. The prescriber's email address
c. The DEA number of the prescriber
d. The pharmacy's inventory level of the drug

Answer: c. The DEA number of the prescriber. Explanation: State regulations typically require that prescription records for controlled substances include the DEA number of the prescriber to ensure the legitimacy of the prescription and facilitate tracking and accountability in the use of controlled substances.

409. In some states, regulations regarding the substitution of biosimilar products for prescribed biologics require that:
a. The pharmacist must obtain the prescriber's explicit consent for each substitution
b. The patient must request the substitution in writing
c. The substitution can be made without informing the prescriber
d. The pharmacist must notify the prescriber of the substitution within a certain timeframe

Answer: d. The pharmacist must notify the prescriber of the substitution within a certain timeframe. Explanation: Regulations in some states allow pharmacists to substitute biosimilar products for prescribed biologics, provided that the pharmacist notifies the prescriber of the substitution within a specified timeframe, ensuring communication and maintaining trust in the therapeutic interchange process.

410. Which requirement is commonly enforced by state boards for the remote management of pharmacy operations, such as telepharmacy?
a. Video surveillance of all telepharmacy sites
b. Direct supervision by a pharmacist at each remote site
c. Secure electronic communication systems
d. A pharmacist on-site at the remote location at all times

Answer: c. Secure electronic communication systems. Explanation: State boards often require secure electronic communication systems for the remote management of pharmacy operations, such as telepharmacy, to ensure the confidentiality, integrity, and security of patient information and remote supervision by pharmacists.

411. What is a primary function of the State Board of Pharmacy?
a. To negotiate drug prices for pharmacies
b. To oversee the licensure and regulation of pharmacists and pharmacies
c. To manage the financial operations of pharmacies within the state
d. To provide continuing education courses for healthcare professionals

Answer: b. To oversee the licensure and regulation of pharmacists and pharmacies. Explanation: The State Board of Pharmacy is responsible for the licensure and regulation of pharmacists and pharmacies within the state. It sets standards for pharmacy practice, oversees compliance with state pharmacy laws, and takes disciplinary action when necessary to protect public health.

412. Under what circumstance might a Board of Pharmacy revoke a pharmacist's license?
a. If the pharmacist decides to work in a non-pharmacy-related field
b. For a single minor error in prescription processing
c. For repeated violations of pharmacy law or professional misconduct
d. If the pharmacist fails to attend annual pharmacy conferences

Answer: c. For repeated violations of pharmacy law or professional misconduct. Explanation: A Board of Pharmacy may revoke a pharmacist's license for serious reasons such as repeated violations of pharmacy law, professional misconduct, or actions that compromise patient safety, not for single minor errors or personal career choices.

413. Which of the following activities requires licensure from the Board of Pharmacy?
a. Selling over-the-counter medications in a convenience store
b. Providing nutritional advice as a health coach

c. Dispensing prescription medications in a pharmacy

d. Writing a blog about personal wellness and health

Answer: c. Dispensing prescription medications in a pharmacy. Explanation: Dispensing prescription medications is a regulated activity that requires licensure from the Board of Pharmacy. This ensures that individuals dispensing medications have the necessary knowledge and skills to do so safely.

414. How often must a pharmacist typically renew their license with the Board of Pharmacy?
a. Monthly
b. Annually
c. Every two years
d. Every five years

Answer: c. Every two years. Explanation: While the specific renewal period can vary by state, most Boards of Pharmacy require pharmacists to renew their licenses every two years. This process often includes completing continuing education credits to ensure ongoing professional competence.

415. What is a common requirement for pharmacy technicians to maintain their certification or registration with the Board of Pharmacy?
a. Publishing an article in a pharmacy journal annually
b. Completing a set number of continuing education hours within a renewal period
c. Attending weekly Board of Pharmacy meetings
d. Passing a comprehensive pharmacy law exam every year

Answer: b. Completing a set number of continuing education hours within a renewal period. Explanation: Pharmacy technicians are often required to complete a specified number of continuing education (CE) hours within a renewal period to maintain their certification or registration. This ensures they stay current with pharmacy practices and knowledge.

416. In the case of a medication error that results in patient harm, what is the FIRST action a pharmacist should take?
a. Contact the Board of Pharmacy to report the error
b. Ensure the patient receives appropriate medical care
c. Modify pharmacy policies to prevent future errors
d. Notify the pharmacy's insurance company

Answer: b. Ensure the patient receives appropriate medical care. Explanation: The immediate priority in the event of a medication error that results in patient harm is to ensure the patient receives the necessary medical care. Subsequent actions include internal reporting and analysis to prevent future errors and, if required, reporting to the Board of Pharmacy.

417. What role does the Board of Pharmacy play in the approval of new medications?
a. The Board directly approves all new medications before they can be sold in pharmacies.
b. The Board advises the FDA on the safety and efficacy of new medications.
c. The Board regulates pharmacy practice but does not approve new medications.
d. The Board conducts clinical trials for new medications.

Answer: c. The Board regulates pharmacy practice but does not approve new medications. Explanation: The approval of new medications falls under the jurisdiction of the FDA (Food and Drug Administration), not the State Board of Pharmacy. The Board's role is to regulate pharmacy practice and ensure compliance with state laws and regulations.

418. When a pharmacist moves from one state to another, what must they typically do to practice in the new state?
a. Apply for reciprocity with the new state's Board of Pharmacy
b. Automatically transfer their license without any additional requirements
c. Retake and pass the pharmacy school entrance exam
d. Complete a new Pharm.D. program in the new state

Answer: a. Apply for reciprocity with the new state's Board of Pharmacy. Explanation: Pharmacists moving to a new state typically need to apply for licensure reciprocity or endorsement with the new state's Board of Pharmacy, which may include meeting specific state requirements, such as additional exams or background checks.

419. What is the purpose of a Board of Pharmacy conducting pharmacy inspections?
a. To assess the financial health of the pharmacy
b. To evaluate compliance with state laws and regulations regarding pharmacy practice
c. To determine the pharmacy's customer service satisfaction ratings
d. To compare the pricing of medications with other pharmacies in the area

Answer: b. To evaluate compliance with state laws and regulations regarding pharmacy practice. Explanation: Pharmacy inspections conducted by the Board of Pharmacy are meant to ensure that pharmacies comply with state laws and regulations, focusing on aspects like medication safety, record-keeping, and the security of drug storage areas, rather than financial health or customer service metrics.

420. Which of the following tasks is generally allowed for pharmacy technicians under most state regulations?
a. Counseling patients on medication use
b. Performing the final check on prescriptions
c. Compounding sterile intravenous (IV) medications under supervision
d. Prescribing medications under certain conditions

Answer: c. Compounding sterile intravenous (IV) medications under supervision. Explanation: Pharmacy technicians are often permitted to compound sterile IV medications under the supervision of a licensed pharmacist. This task is within the scope of practice for technicians in many jurisdictions, provided they have received appropriate training and are following established protocols.

421. What task is typically prohibited for pharmacy technicians?
a. Reconstituting oral antibiotics as directed by a pharmacist
b. Conducting medication therapy management sessions
c. Assisting with inventory management
d. Operating automated dispensing machines

Answer: b. Conducting medication therapy management sessions. Explanation: Medication therapy management (MTM) involves direct patient interaction and clinical decision-making, which are responsibilities reserved for pharmacists. Pharmacy technicians may assist with logistical aspects of MTM but are not permitted to conduct the sessions themselves.

422. In a retail pharmacy setting, a pharmacy technician might be responsible for which of the following tasks?
a. Initiating drug therapy changes based on lab results
b. Transferring prescription authorization to another pharmacy
c. Diagnosing minor health conditions for over-the-counter medication recommendations
d. Administering vaccinations to patients

Answer: b. Transferring prescription authorization to another pharmacy. Explanation: Pharmacy technicians are often allowed to handle administrative tasks such as transferring prescription authorizations between pharmacies under the direction of a pharmacist. This task does not involve clinical judgment or direct patient care, making it suitable for trained technicians.

423. Under the supervision of a pharmacist, pharmacy technicians are generally NOT allowed to:
a. Enter prescription information into the pharmacy computer system
b. Provide a patient with drug-specific information
c. Select the correct medication from the shelf for dispensing
d. Count and pour medications for prescriptions

Answer: b. Provide a patient with drug-specific information. Explanation: Providing drug-specific information, which can be considered a form of patient counseling, typically falls outside the scope of practice for pharmacy technicians. This task requires clinical knowledge and judgment, which are the responsibility of the pharmacist.

424. A pharmacy technician receives a prescription with unclear handwriting. What is the appropriate course of action?
a. Guess the intended medication based on experience
b. Consult a drug reference to determine the most likely medication
c. Contact the prescriber for clarification
d. Ask the patient what medication they were expecting

Answer: c. Contact the prescriber for clarification. Explanation: When faced with unclear handwriting or ambiguity in a prescription, the appropriate action for a pharmacy technician is to refer the issue to the pharmacist, who may then contact the prescriber for clarification. Guessing or making assumptions about prescriptions can lead to medication errors.

425. Which task can a pharmacy technician perform in a hospital setting under the supervision of a pharmacist?
a. Adjusting medication doses based on patient renal function
b. Preparing patient-specific doses of medications for administration
c. Ordering laboratory tests to monitor drug therapy
d. Making rounds with the medical team to provide pharmacotherapy input

Answer: b. Preparing patient-specific doses of medications for administration. Explanation: Pharmacy technicians in hospital settings are often involved in the preparation of patient-specific medication doses, including filling unit-dose carts or preparing doses for immediate administration, under the supervision of a pharmacist.

426. What is a common role for pharmacy technicians in the medication dispensing process?
a. Verifying the accuracy and appropriateness of prescriptions
b. Assessing drug-drug and drug-disease interactions
c. Generating medication labels and affixing them to the appropriate containers
d. Modifying medication regimens based on treatment protocols

Answer: c. Generating medication labels and affixing them to the appropriate containers. Explanation: A common role for pharmacy technicians includes generating medication labels based on the prescription information and affixing them to the correct containers as part of the dispensing process, always under the oversight of a pharmacist.

427. In the context of a community pharmacy, which of the following activities would a pharmacy technician likely be responsible for?
a. Providing immunization services to patients
b. Conducting clinical assessments to prioritize medication fills
c. Managing the pharmacy's social media accounts to engage with customers
d. Independently consulting with patients on over-the-counter medication choices

Answer: c. Managing the pharmacy's social media accounts to engage with customers. Explanation: Pharmacy technicians may be involved in non-clinical tasks such as managing social media accounts or other forms of customer engagement that do not involve direct patient care or clinical decision-making.

428. When dealing with controlled substances, a pharmacy technician's responsibilities might include:
a. Adjusting inventory levels based on prescription trends
b. Witnessing the waste of unused portions of controlled substances
c. Prescribing controlled substances under a collaborative practice agreement
d. Independently counseling patients on opioid safety

Answer: b. Witnessing the waste of unused portions of controlled substances. Explanation: Pharmacy technicians may be involved in controlled substance management tasks, such as witnessing the disposal or wasting of unused portions, to ensure compliance with regulations and maintain accurate inventory records, typically requiring dual verification with a pharmacist or another authorized staff member.

429. In a mail-order pharmacy, what task might a pharmacy technician be expected to perform?
a. Evaluating patient profiles for potential therapy problems
b. Packaging and labeling medications for shipment
c. Providing detailed drug information to patients via telephone
d. Changing a patient's medication regimen based on recent lab results

Answer: b. Packaging and labeling medications for shipment. Explanation: In a mail-order pharmacy setting, pharmacy technicians commonly handle tasks such as packaging and labeling medications for shipment to patients. This role involves logistical and administrative duties and does not require clinical judgment or direct patient interaction.

430. What is the minimum font size generally required on prescription labels to ensure readability for patients?
a. 8 point
b. 10 point
c. 12 point
d. 14 point

Answer: b. 10 point. Explanation: Most regulations recommend a minimum font size of 10 point on prescription labels to ensure that the information is legible and accessible to a wide range of patients, including those with visual impairments, enhancing medication safety and adherence.

431. Which auxiliary label is essential for a prescription that causes drowsiness and may impair the ability to operate heavy machinery or drive?
a. "Take with food"
b. "Shake well before use"
c. "May cause drowsiness"
d. "Keep refrigerated"

Answer: c. "May cause drowsiness." Explanation: For medications that may cause drowsiness or impair cognitive and motor functions, an auxiliary label stating "May cause drowsiness" is crucial to alert patients of the potential risks when performing activities that require full attention, such as driving or operating heavy machinery.

432. In the context of antibiotic prescriptions, which auxiliary label is commonly used to emphasize the importance of completing the full course of therapy?
a. "Take until gone"
b. "Use sunscreen"

c. "On an empty stomach"
d. "With plenty of water"

Answer: a. "Take until gone." Explanation: For antibiotics, it's vital to complete the full course to effectively clear the infection and prevent antibiotic resistance. The auxiliary label "Take until gone" reinforces this message, encouraging patients not to stop the medication prematurely even if they feel better.

433. When a prescription requires storage in a cool environment but not necessarily refrigeration, which auxiliary label is most appropriate?
a. "Keep in freezer"
b. "Store at room temperature"
c. "Keep in a cool place"
d. "Protect from light"

Answer: c. "Keep in a cool place." Explanation: Medications that are sensitive to heat but do not require refrigeration should have an auxiliary label stating "Keep in a cool place" to indicate that they should be stored in a location away from direct heat sources, ensuring their efficacy and stability.

434. For medications that are known to increase the risk of sunburn or photosensitivity, which auxiliary label is most suitable?
a. "Avoid prolonged sunlight exposure"
b. "Take with food"
c. "Do not crush or chew"
d. "For topical use only"

Answer: a. "Avoid prolonged sunlight exposure." Explanation: Drugs that cause photosensitivity necessitate an auxiliary label such as "Avoid prolonged sunlight exposure" to warn patients to protect their skin from the sun and minimize the risk of severe sunburn or photosensitive reactions.

435. Which auxiliary label should be used for a liquid medication that requires shaking before administration to ensure proper dose uniformity?
a. "Shake well before use"
b. "Refrigerate after opening"
c. "Dilute before taking"
d. "Avoid dairy products"

Answer: a. "Shake well before use." Explanation: Suspensions and some liquid medications need to be well shaken before each dose to ensure the active ingredients are evenly distributed throughout the liquid. The "Shake well before use" auxiliary label instructs patients on this essential step for accurate dosing.

436. For a medication that could potentially stain teeth, such as some liquid antibiotic formulations, which auxiliary label would be most appropriate?
a. "Rinse mouth after use"
b. "Take on an empty stomach"
c. "Use a straw to minimize tooth discoloration"
d. "Swallow whole, do not chew"

Answer: c. "Use a straw to minimize tooth discoloration." Explanation: Medications that may cause tooth discoloration, especially in liquid form, often come with the recommendation to use a straw when taking them. This minimizes contact with the teeth and helps prevent staining.

437. What auxiliary label is recommended for enteric-coated tablets to prevent the destruction of the coating which could lead to medication inactivation by stomach acid?
a. "Take with meals"
b. "Do not crush or chew"
c. "Take with plenty of water"
d. "Dissolve under tongue"

Answer: b. "Do not crush or chew." Explanation: Enteric-coated tablets are designed to withstand stomach acid and dissolve in the intestines. The "Do not crush or chew" auxiliary label is crucial to ensure that patients do not compromise the protective coating, maintaining the medication's effectiveness.

438. For a topical cream that has the potential to cause severe irritation if it comes into contact with the eyes, which auxiliary label is necessary?
a. "For external use only"
b. "Apply thinly"
c. "Wear gloves when applying"
d. "Keep out of reach of children"

Answer: a. "For external use only." Explanation: Topical medications, especially those that can cause irritation or damage to sensitive areas, should have an auxiliary label stating "For external use only" to alert patients to avoid contact with the eyes and mucous membranes, ensuring safe application.

439. In the case of a prescription for a diuretic known to deplete potassium levels, which auxiliary label might be added to prompt dietary supplementation or monitoring?
a. "Eat more potassium-rich foods"
b. "Limit fluid intake"
c. "Take on an empty stomach"
d. "Monitor blood pressure regularly"

Answer: a. "Eat more potassium-rich foods." Explanation: Diuretics can lead to potassium depletion, so an auxiliary label such as "Eat more potassium-rich foods" or advice to monitor potassium levels may be provided to prevent hypokalemia, ensuring the patient's safety while on the medication.

440. What is the primary purpose of a Collaborative Practice Agreement (CPA) between pharmacists and physicians?
a. To allow pharmacists to prescribe medications independently
b. To define specific patient care functions that a pharmacist can perform under a physician's oversight
c. To transfer legal responsibility from physicians to pharmacists
d. To increase the pharmacist's salary based on performance metrics

Answer: b. To define specific patient care functions that a pharmacist can perform under a physician's oversight. Explanation: CPAs establish formal agreements between pharmacists and physicians, outlining the specific patient care services that pharmacists are authorized to perform, such as initiating, modifying, or discontinuing medication therapy, under the oversight of a physician, enhancing collaborative patient care.

441. Under a CPA, what type of medication-related decisions can a pharmacist be authorized to make?
a. Prescribe new medications for any condition
b. Change the brand of medications for insurance purposes
c. Adjust medication dosages based on therapeutic goals and laboratory values
d. Dispense medications without a prescription

Answer: c. Adjust medication dosages based on therapeutic goals and laboratory values. Explanation: CPAs can empower pharmacists to adjust medication dosages based on the patient's response, therapeutic goals, and laboratory values within the scope of the agreement, ensuring optimized medication therapy management.

442. Which factor is critical for the successful implementation of a CPA in a pharmacy setting?
a. A large stock of medication samples
b. Advanced diagnostic equipment in the pharmacy
c. Effective communication and trust between the pharmacist and collaborating physician
d. The ability to bill for medical services directly

Answer: c. Effective communication and trust between the pharmacist and collaborating physician. Explanation: The foundation of a successful CPA is built on effective communication and mutual trust between the pharmacist and the collaborating physician, ensuring cohesive teamwork in managing patient care.

443. What is a potential benefit of CPAs to the healthcare system?
a. Reduction in the need for clinical oversight
b. Decreased healthcare costs due to optimized medication therapy management
c. Elimination of pharmacy audits
d. Standardization of medication prices

Answer: b. Decreased healthcare costs due to optimized medication therapy management. Explanation: CPAs can lead to more efficient and effective medication management by leveraging the pharmacist's expertise, potentially reducing healthcare costs through improved patient outcomes, decreased medication errors, and reduced hospital readmissions.

444. In a CPA, how are the specific roles and responsibilities of the pharmacist usually determined?
a. By state legislation exclusively
b. Through mutual agreement between the pharmacist and the collaborating physician, within the framework of state laws
c. By the pharmacy's administrative board
d. By a consensus among patients

Answer: b. Through mutual agreement between the pharmacist and the collaborating physician, within the framework of state laws. Explanation: The roles and responsibilities of the pharmacist in a CPA are typically defined through a mutual agreement between the pharmacist and the collaborating physician, tailored to meet the needs of their specific practice setting while adhering to the guidelines established by state laws.

445. Which patient care activity might a pharmacist perform under a CPA that involves direct patient interaction?
a. Conducting minor surgical procedures
b. Ordering and interpreting laboratory tests related to medication therapy management
c. Admitting patients to a hospital
d. Providing vaccinations without any oversight

Answer: b. Ordering and interpreting laboratory tests related to medication therapy management. Explanation: Under a CPA, pharmacists may be authorized to order and interpret laboratory tests related to medication therapy management, enabling them to make informed decisions about medication adjustments, monitor drug therapy outcomes, and ensure patient safety.

446. How does a CPA benefit patients with chronic conditions like diabetes or hypertension?
a. By allowing self-adjustment of medications without consulting a healthcare provider
b. By providing continuous, coordinated care between the pharmacist and physician to manage medication therapy effectively
c. By eliminating the need for regular physician visits
d. By giving patients total control over their medication choices

Answer: b. By providing continuous, coordinated care between the pharmacist and physician to manage medication therapy effectively. Explanation: CPAs benefit patients with chronic conditions by facilitating a collaborative approach to medication management, allowing for timely adjustments and close monitoring of therapy, leading to better disease management and improved patient outcomes.

447. What legal document typically outlines the scope of practice and responsibilities within a CPA?

a. A general verbal agreement
b. A memorandum of understanding (MOU)
c. A binding contract signed by the pharmacy and medical boards
d. A patient consent form

Answer: b. A memorandum of understanding (MOU). Explanation: A memorandum of understanding (MOU) is a formal legal document that outlines the scope of practice, responsibilities, and specific collaborative activities agreed upon by the pharmacist and the collaborating physician within a CPA, ensuring clarity and mutual understanding of each party's roles.

448. In the context of a CPA, how is the pharmacist's performance and adherence to the agreement typically monitored and evaluated?
a. Through annual patient satisfaction surveys
b. By continuous quality improvement (CQI) processes and regular reviews by the collaborating physician
c. Solely based on pharmacy sales and revenue
d. By random audits conducted by insurance companies

Answer: b. By continuous quality improvement (CQI) processes and regular reviews by the collaborating physician. Explanation: The pharmacist's performance in a CPA is usually monitored and evaluated through continuous quality improvement processes and regular reviews by the collaborating physician, focusing on patient outcomes, adherence to the agreed-upon protocol, and overall effectiveness of the collaborative practice.

449. What mechanism is often included in a CPA to address potential disagreements or conflicts between the pharmacist and collaborating physician?
a. A mandatory arbitration clause
b. An immediate termination policy
c. A conflict resolution process outlined in the agreement
d. A public review board

Answer: c. A conflict resolution process outlined in the agreement. Explanation: CPAs often include a conflict resolution process to address any disagreements or conflicts that may arise between the pharmacist and collaborating physician, ensuring that issues can be resolved constructively and collaboratively, maintaining the integrity of the patient care provided under the agreement.

450. A pharmacy technician discovers a coworker diverting narcotics for personal use. What is the most ethical course of action?
a. Confront the coworker directly and demand they stop immediately.
b. Ignore the behavior, assuming the coworker has a valid reason for their actions.
c. Report the behavior to the pharmacy manager or supervisor immediately.
d. Advise the coworker to seek help from a professional addiction counselor.

Answer: c. Report the behavior to the pharmacy manager or supervisor immediately. Explanation: The ethical responsibility to maintain a safe and legal pharmacy environment mandates reporting any illegal or unethical behavior, such as drug diversion, to a supervisor or manager. This ensures appropriate actions are taken to address the situation and uphold pharmacy standards.

451. If a patient confides in a pharmacy technician about a serious adverse reaction to a medication that seems unrelated to the known side effects, what should the technician do?
a. Advise the patient to stop taking the medication immediately.
b. Document the conversation and inform the pharmacist for further assessment.
c. Suggest alternative medications that might not have the same side effect.
d. Assure the patient that the side effect is likely temporary and will pass.

Answer: b. Document the conversation and inform the pharmacist for further assessment. Explanation: Pharmacy technicians should document any significant patient concerns and relay them to the pharmacist for professional assessment and appropriate action, ensuring patient safety and adherence to ethical standards in patient care.

452. A pharmacy technician receives a prescription with a dosage that appears unusually high. What is the ethical action to take?
a. Fill the prescription as written, trusting the prescriber's judgment.
b. Contact the prescriber to verify the dosage before filling the prescription.
c. Refuse to fill the prescription and suggest the patient go to another pharmacy.
d. Alter the dosage to what the technician believes is a more typical amount.

Answer: b. Contact the prescriber to verify the dosage before filling the prescription. Explanation: The ethical approach involves verifying any unusual or potentially harmful prescription orders with the prescriber to ensure patient safety. Making unauthorized changes or assumptions can lead to serious errors.

453. In a situation where a pharmacy technician faces a conflict of interest due to a close relationship with a patient, what should they do?
a. Proceed with filling the prescription, keeping the relationship confidential.
b. Excuse themselves from handling the prescription and inform their supervisor.
c. Give the patient preferential treatment to ensure faster service.
d. Use their discretion to provide discounts or waivers on pharmacy services.

Answer: b. Excuse themselves from handling the prescription and inform their supervisor. Explanation: Ethical standards require pharmacy staff to avoid conflicts of interest. If a technician's relationship with a patient could influence their professional duties, they should step aside from the transaction and inform a supervisor.

454. When a pharmacy technician encounters a language barrier with a patient, which action aligns with ethical best practices?
a. Use translation software to communicate medication instructions.
b. Attempt to explain the instructions using gestures and pointing.

c. Seek assistance from a bilingual staff member or professional translation service.
d. Provide the medication without instructions, assuming the patient will figure it out.

Answer: c. Seek assistance from a bilingual staff member or professional translation service. Explanation: Ethical practice demands clear communication about medication use. Utilizing bilingual staff or professional services ensures accurate information is conveyed, upholding patient safety and care standards.

455. If a pharmacy technician realizes they have made a dispensing error after the patient has left the pharmacy, what is the ethical response?
a. Wait to see if the patient notices the error and returns.
b. Contact the patient immediately to correct the error and report the incident following pharmacy protocol.
c. Cover up the mistake to avoid personal and pharmacy liability.
d. Report the error to the pharmacist but take no further action unless instructed.

Answer: b. Contact the patient immediately to correct the error and report the incident following pharmacy protocol. Explanation: Ethical responsibility and patient safety require immediate action to rectify dispensing errors. This includes contacting the patient to correct the mistake and reporting the incident internally for documentation and learning purposes.

456. How should a pharmacy technician ethically handle a situation where a patient's insurance denies coverage for a prescribed medication?
a. Inform the patient there is nothing the pharmacy can do.
b. Offer to sell the medication to the patient at cost.
c. Work with the pharmacist to explore alternative solutions, such as contacting the prescriber for a different medication or assisting the patient with insurance issues.
d. Suggest the patient shop around at different pharmacies for better prices.

Answer: c. Work with the pharmacist to explore alternative solutions, such as contacting the prescriber for a different medication or assisting the patient with insurance issues. Explanation: Ethically, pharmacy staff should assist patients in navigating challenges with medication access, including exploring alternatives or helping with insurance matters, ensuring the patient's health needs are met.

457. What is the ethical action for a pharmacy technician if they notice a coworker providing incorrect health advice to a patient?
a. Stay silent to avoid conflict with the coworker.
b. Interrupt the conversation to correct the coworker in front of the patient.
c. Discuss the matter privately with the coworker after the patient leaves.
d. Report the incident to the pharmacist or supervisor for appropriate intervention.

Answer: d. Report the incident to the pharmacist or supervisor for appropriate intervention. Explanation: Ethical practice and patient safety require that incorrect information be corrected. Reporting the incident to a supervisor ensures that the situation is addressed properly and that the patient receives accurate health information.

458. If a pharmacy technician discovers a significant pricing error that is in favor of the pharmacy, what is the ethical course of action?
a. Proceed with the transaction to benefit the pharmacy's revenue.
b. Correct the error immediately, even if it results in lower revenue for the pharmacy.
c. Inform the patient about the error but let them decide what to do.
d. Report the error to management after completing the transaction.

Answer: b. Correct the error immediately, even if it results in lower revenue for the pharmacy. Explanation: Ethical integrity demands that errors, especially those that could unjustly benefit the pharmacy at the expense of the patient, be corrected immediately to ensure fair and honest transactions.

459. Under HIPAA, what information is considered Protected Health Information (PHI)?
a. Any information in a medical record that can be used to identify an individual
b. Only the patient's name and date of birth
c. Medical information that does not include the patient's contact details
d. Prescription details without patient identifiers

Answer: a. Any information in a medical record that can be used to identify an individual. Explanation: Protected Health Information (PHI) under HIPAA includes any information in a medical record or other health-related information that can be used to identify an individual, not limited to, but including diagnoses, treatment information, medical test results, and prescription details.

460. What is the minimum necessary standard as it relates to patient privacy and confidentiality?
a. Disclosing all patient information to anyone involved in healthcare
b. Limiting the sharing of information to the minimum necessary to accomplish the intended purpose
c. Sharing information with the minimum number of people regardless of the need
d. Using patient information only for billing purposes

Answer: b. Limiting the sharing of information to the minimum necessary to accomplish the intended purpose. Explanation: The minimum necessary standard requires healthcare providers and professionals to take reasonable steps to limit the use, disclosure, and requests of PHI to the minimum necessary to accomplish the intended purpose, thereby protecting patient privacy.

461. In which scenario is it appropriate to disclose patient health information without consent?
a. At the request of a family member for curiosity
b. For public health activities, such as reporting a contagious disease to public health authorities
c. To a pharmaceutical company for marketing purposes
d. To friends asking about a patient's condition out of concern

Answer: b. For public health activities, such as reporting a contagious disease to public health authorities. Explanation: HIPAA allows the disclosure of PHI without the patient's consent for specific situations, such as for public health activities, including reporting diseases, injuries, or conditions as required by law to control and prevent disease.

462. What should a pharmacy technician do if they overhear coworkers discussing a patient's health information in a public area of the pharmacy?
a. Join the conversation and provide their opinion
b. Ignore the conversation as it is not their responsibility
c. Report the incident to a supervisor or the privacy officer
d. Share the information with friends or family out of concern

Answer: c. Report the incident to a supervisor or the privacy officer. Explanation: If a pharmacy technician overhears coworkers discussing PHI inappropriately, they should report the incident to a supervisor or the designated privacy officer to address the breach of patient confidentiality and ensure corrective actions are taken.

463. How should electronic PHI (ePHI) be protected in a pharmacy setting to comply with patient privacy regulations?
a. By using a single shared password for all employees
b. By ensuring all electronic devices are left unattended and unlocked
c. Through encryption, secure passwords, and automatic log-off features
d. ePHI does not require any special protection

Answer: c. Through encryption, secure passwords, and automatic log-off features. Explanation: ePHI should be protected using encryption, secure individual passwords, and automatic log-off features to prevent unauthorized access, in compliance with HIPAA Security Rule requirements for safeguarding electronic patient information.

464. What is the role of a pharmacy's privacy officer in maintaining patient confidentiality?
a. To manage the pharmacy's social media accounts
b. To oversee and ensure compliance with privacy laws and regulations
c. To disclose patient information to the public
d. To handle only the technical aspects of data security

Answer: b. To oversee and ensure compliance with privacy laws and regulations. Explanation: A privacy officer in a pharmacy is responsible for developing, implementing, and overseeing policies and procedures that ensure compliance with federal and state privacy laws and regulations, including the protection of patient confidentiality.

465. When is it permissible for a pharmacy technician to access a patient's medication record?
a. Out of personal curiosity about the patient's medications
b. When necessary to perform their job responsibilities

c. To share interesting cases with friends or family
d. Whenever the pharmacy is not busy

Answer: b. When necessary to perform their job responsibilities. Explanation: Pharmacy technicians should only access a patient's medication record or PHI when it is necessary to fulfill their job responsibilities, such as processing a prescription or providing patient care, ensuring adherence to the principle of minimum necessary use of PHI.

466. What should be included in a Notice of Privacy Practices provided to pharmacy patients?
a. A list of all employees in the pharmacy
b. Details about how the pharmacy intends to use and disclose PHI
c. Personal notes from the pharmacy staff
d. Advertising for pharmaceutical products

Answer: b. Details about how the pharmacy intends to use and disclose PHI. Explanation: A Notice of Privacy Practices must include detailed information on how a healthcare entity, including pharmacies, will use and disclose PHI, the patient's rights regarding their health information, and the entity's legal duties concerning that information.

467. How should verbal consent for the use of PHI for treatment, payment, and healthcare operations be documented in a pharmacy?
a. It does not need to be documented
b. Through a written note signed by the patient in every instance
c. By making a log entry or note in the patient's record indicating consent was obtained verbally
d. By recording the conversation

Answer: c. By making a log entry or note in the patient's record indicating consent was obtained verbally. Explanation: While formal written consent may not always be required for uses of PHI related to treatment, payment, and healthcare operations, it's good practice to document that verbal consent was obtained by making a note in the patient's record, ensuring there is a record of the patient's agreement to the use of their information.

468. In what instance might a pharmacy be required to provide an accounting of disclosures of a patient's PHI?
a. Upon request by the patient for disclosures outside of treatment, payment, and healthcare operations
b. Every time the pharmacy dispenses medication
c. Automatically on a monthly basis
d. Only when there is a data breach

Answer: a. Upon request by the patient for disclosures outside of treatment, payment, and healthcare operations. Explanation: Patients have the right to request an accounting of disclosures of their PHI for purposes outside of treatment, payment, and healthcare operations, and the pharmacy must provide this information, typically for the six years prior to the request, excluding certain exceptions.

469. What is the first step a pharmacy technician should take when receiving a new prescription to ensure accurate dispensing?
a. Verify the patient's insurance information
b. Confirm the legibility and completeness of the prescription
c. Select the medication from the shelf
d. Consult with the pharmacist about potential drug interactions

Answer: b. Confirm the legibility and completeness of the prescription. Explanation: The first step in ensuring accurate dispensing is to confirm that the prescription is legible and complete, including the patient's name, medication name, dosage, route, frequency, prescriber's information, and any special instructions. This ensures clarity and accuracy before proceeding with the dispensing process.

470. When using automated dispensing systems, what is a critical check to prevent dispensing errors?
a. Ensuring the machine is located in a well-lit area
b. Regularly updating the software
c. Verifying the barcode of the medication matches the prescription
d. Keeping the machine at a certain temperature

Answer: c. Verifying the barcode of the medication matches the prescription. Explanation: A critical step when using automated dispensing systems is to verify that the barcode of the medication being dispensed matches the prescribed medication's barcode on the prescription. This step ensures that the correct medication is selected by the automated system.

471. In the context of high-alert medications, what additional safety measure is recommended?
a. Dispensing these medications in larger quantities to reduce refill frequency
b. Implementing a mandatory double-check system involving two healthcare professionals
c. Placing high-alert medications in a separate area but within easy reach for efficiency
d. Using distinct packaging colors for each high-alert medication

Answer: b. Implementing a mandatory double-check system involving two healthcare professionals. Explanation: For high-alert medications, an additional safety measure is to implement a mandatory double-check system where two qualified healthcare professionals, such as two pharmacists or a pharmacist and a technician, independently verify the medication, dose, and patient information to minimize the risk of errors.

472. What practice can help in reducing look-alike/sound-alike (LASA) medication errors?
a. Storing LASA medications next to each other for easy comparison
b. Highlighting or "tall man" lettering critical differences in medication names
c. Using abbreviations for medication names to reduce clutter
d. Limiting the availability of LASA medications to decrease selection errors

Answer: b. Highlighting or "tall man" lettering critical differences in medication names. Explanation: To reduce LASA medication errors, the practice of highlighting or using "tall man" lettering to emphasize critical differences in similar-sounding or looking medication names is recommended. This visual cue helps distinguish between similar names, reducing the risk of selection errors.

473. When dispensing a medication that requires patient-specific compounding, what is a key step in ensuring accuracy?
a. Compounding the medication in bulk quantities for efficiency
b. Consulting a reference guide for each individual compounding process
c. Verifying the compounding formula and calculations with a pharmacist
d. Using alternative ingredients if the specified ones are not readily available

Answer: c. Verifying the compounding formula and calculations with a pharmacist. Explanation: For patient-specific compounding, a key step in ensuring accuracy is to verify the compounding formula and any necessary calculations with a pharmacist. This ensures that the compounded medication meets the specific needs and prescription requirements of the patient.

474. How should pharmacy technicians handle verbal prescription orders to minimize errors?
a. Accepting verbal orders for all medication types, including controlled substances
b. Repeating the order back to the prescriber and obtaining confirmation
c. Writing down the verbal order and filing it without confirmation for efficiency
d. Relaying the verbal order directly to the dispensing pharmacist without documentation

Answer: b. Repeating the order back to the prescriber and obtaining confirmation. Explanation: When handling verbal prescription orders, pharmacy technicians should repeat the order back to the prescriber to confirm its accuracy. This read-back process helps ensure that the medication, dose, and patient information are correctly understood and documented.

475. In the event of a dispensing error, what is an appropriate immediate action by the pharmacy technician?
a. Correcting the error silently to avoid drawing attention
b. Informing the supervising pharmacist immediately for proper resolution
c. Discarding any evidence of the error to prevent patient concern
d. Blaming the prescriber to deflect pharmacy responsibility

Answer: b. Informing the supervising pharmacist immediately for proper resolution. Explanation: If a dispensing error occurs, the appropriate immediate action is for the pharmacy technician to inform the supervising pharmacist. This allows for proper assessment, resolution, and, if necessary, patient notification and intervention to correct the error and prevent harm.

476. What strategy helps prevent errors when multiple strengths of the same medication are stocked?
a. Removing less commonly used strengths from the pharmacy inventory
b. Storing different strengths in the same bin for convenience

c. Clearly segregating and labeling shelves or bins for each strength
d. Relying on memory and experience to select the correct strength

Answer: c. Clearly segregating and labeling shelves or bins for each strength. Explanation: To prevent errors when stocking multiple strengths of the same medication, it is recommended to clearly segregate and label shelves or bins designated for each strength. This visual and physical separation helps reduce the risk of selecting the wrong strength during dispensing.

477. For a medication with specific storage requirements (e.g., refrigeration), what practice ensures potency and safety?
a. Storing all doses at room temperature for short periods to simplify dispensing
b. Regularly rotating stock based on expiration dates, regardless of storage conditions
c. Clearly marking and using designated storage areas that meet the required conditions
d. Assuming stability under all conditions if the medication is in a sealed container

Answer: c. Clearly marking and using designated storage areas that meet the required conditions. Explanation: Medications with specific storage requirements, such as refrigeration, must be stored according to manufacturer recommendations to ensure their potency and safety. Clearly marked and appropriately conditioned storage areas, such as refrigerators for temperature-sensitive medications, help maintain stability and efficacy.

478. What is the primary purpose of utilizing aseptic technique in pharmacy compounding?
a. To increase the speed of the compounding process
b. To prevent microbial contamination of compounded sterile preparations (CSPs)
c. To alter the chemical composition of the drugs being compounded
d. To comply with the color-coding system of medications

Answer: b. To prevent microbial contamination of compounded sterile preparations (CSPs). Explanation: Aseptic technique is employed in pharmacy compounding to ensure that compounded sterile preparations are free from microbial contamination, which is crucial for patient safety, particularly for those who are immunocompromised or receiving treatment via routes that bypass natural body defenses, such as intravenous administration.

479. When compounding a sterile product, which of the following actions is NOT recommended as part of aseptic technique?
a. Using sterile gloves and garb
b. Disinfecting the work surface before and after compounding
c. Talking over open sterile containers
d. Using laminar airflow workbenches (LAFWs) or isolators

Answer: c. Talking over open sterile containers. Explanation: Talking over open sterile containers can introduce microbial contaminants from the mouth and respiratory tract into the sterile field, compromising the aseptic environment. Proper aseptic technique involves minimizing any activity that could introduce contaminants, including speaking, coughing, or sneezing over exposed sterile preparations.

480. Which component is essential for personal protective equipment (PPE) when performing aseptic compounding?
a. Jewelry and watches
b. Sterile gloves that have been properly sanitized
c. Loose-fitting clothing for comfort
d. Masks and hair covers

Answer: d. Masks and hair covers. Explanation: Masks and hair covers are crucial components of personal protective equipment (PPE) in aseptic compounding to prevent contamination from particles, skin flakes, and microorganisms that could be shed from the hair and respiratory tract. Sterile gloves are also essential but they must be sterile, not just sanitized, to maintain aseptic conditions.

481. In aseptic compounding, what is the significance of the first air principle?
a. Ensuring that the compounding is completed as quickly as possible
b. Preventing the use of horizontal laminar airflow workbenches
c. Maintaining a direct, unobstructed path of HEPA-filtered air over critical sites
d. Allowing multiple technicians to work in the same laminar flow hood

Answer: c. Maintaining a direct, unobstructed path of HEPA-filtered air over critical sites. Explanation: The first air principle refers to the importance of maintaining a direct, unobstructed flow of HEPA-filtered air to critical sites to prevent contamination. It emphasizes that anything placed between the HEPA filter and the critical site can disrupt the airflow and introduce contaminants, underscoring the need for careful placement of materials and equipment within the laminar flow hood.

482. What is the proper technique for disinfecting a vial's rubber stopper in aseptic compounding?
a. Wiping with a dry cloth
b. Swabbing with 70% isopropyl alcohol and allowing it to air dry
c. Rinsing with sterile water
d. Blowing on it after swabbing to speed up drying

Answer: b. Swabbing with 70% isopropyl alcohol and allowing it to air dry. Explanation: The correct method to disinfect a vial's rubber stopper involves swabbing it with 70% isopropyl alcohol and then allowing it to air dry. This process ensures the removal of contaminants while preventing the introduction of moisture, which could compromise the sterility of the contents.

483. How should ampules be handled during aseptic compounding to maintain sterility?
a. The neck should be flame-sealed after opening
b. The contents should be filtered to remove any glass particles
c. The ampule should be opened away from the laminar flow hood
d. The ampule should be immediately discarded if not used within 5 minutes of opening

Answer: b. The contents should be filtered to remove any glass particles. Explanation: When opening an ampule, it is possible for glass particles to contaminate the solution. Therefore, the contents should be filtered through a sterile filter to remove any potential glass particles, ensuring the safety and sterility of the compounded preparation.

484. In which scenario is it most appropriate to use an ISO Class 5 environment for aseptic compounding?
a. When compounding non-sterile preparations
b. When preparing hazardous drugs that require containment
c. When compounding preparations that require sterility
d. When cleaning the pharmacy at the end of the day

Answer: c. When compounding preparations that require sterility. Explanation: An ISO Class 5 environment, such as a laminar airflow workbench or a compounding isolator, is required for the compounding of sterile preparations to ensure an aseptic environment that meets the necessary air quality standards for sterility.

485. What is the role of a beyond-use date (BUD) in aseptically compounded preparations?
a. To indicate the date when the preparation should be sold by
b. To specify the last date the preparation can be safely used before it is considered at risk for contamination or degradation
c. To mark the date when the preparation was compounded
d. To display the expiration date of the bulk drug powder

Answer: b. To specify the last date the preparation can be safely used before it is considered at risk for contamination or degradation. Explanation: The beyond-use date (BUD) for aseptically compounded preparations indicates the time up to which the preparation is expected to remain stable and sterile, beyond which it should not be used due to potential risks of contamination or degradation.

486. Which practice is crucial to maintaining an aseptic environment when introducing components into a laminar airflow workbench?
a. Pre-warming components to room temperature
b. Spraying components with a disinfectant spray before introduction
c. Performing a double wipe-down of components with sterile 70% isopropyl alcohol
d. Shaking components to remove any dust

Answer: c. Performing a double wipe-down of components with sterile 70% isopropyl alcohol. Explanation: A double wipe-down of components with sterile 70% isopropyl alcohol before introduction into the laminar airflow workbench is essential to remove contaminants from the surfaces of containers and materials, thereby maintaining the sterility of the aseptic environment.

487. What is the recommended action if a critical site is inadvertently touched or contaminated during aseptic compounding?
a. The site should be immediately re-sanitized with 70% isopropyl alcohol
b. Compounding should continue as long as the touch was minimal
c. The contaminated item should be discarded, and the process restarted with new materials
d. The area should be covered with sterile tape to contain any contamination

Answer: c. The contaminated item should be discarded, and the process restarted with new materials. Explanation: If a critical site is touched or contaminated during aseptic compounding, the contaminated item must be discarded, and the process should be restarted with new, sterile materials to ensure the compounded preparation remains sterile and safe for patient use.

488. What is the primary purpose of a cleanroom environment in pharmacy compounding according to USP standards?
a. To facilitate faster compounding processes
b. To provide a comfortable working environment for pharmacy staff
c. To prevent contamination of sterile compounded preparations
d. To store compounded medications for extended periods

Answer: c. To prevent contamination of sterile compounded preparations. Explanation: The primary purpose of a cleanroom environment, as outlined by USP standards, is to maintain a controlled environment that minimizes the risk of contamination in sterile compounded preparations, ensuring their safety and efficacy for patient use.

489. According to USP <797>, which piece of personal protective equipment (PPE) must be donned first before entering the cleanroom?
a. Sterile gloves
b. Gown
c. Shoe covers
d. Hairnet

Answer: c. Shoe covers. Explanation: According to USP <797> guidelines, shoe covers should be donned first to prevent tracking contaminants from the floor into the cleanroom environment. This is part of the proper gowning procedure to maintain the sterility of the compounding area.

490. In USP <800>, what is a critical consideration when handling hazardous drugs in the pharmacy?
a. Ensuring all hazardous drugs are compounded in a positive pressure environment
b. Using appropriate containment strategies and PPE to minimize exposure
c. Compounding hazardous drugs in the same area as non-hazardous drugs to conserve space
d. Disposing of hazardous drug waste with regular pharmacy trash

Answer: b. Using appropriate containment strategies and PPE to minimize exposure. Explanation: USP <800> emphasizes the importance of using containment strategies and personal protective equipment (PPE) to protect personnel from exposure to hazardous drugs, including the use of engineering controls, proper work practices, and appropriate PPE.

491. Which USP chapter provides guidelines for the compounding of nonsterile preparations?
a. USP <795>
b. USP <797>
c. USP <800>
d. USP <825>

Answer: a. USP <795>. Explanation: USP <795> provides guidelines for the compounding of nonsterile preparations, covering aspects such as compounding procedures, facilities, equipment, and components, to ensure the quality and consistency of compounded nonsterile medications.

492. Under USP <797>, how often must personnel demonstrate proficiency in aseptic technique through media fill testing?
a. Annually
b. Semiannually
c. Quarterly
d. Monthly

Answer: b. Semiannually. Explanation: USP <797> requires that personnel involved in the compounding of sterile preparations demonstrate proficiency in aseptic technique through media fill testing at least semiannually (every six months) to ensure ongoing competency and the safety of compounded sterile preparations.

493. What is the role of a laminar airflow workbench (LAFW) in a cleanroom according to USP standards?
a. To provide a comfortable temperature for compounding personnel
b. To reduce the noise level in the compounding area
c. To provide a particulate-free air environment for the preparation of sterile products
d. To store sterile products before dispensing

Answer: c. To provide a particulate-free air environment for the preparation of sterile products. Explanation: A laminar airflow workbench (LAFW) is designed to provide a particulate-free air environment by directing laminar (unidirectional) airflow over the work area, which is crucial for the aseptic preparation of sterile pharmaceutical products, as per USP standards.

494. According to USP <797>, what is the maximum allowable time for a beyond-use date (BUD) for low-risk compounded sterile preparations stored at room temperature?
a. 12 hours
b. 24 hours
c. 48 hours

d. 72 hours

Answer: c. 48 hours. Explanation: For low-risk compounded sterile preparations, USP <797> allows a maximum beyond-use date (BUD) of 48 hours when stored at room temperature, ensuring the sterility and safety of the preparations for patient use within this timeframe.

495. When compounding with hazardous drugs as per USP <800>, what type of engineering control is required for nonsterile compounding?
a. Class I biological safety cabinet (BSC)
b. Compounding aseptic isolator (CAI)
c. Compounding aseptic containment isolator (CACI)
d. Containment ventilated enclosure (CVE)

Answer: d. Containment ventilated enclosure (CVE). Explanation: For nonsterile compounding of hazardous drugs, USP <800> requires the use of a containment ventilated enclosure (CVE) or another appropriate containment strategy to minimize personnel exposure to hazardous drug particles and vapors.

496. In the context of USP standards, what is the significance of the "negative pressure" environment in compounding hazardous drugs?
a. It ensures that air flows into the compounding area to keep it cool.
b. It prevents the escape of hazardous drug particles and vapors into adjacent areas.
c. It allows for faster compounding by reducing air resistance.
d. It increases the efficiency of laminar airflow workbenches.

Answer: b. It prevents the escape of hazardous drug particles and vapors into adjacent areas. Explanation: A "negative pressure" environment is maintained in areas where hazardous drugs are compounded to ensure that air (potentially contaminated with hazardous drug particles and vapors) flows into the compounding area rather than escaping into adjacent areas, protecting personnel and the surrounding environment from exposure.

497. Under USP <797>, what is a requirement for the frequency of cleaning the direct compounding area (DCA)?
a. Before each shift
b. Once a week
c. At least every 12 hours when in use
d. Only after a spill or contamination

Answer: c. At least every 12 hours when in use. Explanation: USP <797> requires that the direct compounding area (DCA), where critical aseptic manipulations occur, be cleaned and disinfected at the beginning of each shift and at least every 12 hours thereafter when in continuous operation, to maintain the sterility and cleanliness of the compounding environment.

498. What is the primary difference in airflow direction between horizontal and vertical laminar airflow hoods?
a. Horizontal hoods direct air towards the operator, while vertical hoods direct air away from the operator.
b. Horizontal hoods direct air away from the operator, while vertical hoods direct air downwards towards the work surface.
c. Horizontal hoods recycle air within the hood, while vertical hoods expel air out of the hood.
d. Horizontal hoods use natural convection, while vertical hoods use forced air.

Answer: b. Horizontal hoods direct air away from the operator, while vertical hoods direct air downwards towards the work surface. Explanation: In horizontal laminar airflow hoods, the air flows horizontally from the back of the hood towards the operator, ensuring a clean work area by sweeping particles away from the sterile field. In contrast, vertical laminar airflow hoods direct the air vertically downwards from a filter positioned above the work surface, minimizing the risk of contamination from the operator into the sterile field.

499. For which type of preparation would a vertical laminar airflow hood be preferred over a horizontal hood?
a. Non-hazardous sterile preparations
b. Preparations that require minimal protection from contamination
c. Hazardous drug compounding, such as chemotherapy agents
d. Simple reconstitutions of antibiotics

Answer: c. Hazardous drug compounding, such as chemotherapy agents. Explanation: Vertical laminar airflow hoods are preferred for compounding hazardous drugs, such as chemotherapy agents, because the vertical airflow directs harmful particles and vapors away from the operator, providing an additional level of safety compared to horizontal hoods where the airflow is directed towards the operator.

500. What is a critical practice when working in a horizontal laminar airflow hood to maintain sterility?
a. Placing all materials directly under the HEPA filter
b. Frequently opening and closing the hood's sash
c. Organizing work from clean to dirty areas within the hood
d. Working at least 6 inches inside the hood from the front edge

Answer: d. Working at least 6 inches inside the hood from the front edge. Explanation: To maintain sterility in a horizontal laminar airflow hood, it is crucial to work at least 6 inches inside the hood from the front edge. This practice ensures that the work is performed within the area of unobstructed first air, minimizing the risk of introducing contaminants from the room environment.

501. How does the placement of items in a laminar airflow hood impact airflow and sterility?
a. Items should be evenly distributed to allow for uniform airflow.
b. Large items placed in the hood can disrupt airflow and create turbulence.
c. All items should be placed as close to the HEPA filter as possible.
d. Airflow is not significantly impacted by the placement of items in the hood.

Answer: b. Large items placed in the hood can disrupt airflow and create turbulence. Explanation: The placement of large items in a laminar airflow hood can disrupt the laminar flow of air, creating turbulence that can potentially introduce contaminants into the sterile field. It's important to strategically place items in the hood to maintain unidirectional airflow and ensure the sterility of preparations.

502. What maintenance procedure is essential for ensuring the effectiveness of laminar airflow hoods?
a. Daily washing of the interior with soap and water
b. Regular replacement of the UV light bulb
c. Certification and HEPA filter integrity testing at specified intervals
d. Continuous operation to prevent particle buildup

Answer: c. Certification and HEPA filter integrity testing at specified intervals. Explanation: Regular certification, which includes HEPA filter integrity testing, airflow velocity measurements, and overall operational checks at specified intervals (typically every six months), is essential to ensure the hood is functioning correctly and maintaining a sterile environment for compounding activities.

503. In a laminar airflow hood, what is the purpose of the HEPA filter?
a. To remove odors and gases from the air
b. To recirculate cooled air within the hood
c. To remove particles and microorganisms from the air to provide a sterile working environment
d. To add humidity to the air to prevent product desiccation

Answer: c. To remove particles and microorganisms from the air to provide a sterile working environment. Explanation: The HEPA (High-Efficiency Particulate Air) filter in a laminar airflow hood is designed to remove 99.97% of particles and microorganisms 0.3 microns or larger from the air, providing a sterile environment for the preparation of sterile products.

504. What is the significance of the "first air" concept in aseptic compounding within laminar airflow hoods?
a. It refers to the initial air that enters the hood after it is turned on.
b. It is the air that first comes into contact with materials in the hood, free from contaminants.
c. It is a special type of air used only in the first few minutes of compounding.
d. It describes the coolest air layer at the bottom of the hood.

Answer: b. It is the air that first comes into contact with materials in the hood, free from contaminants. Explanation: "First air" is the term used to describe the HEPA-filtered air that directly flows over and contacts the materials and critical sites within the hood without any obstruction. This air is free from contaminants and essential for maintaining sterility during the compounding process.

505. When using a vertical laminar airflow hood, what precaution should be taken to protect the operator from exposure to hazardous drugs?
a. Compounding should be done as quickly as possible.
b. Operators should work closer to the hood's sash.

c. The use of personal protective equipment (PPE) and proper containment techniques should be employed.
d. All work should be performed at the back of the hood, farthest from the sash.

Answer: c. The use of personal protective equipment (PPE) and proper containment techniques should be employed. Explanation: When compounding hazardous drugs in a vertical laminar airflow hood, it's crucial to use appropriate personal protective equipment (PPE) and containment techniques to protect the operator from exposure. These might include gloves, gowns, and respiratory protection, depending on the level of risk associated with the specific drugs being handled.

506. How should spills be managed within a laminar airflow hood?
a. By immediately stopping work and evacuating the area
b. By covering the spill with paper towels and continuing work
c. By cleaning the spill from the back of the hood towards the front using a disinfectant
d. By reporting the spill to the facility's environmental services department

Answer: c. By cleaning the spill from the back of the hood towards the front using a disinfectant. Explanation: In the event of a spill within a laminar airflow hood, the spill should be cleaned promptly using an appropriate disinfectant, starting from the back of the hood and moving towards the front. This method helps contain the spill and prevent the spread of contamination while maintaining the integrity of the sterile field.

507. What is a common practice to prevent cross-contamination when using a horizontal laminar airflow hood?
a. Placing a physical barrier between different compounds
b. Using the same set of tools for all compounds to maintain workflow consistency
c. Compounding different products simultaneously to maximize efficiency
d. Frequently turning the hood on and off to save energy

Answer: a. Placing a physical barrier between different compounds. Explanation: To prevent cross-contamination in a horizontal laminar airflow hood, a physical barrier may be used between different compounds being prepared. This practice helps to maintain separation and ensures that the laminar flow of air is not disrupted, preserving the sterility of each preparation.

508. What is the recommended duration for handwashing with soap and water according to USP <797> guidelines before entering a cleanroom environment?
a. At least 10 seconds
b. At least 30 seconds
c. At least 1 minute
d. At least 2 minutes

Answer: b. At least 30 seconds. Explanation: USP <797> guidelines recommend washing hands with soap and water for at least 30 seconds as part of proper hand hygiene before garbing and entering a cleanroom environment to ensure the removal of dirt, debris, and transient microorganisms, reducing the risk of contamination in sterile compounding areas.

509. In what order should garbing components be donned according to aseptic technique principles?
a. Gown, shoe covers, hairnet, mask, gloves
b. Shoe covers, hairnet, gown, mask, gloves
c. Hairnet, shoe covers, gown, gloves, mask
d. Mask, gown, shoe covers, hairnet, gloves

Answer: b. Shoe covers, hairnet, gown, mask, gloves. Explanation: The proper sequence for donning garbing components typically starts with shoe covers to minimize contamination from the floor, followed by a hairnet to secure all hair, then a gown, mask to cover the mouth and nose, and finally gloves, ensuring that hands are covered last after touching other garbing components.

510. How often should gloves be sanitized during compounding activities in a cleanroom?
a. Every 10 minutes
b. Every 30 minutes
c. Whenever they become contaminated
d. Only before starting compounding

Answer: c. Whenever they become contaminated. Explanation: Gloves should be sanitized whenever they become contaminated, and also periodically throughout the compounding process, especially when transitioning between different compounding activities. This ensures the maintenance of aseptic conditions and minimizes the risk of contaminating sterile preparations.

511. What is the significance of wearing a gown in the cleanroom?
a. To protect the wearer's clothing from damage
b. To maintain a comfortable working temperature
c. To provide a barrier that minimizes microbial and particulate contamination
d. To comply with fashion standards in a professional setting

Answer: c. To provide a barrier that minimizes microbial and particulate contamination. Explanation: Wearing a gown in the cleanroom serves as a critical barrier that minimizes the introduction of microbial and particulate contamination into the sterile environment, thereby protecting the integrity of compounded sterile preparations.

512. When is the use of waterless alcohol-based hand sanitizers acceptable in place of traditional handwashing with soap and water?
a. When the hands are visibly soiled
b. As a routine practice before garbing
c. After donning sterile gloves
d. When entering the anteroom from the general pharmacy area

Answer: d. When entering the anteroom from the general pharmacy area. Explanation: Waterless alcohol-based hand sanitizers may be used when entering the anteroom from the general pharmacy area if the hands are not visibly soiled. However, traditional handwashing with soap and water is required before initially donning sterile gloves for compounding activities.

513. What is the appropriate action if a tear is discovered in a glove during compounding activities?
a. Continue compounding until a convenient stopping point is reached
b. Tape the tear and proceed with the compounding process
c. Immediately stop compounding, replace the torn glove, and sanitize the new glove
d. Wash the torn glove with soap and water before continuing

Answer: c. Immediately stop compounding, replace the torn glove, and sanitize the new glove. Explanation: If a tear is discovered in a glove during compounding, the appropriate action is to immediately stop compounding, remove the torn glove, replace it with a new one, and sanitize the new glove before resuming compounding activities to maintain sterility.

514. Under what circumstances should a face mask be replaced in a cleanroom setting?
a. After each compounding activity
b. Every 4 hours during continuous use
c. When it becomes wet or visibly contaminated
d. Only at the end of the workday

Answer: c. When it becomes wet or visibly contaminated. Explanation: A face mask should be replaced if it becomes wet, visibly contaminated, or compromised in any way to ensure that microbial contamination risk is minimized and that the cleanroom environment remains controlled.

515. What is the purpose of shoe covers in the cleanroom garbing process?
a. To prevent slips and falls on the cleanroom floor
b. To provide personal comfort for the staff working long hours
c. To minimize the introduction of particulate and microbial contamination from the floor
d. To indicate different staff roles within the cleanroom based on color

Answer: c. To minimize the introduction of particulate and microbial contamination from the floor. Explanation: Shoe covers are used in the cleanroom garbing process to minimize the introduction of particulate and microbial contamination from the floor into the cleanroom environment, thereby protecting the sterility of the compounded preparations.

516. What is the best practice for handling sterile gowning components when garbing for entry into the cleanroom?
a. Gowning components should be pre-placed inside the cleanroom for convenience
b. Gowning components should be donned outside the anteroom to save space

c. Sterile gowning components should be donned in the anteroom to maintain their sterility
d. Gowning components can be reused if they appear clean and intact

Answer: c. Sterile gowning components should be donned in the anteroom to maintain their sterility. Explanation: Sterile gowning components should be donned in the anteroom, a controlled environment that precedes the cleanroom, to maintain their sterility before entering the cleanroom. This practice ensures that the components remain free from contamination, thereby protecting the aseptic compounding environment.

517. After completing compounding activities, in what order should garbing components be removed?
a. Gloves, gown, mask, hairnet, shoe covers
b. Shoe covers, hairnet, gown, mask, gloves
c. Gloves, shoe covers, gown, hairnet, mask
d. Gown, gloves, mask, shoe covers, hairnet

Answer: a. Gloves, gown, mask, hairnet, shoe covers. Explanation: The recommended order for removing garbing components after compounding activities is to first remove gloves, as they are considered the most contaminated, followed by the gown, mask, hairnet, and finally shoe covers. This sequence minimizes the risk of contaminating the wearer and the surrounding environment.

518. What is the recommended frequency for cleaning a laminar airflow workbench (LAFW) in a pharmacy compounding area?
a. Before each compounding session
b. Once at the end of each day
c. Weekly during general pharmacy cleaning
d. Monthly during scheduled maintenance

Answer: a. Before each compounding session. Explanation: Cleaning a laminar airflow workbench (LAFW) before each compounding session is crucial to maintain a sterile environment and prevent contamination. This practice ensures that any particles or microbes introduced since the last cleaning are removed, providing a safe area for compounding sterile preparations.

519. Which disinfectant is most commonly used for cleaning surfaces in the pharmacy compounding area?
a. Bleach solution
b. Ammonia-based cleaners
c. 70% isopropyl alcohol
d. Vinegar and water solution

Answer: c. 70% isopropyl alcohol. Explanation: 70% isopropyl alcohol is widely used for cleaning surfaces in the pharmacy compounding area due to its effectiveness in disinfecting and its rapid evaporation, which leaves minimal residue. It is particularly effective against bacteria and viruses and is suitable for maintaining the sterility of the compounding environment.

520. After a spill of a hazardous drug occurs in the compounding area, what is the first step in the cleaning process?
a. Wipe the area with a dry cloth
b. Apply a bleach solution directly to the spill
c. Don personal protective equipment (PPE)
d. Mop the area with water

Answer: c. Don personal protective equipment (PPE). Explanation: The first step in responding to a spill of a hazardous drug is to don appropriate personal protective equipment (PPE) to protect oneself from exposure to the hazardous substance. PPE may include gloves, gowns, eye protection, and respiratory protection, depending on the nature and severity of the spill.

521. For cleaning a non-laminar airflow workbench, what is the recommended direction for wiping surfaces?
a. From the dirtiest area to the cleanest
b. In a circular motion starting from the center
c. From the cleanest area to the dirtiest
d. From back to front and top to bottom

Answer: d. From back to front and top to bottom. Explanation: When cleaning a non-laminar airflow workbench, it is recommended to wipe surfaces from back to front and top to bottom. This method ensures that any particles or contaminants are moved away from the work area and towards areas less critical for sterility, reducing the risk of contaminating the compounding area.

522. What is the purpose of using a sporicidal agent in the cleaning protocol of a pharmacy compounding area?
a. To enhance the shine of stainless steel surfaces
b. To remove stains and residues from compounding mats
c. To kill bacterial spores that are resistant to standard disinfectants
d. To clean glassware and utensils used in compounding

Answer: c. To kill bacterial spores that are resistant to standard disinfectants. Explanation: A sporicidal agent is used in the cleaning protocol of a pharmacy compounding area specifically to kill bacterial spores, which are more resistant to standard disinfectants than other forms of bacteria. The use of a sporicidal agent ensures a higher level of sterility, particularly important in environments where sterile compounding takes place.

523. How should cleaning solutions be applied to surfaces in the compounding area to avoid contamination?
a. Sprayed directly onto the surfaces
b. Poured liberally over the surfaces
c. Applied using a soaked sponge or mop
d. Sprayed onto a cleaning cloth and then applied to the surfaces

Answer: d. Sprayed onto a cleaning cloth and then applied to the surfaces. Explanation: Cleaning solutions should be sprayed onto a cleaning cloth or wipe, rather than directly onto surfaces, to avoid generating aerosols that could contaminate sterile areas or products. This method allows for more controlled application of the disinfectant and minimizes the risk of spreading contaminants.

524. What is an appropriate action to take with cleaning cloths used in the aseptic compounding area after use?
a. Reuse for cleaning general pharmacy areas
b. Dispose of as regular trash
c. Launder for reuse in the compounding area
d. Dispose of as biohazardous waste

Answer: d. Dispose of as biohazardous waste. Explanation: Cleaning cloths used in the aseptic compounding area should be disposed of as biohazardous waste, given the potential for them to be contaminated with hazardous drugs, microbes, or other harmful substances. Proper disposal reduces the risk of cross-contamination and ensures compliance with safety protocols.

525. In the event of a significant contamination event in the compounding area, what is a critical next step after initial cleaning and disinfection?
a. Immediate resumption of compounding activities
b. Assessment and certification by an environmental safety officer
c. A brief airing out of the compounding area
d. Application of a fragrant air freshener

Answer: b. Assessment and certification by an environmental safety officer. Explanation: After a significant contamination event in the compounding area, an assessment and certification by an environmental safety officer or other qualified individual are critical to ensure that the area is safe and meets the required standards for sterility and cleanliness before resuming compounding activities.

526. When selecting disinfectants for use in the pharmacy compounding area, what factor must be considered to ensure compatibility with the materials commonly found in the area?
a. The color of the disinfectant
b. The fragrance of the disinfectant
c. The material compatibility, such as with plastics and stainless steel
d. The viscosity of the disinfectant

Answer: c. The material compatibility, such as with plastics and stainless steel. Explanation: When selecting disinfectants for use in the pharmacy compounding area, it is essential to consider the compatibility of the disinfectant with materials commonly found in the area, such as plastics, stainless steel, and other surfaces. This consideration ensures that the disinfectant will not damage equipment or surfaces and maintains the integrity of the compounding environment.

527. When preparing an ointment using the levigation method, which of the following is used as a levigating agent?

a. Purified water
b. Mineral oil
c. Ethanol
d. Glycerin

Answer: b. Mineral oil. Explanation: In the levigation method for preparing ointments, a levigating agent like mineral oil is commonly used to help reduce the particle size of solids, making them smoother and easier to incorporate into the ointment base. Mineral oil is particularly useful for hydrophobic powders.

528. For a compounded capsule, what factor is crucial in ensuring uniformity of dosage units?
a. The color of the capsule shells
b. The geometric dilution technique
c. The use of a high-speed mixer
d. The capsule size number

Answer: b. The geometric dilution technique. Explanation: The geometric dilution technique is critical in ensuring uniformity of dosage units when compounding capsules. This method involves thoroughly mixing a small quantity of the active drug with an equal amount of diluent and then sequentially adding more diluent in equal amounts until homogeneity is achieved.

529. When compounding a suspension, why is it important to consider the particle size of the suspended drug?
a. Larger particles enhance the taste of the suspension.
b. Smaller particles tend to dissolve completely, making the suspension unstable.
c. Larger particles settle more quickly, affecting the uniformity of the dose.
d. Smaller particles increase the viscosity of the suspension significantly.

Answer: c. Larger particles settle more quickly, affecting the uniformity of the dose. Explanation: In a suspension, the particle size of the suspended drug is crucial because larger particles tend to settle more quickly due to gravity, which can affect the uniformity of the dose. Smaller particles remain suspended longer, contributing to a more uniform and stable suspension.

530. What is the primary purpose of using a mortar and pestle in non-sterile compounding?
a. To measure liquid volumes accurately
b. To mix ingredients of different densities uniformly
c. To reduce particle size and achieve finer powder
d. To heat substances for better solubility

Answer: c. To reduce particle size and achieve finer powder. Explanation: The primary purpose of using a mortar and pestle in non-sterile compounding is to triturate solids, reducing particle size to achieve a finer powder. This is essential for improving the uniformity of the mix and ensuring a consistent dosage in the final compounded product.

531. In non-sterile compounding, what is the significance of the "Beyond Use Date" (BUD)?
a. It indicates the date by which the manufacturer guarantees the potency of the drug.
b. It is the expiration date of the raw materials used in the compound.
c. It represents the date after which the compounded preparation should not be used.
d. It is the same as the expiration date found on commercially available products.

Answer: c. It represents the date after which the compounded preparation should not be used. Explanation: The Beyond Use Date (BUD) in non-sterile compounding is determined based on the stability of the compounded preparation and represents the date after which the preparation is no longer considered safe or effective to use. It is not the same as the manufacturer's expiration date but is determined by the compounding pharmacist based on various factors, including the nature of the drug and compounding process.

532. When compounding a cream, what is the purpose of incorporating a preservative into the formulation?
a. To increase the viscosity of the cream
b. To enhance the therapeutic effect of the active ingredient
c. To prevent microbial growth during the cream's shelf life
d. To improve the cream's fragrance

Answer: c. To prevent microbial growth during the cream's shelf life. Explanation: The purpose of incorporating a preservative into a cream formulation during non-sterile compounding is to prevent microbial growth, which can contaminate the product and potentially harm the user. Preservatives ensure the safety and stability of the cream throughout its intended shelf life.

533. In the process of compounding a non-sterile oral solution, what is the role of a suspending agent?
a. To dissolve hydrophobic substances
b. To thicken the solution and stabilize suspended particles
c. To act as a sweetener to improve taste
d. To serve as a coloring agent for aesthetic purposes

Answer: b. To thicken the solution and stabilize suspended particles. Explanation: A suspending agent in a non-sterile oral solution serves to thicken the solution and stabilize suspended particles, preventing them from settling quickly. This ensures a uniform distribution of particles in each dose and maintains the physical stability of the suspension.

534. When compounding a dermatological gel, why is it important to consider the pH of the final product?
a. The pH can influence the gel's color and opacity.
b. The pH affects the solubility and stability of active ingredients and can impact skin irritation.
c. The pH determines the gel's viscosity.
d. The pH is crucial for the gel's fragrance stability.

Answer: b. The pH affects the solubility and stability of active ingredients and can impact skin irritation. Explanation: When compounding a dermatological gel, the pH of the final product is crucial because it can significantly affect the solubility and stability of active ingredients. Additionally, an inappropriate pH level can lead to skin irritation or discomfort upon application, making it an essential factor to consider for patient safety and product efficacy.

535. What technique is recommended when mixing two powders of unequal quantities in non-sterile compounding?
a. Trituration
b. Levigation
c. Geometric dilution
d. Pulverization by intervention

Answer: c. Geometric dilution. Explanation: Geometric dilution is the recommended technique when mixing two powders of unequal quantities in non-sterile compounding. It involves adding the smaller quantity of powder to an equal amount of the larger quantity and mixing thoroughly before progressively adding the remaining larger quantity in equal parts. This ensures a uniform distribution of the smaller quantity throughout the mixture.

536. What is the primary difference between an ointment and a cream in terms of their base composition?
a. Ointments are primarily water-based, while creams are oil-based.
b. Ointments are primarily oil-based, providing a more occlusive effect, while creams are a mix of oil and water, making them less occlusive.
c. Creams are used for internal purposes, while ointments are used externally.
d. Ointments contain alcohol, while creams do not.

Answer: b. Ointments are primarily oil-based, providing a more occlusive effect, while creams are a mix of oil and water, making them less occlusive. Explanation: Ointments are oil-based and provide a barrier that enhances medication absorption through the skin by providing an occlusive effect. Creams, being a mix of oil and water, are less occlusive, more absorbent, and easier to spread on the skin, making them suitable for moist or weeping areas.

537. Which type of formulation is typically preferred for delivering medication to a dry, scaly skin condition?
a. Gel
b. Lotion
c. Ointment
d. Solution

Answer: c. Ointment. Explanation: Ointments, due to their oil-based formulation, are preferred for treating dry, scaly skin conditions as they help to moisturize and provide a barrier to the affected area, promoting healing and medication absorption.

538. For a patient with an oozing dermatological condition, which formulation would be most appropriate?
a. Cream
b. Ointment
c. Paste

d. Powder

Answer: a. Cream. Explanation: Creams, being less occlusive and more absorbent than ointments due to their water content, are more suitable for oozing skin conditions as they allow the skin to breathe and do not trap moisture over the lesion, which could potentially worsen the condition.

539. What is the key advantage of using a solution formulation for a medication applied to the scalp?
a. Increased occlusivity
b. Easier application and spreadability over hair-covered areas
c. Thicker consistency for targeted application
d. Longer duration of action

Answer: b. Easier application and spreadability over hair-covered areas. Explanation: Solution formulations are liquid and therefore can be easily applied and spread over hair-covered areas like the scalp, making them ideal for treating conditions in these regions without the messiness or difficulty in application associated with thicker formulations like ointments or creams.

540. In compounding a suspension, what is the primary purpose of incorporating a suspending agent?
a. To dissolve the active ingredient completely
b. To enhance the flavor of the formulation
c. To maintain the uniform dispersion of insoluble solids within the liquid
d. To increase the absorption of the medication through the skin

Answer: c. To maintain the uniform dispersion of insoluble solids within the liquid. Explanation: Suspending agents are used in suspension formulations to keep insoluble solid particles uniformly dispersed throughout the liquid carrier. This prevents the particles from settling at the bottom, ensuring consistent dosing with each administration.

541. What is the main reason for prescribing a medicated gel for acne treatment?
a. To provide an occlusive layer over the skin
b. To deliver medication in a cooling and drying base suitable for oily skin
c. To cover large areas of the body easily
d. To create a protective barrier against UV radiation

Answer: b. To deliver medication in a cooling and drying base suitable for oily skin. Explanation: Medicated gels are often used for acne treatment as they are water-based, which provides a cooling effect, and they dry quickly, making them suitable for the oily skin commonly associated with acne. Gels can deliver medication effectively without adding extra oil to the skin.

542. When would a pharmacist choose to compound a medication into a paste rather than a cream?
a. When a cooling effect on the skin is desired

b. For deeper penetration of the medication into the skin
c. For a protective barrier effect on weeping or inflamed skin areas
d. For easier application over large surface areas

Answer: c. For a protective barrier effect on weeping or inflamed skin areas. Explanation: Pastes are thicker than creams and ointments and contain a higher concentration of solid particles, making them ideal for providing a protective barrier on the skin. They are particularly useful for weeping or inflamed areas as they adhere well to the skin and absorb moisture, promoting healing.

543. In what situation is a transdermal patch an advantageous formulation for medication delivery?
a. When rapid onset of action is required
b. For localized treatment of skin conditions
c. For sustained release of medication over an extended period
d. When high concentrations of medication are needed at the site of application

Answer: c. For sustained release of medication over an extended period. Explanation: Transdermal patches are designed to deliver medication through the skin and into the bloodstream over an extended period, providing sustained therapeutic levels with minimal peaks and troughs. This is particularly advantageous for chronic conditions requiring consistent medication levels.

544. What distinguishes a lotion from a cream in terms of application and use?
a. Lotions are oil-free, whereas creams contain oil
b. Lotions are thicker and more suitable for very dry skin
c. Lotions are more liquid and easier to apply over larger areas of the body
d. Lotions require refrigeration to maintain stability

Answer: c. Lotions are more liquid and easier to apply over larger areas of the body. Explanation: Lotions have a higher water content compared to creams, making them more liquid. This property makes lotions easier to spread and more suitable for application over large areas of the body, especially when a lighter moisturizing effect is desired.

545. Why might a healthcare provider prescribe a medicated shampoo formulation for a scalp condition?
a. To provide a protective coating on the scalp
b. To facilitate the removal of scales and crusts while delivering medication
c. For the sustained release of medication over several days
d. To create a barrier against external irritants

Answer: b. To facilitate the removal of scales and crusts while delivering medication. Explanation: Medicated shampoos are formulated to treat scalp conditions by facilitating the removal of scales and crusts associated with conditions like psoriasis or seborrheic dermatitis. They deliver therapeutic agents directly to the scalp, often with ingredients that help soothe inflammation and treat the underlying condition.

546. To prepare a 1:20 dilution of a solution, how much stock solution and diluent are needed to make 200 mL of the final dilution?
a. 10 mL stock solution and 190 mL diluent
b. 20 mL stock solution and 180 mL diluent
c. 50 mL stock solution and 150 mL diluent
d. 100 mL stock solution and 100 mL diluent

Answer: a. 10 mL stock solution and 190 mL diluent. Explanation: A 1:20 dilution means 1 part of stock solution to 20 parts of the final solution. For 200 mL of final solution, divide 200 mL by the sum of the parts in the ratio (1+20=21) to find the volume per part, which is approximately 9.52 mL, rounded to 10 mL for simplicity. Thus, 10 mL of stock solution and 190 mL of diluent (200 mL - 10 mL) are needed.

547. If a cream is prescribed with a 2% w/w strength, how much active ingredient is needed to prepare 100g of this cream?
a. 2 g
b. 20 g
c. 0.2 g
d. 200 g

Answer: a. 2 g. Explanation: A 2% w/w (weight/weight) concentration means that there are 2 grams of active ingredient for every 100 grams of the final product. Therefore, to prepare 100g of a 2% w/w cream, 2 grams of the active ingredient are needed.

548. To make a 1:5 dilution of a 10 mL solution, how much diluent should be added?
a. 2 mL
b. 40 mL
c. 50 mL
d. 8 mL

Answer: b. 40 mL. Explanation: A 1:5 dilution means 1 part of the solution to 4 parts diluent (since the total is 5 parts and 1 part is already the solution). If the solution is 10 mL, you need 4 times that amount in diluent, which is 40 mL.

549. What is the percent strength of a solution that contains 5g of solute in 250 mL of solution?
a. 2%
b. 5%
c. 20%
d. 0.5%

Answer: a. 2%. Explanation: Percent strength is calculated as (weight of solute/volume of solution) x 100. Thus, (5g/250mL) x 100 = 2%.

550. How much water must be added to 15 mL of a 50% solution to dilute it to a 10% solution?
a. 60 mL
b. 45 mL
c. 75 mL
d. 30 mL

Answer: a. 60 mL. Explanation: Using the dilution equation C1V1 = C2V2, where C1 is the initial concentration (50%), V1 is the initial volume (15 mL), C2 is the final concentration (10%), and V2 is the final volume, we can solve for V2 and then subtract V1 to find the amount of water to add. (0.50)(15 mL) = (0.10)V2, V2 = 75 mL. Thus, 75 mL - 15 mL = 60 mL of water must be added.

551. A pharmacist needs to prepare 250 mL of a 20% (v/v) alcohol solution. How much pure alcohol and how much water are needed?
a. 50 mL alcohol and 200 mL water
b. 100 mL alcohol and 150 mL water
c. 200 mL alcohol and 50 mL water
d. 20 mL alcohol and 230 mL water

Answer: a. 50 mL alcohol and 200 mL water. Explanation: A 20% v/v solution means 20 mL of solute in every 100 mL of solution. For 250 mL of a 20% solution, (20/100) x 250 = 50 mL of alcohol is needed, and the rest is water, so 250 mL - 50 mL = 200 mL of water.

552. To adjust a 1 L saline solution from 0.9% w/v to 0.45% w/v, how much water should be added?
a. 1 L
b. 500 mL
c. 250 mL
d. 2 L

Answer: a. 1 L. Explanation: To halve the concentration from 0.9% w/v to 0.45% w/v, you need to double the total volume while keeping the amount of solute constant. Therefore, adding 1 L of water to the existing 1 L solution will achieve the desired 0.45% w/v concentration.

553. If a prescription requires 200 mg of a drug to be dispensed, and the stock solution contains 50 mg/mL, how many mL of the stock solution is needed?
a. 4 mL
b. 10 mL
c. 2 mL
d. 5 mL

Answer: a. 4 mL. Explanation: To find out how many mL are needed to obtain 200 mg from a 50 mg/mL solution, divide the required dose by the concentration: 200 mg / 50 mg/mL = 4 mL.

554. A 3% hydrogen peroxide solution needs to be diluted to a 1% solution. If you start with 100 mL of the 3% solution, how much water do you need to add?
a. 100 mL
b. 200 mL
c. 300 mL
d. 50 mL

Answer: b. 200 mL. Explanation: To dilute a 3% solution to a 1% solution, you need to triple the volume while keeping the amount of solute constant. Therefore, adding 200 mL of water to the existing 100 mL of 3% solution will give you 300 mL of a 1% solution.

555. When compounding a medication, if the formula calls for a 25% concentration of a drug and you need to prepare 200 g of the final product, how much of the drug is needed?
a. 50 g
b. 25 g
c. 75 g
d. 100 g

Answer: a. 50 g. Explanation: A 25% concentration means that 25% of the weight of the final product should be the drug. Therefore, for 200 g of the final product, (25/100) x 200 = 50 g of the drug is needed.

556. What primary factor influences the Beyond Use Date (BUD) of a non-sterile compounded preparation?
a. The expiration date of the bulk drug substance
b. The color of the final preparation
c. The flavoring agents used in the preparation
d. The container in which the final preparation is stored

Answer: a. The expiration date of the bulk drug substance. Explanation: The BUD of a non-sterile compounded preparation is significantly influenced by the expiration date of the bulk drug substance used. The BUD cannot exceed the expiration date of any individual component or the maximum allowable BUD based on the type of preparation and storage conditions, as per USP guidelines.

557. For a compounded sterile intravenous (IV) solution stored at room temperature, what is the typical BUD according to USP <797> standards?
a. 24 hours
b. 48 hours
c. 30 days
d. 6 hours

Answer: a. 24 hours. Explanation: According to USP <797> standards, a compounded sterile intravenous (IV) solution stored at room temperature typically has a BUD of 24 hours. This BUD is established to minimize the risk of microbial growth and ensure the safety and efficacy of the sterile preparation.

558. When determining the BUD for a water-containing oral formulation, what is the maximum BUD recommended by USP guidelines?
a. 14 days when refrigerated
b. 30 days when refrigerated
c. 90 days at room temperature
d. 1 year when frozen

Answer: a. 14 days when refrigerated. Explanation: For water-containing oral formulations, USP guidelines recommend a maximum BUD of 14 days when stored in a refrigerator. This limitation is due to the potential for microbial growth in aqueous environments, which can compromise the safety of the preparation.

559. In the absence of stability data, what BUD should be assigned to an ointment compounded in a water-free base?
a. 30 days
b. 6 months
c. 1 year
d. 3 days

Answer: b. 6 months. Explanation: In the absence of specific stability data, an ointment compounded in a water-free base can generally be assigned a BUD of up to 6 months, assuming it is stored under appropriate conditions. The absence of water reduces the risk of microbial growth, allowing for a longer BUD than aqueous formulations.

560. How does the complexity of a compounded preparation affect its BUD?
a. More complex preparations have a longer BUD due to increased stability.
b. Complexity does not affect BUD; only storage conditions matter.
c. More complex preparations may have a shorter BUD due to potential for incompatibilities and degradation.
d. All compounded preparations, regardless of complexity, have the same BUD.

Answer: c. More complex preparations may have a shorter BUD due to potential for incompatibilities and degradation. Explanation: The complexity of a compounded preparation can affect its BUD, with more complex mixtures potentially having a shorter BUD due to increased risks of chemical incompatibilities and degradation pathways. Each component and their interactions must be considered in determining an appropriate BUD.

561. What is the role of a stability-indicating assay in determining the BUD of a compounded preparation?
a. It determines the flavor stability of the preparation.
b. It identifies the physical appearance changes over time.
c. It detects the presence of preservatives in the preparation.

d. It quantitatively measures the degradation of the active ingredient over time.

Answer: d. It quantitatively measures the degradation of the active ingredient over time. Explanation: A stability-indicating assay is a quantitative analytical method that specifically measures the degradation of the active ingredient over time, under various storage conditions. This information is crucial for accurately determining the BUD of a compounded preparation, ensuring its safety and efficacy throughout its intended use period.

562. How should the BUD of a compounded preparation be affected if stored under less than optimal conditions?
a. The BUD should be extended to account for accelerated stability testing.
b. The BUD remains unchanged, as it is determined at the time of compounding.
c. The BUD should be shortened to reflect the potential for increased degradation.
d. Storage conditions do not influence the BUD of a compounded preparation.

Answer: c. The BUD should be shortened to reflect the potential for increased degradation. Explanation: If a compounded preparation is stored under less than optimal conditions (e.g., higher temperatures, exposure to light), the BUD should be shortened to account for the potential for increased degradation or loss of potency. Proper storage conditions are critical to maintaining the stability and effectiveness of compounded medications.

563. In what scenario might a pharmacist need to consult with the prescriber to determine an appropriate BUD for a compounded medication?
a. When the medication is intended for use in a clinical trial
b. When the medication contains a particularly unstable active ingredient
c. When the medication is compounded in a novel dosage form
d. All of the above

Answer: d. All of the above. Explanation: A pharmacist may need to consult with the prescriber to determine an appropriate BUD in various scenarios, including when the medication is intended for a clinical trial, contains an unstable active ingredient, or is compounded in a novel dosage form. Collaboration between the pharmacist and prescriber is essential in these cases to ensure the medication's safety, efficacy, and stability.

564. What impact does the incorporation of a preservative in a compounded aqueous preparation have on its BUD?
a. It allows for an indefinite extension of the BUD.
b. It generally allows for a longer BUD within USP-recommended limits.
c. It shortens the BUD due to chemical instability.
d. It has no impact on the BUD determination.

Answer: b. It generally allows for a longer BUD within USP-recommended limits. Explanation: The incorporation of an appropriate preservative in a compounded aqueous preparation can allow for a longer BUD by inhibiting microbial growth. However, the BUD must still comply with USP-recommended limits and consider other factors like chemical stability and compatibility.

565. When assigning a BUD to a compounded preparation, what documentation is essential for the pharmacist to maintain?
a. A record of the weather conditions at the time of compounding
b. A detailed compounding log including ingredients, procedures, and assigned BUD
c. The personal preferences of the patient regarding medication storage
d. The sales history of the active ingredients used in the preparation

Answer: b. A detailed compounding log including ingredients, procedures, and assigned BUD. Explanation: Maintaining a detailed compounding log that includes information on the ingredients used, compounding procedures followed, and the rationale for the assigned BUD is essential for ensuring traceability, quality control, and compliance with regulatory standards. This documentation is critical for verifying the safety and efficacy of the compounded preparation.

566. What is the primary role of a binder in tablet formulations?
a. To enhance the dissolution rate of the tablet
b. To ensure the tablet disintegrates properly in the body
c. To provide color and taste to the tablet
d. To hold the constituents of the tablet together

Answer: d. To hold the constituents of the tablet together. Explanation: Binders are added to tablet formulations to agglomerate the powder mixture, ensuring that the tablet remains intact after compression by providing cohesion to the powder blend.

567. Which excipient is commonly used as a disintegrant in tablet formulations to facilitate breakup after administration?
a. Magnesium stearate
b. Croscarmellose sodium
c. Propylene glycol
d. Glycerin

Answer: b. Croscarmellose sodium. Explanation: Croscarmellose sodium is a widely used superdisintegrant in tablet formulations. Its primary function is to facilitate the breakup of the tablet into smaller fragments in the aqueous environment of the gastrointestinal tract, enhancing dissolution and absorption of the drug.

568. In a suspension, what is the purpose of adding a viscosity enhancer?
a. To increase the solubility of the active ingredient
b. To stabilize the suspension and prevent sedimentation
c. To act as a preservative against microbial growth
d. To mask the taste of the active ingredient

Answer: b. To stabilize the suspension and prevent sedimentation. Explanation: Viscosity enhancers, or thickeners, are added to suspensions to increase the viscosity of the liquid medium, which helps in stabilizing the suspension by reducing the rate of sedimentation of suspended particles, ensuring uniform distribution of the active ingredient throughout the product.

569. What is the function of a lubricant like magnesium stearate in tablet manufacturing?
a. To enhance the flow properties of the tablet granules during compression
b. To increase the tablet's hardness
c. To act as a disintegrant
d. To improve the tablet's taste

Answer: a. To enhance the flow properties of the tablet granules during compression. Explanation: Lubricants like magnesium stearate are used in tablet formulations to improve the flow properties of the granules/powder mixture during the compression process, reducing friction between the tablet material and the die walls, which facilitates tablet ejection and prevents sticking.

570. In compounding a cream, what is the role of an emulsifying agent?
a. To increase the cream's absorption into the skin
b. To maintain the homogeneity of the cream by preventing the separation of oil and water phases
c. To act as a preservative
d. To color the cream for aesthetic purposes

Answer: b. To maintain the homogeneity of the cream by preventing the separation of oil and water phases. Explanation: Emulsifying agents are added to cream formulations to stabilize emulsions, which are mixtures of oil and water phases. They work by reducing the surface tension between the two immiscible liquids, preventing their separation and maintaining the homogeneity of the cream.

571. What is the purpose of using a sweetening agent in a pediatric syrup formulation?
a. To enhance the viscosity of the syrup
b. To improve the taste for better patient compliance
c. To act as a thickening agent
d. To preserve the syrup against microbial contamination

Answer: b. To improve the taste for better patient compliance. Explanation: Sweetening agents are added to pediatric syrup formulations to improve the taste, making the medication more palatable for children. This is important for ensuring better patient compliance, especially among pediatric patients who may be sensitive to bitter or unpleasant tastes.

572. Why is propylene glycol commonly used in topical formulations?
a. As a solvent to dissolve poorly water-soluble drugs
b. To increase the melting point of the formulation
c. As a buffering agent to maintain pH

d. To act as a coating agent for tablets

Answer: a. As a solvent to dissolve poorly water-soluble drugs. Explanation: Propylene glycol is frequently used in topical formulations as a solvent due to its ability to dissolve many poorly water-soluble drugs, enhancing their availability on the skin surface for absorption.

573. In a capsule formulation, what is the role of a glidant like colloidal silicon dioxide?
a. To prevent the oxidation of the active ingredient
b. To improve the flow properties of the powder blend during encapsulation
c. To serve as the active ingredient
d. To color the capsule shell for identification

Answer: b. To improve the flow properties of the powder blend during encapsulation. Explanation: Glidants like colloidal silicon dioxide are added to capsule formulations to improve the flow properties of the powder blend. This ensures that the powder flows smoothly through the machinery during the encapsulation process, promoting uniform filling of the capsules.

574. When compounding an ointment, what is the function of a humectant like glycerin?
a. To reduce microbial contamination
b. To increase the product's viscosity
c. To prevent the ointment from drying out by retaining moisture
d. To serve as the active ingredient for skin conditions

Answer: c. To prevent the ointment from drying out by retaining moisture. Explanation: Humectants like glycerin are added to ointment formulations to retain moisture within the product. They attract water from the air and the underlying skin layers, preventing the ointment from drying out and helping to keep the skin moist.

575. In the formulation of a transdermal patch, what is the primary function of the adhesive component?
a. To act as a preservative and extend the shelf life of the patch
b. To ensure the patch adheres securely to the patient's skin for the intended duration
c. To control the release rate of the active drug
d. To protect the active ingredient from environmental degradation

Answer: b. To ensure the patch adheres securely to the patient's skin for the intended duration. Explanation: The adhesive component of a transdermal patch is crucial for ensuring that the patch remains securely attached to the patient's skin for the intended duration of therapy, allowing for consistent and controlled delivery of the active drug through the skin.

576. What is the primary purpose of using a laminar airflow workbench (LAFW) in sterile compounding?
a. To increase the speed of the compounding process

b. To provide a particle-free environment by directing airflow
c. To eliminate the need for personal protective equipment (PPE)
d. To reduce the cost of compounding medications

Answer: b. To provide a particle-free environment by directing airflow. Explanation: The primary purpose of using a laminar airflow workbench (LAFW) in sterile compounding is to create a particle-free environment, where the air flows in a laminar (unidirectional) stream, significantly reducing the risk of contamination in sterile preparations.

577. When compounding sterile preparations, what is the significance of using an ISO Class 5 environment?
a. It specifies the maximum number of preparations that can be compounded per hour.
b. It defines an environment where the air quality meets specific particle count limits conducive to sterile compounding.
c. It indicates the temperature range suitable for compounding activities.
d. It designates areas where only non-hazardous drugs can be compounded.

Answer: b. It defines an environment where the air quality meets specific particle count limits conducive to sterile compounding. Explanation: An ISO Class 5 environment is critical for sterile compounding as it specifies an area where the air quality, including the particle count (particles per cubic meter of air), is controlled to levels that minimize the risk of microbial and particulate contamination of sterile preparations.

578. In sterile compounding, what is the primary role of a biological safety cabinet (BSC)?
a. To store sterile products before dispensing
b. To protect the operator, environment, and product during the compounding of hazardous drugs
c. To refrigerate compounds that require low temperatures
d. To record and monitor the compounding process for quality assurance

Answer: b. To protect the operator, environment, and product during the compounding of hazardous drugs. Explanation: A biological safety cabinet (BSC) is designed to provide protection for the operator, the environment, and the product when compounding hazardous drugs. It uses HEPA-filtered air and containment principles to ensure safety and sterility during the compounding process.

579. Which technique is essential to maintain sterility when transferring a solution from a vial to a sterile compounding container?
a. The pour technique
b. The syringe filter technique
c. The needle and syringe technique
d. The vacuum transfer technique

Answer: c. The needle and syringe technique. Explanation: The needle and syringe technique is essential for maintaining sterility when transferring solutions in sterile compounding. This method involves using a sterile syringe and needle to withdraw the solution from the vial and then injecting it into the compounding container, minimizing the risk of contamination.

580. How often should the air quality in areas used for sterile compounding be tested to ensure compliance with USP <797> standards?
a. Daily
b. Weekly
c. Monthly
d. Semiannually

Answer: d. Semiannually. Explanation: According to USP <797> standards, air quality in areas used for sterile compounding should be tested at least semiannually (every six months) to ensure that the environment continues to meet the required standards for particulate and microbial cleanliness, ensuring the safety and efficacy of compounded sterile preparations.

581. What is the significance of "first air" in the context of sterile compounding?
a. It refers to the initial air entering the cleanroom, which must be discarded.
b. It describes the air that directly exits the HEPA filter, free from contamination.
c. It indicates the air used in the first compounding procedure of the day.
d. It represents the warm-up period for the laminar airflow workbench.

Answer: b. It describes the air that directly exits the HEPA filter, free from contamination. Explanation: "First air" refers to the air that directly exits the HEPA filter in a laminar airflow workbench or biological safety cabinet, which is free from particulate and microbial contamination. Ensuring that "first air" flows directly onto critical sites is essential for maintaining sterility during the compounding process.

582. What action should be taken if a sterility breach is suspected during the compounding process?
a. Continue compounding while increasing the airflow in the LAFW.
b. Immediately stop compounding, discard the preparation, and start anew.
c. Place the suspected preparation in quarantine for further testing.
d. Decrease the compounding volume to minimize potential waste.

Answer: b. Immediately stop compounding, discard the preparation, and start anew. Explanation: If a sterility breach is suspected during the compounding process, the correct action is to immediately stop compounding, discard the potentially contaminated preparation, and start the compounding process anew to ensure the sterility and safety of the final product.

583. What is the role of garbing in sterile compounding?
a. To identify staff members' roles within the cleanroom
b. To protect the compounded preparations from contamination by the compounding personnel
c. To keep the compounding personnel comfortable during long compounding sessions
d. To comply with the fashion standards of the healthcare facility

Answer: b. To protect the compounded preparations from contamination by the compounding personnel. Explanation: Garbing, which includes wearing gowns, gloves, masks, and other protective apparel, is a critical procedure in sterile compounding designed to protect the sterile preparations from contamination by skin flakes, microbes, and particulates that may be shed by the compounding personnel.

584. When selecting gloves for use in sterile compounding, what characteristic is most important?
a. Color and design
b. Powder-free and sterile
c. Thickness for durability
d. Elasticity for comfort

Answer: b. Powder-free and sterile. Explanation: The most important characteristics of gloves for use in sterile compounding are that they should be powder-free to avoid particulate contamination and sterile to ensure that they do not introduce microbes into the sterile field or compounded preparations.

585. When preparing Total Parenteral Nutrition (TPN) admixtures, what is the primary reason for the careful management of electrolyte concentrations?
a. To enhance the flavor of the TPN solution
b. To prevent precipitation and ensure stability of the solution
c. To color-code the TPN for different patients
d. To increase the viscosity of the TPN solution for slower infusion rates

Answer: b. To prevent precipitation and ensure stability of the solution. Explanation: Careful management of electrolyte concentrations in TPN admixtures is crucial to prevent precipitation and ensure the stability of the solution. Precipitation can occur when incompatible electrolytes are mixed in improper ratios, leading to potential harm if infused into a patient.

586. In chemotherapy admixture preparation, what is the significance of using a biological safety cabinet (BSC)?
a. To speed up the preparation process
b. To provide a sterile environment for compounding
c. To protect the operator from exposure to hazardous drugs
d. To keep the chemotherapy at a stable temperature

Answer: c. To protect the operator from exposure to hazardous drugs. Explanation: The use of a biological safety cabinet (BSC) in the preparation of chemotherapy admixtures is primarily to protect the operator from exposure to hazardous drugs. BSCs are designed to provide both a sterile environment for compounding and containment of hazardous aerosols and drug particles.

587. What is the purpose of using a filter needle when drawing up medications for IV admixtures?

a. To prevent air bubbles from entering the syringe
b. To remove particulate matter from the medication
c. To increase the flow rate of the medication into the syringe
d. To mix the medication more thoroughly before administration

Answer: b. To remove particulate matter from the medication. Explanation: The purpose of using a filter needle when drawing up medications for IV admixtures is to remove particulate matter from the medication. This ensures that the final admixture is free from contamination that could potentially cause harm to the patient upon administration.

588. When compounding IV admixtures, why is it important to adhere to USP <797> guidelines?
a. To ensure rapid delivery of the medication to the patient
b. To maintain the potency of the medication over time
c. To prevent microbial contamination and ensure patient safety
d. To comply with insurance reimbursement policies

Answer: c. To prevent microbial contamination and ensure patient safety. Explanation: Adhering to USP <797> guidelines when compounding IV admixtures is important to prevent microbial contamination and ensure patient safety. These guidelines set standards for the compounding process, including environmental control, personnel training, and quality assurance, to ensure that compounded sterile preparations are safe for patient use.

589. In TPN preparation, why is it necessary to adjust the pH of the solution?
a. To allow for the addition of flavorings to improve patient acceptance
b. To prevent the degradation of vitamins and other sensitive components
c. To ensure compatibility of all components and prevent precipitation
d. To match the pH of blood for direct infusion compatibility

Answer: c. To ensure compatibility of all components and prevent precipitation. Explanation: Adjusting the pH of TPN solutions is necessary to ensure the compatibility of all components and prevent precipitation. Certain nutrients and medications may only remain soluble within specific pH ranges, and failure to maintain an appropriate pH can lead to precipitation, which can be harmful if infused.

590. What is a critical consideration when preparing admixtures containing lipids for parenteral nutrition?
a. The need to shake the admixture vigorously before administration
b. The risk of lipid peroxidation and the potential for generating toxic compounds
c. The requirement to infuse the admixture over a shorter period than aqueous solutions
d. The color change of the solution as an indicator of lipid concentration

Answer: b. The risk of lipid peroxidation and the potential for generating toxic compounds. Explanation: When preparing admixtures containing lipids for parenteral nutrition, a critical consideration is the risk of lipid peroxidation, which can lead to the generation of toxic compounds. Lipid peroxidation can occur when lipids are exposed to oxygen, light, or certain temperatures, and it can compromise the safety of the admixture.

591. How does the use of an inline filter benefit IV admixture administration?
a. By regulating the infusion rate to prevent fluid overload
b. By removing air bubbles to prevent air embolism
c. By trapping particulate matter to reduce the risk of phlebitis and embolism
d. By warming the solution to body temperature for patient comfort

Answer: c. By trapping particulate matter to reduce the risk of phlebitis and embolism. Explanation: The use of an inline filter during IV admixture administration benefits by trapping particulate matter, which can reduce the risk of complications such as phlebitis (inflammation of the veins) and embolism (obstruction of a blood vessel by a foreign substance).

592. What is the role of a compatibility chart in IV admixture preparation?
a. To determine the nutritional value of TPN admixtures
b. To ensure that combined medications do not interact adversely
c. To track the expiration dates of compounded admixtures
d. To calculate the required infusion rates for different medications

Answer: b. To ensure that combined medications do not interact adversely. Explanation: The role of a compatibility chart in IV admixture preparation is to ensure that combined medications do not interact adversely. Compatibility charts provide information on the physical and chemical compatibility of various medications when mixed, helping to prevent adverse reactions or inactivation of drugs when they are compounded together.

593. Why is it important to label IV admixtures with beyond-use dates (BUDs)?
a. To indicate the date after which the admixture can be safely administered
b. To provide legal protection for the pharmacy in case of an adverse reaction
c. To track inventory and manage stock rotation effectively
d. To indicate the date after which the admixture should not be used due to potential instability or contamination

Answer: d. To indicate the date after which the admixture should not be used due to potential instability or contamination. Explanation: Labeling IV admixtures with beyond-use dates (BUDs) is important to indicate the date after which the admixture should not be used. This is due to potential instability or contamination risks that could arise after the BUD, ensuring patient safety by preventing the use of compromised admixtures.

594. When preparing an IV chemotherapy admixture, what safety precaution is essential to protect pharmacy personnel?
a. Using tinted IV bags to protect the solution from light
b. Working within a dedicated chemotherapy laminar flow hood
c. Infusing the chemotherapy over a longer period to reduce side effects
d. Refrigerating the admixture immediately after preparation to preserve potency

Answer: b. Working within a dedicated chemotherapy laminar flow hood. Explanation: When preparing an IV chemotherapy admixture, it is essential for pharmacy personnel to work within a dedicated chemotherapy laminar flow hood. This specialized equipment is designed to provide containment and protection from exposure to hazardous chemotherapy agents, ensuring the safety of personnel during the compounding process.

595. When withdrawing medication from a vial, why is it important to inject an equal amount of air into the vial before withdrawal?
a. To increase the pressure inside the vial, facilitating easier withdrawal of the liquid
b. To sterilize the contents of the vial with air
c. To prevent the vial from collapsing
d. To mix the medication more thoroughly before withdrawal

Answer: a. To increase the pressure inside the vial, facilitating easier withdrawal of the liquid. Explanation: Injecting air into a vial before withdrawing medication equalizes the pressure, making it easier to withdraw the liquid. Without this step, a vacuum can form, making withdrawal difficult and potentially leading to inaccurate dosing.

596. What is the primary reason for using a filter needle when drawing up medication from an ampule?
a. To prevent air bubbles from entering the syringe
b. To ensure the medication is mixed properly
c. To remove any potential glass particles that may have been introduced during ampule opening
d. To increase the flow rate of the medication into the syringe

Answer: c. To remove any potential glass particles that may have been introduced during ampule opening. Explanation: When an ampule is snapped open, tiny glass particles can sometimes be introduced into the medication. A filter needle is designed to remove these particles, ensuring that the preparation administered to the patient is free from contamination.

597. In sterile compounding, what is the purpose of using a Luer-Lok syringe over a traditional slip-tip syringe?
a. To provide a more ergonomic grip for the pharmacist
b. To allow for larger volumes of medication to be drawn up
c. To prevent accidental disconnection of the syringe from the needle or IV line
d. To reduce the required force for plunger operation

Answer: c. To prevent accidental disconnection of the syringe from the needle or IV line. Explanation: Luer-Lok syringes have a threaded tip that securely locks needles or other devices in place, preventing accidental disconnections that could lead to contamination or loss of medication, which is crucial in maintaining the sterility and integrity of compounded sterile preparations.

598. Why is it advised to visually inspect a vial's rubber stopper and the medication within before use?
a. To check for the expiration date printed on the stopper
b. To ensure there is no discoloration, precipitation, or damage that could indicate contamination or degradation

c. To verify the brand name of the medication
d. To confirm the volume of medication left in the vial

Answer: b. To ensure there is no discoloration, precipitation, or damage that could indicate contamination or degradation. Explanation: Visual inspection of the vial's rubber stopper and the medication is critical to identify any signs of contamination, degradation, or damage, such as discoloration or precipitation, ensuring the safety and efficacy of the medication before it is administered to a patient.

599. What is the key difference between a single-dose vial and a multi-dose vial?
a. Single-dose vials contain preservatives, while multi-dose vials do not
b. Multi-dose vials are larger in size
c. Single-dose vials are intended for one-time use, while multi-dose vials contain preservatives allowing for multiple withdrawals
d. Multi-dose vials have a rubber stopper that single-dose vials lack

Answer: c. Single-dose vials are intended for one-time use, while multi-dose vials contain preservatives allowing for multiple withdrawals. Explanation: Single-dose vials are designed for a single use and do not contain preservatives, making them susceptible to contamination after the first breach. Multi-dose vials, on the other hand, contain preservatives that allow for the vial to be accessed multiple times while minimizing the risk of microbial growth.

600. How should the bevel of the needle be oriented when penetrating the rubber stopper of a vial to maintain sterility?
a. The bevel should face downward to minimize contact with the stopper
b. The bevel should face upward to ensure a smooth entry and reduce coring
c. Orientation of the bevel does not affect sterility
d. The bevel should be parallel to the stopper for easier insertion

Answer: b. The bevel should face upward to ensure a smooth entry and reduce coring. Explanation: Orienting the bevel of the needle upward when penetrating the rubber stopper of a vial helps ensure a smooth entry and reduces the risk of coring, where small pieces of the rubber stopper may be cored out by the needle, potentially contaminating the medication.

601. What is the primary advantage of using pre-filled syringes in a healthcare setting?
a. They eliminate the need for preservatives in the medication
b. They reduce preparation time and minimize dosing errors
c. They can be reused for multiple patients
d. They are less expensive than vials

Answer: b. They reduce preparation time and minimize dosing errors. Explanation: Pre-filled syringes come with a set dose of medication, reducing the time needed for preparation and significantly minimizing the potential for dosing errors, thereby enhancing patient safety and efficiency in medication administration.

602. When preparing an injection from a vial, why is it important to swab the rubber stopper with an antiseptic?
a. To lubricate the stopper for easier needle penetration
b. To remove any visible debris from the stopper
c. To disinfect the stopper and reduce the risk of introducing contaminants into the vial
d. To mark the spot for needle insertion

Answer: c. To disinfect the stopper and reduce the risk of introducing contaminants into the vial. Explanation: Swabbing the rubber stopper with an antiseptic, such as alcohol, is crucial to disinfect the surface before needle penetration, reducing the risk of introducing microbial contaminants into the vial and maintaining the sterility of the medication.

603. In the context of syringes, what does the term "dead space" refer to, and why is it significant?
a. The area where additional medication can be stored for later use
b. The space within the syringe and needle that holds residual medication after administration
c. The gap between the syringe plunger and the barrel that affects the accuracy of small volume measurements
d. The length of the needle that affects the depth of medication delivery

Answer: b. The space within the syringe and needle that holds residual medication after administration. Explanation: "Dead space" refers to the volume within a syringe and needle that remains filled with medication after the plunger has been fully depressed. This is significant because it can lead to medication waste and inaccuracies in dosing, especially in low-volume administrations.

604. What precaution should be taken when opening an ampule to prevent injury and contamination?
a. Open the ampule away from the face and use a sterile gauze pad to protect the fingers
b. Heat the neck of the ampule to soften the glass before opening
c. Freeze the ampule briefly to strengthen the glass
d. Tap the ampule neck sharply on a hard surface to initiate a clean break

Answer: a. Open the ampule away from the face and use a sterile gauze pad to protect the fingers. Explanation: When opening an ampule, it's important to protect oneself from glass shards and prevent contamination of the contents. Using a sterile gauze pad to hold the ampule and opening it away from the face and body helps achieve this by providing a barrier and ensuring that any potential glass particles or medication do not come into contact with the operator or contaminate the sterile field.

605. What pore size is commonly used in filters for sterile filtration of pharmaceutical solutions?
a. 5.0 μm
b. 1.2 μm
c. 0.45 μm
d. 0.22 μm

Answer: d. 0.22 μm. Explanation: A pore size of 0.22 μm is commonly used in filters for sterile filtration of pharmaceutical solutions. This size is effective in removing bacteria and other pathogens, ensuring the sterility of the solution.

606. In the context of sterile compounding, why is pre-filtration sometimes necessary before final sterile filtration?
a. To increase the pH of the solution
b. To remove larger particles and protect the final filter from clogging
c. To add essential nutrients to the solution
d. To change the color of the solution for identification purposes

Answer: b. To remove larger particles and protect the final filter from clogging. Explanation: Pre-filtration is used to remove larger particles from the solution, which protects the final sterile filter from clogging. This step ensures the longevity of the final filter and maintains the efficiency of the filtration process.

607. Which of the following best describes the principle of membrane filtration in sterile compounding?
a. The solution is heated to a temperature that kills all microorganisms.
b. A chemical agent is added to the solution to sterilize it.
c. The solution passes through a membrane that traps microorganisms based on size exclusion.
d. The solution undergoes irradiation to destroy all microbial life.

Answer: c. The solution passes through a membrane that traps microorganisms based on size exclusion. Explanation: Membrane filtration works on the principle of size exclusion, where the solution is passed through a membrane filter that traps microorganisms and other particulates based on their size, allowing only the sterile solution to pass through.

608. When selecting a filter for sterile filtration, what factor is crucial in ensuring the compatibility of the filter with the solution being filtered?
a. The color of the filter membrane
b. The pH range that the filter can withstand
c. The filter's pore size
d. The chemical compatibility of the filter material with the solution

Answer: d. The chemical compatibility of the filter material with the solution. Explanation: The chemical compatibility of the filter material with the solution is crucial to ensure that the filter does not interact negatively with the solution, such as by leaching contaminants or being degraded by the solution. This ensures the integrity of the filtration process and the safety of the final product.

609. What is the primary purpose of using a bubble point test in sterile filtration?
a. To determine the pH of the solution
b. To measure the viscosity of the solution
c. To assess the integrity of the filter membrane

d. To evaluate the color clarity of the filtered solution

Answer: c. To assess the integrity of the filter membrane. Explanation: The bubble point test is used to assess the integrity of the filter membrane by determining the pressure at which air bubbles pass through the wetted membrane. A failure to reach the expected bubble point indicates a compromise in the filter's integrity, potentially allowing passage of microorganisms.

610. In sterile filtration, what is the significance of using a positive pressure in the filtration system?
a. To decrease the filtration speed for better accuracy
b. To prevent the backflow of air into the sterile solution
c. To force the solution through the filter membrane, aiding in the removal of microorganisms
d. To increase the temperature of the solution for better solubility

Answer: c. To force the solution through the filter membrane, aiding in the removal of microorganisms. Explanation: Using positive pressure in the filtration system helps to force the solution through the filter membrane, aiding in the efficient removal of microorganisms and ensuring the sterility of the solution.

611. Why is it important to avoid touching the membrane surface of a sterile filter during setup?
a. To prevent static electricity buildup
b. To maintain the aesthetic appearance of the filter
c. To prevent the introduction of contaminants that could compromise sterility
d. To keep the filter dry for storage

Answer: c. To prevent the introduction of contaminants that could compromise sterility. Explanation: Touching the membrane surface of a sterile filter can introduce contaminants, such as bacteria from the skin, which could compromise the sterility of the filtered solution. It is crucial to handle sterile filters aseptically to maintain their sterility and the integrity of the filtration process.

612. What role does the flow rate play in the sterile filtration process?
a. A faster flow rate improves the clarity of the solution.
b. A slower flow rate ensures complete evaporation of the solvent.
c. The flow rate must be controlled to prevent damage to the filter and ensure effective removal of microorganisms.
d. The flow rate determines the final pH of the solution.

Answer: c. The flow rate must be controlled to prevent damage to the filter and ensure effective removal of microorganisms. Explanation: The flow rate in sterile filtration must be carefully controlled to prevent damage to the filter membrane from excessive pressure and to ensure that the filtration process effectively removes microorganisms. Too high a flow rate can lead to filter failure or bypassing of the filter by microorganisms.

613. How does the use of a pre-filter benefit the sterile filtration process?

a. It enhances the color of the final solution.
b. It increases the final pH of the solution.
c. It extends the life of the sterile filter by removing larger particles that could cause clogging.
d. It decreases the need for chemical preservatives in the solution.

Answer: c. It extends the life of the sterile filter by removing larger particles that could cause clogging. Explanation: The use of a pre-filter in the sterile filtration process removes larger particles from the solution before it reaches the sterile filter. This reduces the risk of clogging the sterile filter, extending its life and maintaining the efficiency of the filtration process.

614. What is the maximum Beyond Use Date (BUD) for a compounded sterile preparation classified under low-risk level with immediate use, stored at room temperature?
a. 1 hour
b. 12 hours
c. 24 hours
d. 48 hours

Answer: a. 1 hour. Explanation: Low-risk level compounded sterile preparations with immediate use are intended for emergency situations where the standard aseptic compounding conditions cannot be met. These preparations have a maximum BUD of 1 hour at room temperature to minimize the risk of microbial growth.

615. In medium-risk level compounding, what is the BUD for preparations stored in a refrigerator?
a. 9 days
b. 14 days
c. 30 days
d. 45 days

Answer: b. 14 days. Explanation: Medium-risk level compounded sterile preparations, which involve multiple doses or complex aseptics, typically have a BUD of 14 days when stored in a refrigerator. This accounts for the increased risk of contamination due to the complexity of the compounding process and the number of components involved.

616. For high-risk level compounded sterile preparations stored at room temperature, what is the recommended BUD?
a. 12 hours
b. 24 hours
c. 48 hours
d. 72 hours

Answer: b. 24 hours. Explanation: High-risk level compounded sterile preparations, which involve non-sterile ingredients or exposure to non-sterile environments, have a BUD of 24 hours at room temperature. This limited BUD reflects the higher risk of contamination and the need for stringent control to ensure patient safety.

617. What determines the risk level classification of a compounded sterile preparation?
a. The cost of the ingredients used
b. The complexity of the compounding procedure
c. The sterility of the starting components and the environment
d. The color and viscosity of the final product

Answer: c. The sterility of the starting components and the environment. Explanation: The risk level classification of a compounded sterile preparation is primarily determined by the sterility of the starting components and the compounding environment. Factors include whether ingredients are sterile, the sterility of the compounding environment, and the potential for microbial contamination during the compounding process.

618. How does the use of non-sterile ingredients affect the risk level classification of a compounded sterile preparation?
a. It does not affect the risk level as long as the final product is sterile.
b. It automatically classifies the preparation as low-risk.
c. It typically results in a high-risk level classification.
d. It classifies the preparation as medium-risk if aseptic techniques are used.

Answer: c. It typically results in a high-risk level classification. Explanation: The use of non-sterile ingredients in the preparation of sterile compounds typically results in a high-risk classification due to the significant risk of contamination. Such preparations require sterilization processes and are subject to stricter controls to ensure the sterility and safety of the final product.

619. What is the BUD for a low-risk level compounded sterile preparation stored in a freezer?
a. 9 days
b. 14 days
c. 45 days
d. 6 months

Answer: d. 6 months. Explanation: Low-risk level compounded sterile preparations stored in a freezer can have a BUD of up to 6 months. This extended BUD takes advantage of the reduced microbial growth rates at lower temperatures, allowing for longer storage while maintaining the safety and efficacy of the preparation.

620. For a compounded sterile preparation involving multiple small volumes combined into a final product, what is the typical risk level classification?
a. Low-risk
b. Medium-risk
c. High-risk
d. Cannot be determined without more information

Answer: b. Medium-risk. Explanation: Combining multiple small volumes into a final compounded sterile preparation is typically classified as medium-risk. This classification accounts for the increased complexity and potential for contamination compared to single-volume compounding, requiring more stringent aseptic techniques.

621. In the context of sterile compounding, what factor contributes to a preparation being classified as high-risk?
a. Use of sterile gloves and garb during compounding
b. Compounding within an ISO Class 5 environment
c. Exposure of sterile ingredients to air quality worse than ISO Class 5
d. The preparation being intended for ophthalmic use

Answer: c. Exposure of sterile ingredients to air quality worse than ISO Class 5. Explanation: A preparation is classified as high-risk if sterile ingredients are exposed to an environment with air quality worse than ISO Class 5 during compounding, significantly increasing the potential for microbial contamination.

622. When assigning a BUD to a sterile compounded preparation, which factor is NOT typically considered?
a. The risk level of the compounding process
b. The patient's age and medical history
c. The storage conditions of the final preparation
d. The sterility of the components and environment

Answer: b. The patient's age and medical history. Explanation: While patient-specific factors like age and medical history are critical for medication selection and dosing, they do not directly influence the BUD assignment of a sterile compounded preparation. The BUD is determined based on factors related to the compounding process, sterility, and storage conditions.

623. What BUD should be applied to a medium-risk level compounded sterile preparation stored at room temperature?
a. 12 hours
b. 24 hours
c. 30 days
d. 72 hours

Answer: d. 72 hours. Explanation: Medium-risk level compounded sterile preparations stored at room temperature typically have a BUD of up to 72 hours. This BUD reflects the balance between the complexity of the compounding process, which involves multiple steps or mixing sterile ingredients, and the need to limit the potential for microbial growth at room temperature.

624. What strategy is recommended to prevent medication errors related to look-alike/sound-alike (LASA) drugs?
a. Storing LASA drugs in the same bin for easy comparison
b. Using tall man lettering to differentiate similar drug names
c. Limiting access to LASA drugs to senior pharmacy staff only

d. Placing LASA drugs in high-traffic areas for increased awareness

Answer: b. Using tall man lettering to differentiate similar drug names. Explanation: Using tall man lettering to differentiate similar drug names is an effective strategy to prevent medication errors related to look-alike/sound-alike (LASA) drugs. This approach highlights differences in drug names, reducing the risk of confusion and selection errors.

625. How does implementing a barcoding system at the point of care contribute to error prevention in medication administration?
a. By ensuring the correct medication is administered at the right time to the right patient
b. By automatically updating the patient's medical records with medication administration details
c. By reducing the need for manual documentation, thus saving time
d. By eliminating the need for pharmacist verification of medication orders

Answer: a. By ensuring the correct medication is administered at the right time to the right patient. Explanation: Implementing a barcoding system at the point of care ensures that the correct medication is administered at the right time to the right patient by matching the medication barcode to the patient's barcode on their wristband, significantly reducing administration errors.

626. What is the role of automated dispensing cabinets in reducing medication errors in inpatient settings?
a. They eliminate the need for nurses to administer medications
b. They provide a direct link to the patient's electronic health record for real-time updates
c. They allow for centralized control of medication distribution
d. They control access to medications and track usage, reducing the risk of errors and diversion

Answer: d. They control access to medications and track usage, reducing the risk of errors and diversion. Explanation: Automated dispensing cabinets control access to medications and track usage, which helps reduce the risk of medication errors and diversion by ensuring that medications are securely stored and dispensed according to authorized prescriptions and protocols.

627. In the context of error prevention, what is the significance of a "time-out" procedure before surgical procedures?
a. It ensures all surgical instruments are accounted for
b. It provides a final check to confirm the correct patient, procedure, and site
c. It allows the surgical team to rest briefly before proceeding
d. It confirms that all required documentation is complete

Answer: b. It provides a final check to confirm the correct patient, procedure, and site. Explanation: A "time-out" procedure before surgical procedures is significant as it provides a final check to confirm the correct patient, procedure, and site. This pause allows the surgical team to verify critical information, reducing the risk of wrong-site, wrong-procedure, and wrong-patient errors.

628. How does the use of standardized medication concentration help in minimizing medication errors in IV therapy?
a. By reducing the variety of medication concentrations that staff need to calculate
b. By allowing for easier substitution of generic drugs
c. By facilitating bulk purchasing and reducing pharmacy costs
d. By making it easier to administer medications without pharmacist oversight

Answer: a. By reducing the variety of medication concentrations that staff need to calculate. Explanation: The use of standardized medication concentrations helps in minimizing medication errors in IV therapy by reducing the variety of medication concentrations that healthcare staff need to calculate, thereby simplifying dosing and reducing the potential for calculation errors.

629. What is the purpose of employing double-check systems for high-alert medications?
a. To increase the workload and accountability of healthcare staff
b. To provide legal protection to healthcare institutions
c. To ensure accuracy in dosing and administration of medications with a higher risk of causing harm
d. To comply with pharmaceutical advertising regulations

Answer: c. To ensure accuracy in dosing and administration of medications with a higher risk of causing harm. Explanation: Employing double-check systems for high-alert medications serves the purpose of ensuring accuracy in dosing and administration. These medications have a higher risk of causing significant harm if used incorrectly, and the double-check system acts as a safeguard against potential errors.

630. What impact does computerized provider order entry (CPOE) have on medication error rates?
a. It increases error rates due to complex interfaces
b. It has no significant impact on error rates
c. It reduces error rates by eliminating handwritten prescriptions
d. It shifts error responsibility from physicians to pharmacists

Answer: c. It reduces error rates by eliminating handwritten prescriptions. Explanation: Computerized provider order entry (CPOE) systems significantly reduce medication error rates by eliminating the need for handwritten prescriptions, which can be prone to misinterpretation due to illegible handwriting or ambiguous abbreviations.

631. How do clinical decision support systems (CDSS) integrated with electronic health records (EHR) contribute to error prevention?
a. By providing entertainment to healthcare staff during breaks
b. By automatically filling prescriptions without pharmacist review
c. By offering alerts and recommendations based on patient-specific information and evidence-based guidelines
d. By transferring responsibility for clinical decisions to the software

Answer: c. By offering alerts and recommendations based on patient-specific information and evidence-based guidelines. Explanation: Clinical decision support systems (CDSS) integrated with electronic health records (EHR) contribute to error prevention by offering alerts and recommendations to healthcare providers. These are based on patient-specific information, such as allergies or potential drug interactions, and evidence-based guidelines, assisting in making safer clinical decisions.

632. In what way does a pharmacist's involvement in medication reconciliation at hospital admission and discharge reduce medication errors?
a. By ensuring that patients receive a complete list of their medications for future reference
b. By verifying and documenting the accuracy of patients' medication lists, preventing discrepancies
c. By reducing the time physicians spend on reviewing medications
d. By allowing nurses more time for patient care activities

Answer: b. By verifying and documenting the accuracy of patients' medication lists, preventing discrepancies. Explanation: A pharmacist's involvement in medication reconciliation at hospital admission and discharge plays a crucial role in verifying and documenting the accuracy of patients' medication lists. This process helps in identifying and resolving discrepancies, which can prevent potential medication errors and ensure continuity of care.

633. What is the primary purpose of employing Tall Man lettering in medication labeling?
a. To highlight the brand name over the generic name
b. To enhance the aesthetic appeal of the label
c. To differentiate look-alike/sound-alike medication names
d. To indicate medications that are available over the counter

Answer: c. To differentiate look-alike/sound-alike medication names. Explanation: Tall Man lettering is used to help distinguish between medication names that look or sound similar by capitalizing certain parts of the names, reducing the risk of medication errors.

634. Which pair of medications is commonly cited as an example where Tall Man lettering can be beneficial to prevent confusion?
a. Aspirin and atorvastatin
b. Hydrocodone and oxycodone
c. Metformin and metronidazole
d. Prednisone and prednisolone

Answer: b. Hydrocodone and oxycodone. Explanation: Hydrocodone and oxycodone are two medications that have similar names and are both opioids, but they have different potencies and indications. Using Tall Man lettering (e.g., hydrOXYcodone and oxyCODONE) can help reduce the risk of confusing these two medications.

635. In which setting is the implementation of Tall Man lettering particularly critical?
a. Retail pharmacies only
b. Online pharmacies
c. All healthcare settings where medications are prescribed, dispensed, or administered
d. Veterinary clinics

Answer: c. All healthcare settings where medications are prescribed, dispensed, or administered. Explanation: Tall Man lettering is critical in all healthcare settings to prevent medication errors, as look-alike/sound-alike medication errors can occur anywhere medications are handled.

636. What regulatory or advisory body recommends the use of Tall Man lettering to reduce medication errors?
a. The Food and Drug Administration (FDA)
b. The World Health Organization (WHO)
c. The Institute for Safe Medication Practices (ISMP)
d. The American Pharmacists Association (APhA)

Answer: c. The Institute for Safe Medication Practices (ISMP). Explanation: The Institute for Safe Medication Practices (ISMP) is a leading organization that advocates for the safe use of medications and recommends the use of Tall Man lettering to help reduce the risk of medication errors related to look-alike/sound-alike names.

637. How should Tall Man lettering be applied to medication labels to maximize its effectiveness?
a. By capitalizing the entire name of the medication
b. By using it for the first letter of each word in the medication name
c. By capitalizing the distinct parts of look-alike/sound-alike medication names
d. By applying it randomly to various letters in the medication name

Answer: c. By capitalizing the distinct parts of look-alike/sound-alike medication names. Explanation: The effectiveness of Tall Man lettering is maximized by capitalizing the distinct syllables or parts of medication names that differ from those of similar names, making the differences more noticeable and reducing the risk of confusion.

638. What is a potential limitation of Tall Man lettering in preventing medication errors?
a. It can be overused, leading to desensitization and reduced effectiveness
b. It is not recognized by electronic health record (EHR) systems
c. It is only applicable to medications with long names
d. It increases the time required for pharmacists to label medications

Answer: a. It can be overused, leading to desensitization and reduced effectiveness. Explanation: If Tall Man lettering is overused or applied to too many medications, healthcare professionals may become desensitized to its significance, potentially reducing its effectiveness in highlighting critical differences between look-alike/sound-alike medication names.

639. In the context of medication safety, what does the term "look-alike/sound-alike" (LASA) refer to?
a. Medications that have similar packaging
b. Medications with names that look alike or sound alike, posing a risk for errors
c. Generic and brand-name medications that are therapeutically equivalent

d. Medications that are chemically similar but used for different indications

Answer: b. Medications with names that look alike or sound alike, posing a risk for errors. Explanation: Look-alike/sound-alike (LASA) refers to medications with names that are visually similar or phonetically similar, increasing the risk of medication errors due to confusion between the names.

640. What strategy, in addition to Tall Man lettering, can be employed to reduce the risk of errors with LASA medications?
a. Using different color labels for all medications
b. Separating LASA medications physically in storage
c. Placing a warning sticker on all medication bottles
d. Writing the indication for use on every medication label

Answer: b. Separating LASA medications physically in storage. Explanation: Physically separating look-alike/sound-alike medications in storage is an effective strategy to reduce the risk of errors by minimizing the chance of selecting the wrong medication, especially in busy or stressful environments.

641. How does the integration of clinical decision support (CDS) tools in electronic prescribing systems help mitigate risks associated with LASA medications?
a. By automatically selecting the cheapest medication option
b. By providing real-time alerts when a LASA medication is prescribed
c. By limiting prescribing rights to certain classes of medications
d. By requiring manual entry of all medication orders

Answer: b. By providing real-time alerts when a LASA medication is prescribed. Explanation: Clinical decision support (CDS) tools integrated into electronic prescribing systems can provide real-time alerts to prescribers when a medication with a look-alike/sound-alike name is selected, prompting a review to ensure the correct medication is prescribed, thereby reducing the risk of errors.

642. What role do standardized medication protocols play in minimizing risks associated with LASA medications?
a. They restrict the use of high-risk medications to specific patients
b. They provide a uniform approach to prescribing, dispensing, and administering medications, including LASA medications
c. They eliminate the need for verbal medication orders
d. They ensure that all medications are dispensed in child-resistant containers

Answer: b. They provide a uniform approach to prescribing, dispensing, and administering medications, including LASA medications. Explanation: Standardized medication protocols offer a systematic approach to handling medications, including those with look-alike/sound-alike names, by establishing consistent procedures for prescribing, dispensing, and administering, which helps reduce the likelihood of errors.

643. What primary benefit does barcode scanning provide in medication dispensing?
a. Reduces the need for pharmacist oversight
b. Eliminates the need for manual inventory counts
c. Enhances the speed of the dispensing process
d. Increases accuracy and reduces dispensing errors

Answer: d. Increases accuracy and reduces dispensing errors. Explanation: Barcode scanning in medication dispensing primarily increases accuracy and reduces dispensing errors by ensuring that the correct medication is selected and dispensed according to the prescription. This technology verifies medication against the prescription details, minimizing human error.

644. How does automation in pharmacy inventory management impact stock levels?
a. It increases stock levels due to bulk purchasing
b. It reduces stock variability and prevents overstocking or stockouts
c. It eliminates the need for stock management
d. It decreases stock levels by increasing medication waste

Answer: b. It reduces stock variability and prevents overstocking or stockouts. Explanation: Automation in pharmacy inventory management helps maintain optimal stock levels by using software to track inventory in real-time, predict demand, and automate reordering processes. This reduces stock variability and prevents overstocking or stockouts, ensuring that medications are available when needed without excessive inventory.

645. In what way does the integration of barcode scanning with electronic health records (EHRs) improve patient safety?
a. By providing easy access to medication administration guidelines
b. By ensuring real-time documentation of medication administration
c. By facilitating faster communication between pharmacists and prescribers
d. By allowing patients to self-administer medications safely

Answer: b. By ensuring real-time documentation of medication administration. Explanation: Integrating barcode scanning with electronic health records (EHRs) improves patient safety by ensuring real-time documentation of medication administration. This integration allows for immediate recording of administered medications, dosages, and times in the patient's EHR, enhancing medication tracking and reducing the risk of errors.

646. What challenge can arise with the implementation of pharmacy automation systems?
a. Decreased efficiency due to frequent system updates
b. Increased medication errors from over-reliance on technology
c. Initial costs and staff training requirements
d. Reduction in patient interaction and counseling opportunities

Answer: c. Initial costs and staff training requirements. Explanation: Implementing pharmacy automation systems can present challenges, including initial costs associated with purchasing equipment and software, as well as the need for comprehensive staff training to ensure effective and safe use of the new systems.

647. How does automated compounding of IV admixtures benefit pharmacy operations?
a. By allowing the use of lower-quality medication to save costs
b. By standardizing the compounding process and improving preparation consistency
c. By eliminating the need for cleanroom facilities
d. By completely removing pharmacists from the compounding process

Answer: b. By standardizing the compounding process and improving preparation consistency. Explanation: Automated compounding of IV admixtures benefits pharmacy operations by standardizing the compounding process, which improves the consistency and accuracy of preparations. Automation helps ensure that each admixture is prepared according to precise specifications, reducing the variability associated with manual compounding.

648. What role does automation play in enhancing medication reconciliation processes?
a. It eliminates the need for patient interviews during reconciliation
b. It provides automatic translation of medication names into different languages
c. It facilitates the identification and resolution of discrepancies in medication orders
d. It allows patients to verify their medication lists without pharmacist intervention

Answer: c. It facilitates the identification and resolution of discrepancies in medication orders. Explanation: Automation enhances medication reconciliation processes by facilitating the identification and resolution of discrepancies in medication orders. Automated systems can compare medication orders with patient records and alert healthcare providers to potential inconsistencies, helping to ensure accurate and up-to-date medication lists.

649. How does the use of robotic dispensing systems impact pharmacy workflow?
a. It increases the time pharmacists spend on routine dispensing tasks
b. It reallocates pharmacist time to patient care and clinical duties
c. It requires more frequent manual checks for dispensing accuracy
d. It reduces the variety of medications that can be dispensed

Answer: b. It reallocates pharmacist time to patient care and clinical duties. Explanation: The use of robotic dispensing systems impacts pharmacy workflow by reallocating pharmacist time away from routine dispensing tasks to focus more on patient care and clinical duties. Automation handles repetitive tasks, allowing pharmacists to engage in activities that require their clinical expertise.

650. In the context of error prevention, what advantage does automated dose dispensing (ADD) offer for multi-dose packaged medications?
a. It ensures that all medications are dispensed in liquid form for easier administration
b. It provides patients with detailed written instructions for each medication
c. It pre-packages medications by dose and time, reducing administration errors

d. It allows patients to alter their medication doses based on symptoms

Answer: c. It pre-packages medications by dose and time, reducing administration errors. Explanation: Automated dose dispensing (ADD) offers the advantage of pre-packaging medications according to the dose and time of administration. This system helps to organize medications for patients, particularly those on complex regimens, reducing the risk of administration errors by ensuring that the right medication is taken at the right time.

651. What is a potential drawback of relying heavily on barcode scanning for medication verification?
a. Increased likelihood of allergic reactions in patients
b. Barcode scanners can misinterpret barcodes, leading to selection errors
c. Patients may develop a dependency on technology for medication management
d. Barcode scanning significantly increases the time required for medication dispensing

Answer: b. Barcode scanners can misinterpret barcodes, leading to selection errors. Explanation: While barcode scanning significantly reduces medication errors, a potential drawback is that scanners can misinterpret barcodes due to factors like damage, poor printing quality, or scanner malfunctions, which could lead to selection errors. Proper maintenance and quality control measures are necessary to mitigate this risk.

652. How does real-time inventory tracking through automation influence pharmacy procurement decisions?
a. It limits the procurement to generic medications only
b. It provides data-driven insights into usage patterns, optimizing stock levels
c. It mandates bulk purchasing for all medications
d. It eliminates the need for manual inventory audits

Answer: b. It provides data-driven insights into usage patterns, optimizing stock levels. Explanation: Real-time inventory tracking through automation influences pharmacy procurement decisions by providing data-driven insights into medication usage patterns and trends. This information helps pharmacies to optimize stock levels, ensuring that medications are available when needed while minimizing excess inventory and reducing waste.

653. What is the primary purpose of implementing independent double-checks for high-risk medications?
a. To ensure that medications are stored correctly
b. To provide training for new pharmacy staff
c. To reduce the risk of medication errors by verifying accuracy at critical points
d. To comply with pharmaceutical marketing standards

Answer: c. To reduce the risk of medication errors by verifying accuracy at critical points. Explanation: Independent double-checks are a safety measure designed to catch and correct potential errors by having a second, independent clinician verify the medication, dose, route, timing, and patient, particularly for high-risk medications where errors could have severe consequences.

654. Which step is crucial for the effectiveness of an independent double-check process?
a. The second checker must be the one who prepared the medication.
b. The check must be performed in the presence of the first checker.
c. The second checker must review the medication order independently without bias from the first checker's process.
d. The check should be documented after medication administration to the patient.

Answer: c. The second checker must review the medication order independently without bias from the first checker's process. Explanation: For an independent double-check to be effective, the second clinician must review the order and the medication independently, without influence from the first checker's process, to ensure an unbiased verification.

655. When should an independent double-check be performed for high-risk medications?
a. Only at the end of the shift
b. Before the medication is dispensed from the pharmacy
c. Immediately after the medication is administered to the patient
d. At critical points, such as before preparation, before dispensing, and before administration

Answer: d. At critical points, such as before preparation, before dispensing, and before administration. Explanation: Independent double-checks for high-risk medications should be performed at critical points in the medication use process, including before preparation, before dispensing, and before administration to the patient, to maximize the opportunity to catch and correct errors.

656. What is a key factor that can undermine the effectiveness of independent double-checks?
a. Performing the check in a quiet environment
b. Having a standardized process for the check
c. Time pressure that may rush the checking process
d. Documentation of the check in the patient's medical record

Answer: c. Time pressure that may rush the checking process. Explanation: Time pressure is a significant factor that can undermine the effectiveness of independent double-checks by rushing the process, potentially leading to oversight of errors. It's essential that checks are performed thoroughly and without haste, even in busy settings.

657. In what scenario might independent double-checks be most critical?
a. When refilling a routine prescription for a chronic condition
b. When dispensing a high-risk medication like insulin or anticoagulants
c. When a medication is available over the counter
d. When dispensing a placebo in a clinical trial

Answer: b. When dispensing a high-risk medication like insulin or anticoagulants. Explanation: Independent double-checks are most critical when dispensing high-risk medications, such as insulin or anticoagulants, due to the significant harm that can result from errors with these medications. These checks serve as a vital safeguard to enhance patient safety.

658. How does the "independence" aspect of double-checks impact its effectiveness?
a. It requires the check to be performed by a supervisor only.
b. It ensures that the second checker has no prior knowledge of the original order to avoid confirmation bias.
c. It mandates that checks are performed by individuals from different departments.
d. It specifies that checks must be conducted at different times of the day.

Answer: b. It ensures that the second checker has no prior knowledge of the original order to avoid confirmation bias.
Explanation: The independence of the second checker, who should have no prior knowledge of the medication order or the initial preparation process, is crucial to avoid confirmation bias and ensure a truly objective verification process.

659. What role does documentation play in the independent double-check process?
a. It is unnecessary if the check confirms accuracy.
b. It provides a legal record of the checking process but has no impact on patient safety.
c. It is critical for tracking the effectiveness of the process and identifying areas for improvement.
d. It should be avoided to reduce paperwork.

Answer: c. It is critical for tracking the effectiveness of the process and identifying areas for improvement.
Explanation: Documentation of independent double-checks is essential for tracking the process's effectiveness, providing a record of checks performed, and identifying patterns or areas where improvements can be made to enhance safety.

660. What is a potential drawback of relying solely on independent double-checks for ensuring medication safety?
a. It can lead to overconfidence and complacency, potentially bypassing other safety measures.
b. It increases the efficiency of the medication dispensing process.
c. It reduces the need for electronic prescribing systems.
d. It eliminates all types of medication errors.

Answer: a. It can lead to overconfidence and complacency, potentially bypassing other safety measures. Explanation: While independent double-checks can significantly reduce errors, relying solely on them can lead to overconfidence and complacency, potentially causing individuals to bypass or undervalue other critical safety measures and checks within the medication use process.

661. In what way can technology complement independent double-checks in medication safety?
a. By completely replacing the need for human checks
b. By providing automated alerts and reminders for high-risk medications that require double-checks
c. By eliminating the need for any checks for low-risk medications
d. By reducing the importance of clinical judgment in medication administration

Answer: b. By providing automated alerts and reminders for high-risk medications that require double-checks. Explanation: Technology, such as clinical decision support systems, can complement independent double-checks by providing automated alerts and reminders for high-risk medications, enhancing the process's overall effectiveness and ensuring that critical checks are not overlooked.

662. When counseling a patient on the use of an inhaler for asthma, what safety information is crucial to emphasize?
a. The importance of shaking the inhaler well before use
b. The need to store the inhaler in the refrigerator
c. The option to use the inhaler more frequently for better results
d. The ability to share the inhaler with family members who have similar symptoms

Answer: a. The importance of shaking the inhaler well before use. Explanation: It's crucial to shake the inhaler well before use to ensure the medication is properly mixed and the correct dose is delivered with each inhalation. This helps in achieving the desired therapeutic effect and maintaining effective asthma control.

663. During counseling on warfarin therapy, what dietary advice should be provided to ensure safety?
a. Increase intake of vitamin K-rich foods like green leafy vegetables
b. Maintain a consistent intake of vitamin K-rich foods to ensure stable drug activity
c. Avoid foods high in vitamin C as they can counteract the medication's effects
d. Consume grapefruit juice daily to enhance the medication's absorption

Answer: b. Maintain a consistent intake of vitamin K-rich foods to ensure stable drug activity. Explanation: Patients on warfarin therapy should maintain a consistent intake of vitamin K-rich foods because vitamin K can affect how warfarin works, potentially leading to fluctuations in the INR (International Normalized Ratio). Sudden changes in vitamin K intake can lead to either an increased risk of bleeding or decreased effectiveness of the medication.

664. What key information should be provided when counseling a patient starting on insulin therapy for diabetes management?
a. The possibility of skipping doses if blood sugar levels are normal
b. The importance of rotating injection sites to prevent lipodystrophy
c. The need to decrease insulin doses during periods of physical activity
d. The recommendation to store all insulin vials in the freezer

Answer: b. The importance of rotating injection sites to prevent lipodystrophy. Explanation: Rotating injection sites is crucial when using insulin to prevent lipodystrophy, a condition that affects the fat tissue under the skin and can interfere with insulin absorption. Patients should be advised to use different sites for each injection to ensure consistent insulin absorption and effectiveness.

665. When counseling a patient on the use of a nitroglycerin patch for angina, what safety precaution is essential to mention?

a. The patch can be cut into smaller pieces for a lower dose
b. The patch should be applied directly over the heart for best results
c. The patch should be worn continuously, without taking breaks
d. Avoid exposure of the patch to heat sources, such as heating pads or hot water bottles

Answer: d. Avoid exposure of the patch to heat sources, such as heating pads or hot water bottles. Explanation: Patients should be cautioned to avoid exposing the nitroglycerin patch to heat sources because heat can increase nitroglycerin absorption, potentially leading to an excessive drop in blood pressure or other adverse effects.

666. In counseling a patient on the use of an oral contraceptive pill, what is a critical piece of safety information to provide?
a. The effectiveness of the pill is enhanced by taking it with grapefruit juice
b. Antibiotics can decrease the effectiveness of the pill, increasing the risk of unintended pregnancy
c. Missing one pill requires immediate discontinuation of the pack and starting a new pack
d. The pill should be discontinued if the patient experiences mild headaches

Answer: b. Antibiotics can decrease the effectiveness of the pill, increasing the risk of unintended pregnancy. Explanation: It's important to inform patients that certain antibiotics (and other medications) can decrease the effectiveness of oral contraceptives, leading to an increased risk of unintended pregnancy. Patients should be advised to use an additional method of contraception during antibiotic therapy and for a short period after completing the antibiotics.

667. What safety advice should be given to a patient prescribed a fentanyl transdermal patch for chronic pain?
a. The patch should be changed every day, even if pain relief is adequate
b. Used patches can be folded in half and discarded in regular trash
c. The patch application site should be rotated to avoid skin irritation
d. Avoid exposing the patch to heat as it can increase the risk of overdose

Answer: d. Avoid exposing the patch to heat as it can increase the risk of overdose. Explanation: Patients using fentanyl patches should be advised to avoid exposing the patch to heat sources such as heating pads, electric blankets, heated water beds, or saunas, as heat can increase the release rate of fentanyl from the patch, leading to increased absorption and potentially life-threatening overdose.

668. When providing counseling for sildenafil, what important safety information should be emphasized regarding concurrent medication use?
a. ACE inhibitors should be avoided as they can reduce sildenafil's effectiveness
b. Nonsteroidal anti-inflammatory drugs (NSAIDs) enhance sildenafil's action and can be used for better results
c. Nitrates should not be taken concomitantly due to the risk of severe hypotension
d. Antihistamines should be avoided as they can nullify sildenafil's effects

Answer: c. Nitrates should not be taken concomitantly due to the risk of severe hypotension. Explanation: It is critical to advise patients against the concurrent use of sildenafil and nitrates, as this combination can lead to severe hypotension (low blood pressure), which can be life-threatening.

669. For a patient starting on lithium therapy for bipolar disorder, what monitoring parameter is vital to discuss during counseling?
a. Daily cholesterol levels
b. Weekly liver function tests
c. Regular blood lithium levels to avoid toxicity
d. Monthly thyroid hormone tests only

Answer: c. Regular blood lithium levels to avoid toxicity. Explanation: Patients on lithium therapy need regular monitoring of blood lithium levels to ensure they are within the therapeutic range and to avoid toxicity. Lithium has a narrow therapeutic window, and levels that are too high can lead to serious adverse effects.

670. What precaution is important to communicate to a patient prescribed a tetracycline antibiotic for acne treatment?
a. The medication will cause permanent teeth discoloration in adults
b. Sun exposure should be limited due to increased risk of photosensitivity
c. The medication should be taken with a full glass of milk for better absorption
d. The treatment effectiveness is significantly reduced when used with topical acne medications

Answer: b. Sun exposure should be limited due to increased risk of photosensitivity. Explanation: Patients taking tetracycline antibiotics should be cautioned about the increased risk of photosensitivity and advised to limit sun exposure and use sun protection measures (e.g., sunscreen, protective clothing) to prevent sunburn-like reactions.

671. When counseling a patient on the use of a metered-dose inhaler (MDI) with a corticosteroid for asthma, what instruction is crucial for preventing oral thrush?
a. Rinse the mouth with water and spit after each use of the inhaler
b. The inhaler should be used immediately after meals for better efficacy
c. The inhaler must be shaken for at least 30 seconds before use
d. Use the inhaler only once daily, regardless of symptoms

Answer: a. Rinse the mouth with water and spit after each use of the inhaler. Explanation: It is crucial to instruct patients to rinse their mouth with water and spit it out after each use of a corticosteroid metered-dose inhaler to reduce the risk of developing oral thrush, a common side effect of inhaled corticosteroids.

672. What is the most common immediate hypersensitivity reaction to penicillin?
a. Nephrotoxicity
b. Anaphylaxis
c. Photosensitivity
d. Ototoxicity

Answer: b. Anaphylaxis. Explanation: Anaphylaxis is the most severe and immediate hypersensitivity reaction to penicillin, characterized by rapid onset and potentially life-threatening symptoms such as difficulty breathing, hypotension, and swelling of the face, lips, or throat.

673. A patient reports a rash after taking amoxicillin. What type of allergic reaction is this most indicative of?
a. Type I hypersensitivity
b. Type II hypersensitivity
c. Type III hypersensitivity
d. Type IV hypersensitivity

Answer: d. Type IV hypersensitivity. Explanation: A rash developing after taking amoxicillin is most indicative of a Type IV hypersensitivity reaction, also known as a delayed hypersensitivity reaction, which typically occurs days after exposure to the allergen.

674. When a patient has a known allergy to sulfonamides, which of the following medications should be used with caution due to cross-reactivity?
a. Metformin
b. Furosemide
c. Acetaminophen
d. Levothyroxine

Answer: b. Furosemide. Explanation: Furosemide, a loop diuretic, should be used with caution in patients with a known allergy to sulfonamides due to potential cross-reactivity, as both sulfonamide antibiotics and some non-antibiotic sulfonamides (like furosemide) contain a sulfonamide moiety.

675. What is the appropriate first step when a patient presents with a suspected drug allergy?
a. Prescribe an antihistamine
b. Discontinue the suspected drug
c. Administer epinephrine immediately
d. Increase the dosage of the suspected drug to build tolerance

Answer: b. Discontinue the suspected drug. Explanation: The appropriate first step when a patient presents with a suspected drug allergy is to discontinue the suspected drug to prevent further exposure and potential exacerbation of the allergic reaction.

676. Which class of drugs is commonly associated with causing angioedema?
a. Beta-blockers
b. Angiotensin-converting enzyme (ACE) inhibitors
c. Statins

d. Proton pump inhibitors

Answer: b. Angiotensin-converting enzyme (ACE) inhibitors. Explanation: ACE inhibitors are commonly associated with causing angioedema, which is a serious allergic reaction characterized by deep tissue swelling, often around the eyes and lips, and sometimes the throat.

677. In managing a patient with a severe penicillin allergy, what alternative antibiotic class is generally considered safe?
a. Cephalosporins
b. Macrolides
c. Aminoglycosides
d. Fluoroquinolones

Answer: b. Macrolides. Explanation: Macrolides, such as erythromycin, azithromycin, and clarithromycin, are generally considered safe alternatives for patients with severe penicillin allergies due to their different chemical structure and low cross-reactivity with penicillins.

678. What is the role of skin testing in the context of drug allergies?
a. To confirm the effectiveness of antihistamines
b. To determine the severity of allergic reactions
c. To identify specific drug allergies and potential cross-reactivities
d. To predict future allergic reactions to unrelated drugs

Answer: c. To identify specific drug allergies and potential cross-reactivities. Explanation: Skin testing plays a crucial role in identifying specific drug allergies and potential cross-reactivities by exposing the skin to small amounts of the drug allergen and observing for a reaction, aiding in safe medication selection for the patient.

679. When documenting a patient's drug allergy, what information is crucial to include?
a. Only the name of the drug
b. The specific reaction experienced and the drug involved
c. The dosage of the drug that caused the reaction
d. The date and time the drug was last administered

Answer: b. The specific reaction experienced and the drug involved. Explanation: When documenting a patient's drug allergy, it is crucial to include both the specific reaction experienced (e.g., rash, anaphylaxis) and the drug involved to inform future healthcare providers of the potential risk and guide safe medication prescribing.

680. What is desensitization therapy in the context of drug allergies?
a. A process to strengthen the immune system
b. Administering increasing doses of the allergen to induce tolerance

c. Replacing the allergic drug with a stronger medication
d. Using antihistamines to suppress allergic symptoms

Answer: b. Administering increasing doses of the allergen to induce tolerance. Explanation: Desensitization therapy involves administering gradually increasing doses of the allergen (the drug to which the patient is allergic) in a controlled setting to induce a state of temporary tolerance, allowing the patient to receive a medication necessary for treatment despite a known allergy.

681. In the case of a non-severe allergic reaction to a medication, what is a potential management strategy?
a. Immediate discontinuation of all medications
b. Administration of a therapeutic challenge with the suspected drug
c. Use of genetic testing to predict future reactions
d. Permanent avoidance of all drugs within the same class

Answer: b. Administration of a therapeutic challenge with the suspected drug. Explanation: In cases of non-severe allergic reactions, a therapeutic challenge with the suspected drug may be considered, where the drug is re-administered under close medical supervision to confirm the allergy and assess the reaction, guiding future treatment decisions.

682. When documenting a patient's allergic reaction to penicillin, which of the following details is essential to include for comprehensive understanding?
a. The color of the medication
b. The specific symptoms experienced by the patient
c. The pharmacy that dispensed the medication
d. The cost of the medication

Answer: b. The specific symptoms experienced by the patient. Explanation: Documenting the specific symptoms experienced by the patient during an allergic reaction to penicillin is crucial. This information helps healthcare providers understand the severity of the allergy and aids in making informed decisions regarding alternative treatments.

683. In assessing the severity of a drug reaction, which factor is NOT typically considered?
a. The duration of symptoms after medication administration
b. The patient's previous exposure to the drug
c. The patient's preference for the drug's brand
d. The need for medical intervention to manage symptoms

Answer: c. The patient's preference for the drug's brand. Explanation: The patient's preference for the drug's brand is not a factor in assessing the severity of a drug reaction. The focus is on clinical outcomes, such as symptom duration, previous exposure, and the need for medical intervention.

684. Which of the following best describes cross-reactivity in drug allergies?
a. An allergic reaction that occurs due to the drug's color or flavoring agents
b. An allergic reaction to a drug that is chemically unrelated to a previously identified allergen
c. An allergic reaction to a drug with a similar chemical structure to a previously identified allergen
d. A non-allergic adverse reaction that mimics allergic symptoms

Answer: c. An allergic reaction to a drug with a similar chemical structure to a previously identified allergen. Explanation: Cross-reactivity in drug allergies refers to an allergic reaction to a drug that has a similar chemical structure to another drug to which the patient has previously been identified as allergic. This similarity in structure can trigger a similar immune response.

685. How should a pharmacy technician document a medication error for quality improvement purposes?
a. By anonymously reporting the error to a supervisor
b. By including the names of all staff involved in internal communications
c. By detailing the error, corrective actions taken, and recommendations for prevention in the pharmacy's error log
d. By discussing the error informally with colleagues to ensure it is not repeated

Answer: c. By detailing the error, corrective actions taken, and recommendations for prevention in the pharmacy's error log. Explanation: Documenting a medication error should include a detailed description of the error, the corrective actions taken to resolve the issue, and recommendations for preventing similar errors in the future. This documentation in the pharmacy's error log is crucial for quality improvement and ensuring patient safety.

686. In the context of adverse drug reactions (ADRs), what does the term 'severity' refer to?
a. The cost implications of the ADR for the healthcare system
b. The patient's ability to tolerate the discomfort caused by the ADR
c. The clinical impact of the ADR and the level of intervention required
d. The frequency of the ADR occurrence within the patient population

Answer: c. The clinical impact of the ADR and the level of intervention required. Explanation: The 'severity' of an adverse drug reaction refers to the clinical impact on the patient and the level of medical intervention required to address the ADR. Severity can range from mild, requiring no intervention, to severe, which may necessitate significant medical intervention or hospitalization.

687. What is the importance of documenting the lot number of a medication in the event of an adverse reaction?
a. To track the medication's price changes over time
b. To identify potential manufacturing issues or recalls associated with that batch
c. To ensure the patient can request the same lot in the future
d. To monitor the expiration date of the medication

Answer: b. To identify potential manufacturing issues or recalls associated with that batch. Explanation: Documenting the lot number of a medication in the event of an adverse reaction is important to trace the specific batch of the medication. This information can help identify if the adverse reaction is isolated or if there are broader manufacturing issues or recalls associated with that batch.

688. When educating a patient on recognizing signs of medication toxicity, which of the following is a critical point to emphasize?
a. The appearance of the medication
b. Sudden changes in taste preferences
c. Specific symptoms that may indicate toxicity
d. The color of the medication packaging

Answer: c. Specific symptoms that may indicate toxicity. Explanation: When educating a patient on recognizing signs of medication toxicity, it is critical to emphasize specific symptoms that may indicate toxicity. These symptoms can vary depending on the medication but may include things like jaundice, severe gastrointestinal distress, or changes in mental status.

689. How does documenting a patient's medication history contribute to preventing cross-reactivity errors?
a. By ensuring the patient receives medications from the same manufacturer
b. By identifying potential allergies or intolerances to medication classes or families
c. By keeping a record of medications the patient prefers
d. By tracking the frequency of medication administration

Answer: b. By identifying potential allergies or intolerances to medication classes or families. Explanation: Documenting a patient's medication history, including any known allergies or adverse reactions, helps in identifying potential cross-reactivity with new medications. This information is crucial for avoiding medications that are chemically similar to those the patient has reacted to in the past.

690. What role does patient counseling play in minimizing the risk of severe adverse drug reactions?
a. It allows the pharmacy to shift liability to the patient for any adverse reactions
b. It ensures the patient is aware of the financial cost of their medication regimen
c. It provides the patient with knowledge to identify and respond to adverse reactions promptly
d. It encourages the patient to self-manage their medication regimen without medical advice

Answer: c. It provides the patient with knowledge to identify and respond to adverse reactions promptly. Explanation: Patient counseling plays a crucial role in minimizing the risk of severe adverse drug reactions by educating the patient on potential side effects and what actions to take if they occur. This knowledge empowers patients to recognize adverse reactions early and seek medical intervention promptly, potentially mitigating the severity of the reaction.

691. Which medication class is most commonly associated with allergic reactions, prompting the need for allergy status verification before administration?
a. Nonsteroidal anti-inflammatory drugs (NSAIDs)

b. Penicillins
c. Calcium channel blockers
d. Thiazide diuretics

Answer: b. Penicillins. Explanation: Penicillins are well-documented for their potential to cause allergic reactions, ranging from mild rashes to severe anaphylaxis. Therefore, verifying a patient's allergy status is crucial before administering any medication from this class to avoid potentially life-threatening reactions.

692. A patient reports a history of hives after taking sulfamethoxazole/trimethoprim. This reaction suggests an allergy to which type of drug?
a. Beta-lactams
b. Sulfa drugs
c. ACE inhibitors
d. Statins

Answer: b. Sulfa drugs. Explanation: Sulfamethoxazole/trimethoprim contains sulfamethoxazole, a sulfa drug. Hives or urticaria following its intake indicate a sulfa drug allergy, warranting caution with other medications containing sulfa compounds.

693. In the context of drug allergies, what is the significance of a patient having a reaction to local anesthetics such as lidocaine?
a. It indicates a cross-reactivity with all anesthetic agents.
b. It suggests a potential allergy to ester-type local anesthetics but not necessarily to amide-type local anesthetics like lidocaine.
c. It often points to an allergy to the amide group, which includes lidocaine and similar compounds.
d. It typically signifies an allergy to preservatives in the anesthetic solution rather than the anesthetic itself.

Answer: d. It typically signifies an allergy to preservatives in the anesthetic solution rather than the anesthetic itself. Explanation: True allergies to amide-type local anesthetics like lidocaine are rare. Reactions are more commonly associated with other components in the solution, such as preservatives or epinephrine, rather than the anesthetic compound itself.

694. Which component in some intravenous contrast media can cause allergic-type reactions in susceptible individuals?
a. Iodine
b. Barium
c. Magnesium
d. Potassium

Answer: a. Iodine. Explanation: Iodinated contrast media used in radiographic procedures can cause allergic-type reactions in susceptible individuals, ranging from mild (nausea, vomiting) to severe (anaphylaxis), particularly in those with a history of iodine allergy or previous reactions to contrast media.

695. For patients with a documented penicillin allergy, which of the following antibiotics should be prescribed with caution due to potential cross-reactivity?
a. Cephalexin
b. Azithromycin
c. Vancomycin
d. Doxycycline

Answer: a. Cephalexin. Explanation: Cephalexin, a cephalosporin antibiotic, may have cross-reactivity with penicillins due to structural similarities. Although cross-reactivity rates are low, especially with later generations of cephalosporins, caution is advised when prescribing to patients with a known penicillin allergy.

696. What is the recommended approach for managing patients with a history of severe allergic reactions to multiple drug classes?
a. Prescribe only herbal medications
b. Conduct allergy testing for all commonly used medications
c. Utilize a thorough drug history and consultation with an allergist when necessary
d. Limit medication use to only life-threatening conditions

Answer: c. Utilize a thorough drug history and consultation with an allergist when necessary. Explanation: For patients with complex drug allergies, a detailed drug history to identify specific triggers, along with consultation with an allergist for possible testing and desensitization protocols, is recommended to safely manage their medication needs.

697. How should a pharmacy technician respond if a patient reports a "sulfa" allergy when filling a prescription for a thiazide diuretic?
a. Automatically substitute the thiazide diuretic with a potassium-sparing diuretic
b. Note the allergy in the patient's profile and consult the pharmacist for an appropriate action
c. Ignore the allergy since "sulfa" allergies are typically not serious
d. Recommend over-the-counter antihistamines to prevent an allergic reaction

Answer: b. Note the allergy in the patient's profile and consult the pharmacist for an appropriate action. Explanation: If a patient reports a "sulfa" allergy, the pharmacy technician should document this in the patient's profile and consult with the pharmacist. The pharmacist can then assess the relevance of the allergy to the prescribed medication and decide on the appropriate course of action, which may involve contacting the prescriber for an alternative medication if necessary.

698. What is an important consideration when a patient with a known allergy to aspirin needs a nonsteroidal anti-inflammatory drug (NSAID)?
a. All NSAIDs are safe alternatives to aspirin

b. NSAIDs should be avoided due to the risk of cross-reactivity
c. Only COX-2 inhibitors are safe in the context of aspirin allergy
d. Acetaminophen can be used as an alternative, although it is not an NSAID

Answer: d. Acetaminophen can be used as an alternative, although it is not an NSAID. Explanation: Patients with aspirin allergies may also react to other NSAIDs due to cross-reactivity. While COX-2 inhibitors may be safer alternatives, they still pose some risk. Acetaminophen is often considered a safer alternative for pain relief, though it lacks the anti-inflammatory properties of NSAIDs.

699. When a patient reports an allergy to latex, which of the following should be closely reviewed for potential cross-reactivity?
a. Medications with red dye
b. Injectable medications with rubber stoppers
c. Oral medications in gelatin capsules
d. Medications in glass vials

Answer: b. Injectable medications with rubber stoppers. Explanation: Patients with latex allergies may react to the natural rubber latex used in some medication vial stoppers and syringe plungers. Injectable medications with rubber components should be reviewed and possibly avoided or substituted with latex-free alternatives to prevent allergic reactions.

700. Which of the following is a Type A adverse drug reaction (ADR)?
a. An unexpected allergic reaction to a newly prescribed antibiotic
b. Nephrotoxicity associated with long-term use of NSAIDs
c. A rare but severe skin reaction to an antiepileptic drug
d. Discoloration of teeth in children due to tetracycline therapy

Answer: b. Nephrotoxicity associated with long-term use of NSAIDs. Explanation: Type A adverse drug reactions are those that are predictable and often dose-dependent, related to the pharmacological action of the drug. Nephrotoxicity from long-term use of NSAIDs is a known and predictable side effect related to their mechanism of action on prostaglandin synthesis, which can affect renal function.

701. A patient presents with acute onset of muscle pain, weakness, and dark-colored urine after starting a new medication. Which drug class is most likely responsible?
a. Statins, due to the risk of rhabdomyolysis
b. Antihypertensives, due to blood pressure fluctuations
c. Antibiotics, due to potential allergic reactions
d. Anticoagulants, due to risk of internal bleeding

Answer: a. Statins, due to the risk of rhabdomyolysis. Explanation: Statins are associated with a risk of rhabdomyolysis, a severe condition characterized by muscle breakdown, leading to symptoms such as muscle pain, weakness, and dark-colored urine from the presence of myoglobin. This condition requires immediate medical attention.

702. In the case of a patient developing a dry cough after starting medication for hypertension, which class of drugs is most likely responsible?
a. Beta-blockers
b. Calcium channel blockers
c. Angiotensin-converting enzyme (ACE) inhibitors
d. Diuretics

Answer: c. Angiotensin-converting enzyme (ACE) inhibitors. Explanation: A common side effect of ACE inhibitors, used for hypertension, is a persistent dry cough. This side effect is related to the accumulation of bradykinin in the respiratory tract, which ACE inhibitors can cause.

703. What is the mechanism behind aspirin-induced asthma in susceptible individuals?
a. Activation of histamine receptors leading to bronchoconstriction
b. Inhibition of COX enzymes, leading to an imbalance in prostaglandin production
c. Direct damage to the respiratory mucosa
d. Stimulation of the immune system causing an allergic response

Answer: b. Inhibition of COX enzymes, leading to an imbalance in prostaglandin production. Explanation: Aspirin-induced asthma is caused by the inhibition of cyclooxygenase (COX) enzymes by aspirin, leading to an imbalance in prostaglandin and leukotriene production. This imbalance can result in bronchoconstriction in susceptible individuals.

704. A patient develops acute kidney injury after receiving a high dose of a medication during surgery. Which medication is most likely responsible?
a. Acetaminophen
b. Ibuprofen
c. Vancomycin
d. Radiocontrast dye

Answer: d. Radiocontrast dye. Explanation: Radiocontrast dyes, used in imaging studies, are known to cause nephrotoxicity, particularly at high doses or in patients with pre-existing kidney conditions. This acute kidney injury is often referred to as contrast-induced nephropathy.

705. What is the primary concern with the use of fluoroquinolone antibiotics in pediatric patients?
a. Risk of developing type 2 diabetes
b. Potential for causing tendon damage and rupture
c. High likelihood of causing severe allergic reactions
d. Increased risk of dental caries

Answer: b. Potential for causing tendon damage and rupture. Explanation: Fluoroquinolone antibiotics have been associated with an increased risk of tendon damage and rupture, particularly the Achilles tendon. This risk is considered higher in pediatric patients, leading to recommendations to use these antibiotics cautiously in children.

706. A patient on anticoagulant therapy with warfarin starts taking St. John's Wort. What is the most likely outcome of this interaction?
a. Increased risk of bleeding due to enhanced warfarin effect
b. Reduced effectiveness of warfarin leading to potential clot formation
c. No significant interaction between St. John's Wort and warfarin
d. Increased risk of hypertension due to additive effects

Answer: b. Reduced effectiveness of warfarin leading to potential clot formation. Explanation: St. John's Wort induces the activity of cytochrome P450 enzymes, which can lead to increased metabolism of warfarin, reducing its effectiveness and potentially leading to inadequate anticoagulation and risk of clot formation.

707. When considering the use of NSAIDs in elderly patients, what is a major safety concern?
a. Increased risk of insomnia
b. Heightened susceptibility to muscle spasms
c. Potential for gastrointestinal bleeding
d. Enhanced risk of developing cataracts

Answer: c. Potential for gastrointestinal bleeding. Explanation: NSAIDs are associated with an increased risk of gastrointestinal bleeding, especially in elderly patients who may have a higher baseline risk due to other factors like concurrent medication use or pre-existing GI conditions.

708. In the context of adverse drug reactions, what does the term "idiosyncratic reaction" refer to?
a. A predictable reaction based on the drug's pharmacological action
b. An unpredictable reaction not related to the drug's pharmacological action
c. A mild reaction that does not require medical intervention
d. A reaction that occurs only after long-term drug use

Answer: b. An unpredictable reaction not related to the drug's pharmacological action. Explanation: Idiosyncratic reactions are unpredictable and not related to the pharmacological action of a drug. These reactions are typically rare and can vary widely in clinical presentation, often involving genetic, immunologic, or other unknown factors.

709. A patient on monoamine oxidase inhibitors (MAOIs) for depression reports consuming aged cheese at a party and now experiences a severe headache and hypertension. What is this reaction called?
a. Serotonin syndrome
b. Tyramine reaction
c. Histamine reaction
d. Dopamine excess syndrome

Answer: b. Tyramine reaction. Explanation: Patients on monoamine oxidase inhibitors (MAOIs) are at risk for a tyramine reaction when consuming foods high in tyramine, such as aged cheese. Tyramine can cause hypertensive crises in these patients due to the inhibition of MAO, which normally metabolizes tyramine in the body.

710. What is a common side effect associated with ACE inhibitors such as lisinopril?
a. Constipation
b. Dry, persistent cough
c. Tachycardia
d. Hyperkalemia

Answer: b. Dry, persistent cough. Explanation: ACE inhibitors, like lisinopril, can cause a dry, persistent cough in some patients due to the accumulation of bradykinin in the lungs. This side effect is reversible upon discontinuation of the medication.

711. Which side effect is commonly associated with the use of opioid medications like morphine?
a. Diarrhea
b. Insomnia
c. Constipation
d. Hypertension

Answer: c. Constipation. Explanation: Opioid medications, including morphine, often cause constipation due to their action on mu receptors in the gastrointestinal tract, which reduces gastrointestinal motility and fluid secretion.

712. What is a well-known side effect of corticosteroids such as prednisone when used long-term?
a. Weight loss
b. Bone demineralization
c. Hypoglycemia
d. Bradycardia

Answer: b. Bone demineralization. Explanation: Long-term use of corticosteroids like prednisone can lead to bone demineralization, increasing the risk of osteoporosis and fractures due to their effects on calcium metabolism and bone turnover.

713. Which side effect is commonly associated with the use of nonsteroidal anti-inflammatory drugs (NSAIDs) like ibuprofen?
a. Gastric ulcers
b. Hyperglycemia
c. Urinary retention
d. Tinnitus

Answer: a. Gastric ulcers. Explanation: NSAIDs like ibuprofen can cause gastric ulcers due to their mechanism of action, which involves inhibition of COX-1 enzyme, leading to reduced protection of the gastric mucosa against stomach acid.

714. What is a notable side effect of statins, such as atorvastatin, used for lowering cholesterol?
a. Muscle pain and weakness
b. Hyperactivity
c. Increased appetite
d. Hypotension

Answer: a. Muscle pain and weakness. Explanation: Statins, such as atorvastatin, can cause muscle pain and weakness (myalgia or, in severe cases, rhabdomyolysis) due to their effect on muscle cells, potentially leading to muscle injury.

715. What common side effect is associated with the use of metformin, a first-line medication for type 2 diabetes?
a. Dry mouth
b. Gastrointestinal upset
c. Cough
d. Skin rash

Answer: b. Gastrointestinal upset. Explanation: Metformin commonly causes gastrointestinal upset, including diarrhea, nausea, and abdominal discomfort, particularly when initiating treatment or increasing the dose.

716. Which side effect is frequently observed with the use of anticholinergic medications like atropine?
a. Excessive salivation
b. Bradycardia
c. Dry mouth
d. Hypertension

Answer: c. Dry mouth. Explanation: Anticholinergic medications like atropine often cause dry mouth (xerostomia) due to their inhibitory effect on muscarinic receptors, which reduces saliva production.

717. What is a common adverse effect of using loop diuretics such as furosemide?
a. Hyperkalemia
b. Edema
c. Hypokalemia
d. Weight gain

Answer: c. Hypokalemia. Explanation: Loop diuretics like furosemide can lead to hypokalemia, a condition characterized by low potassium levels in the blood, due to increased urinary excretion of potassium.

718. Which side effect is most commonly associated with the use of selective serotonin reuptake inhibitors (SSRIs) like sertraline?
a. Hypertension
b. Sexual dysfunction
c. Hyperkalemia
d. Urinary retention

Answer: b. Sexual dysfunction. Explanation: SSRIs, such as sertraline, are commonly associated with sexual dysfunction, including decreased libido, delayed ejaculation, and anorgasmia, due to their effects on serotonin levels in the brain.

719. What is a common side effect of beta-blockers like metoprolol used for hypertension?
a. Hyperglycemia
b. Tachycardia
c. Bronchospasm
d. Diarrhea

Answer: c. Bronchospasm. Explanation: Beta-blockers, such as metoprolol, can cause bronchospasm, especially in patients with pre-existing respiratory conditions like asthma, due to their blocking effect on beta-2 adrenergic receptors in the lungs.

720. What is the primary purpose of the FDA's MedWatch program?
a. To provide consumers with the latest drug pricing information
b. To facilitate the reporting of adverse events and product problems
c. To announce new drug approvals and indications
d. To track prescription drug sales and marketing practices

Answer: b. To facilitate the reporting of adverse events and product problems. Explanation: The FDA's MedWatch program is designed to facilitate the reporting of adverse events and product problems associated with medical products, including drugs, biologics, medical devices, and dietary supplements, to monitor product safety and protect public health.

721. Which organization focuses on improving patient safety by reducing errors related to medication and health care products?
a. American Pharmacists Association (APhA)
b. Institute for Safe Medication Practices (ISMP)
c. National Association of Boards of Pharmacy (NABP)
d. American Medical Association (AMA)

Answer: b. Institute for Safe Medication Practices (ISMP). Explanation: The Institute for Safe Medication Practices (ISMP) is a nonprofit organization dedicated to preventing medication errors and improving patient safety by providing error-reduction strategies, risk assessment tools, and educational resources for healthcare professionals.

722. When should a healthcare professional submit a report to MedWatch?
a. After every prescription is dispensed
b. When a medication error results in no harm to the patient
c. Upon encountering an adverse event or product problem that could harm patients
d. Only when mandated by state law

Answer: c. Upon encountering an adverse event or product problem that could harm patients. Explanation: Healthcare professionals should submit a report to MedWatch upon encountering any adverse event or product problem associated with medical products that has the potential to harm patients, even if harm has not yet occurred, to help the FDA monitor product safety.

723. What kind of information is crucial to include in a MedWatch report?
a. The patient's full medical history
b. Specific details about the adverse event or product problem
c. The healthcare professional's personal opinion on the product
d. The cost of the medication involved

Answer: b. Specific details about the adverse event or product problem. Explanation: A MedWatch report should include specific details about the adverse event or product problem, such as the nature of the event, the product involved, the outcome, and any relevant clinical information, to help the FDA assess the report and take necessary actions.

724. How does ISMP disseminate information on medication error prevention?
a. Through mandatory training programs for all healthcare workers
b. By publishing newsletters and alerts based on reported errors and research
c. Via direct emails to patients who have experienced medication errors
d. Through annual conferences for pharmaceutical companies only

Answer: b. By publishing newsletters and alerts based on reported errors and research. Explanation: ISMP disseminates information on medication error prevention through various channels, including newsletters, alerts, and educational resources that share insights and recommendations based on reported errors, research, and best practices in medication safety.

725. What is a unique feature of the ISMP's reporting system compared to MedWatch?
a. ISMP focuses solely on medication errors, while MedWatch covers all types of adverse events.
b. ISMP reports are only accessible to pharmacists, whereas MedWatch reports are public.

c. ISMP requires a fee for each report submitted, whereas MedWatch is a free service.
d. ISMP allows for anonymous reporting, while MedWatch requires reporter identification.

Answer: a. ISMP focuses solely on medication errors, while MedWatch covers all types of adverse events.
Explanation: The unique feature of ISMP's reporting system is its specific focus on medication errors and practices that lead to errors, while MedWatch is a broader system that covers a wide range of adverse events and product problems related to medical products.

726. In the event of a serious and unexpected adverse drug reaction, what timeline is recommended for reporting to MedWatch?
a. Within 24 hours
b. Within 7 days
c. Within 15 days
d. Within 30 days

Answer: c. Within 15 days. Explanation: In the event of a serious and unexpected adverse drug reaction, it is recommended to report the incident to MedWatch within 15 days to ensure timely review and action by the FDA to address potential public health concerns.

727. How can healthcare facilities utilize the information provided by ISMP to enhance medication safety?
a. By implementing ISMP's recommended best practices and error-prevention strategies
b. By requiring all patients to read ISMP publications before receiving medications
c. By using ISMP newsletters as the sole source of continuing education for staff
d. By reporting only to ISMP and not to the FDA's MedWatch program

Answer: a. By implementing ISMP's recommended best practices and error-prevention strategies. Explanation: Healthcare facilities can enhance medication safety by implementing the best practices and error-prevention strategies recommended by ISMP, which are based on evidence and analysis of medication errors, to reduce the risk of errors in their own settings.

728. What action might the FDA take based on reports received through the MedWatch program?
a. Immediate removal of all reported products from the market
b. Issuing safety alerts, recalls, or modifications to product labeling
c. Mandatory retraining of the healthcare professional who submitted the report
d. Compensation to patients who experienced adverse events

Answer: b. Issuing safety alerts, recalls, or modifications to product labeling. Explanation: Based on reports received through the MedWatch program, the FDA might take actions such as issuing safety alerts to inform the public and healthcare professionals about potential risks, initiating product recalls, or requiring modifications to product labeling to enhance safety information.

729. What is the primary goal of reporting medication errors and adverse drug reactions to organizations like MedWatch and ISMP?
a. To attribute blame to specific healthcare providers or manufacturers
b. To collect data for pharmaceutical marketing purposes
c. To improve medication safety and prevent future errors
d. To track the financial impact of errors on healthcare systems

Answer: c. To improve medication safety and prevent future errors. Explanation: The primary goal of reporting medication errors and adverse drug reactions to organizations like MedWatch and ISMP is to improve medication safety by identifying risk factors and patterns that lead to errors. This information is used to develop recommendations and strategies to prevent future errors, enhancing patient safety across the healthcare system.

730. What is the first-line treatment for anaphylaxis?
a. Oral antihistamines
b. Intravenous corticosteroids
c. Intramuscular epinephrine
d. Nebulized bronchodilators

Answer: c. Intramuscular epinephrine. Explanation: Intramuscular epinephrine is the first-line treatment for anaphylaxis due to its rapid onset of action in reversing the symptoms by decreasing vascular permeability, increasing cardiac output, and dilating constricted airways.

731. Which route of administration is preferred for epinephrine in the emergency treatment of anaphylaxis?
a. Oral
b. Intravenous
c. Intramuscular
d. Subcutaneous

Answer: c. Intramuscular. Explanation: The intramuscular route, particularly in the lateral thigh, is preferred for administering epinephrine in the emergency treatment of anaphylaxis because it provides rapid absorption and onset of action, crucial in a life-threatening situation.

732. After administering epinephrine for anaphylaxis, what is the next best step in patient management?
a. Discharge the patient with oral antihistamines
b. Observe the patient for at least 4 to 6 hours for biphasic reactions
c. Administer a second dose of epinephrine immediately
d. Start antibiotic therapy

Answer: b. Observe the patient for at least 4 to 6 hours for biphasic reactions. Explanation: After administering epinephrine for anaphylaxis, it's important to observe the patient in a medical facility for at least 4 to 6 hours due to the risk of biphasic reactions, which are delayed recurrences of anaphylaxis without further exposure to the allergen.

733. In anaphylaxis management, what role do antihistamines play?
a. They are the primary treatment to reverse anaphylaxis.
b. They provide symptomatic relief for skin symptoms and are adjunctive to epinephrine.
c. They prevent the occurrence of anaphylaxis when taken prophylactically.
d. They replace the need for corticosteroids in all patients.

Answer: b. They provide symptomatic relief for skin symptoms and are adjunctive to epinephrine. Explanation: Antihistamines are used as adjunctive therapy in anaphylaxis management to provide symptomatic relief, particularly for cutaneous symptoms like urticaria and itching, but they are not a substitute for epinephrine.

734. What is a biphasic anaphylactic reaction?
a. A mild allergic reaction that does not require epinephrine
b. An initial anaphylactic reaction followed by a second, potentially more severe reaction hours later
c. An immediate severe reaction to an allergen without prior exposure
d. A secondary reaction exclusively treated with corticosteroids

Answer: b. An initial anaphylactic reaction followed by a second, potentially more severe reaction hours later. Explanation: A biphasic anaphylactic reaction refers to the recurrence of anaphylaxis a few hours after the initial reaction has been treated and resolved, making prolonged observation after the first episode crucial.

735. Why is epinephrine considered the drug of choice for treating anaphylaxis over other vasopressors?
a. It has a slower onset of action, allowing for more controlled management.
b. It specifically targets gastrointestinal symptoms of anaphylaxis.
c. It has multiple physiological effects that are beneficial in reversing the pathophysiology of anaphylaxis.
d. It is less likely to cause hypertension than other vasopressors.

Answer: c. It has multiple physiological effects that are beneficial in reversing the pathophysiology of anaphylaxis. Explanation: Epinephrine is the drug of choice because it acts on alpha and beta-adrenergic receptors, leading to vasoconstriction, bronchodilation, increased cardiac output, and prevention of further release of allergic mediators, effectively countering the symptoms of anaphylaxis.

736. In an emergency setting, how should a healthcare provider determine the need for epinephrine administration in a suspected anaphylaxis case?
a. Wait for laboratory confirmation of elevated tryptase levels
b. Administer epinephrine if there is any doubt about the diagnosis, considering the potential for rapid deterioration
c. Only administer epinephrine after antihistamines have failed to improve symptoms
d. Use epinephrine exclusively in cases of respiratory distress

Answer: b. Administer epinephrine if there is any doubt about the diagnosis, considering the potential for rapid deterioration. Explanation: In emergencies, if anaphylaxis is suspected, epinephrine should be administered immediately, even if the diagnosis is uncertain, due to the potential for rapid progression of symptoms and the greater risk associated with delayed treatment compared to the relatively low risk of administering epinephrine.

737. What is the recommended observation period in a hospital setting after epinephrine administration for anaphylaxis, to monitor for biphasic reactions?
a. 30 minutes to 1 hour
b. 1 to 2 hours
c. 4 to 6 hours
d. 12 to 24 hours

Answer: c. 4 to 6 hours. Explanation: The recommended observation period in a hospital setting after administering epinephrine for anaphylaxis is 4 to 6 hours to monitor for biphasic reactions, ensuring prompt treatment if symptoms recur.

738. When educating a patient on using an epinephrine auto-injector, what is important to emphasize about the administration technique?
a. Inject epinephrine into the upper arm muscle.
b. Hold the auto-injector in place for at least 3 to 5 seconds after activation.
c. The auto-injector should be used through clothing in the abdominal area.
d. Reuse the auto-injector if the anaphylactic symptoms persist after 10 minutes.

Answer: b. Hold the auto-injector in place for at least 3 to 5 seconds after activation. Explanation: When educating a patient on using an epinephrine auto-injector, it's important to emphasize holding the auto-injector against the lateral thigh muscle for at least 3 to 5 seconds after activation to ensure the full dose of epinephrine is delivered.

739. What is the primary goal of medication reconciliation in a healthcare setting?
a. To ensure that a patient's medication costs are minimized
b. To confirm that the pharmacy inventory is accurately tracked
c. To verify that the patient's medication list is accurate across all transitions of care
d. To guarantee that all patients receive brand-name medications instead of generics

Answer: c. To verify that the patient's medication list is accurate across all transitions of care. Explanation: The primary goal of medication reconciliation is to ensure accuracy and consistency in a patient's medication regimen across different healthcare settings, such as at admission, transfer, and discharge, to prevent medication errors.

740. During medication reconciliation, what is a critical step when a patient is admitted to the hospital?
a. Immediately discontinuing all of the patient's home medications
b. Comparing the patient's home medication list with the hospital's formulary

c. Obtaining a comprehensive list of medications the patient was taking prior to admission
d. Prescribing new medications to replace the patient's home medications

Answer: c. Obtaining a comprehensive list of medications the patient was taking prior to admission. Explanation: A critical step in medication reconciliation upon hospital admission is obtaining a comprehensive and accurate list of all medications the patient was taking before admission, including prescription drugs, over-the-counter medications, and supplements, to ensure continuity and safety in medication management.

741. Which healthcare professional is typically responsible for conducting medication reconciliation at hospital discharge?
a. The attending physician only
b. The primary nurse on the patient's unit
c. A pharmacist or pharmacy technician as part of the healthcare team
d. The hospital administrator

Answer: c. A pharmacist or pharmacy technician as part of the healthcare team. Explanation: Pharmacists and pharmacy technicians, as part of the multidisciplinary healthcare team, often play a key role in conducting medication reconciliation at hospital discharge to ensure that patients understand their post-discharge medication regimen, including any changes made during their hospital stay.

742. What is a potential consequence of failing to accurately reconcile a patient's medications?
a. Increased length of hospital stay
b. Unnecessary duplication of medications
c. Reduced hospital pharmacy costs
d. Faster patient recovery times

Answer: b. Unnecessary duplication of medications. Explanation: Failing to accurately reconcile medications can lead to unnecessary duplication of medications, which can increase the risk of adverse drug reactions, medication non-adherence, and additional healthcare costs.

743. In medication reconciliation, what does the term "medication discrepancy" refer to?
a. A difference between two generic drugs
b. A variance between a patient's current medication list and what is clinically appropriate
c. The absence of over-the-counter drugs on the medication list
d. A change in the medication's appearance due to a new manufacturer

Answer: b. A variance between a patient's current medication list and what is clinically appropriate. Explanation: A medication discrepancy in the context of medication reconciliation refers to any inconsistency or unexplained difference between a patient's documented medication regimen and what is clinically appropriate, based on current health status, indications, and best practice guidelines.

744. How should a pharmacy technician address a medication discrepancy found during reconciliation?
a. Make an independent decision to adjust the medication regimen
b. Document the discrepancy and notify the prescribing healthcare provider for resolution
c. Ignore the discrepancy if it appears minor
d. Advise the patient to stop taking the discrepant medication immediately

Answer: b. Document the discrepancy and notify the prescribing healthcare provider for resolution. Explanation: Pharmacy technicians should document any medication discrepancies identified during reconciliation and communicate them to the prescribing healthcare provider or a pharmacist for review and resolution to ensure patient safety.

745. When reconciling medications, why is it important to include over-the-counter (OTC) medications and supplements in the review?
a. OTC medications and supplements do not impact prescription drug therapy
b. They may interact with prescription medications and affect drug therapy
c. OTC medications are typically more effective than prescription medications
d. To ensure that the patient is spending money wisely on supplements

Answer: b. They may interact with prescription medications and affect drug therapy. Explanation: Including over-the-counter medications and supplements in medication reconciliation is important because they can interact with prescription medications, potentially affecting the efficacy and safety of drug therapy.

746. What information is essential to collect for each medication during the reconciliation process?
a. The medication's color and shape
b. The patient's reason for taking each medication, dosage, route, and frequency
c. The cost of each medication
d. The pharmacy where the medication was last filled

Answer: b. The patient's reason for taking each medication, dosage, route, and frequency. Explanation: Essential information to collect for each medication during reconciliation includes the patient's reason for taking the medication, the dosage, the route of administration, and the frequency. This information ensures that the medication regimen is appropriate and safe for the patient.

747. In what setting is medication reconciliation particularly critical?
a. During pharmaceutical company audits
b. When a patient is transitioning between different levels of care within the healthcare system
c. At the beginning of each month
d. When a new brand-name medication is released

Answer: b. When a patient is transitioning between different levels of care within the healthcare system. Explanation: Medication reconciliation is particularly critical when a patient is transitioning between different levels of care, such as from the hospital to home care or from an outpatient setting to inpatient care, to ensure continuity and safety in medication management.

748. What role does patient or caregiver input play in medication reconciliation?
a. It is unnecessary if the healthcare provider has access to electronic medical records
b. It can provide valuable information about adherence and response to therapy
c. It should be disregarded in favor of professional medical advice
d. It is only useful for pediatric patients

Answer: b. It can provide valuable information about adherence and response to therapy. Explanation: Patient or caregiver input is crucial in medication reconciliation as it can provide valuable insights into the patient's adherence to the medication regimen, response to therapy, and experience with side effects, which are important for tailoring medication management to individual needs.

749. What is the most reliable method for obtaining an accurate medication list during a patient's hospital admission?
a. Asking the patient to recall their medications from memory
b. Reviewing the patient's previous medical records available in the hospital's electronic health system
c. Conducting a "brown bag" review where the patient brings all their current medications to the hospital
d. Relying on the list provided by the patient's primary care physician

Answer: c. Conducting a "brown bag" review where the patient brings all their current medications to the hospital. Explanation: A "brown bag" review, where patients bring all their medications, supplements, and over-the-counter drugs to the hospital, is considered highly reliable for obtaining an accurate medication list. It allows healthcare providers to visually verify the medications, their dosages, and frequency of use.

750. During transitions of care, such as discharge from hospital to home, what is essential to ensure medication safety?
a. Providing the patient with a new list of medications without consulting the home medications
b. Ensuring there is a comprehensive medication reconciliation comparing pre-admission and discharge medications
c. Advising the patient to continue with their regular medication regimen prior to hospital admission
d. Only focusing on the medications administered during the hospital stay

Answer: b. Ensuring there is a comprehensive medication reconciliation comparing pre-admission and discharge medications. Explanation: Comprehensive medication reconciliation during transitions of care is crucial. It involves comparing the patient's medication orders at discharge with those taken before admission to ensure continuity, avoid duplications, omissions, or interactions, and ensure the patient's safety.

751. What is a key step in verifying the accuracy of a patient's medication list upon hospital admission?
a. Guessing based on the patient's age and known conditions
b. Consulting a standard medication textbook

c. Cross-referencing with pharmacy records and previous hospital visits
d. Assuming the list provided by the patient is accurate without verification

Answer: c. Cross-referencing with pharmacy records and previous hospital visits. Explanation: Cross-referencing the patient's provided medication list with pharmacy dispensing records and previous hospital or clinic visit records is a key step in verifying accuracy. This helps identify any discrepancies, omissions, or duplications in the patient's medication regimen.

752. In the context of medication reconciliation, what does the term "medication discrepancy" refer to?
a. A difference between what the patient reports taking and what is documented in the medical record
b. The process of changing a patient's medication regimen without consulting a physician
c. An error made by the pharmacy in dispensing the medication
d. A new medication added to the patient's regimen during hospitalization

Answer: a. A difference between what the patient reports taking and what is documented in the medical record. Explanation: A medication discrepancy during reconciliation refers to any inconsistency between the medications a patient reports taking and what is documented in their medical records. Identifying and resolving these discrepancies is crucial for patient safety.

753. How should a healthcare provider handle over-the-counter (OTC) medications and supplements during medication reconciliation?
a. Ignore them as they are not considered as important as prescription medications
b. Include them in the medication list and consider their potential interactions with prescription medications
c. Only consider OTC medications if they are for treating chronic conditions
d. Advise the patient to stop all OTC medications and supplements immediately

Answer: b. Include them in the medication list and consider their potential interactions with prescription medications. Explanation: OTC medications and supplements should be included in the medication reconciliation process. Their potential interactions with prescription medications can have significant implications on the patient's overall medication regimen and health.

754. What role do family members or caregivers play in obtaining an accurate medication list for a patient?
a. Their input is generally unreliable and should be disregarded
b. They should be consulted, especially if the patient has cognitive impairments or difficulty communicating
c. They should only be involved if the patient gives explicit permission
d. Their observations should be noted but not included in the official medical record

Answer: b. They should be consulted, especially if the patient has cognitive impairments or difficulty communicating. Explanation: Family members or caregivers often provide valuable information for compiling an accurate medication list, especially for patients with cognitive impairments, communication difficulties, or complex medication regimens.

755. When a patient is transferred from one healthcare facility to another, what is a critical component for ensuring medication safety?
a. Immediately discontinuing all previous medications to start a new regimen
b. Sending the patient's medication bottles along with them without a written list
c. Providing a detailed medication list to the receiving facility, including dosages and administration times
d. Relying on the patient's memory for medication reconciliation at the new facility

Answer: c. Providing a detailed medication list to the receiving facility, including dosages and administration times. Explanation: Ensuring a detailed medication list accompanies the patient during transfers between healthcare facilities is critical. This list should include all current medications, dosages, and administration times to maintain continuity of care and prevent errors.

756. What is the significance of including the "indication" for each medication in the medication list during reconciliation?
a. It is only necessary for high-risk medications
b. It helps in identifying potentially unnecessary medications or therapeutic duplications
c. Indications are only relevant for inpatient settings and not needed for outpatient medications
d. It is a legal requirement but does not contribute to patient care

Answer: b. It helps in identifying potentially unnecessary medications or therapeutic duplications. Explanation: Including the "indication" for each medication in the list during reconciliation helps healthcare providers understand why each medication is prescribed, which aids in identifying potentially unnecessary medications, therapeutic duplications, or alternative treatments that could be more effective.

757. What strategy can minimize errors during medication reconciliation at hospital discharge?
a. Only focusing on new medications added during the hospital stay
b. Having the patient's primary care physician conduct the reconciliation after discharge
c. Involving a multidisciplinary team, including pharmacists, to review the discharge medication list
d. Using generic names only to avoid confusion with brand names

Answer: c. Involving a multidisciplinary team, including pharmacists, to review the discharge medication list. Explanation: Involving a multidisciplinary team, including pharmacists, in reviewing the discharge medication list can minimize errors. Pharmacists can provide expert insight into medication interactions, appropriateness, and continuity with the patient's pre-admission regimen.

758. What is the first step in identifying potential medication discrepancies during a patient's hospital admission?
a. Conducting a physical examination
b. Reviewing the patient's previous hospital records
c. Performing a thorough medication reconciliation
d. Consulting with the patient's primary care physician

Answer: c. Performing a thorough medication reconciliation. Explanation: Medication reconciliation is the process of creating the most accurate list possible of all medications a patient is taking — including drug name, dosage, frequency, and route — and comparing that list against the physician's admission, transfer, and/or discharge orders to identify and rectify any discrepancies.

759. A patient is prescribed warfarin and is newly prescribed a course of antibiotics. What is a potential interaction that should be monitored?
a. Increased risk of hypertension
b. Decreased effectiveness of warfarin
c. Increased risk of bleeding due to enhanced warfarin effect
d. Reduced absorption of antibiotics

Answer: c. Increased risk of bleeding due to enhanced warfarin effect. Explanation: Some antibiotics can alter the gut flora, affecting vitamin K production and metabolism, or directly interact with warfarin, potentially enhancing its anticoagulant effect and increasing the risk of bleeding.

760. During a transition of care, a patient's medication list includes both omeprazole and pantoprazole. What does this indicate?
a. A therapeutic duplication
b. A necessary combination therapy for complex conditions
c. An oversight in medication reconciliation
d. Complementary mechanisms of action

Answer: a. A therapeutic duplication. Explanation: Omeprazole and pantoprazole are both proton pump inhibitors (PPIs) with a similar mechanism of action, used to reduce stomach acid. Having both on a medication list without a specific indication could indicate therapeutic duplication, increasing the risk of side effects without additional therapeutic benefit.

761. What is a critical consideration when a patient on monoamine oxidase inhibitors (MAOIs) is prescribed a sympathomimetic drug?
a. Risk of sedation
b. Potential for hypertensive crisis
c. Decreased efficacy of the MAOI
d. Increased risk of gastrointestinal disturbances

Answer: b. Potential for hypertensive crisis. Explanation: Combining MAOIs with sympathomimetic drugs can lead to a hypertensive crisis due to excessive accumulation of neurotransmitters like norepinephrine, requiring careful monitoring and potentially alternative treatments.

762. When a patient taking sildenafil is prescribed a nitrate for chest pain, what is a potential risk?
a. Reduced effectiveness of sildenafil

b. Hypotensive crisis
c. Increased risk of thrombosis
d. Hyperglycemia

Answer: b. Hypotensive crisis. Explanation: The concurrent use of sildenafil, a phosphodiesterase inhibitor, with nitrates can lead to severe hypotension due to synergistic vasodilatory effects, posing a significant risk to the patient.

763. A patient is taking both a loop diuretic and digoxin. What potential interaction should be monitored?
a. Digoxin toxicity due to hypokalemia
b. Increased risk of dehydration
c. Reduced efficacy of the loop diuretic
d. Hyperkalemia

Answer: a. Digoxin toxicity due to hypokalemia. Explanation: Loop diuretics can cause hypokalemia, which increases the risk of digoxin toxicity by affecting cardiac conduction. Monitoring electrolyte levels and digoxin concentrations is essential in patients receiving this combination.

764. In identifying a drug-drug interaction, what is a significant concern with co-administration of a CYP3A4 inhibitor and a drug metabolized by CYP3A4?
a. Decreased plasma levels of the CYP3A4 substrate, reducing efficacy
b. Increased risk of metabolic alkalosis
c. Increased plasma levels of the CYP3A4 substrate, potentially leading to toxicity
d. Induction of CYP2D6 enzymes

Answer: c. Increased plasma levels of the CYP3A4 substrate, potentially leading to toxicity. Explanation: CYP3A4 inhibitors can significantly increase the plasma concentration of drugs metabolized by CYP3A4 by reducing their metabolic clearance, leading to an increased risk of adverse effects and toxicity.

765. What should be done if a patient's medication list includes both aspirin and ibuprofen, and the patient has a history of cardiovascular disease?
a. Continue both medications as they provide complementary benefits
b. Monitor for signs of gastrointestinal bleeding
c. Consult with the healthcare provider to address potential interference of ibuprofen with aspirin's antiplatelet effect
d. Increase the dose of aspirin to counteract ibuprofen's effect

Answer: c. Consult with the healthcare provider to address potential interference of ibuprofen with aspirin's antiplatelet effect. Explanation: Ibuprofen can interfere with the antiplatelet effect of low-dose aspirin, potentially reducing its cardiovascular protective benefits. A healthcare provider should review the necessity of both medications and consider alternative pain management strategies.

766. When reviewing a patient's medication list, you notice the concurrent use of two anticholinergic drugs. What is a primary concern with this combination?
a. Increased risk of cholinergic crisis
b. Exacerbation of anticholinergic side effects such as dry mouth, urinary retention, and constipation
c. Diminished effectiveness of both medications
d. Risk of serotonin syndrome

Answer: b. Exacerbation of anticholinergic side effects such as dry mouth, urinary retention, and constipation. Explanation: The concurrent use of multiple anticholinergic drugs can lead to an additive effect, exacerbating anticholinergic side effects, which may impact the patient's quality of life and increase the risk of complications, particularly in elderly patients.

767. What is the primary purpose of using a perpetual inventory system in pharmacy ordering and receiving?
a. To minimize the physical space needed for storage
b. To ensure that medication orders are automatically placed when stock is low
c. To track the sales and prescriptions filled per day
d. To comply with regulatory requirements for controlled substances

Answer: b. To ensure that medication orders are automatically placed when stock is low. Explanation: A perpetual inventory system continuously updates the quantity and value of stock on hand, ensuring that medication orders are automatically placed when stock levels reach a predefined threshold, thus maintaining an optimal inventory level and preventing stockouts.

768. When receiving a shipment of medications, what is the FIRST step that should be taken?
a. Stocking the medications on the shelves immediately to avoid clutter
b. Verifying the shipment against the purchase order and invoice for accuracy
c. Disposing of the shipping materials and containers
d. Recording the received medications in the sales system

Answer: b. Verifying the shipment against the purchase order and invoice for accuracy. Explanation: The first step upon receiving a shipment of medications is to verify the contents against the purchase order and invoice to ensure that the correct items, quantities, and prices are received. This step is crucial for maintaining inventory accuracy and identifying any discrepancies early in the process.

769. In the context of controlled substances, what additional step must be taken during the receiving process?
a. Reporting the received quantities to the marketing department
b. Placing the substances directly on retail shelves for easy access
c. Documenting the received quantities in a controlled substances log
d. Sending a thank-you note to the supplier for timely delivery

Answer: c. Documenting the received quantities in a controlled substances log. Explanation: When receiving controlled substances, it is essential to document the received quantities in a controlled substances log, detailing the name, strength, quantity, and date received. This step is critical for regulatory compliance and for maintaining strict control over these substances.

770. How should a pharmacy technician handle a medication that arrives damaged or with a compromised seal?
a. Accept the delivery and apply a discount to the damaged items
b. Quarantine the item and notify the supplier for return or replacement
c. Use the medication first to avoid wastage
d. Repackage the medication in a new container for dispensing

Answer: b. Quarantine the item and notify the supplier for return or replacement. Explanation: Any medication that arrives damaged or with a compromised seal should be quarantined immediately and should not be used. The supplier must be notified promptly to arrange for the return or replacement of the damaged items to ensure patient safety and maintain inventory integrity.

771. What is the significance of checking the expiration dates of medications during the receiving process?
a. To determine the price at which the medication should be sold
b. To ensure that medications are used for employee training before they expire
c. To prevent the stocking of medications that are close to or past their expiration date
d. To comply with the aesthetic standards of the pharmacy

Answer: c. To prevent the stocking of medications that are close to or past their expiration date. Explanation: Checking expiration dates during the receiving process is crucial to prevent the stocking and subsequent dispensing of medications that are close to or past their expiration date, ensuring the effectiveness and safety of medications provided to patients.

772. When a new medication is added to the pharmacy inventory, what critical information must be updated in the pharmacy management system?
a. The preferred manufacturer for future orders
b. The medication's name, dosage form, strength, and storage requirements
c. The color and shape of the medication for identification purposes
d. The sales predictions for the upcoming fiscal year

Answer: b. The medication's name, dosage form, strength, and storage requirements. Explanation: When adding a new medication to the pharmacy inventory, it is essential to update the pharmacy management system with critical information such as the medication's name, dosage form, strength, and storage requirements to ensure proper handling, storage, and dispensing.

773. What role does temperature monitoring play in the receiving process of medications?
a. It is only necessary for medications that require room temperature storage
b. It ensures that temperature-sensitive medications are stored appropriately upon receipt

c. It is a regulatory requirement for all non-prescription medications
d. Temperature monitoring is conducted solely for record-keeping purposes

Answer: b. It ensures that temperature-sensitive medications are stored appropriately upon receipt. Explanation: Temperature monitoring during the receiving process is crucial for temperature-sensitive medications, such as vaccines and certain biologics, to ensure that they have been transported and will be stored under the correct conditions to maintain their efficacy and safety.

774. In a scenario where a received medication is not on the original purchase order, what is the appropriate action?
a. Dispense the medication to patients without recording it in the inventory
b. Return the medication to the supplier immediately without documentation
c. Add the medication to the inventory and adjust the purchase order retroactively
d. Quarantine the medication and contact the supplier for clarification

Answer: d. Quarantine the medication and contact the supplier for clarification. Explanation: If a medication that was not ordered is received, it should be quarantined and not added to the inventory. The supplier should be contacted for clarification to resolve the discrepancy, whether it involves returning the medication or amending the purchase order if the medication is needed.

775. How should back-ordered medications be managed upon receipt to ensure continuity of care?
a. By immediately dispensing them to the patients on the waiting list
b. By storing them until the next inventory cycle
c. By updating the inventory system and notifying healthcare providers of their availability
d. By offering them to the first patient who requests medication, regardless of prior reservations

Answer: c. By updating the inventory system and notifying healthcare providers of their availability. Explanation: Upon receipt of back-ordered medications, the inventory system should be updated, and healthcare providers, as well as patients who were waiting for these medications, should be notified of their availability to ensure timely dispensing and continuity of care for those in need.

776. What is a best practice for managing the inventory of fast-moving medications to prevent stockouts?
a. Ordering in bulk quantities to last for a year
b. Implementing an automatic reordering system based on minimum and maximum levels
c. Relying on manual checks once every six months
d. Waiting for patient requests before reordering

Answer: b. Implementing an automatic reordering system based on minimum and maximum levels. Explanation: For fast-moving medications, implementing an automatic reordering system that triggers orders based on predefined minimum and maximum inventory levels is a best practice. This approach ensures a continuous supply, preventing stockouts while avoiding excessive inventory.

777. What is the primary role of pharmaceutical wholesalers in the supply chain?
a. To prescribe medications to patients
b. To act as intermediaries between manufacturers and pharmacies, ensuring efficient distribution of medications
c. To regulate drug prices and enforce drug laws
d. To provide direct patient care and consultation

Answer: b. To act as intermediaries between manufacturers and pharmacies, ensuring efficient distribution of medications. Explanation: Pharmaceutical wholesalers serve as the crucial link between drug manufacturers and healthcare providers, including pharmacies, by purchasing large quantities of medications and distributing them in smaller quantities to various healthcare settings, thereby ensuring an efficient and steady supply of medications.

778. In a contract between a pharmacy and a wholesaler, what is a "prime vendor agreement" (PVA)?
a. A legal requirement for all pharmacies to report drug shortages
b. An agreement where the pharmacy commits to purchasing a majority of its inventory from one wholesaler in exchange for discounts or favorable terms
c. A contract that allows the pharmacy to return all unsold medications for a full refund
d. An agreement that requires the wholesaler to exclusively sell specific medications to one pharmacy

Answer: b. An agreement where the pharmacy commits to purchasing a majority of its inventory from one wholesaler in exchange for discounts or favorable terms. Explanation: A prime vendor agreement is a contractual arrangement where a pharmacy agrees to buy most, if not all, of its pharmaceutical products from a single wholesaler. In return, the wholesaler typically offers the pharmacy better prices, discounts, or other favorable terms, benefiting both parties by ensuring consistent business for the wholesaler and cost savings for the pharmacy.

779. How do wholesalers contribute to drug shortage management?
a. By manufacturing alternative medications
b. By implementing allocation strategies to distribute limited drug supplies equitably among pharmacies
c. By setting higher prices for drugs in short supply
d. By advising the FDA on which drugs to approve

Answer: b. By implementing allocation strategies to distribute limited drug supplies equitably among pharmacies. Explanation: During drug shortages, wholesalers play a critical role by implementing allocation strategies that distribute the limited available stock of the drug as equitably as possible among their pharmacy customers. This may involve limiting the quantity that each pharmacy can purchase or prioritizing distribution based on the urgency of need, thereby helping to manage the shortage and ensure that patients have access to essential medications.

780. What is a key consideration for pharmacies when selecting a wholesaler?
a. The wholesaler's stock price and financial performance
b. The geographic proximity of the wholesaler's distribution centers to the pharmacy
c. The wholesaler's advertising and marketing capabilities
d. The wholesaler's ability to offer legal advice

Answer: b. The geographic proximity of the wholesaler's distribution centers to the pharmacy. Explanation: One key consideration for pharmacies in selecting a wholesaler is the geographic proximity of the wholesaler's distribution centers to the pharmacy. Closer proximity can lead to shorter delivery times, fresher stock, lower shipping costs, and more responsive service, all of which can significantly impact the pharmacy's ability to serve its patients effectively.

781. What does a "service level agreement" (SLA) in a wholesaler contract typically specify?
a. The educational qualifications required for pharmacy staff
b. The minimum stock levels the wholesaler must maintain for certain medications
c. The percentage of orders that must be fulfilled within a specified time frame
d. The social media strategy for promoting new medications

Answer: c. The percentage of orders that must be fulfilled within a specified time frame. Explanation: A service level agreement (SLA) within a wholesaler contract typically specifies performance metrics that the wholesaler agrees to meet, such as the percentage of orders that must be fulfilled within a specified time frame. This ensures that the pharmacy can rely on timely deliveries to meet patient needs.

782. How can a pharmacy benefit from a wholesaler's "generic sourcing program"?
a. By obtaining exclusive access to patented medications
b. By receiving larger rebates for purchasing brand-name drugs
c. By accessing a broader range of over-the-counter products
d. By purchasing generic drugs at competitive prices, potentially increasing the pharmacy's profit margins

Answer: d. By purchasing generic drugs at competitive prices, potentially increasing the pharmacy's profit margins. Explanation: A generic sourcing program offered by a wholesaler typically allows pharmacies to purchase generic drugs at highly competitive prices. This can lead to increased profit margins for the pharmacy on generic medications, as they can offer these drugs to their patients at lower prices while maintaining or even improving their profitability.

783. In negotiating contracts with wholesalers, why might a pharmacy consider the wholesaler's "return policy"?
a. To ensure they can exchange medications for newer versions
b. To be able to return unsold or expired medications for credit, reducing financial loss
c. To comply with local recycling regulations
d. To participate in pharmaceutical research and development

Answer: b. To be able to return unsold or expired medications for credit, reducing financial loss. Explanation: A wholesaler's return policy is an important consideration for pharmacies because it outlines the terms under which the pharmacy can return unsold, expired, or overstocked medications. A favorable return policy allows the pharmacy to receive credit for these returns, thereby minimizing financial loss associated with unsold inventory.

784. What role do wholesalers play in maintaining the "cold chain" for temperature-sensitive medications?
a. Providing specialized storage units for patients' homes

b. Ensuring that temperature-sensitive medications are stored and transported within required temperature ranges
c. Developing new refrigeration technologies for retail pharmacies
d. Setting temperature standards for medication manufacturing

Answer: b. Ensuring that temperature-sensitive medications are stored and transported within required temperature ranges. Explanation: Wholesalers are responsible for maintaining the cold chain for temperature-sensitive medications by ensuring that such medications are properly stored and transported within the required temperature ranges from the point of manufacture to delivery at the pharmacy. This is crucial for preserving the efficacy and safety of these medications.

785. How might a wholesaler's "technology integration services" benefit a pharmacy?
a. By replacing pharmacists with automated systems
b. By providing software that integrates with the pharmacy's inventory and point-of-sale systems for streamlined operations
c. By offering online-only medication sales
d. By mandating the use of specific medical devices

Answer: b. By providing software that integrates with the pharmacy's inventory and point-of-sale systems for streamlined operations. Explanation: A wholesaler's technology integration services can offer significant benefits to a pharmacy by providing software solutions that integrate seamlessly with the pharmacy's existing inventory management, point-of-sale systems, and electronic health records. This integration can streamline operations, improve accuracy, and enhance the efficiency of the pharmacy's workflow.

786. When evaluating a wholesaler's contract, why is it important for a pharmacy to consider the "compliance support" offered by the wholesaler?
a. To ensure the pharmacy adheres to social media policies
b. To assist the pharmacy in meeting regulatory and compliance requirements related to medication storage, handling, and dispensing
c. To guarantee a fixed number of social events for pharmacy staff
d. To mandate participation in specific political campaigns

Answer: b. To assist the pharmacy in meeting regulatory and compliance requirements related to medication storage, handling, and dispensing. Explanation: Compliance support offered by a wholesaler is crucial as it helps the pharmacy navigate the complex regulatory environment associated with the pharmaceutical industry. This support can include guidance on proper medication storage, handling, dispensing, and record-keeping practices, ensuring the pharmacy remains compliant with state and federal regulations, thereby minimizing the risk of legal issues or penalties.

787. What is the primary purpose of a purchase order in the pharmacy's procurement process?
a. To serve as a legal contract between the pharmacy and the supplier for the requested items
b. To track the pharmacy's sales and revenue
c. To record adverse drug reactions for medications
d. To serve as a marketing tool for new pharmaceutical products

Answer: a. To serve as a legal contract between the pharmacy and the supplier for the requested items. Explanation: A purchase order is primarily used in the pharmacy's procurement process as a formal, legal document issued to a supplier, detailing the types, quantities, and agreed prices for products or services. It serves as a binding contract once accepted by the supplier.

788. When reconciling an invoice with a purchase order, what discrepancy should prompt immediate action?
a. A difference in the color of the packaging noted on the invoice
b. A minor spelling error in the drug name on the invoice
c. A discrepancy in the quantity or price of items received
d. Different fonts used between the purchase order and invoice

Answer: c. A discrepancy in the quantity or price of items received. Explanation: Any discrepancies in the quantity or price of items between the purchase order and the invoice should prompt immediate action, as these can affect the pharmacy's inventory levels and financial accuracy. It is crucial to resolve these discrepancies to ensure proper payment and inventory management.

789. How should a pharmacy technician respond if a received shipment does not match the purchase order?
a. Accept the shipment and adjust the pharmacy's inventory to match
b. Refuse the entire shipment and return it to the supplier
c. Document the discrepancy and contact the supplier to resolve the issue
d. Distribute the extra products as free samples to patients

Answer: c. Document the discrepancy and contact the supplier to resolve the issue. Explanation: When a shipment does not match the purchase order, the pharmacy technician should document the discrepancy and contact the supplier to resolve the issue. This may involve returning incorrect items, receiving missing items, or adjusting the invoice to reflect what was actually received.

790. What information is typically included on a pharmacy's purchase order?
a. Patient prescription records
b. Detailed descriptions of each item, including quantity and price
c. The pharmacy's marketing strategies for the quarter
d. Personal information of the pharmacy staff

Answer: b. Detailed descriptions of each item, including quantity and price. Explanation: A pharmacy's purchase order typically includes detailed descriptions of each item being ordered, including the quantity and price of each item, to ensure clarity and accuracy in the procurement process.

791. In what scenario might a pharmacy receive a credit note from a supplier?
a. When the pharmacy orders an excess quantity of a medication
b. After submitting a successful marketing proposal to the supplier

c. If the pharmacy returns damaged or incorrect items from a shipment
d. When the pharmacy staff completes supplier-provided training

Answer: c. If the pharmacy returns damaged or incorrect items from a shipment. Explanation: A pharmacy might receive a credit note from a supplier if it returns damaged or incorrect items from a shipment. The credit note acknowledges the return and indicates that the pharmacy's account has been credited for the returned items, which can be used against future purchases or to correct the invoice.

792. What role does electronic data interchange (EDI) play in the ordering and receiving process in modern pharmacies?
a. It eliminates the need for physical inventory in pharmacies
b. It allows for the electronic exchange of purchase orders, invoices, and other documents
c. It is used exclusively for tracking employee hours and wages
d. It serves as an online platform for direct patient counseling

Answer: b. It allows for the electronic exchange of purchase orders, invoices, and other documents. Explanation: Electronic Data Interchange (EDI) plays a crucial role in modern pharmacies by allowing for the electronic exchange of business documents, such as purchase orders and invoices, between the pharmacy and suppliers. This technology streamlines the ordering and receiving process, reduces errors, and improves efficiency.

793. What is a backorder, and how should it be handled in the pharmacy's inventory system?
a. A special order for rare medications, marked as high priority in the system
b. An order that cannot be fulfilled by the supplier at the time of ordering, requiring monitoring for eventual fulfillment
c. A discounted order placed at the end of the fiscal year, to be stored separately
d. An order for over-the-counter medications, to be processed immediately

Answer: b. An order that cannot be fulfilled by the supplier at the time of ordering, requiring monitoring for eventual fulfillment. Explanation: A backorder occurs when an ordered item is not currently in stock with the supplier. In the pharmacy's inventory system, backorders should be carefully monitored to ensure that they are fulfilled when the item becomes available, to maintain inventory levels and meet patient needs.

794. When verifying the accuracy of an invoice, which element is crucial to review for preventing overpayment?
a. The aesthetic layout of the invoice
b. The terms and conditions of the return policy
c. The alignment of product descriptions and associated costs
d. The supplier's contact information and address

Answer: c. The alignment of product descriptions and associated costs. Explanation: When verifying an invoice, it is crucial to review the alignment of product descriptions with their associated costs to prevent overpayment. This involves ensuring that the prices, quantities, and products listed match the original purchase order and the goods received, and that any discounts or agreed-upon terms are accurately applied.

795. How does maintaining accurate records of purchase orders and invoices benefit a pharmacy?
a. It ensures that all medications are dispensed for free
b. It provides a basis for legal action against difficult patients
c. It aids in financial management, inventory control, and regulatory compliance
d. It allows for automatic prescription refills without patient consent

Answer: c. It aids in financial management, inventory control, and regulatory compliance. Explanation: Maintaining accurate records of purchase orders and invoices is essential for effective financial management, inventory control, and compliance with regulatory requirements. These records help track expenditures, manage stock levels, and provide documentation for audits and regulatory reviews, ensuring the pharmacy operates efficiently and within legal guidelines.

796. In the context of group purchasing organizations (GPOs), how do purchase orders and invoices differ when compared to direct purchases from suppliers?
a. GPOs require purchase orders and invoices to be submitted in person
b. There is no need for purchase orders or invoices when using GPOs
c. GPOs consolidate orders from multiple pharmacies, potentially altering pricing and invoicing processes
d. Purchase orders are replaced by verbal agreements, and invoices are not used

Answer: c. GPOs consolidate orders from multiple pharmacies, potentially altering pricing and invoicing processes.

797. What is the primary goal of implementing a First Expired, First Out (FEFO) stock rotation system in a pharmacy?
a. To maximize the shelf life of products on display
b. To ensure the oldest stock with the nearest expiration date is used first
c. To prioritize the sale of the most expensive medications
d. To reduce the frequency of inventory audits

Answer: b. To ensure the oldest stock with the nearest expiration date is used first. Explanation: The FEFO system prioritizes dispensing or using products that are closest to their expiration date before those with later dates, minimizing waste due to expired medications and ensuring medication efficacy for patients.

798. In a FEFO system, how should newly received stock be placed in relation to existing stock?
a. Behind or below existing stock to ensure older items are used first
b. In front of or above existing stock for easy access
c. Randomly, as long as the stock is within the pharmacy
d. In a separate area designated for new stock only

Answer: a. Behind or below existing stock to ensure older items are used first. Explanation: In a FEFO system, new stock should be placed behind or below existing items. This placement ensures that older stock, especially those with approaching expiration dates, is used or dispensed first, reducing the risk of having to discard expired medications.

799. What should a pharmacy technician do if they notice a medication near the front of the shelf has a later expiration date than one behind it?
a. Leave the medications as they are to avoid confusion
b. Move the medication with the later expiration date behind the one with the earlier date
c. Discard the medication with the earlier expiration date immediately
d. Report the discrepancy to the manufacturer

Answer: b. Move the medication with the later expiration date behind the one with the earlier date. Explanation: If a medication with a later expiration date is in front of one with an earlier date, the technician should reorder them so the item with the earlier expiration date is used first, adhering to the FEFO principle.

800. How does the FEFO system impact pharmacy inventory management during a recall?
a. It has no impact on recall management
b. It complicates the recall process by mixing lot numbers
c. It simplifies the recall process by keeping older stock at the front
d. It ensures only the newest products are recalled

Answer: c. It simplifies the recall process by keeping older stock at the front. Explanation: The FEFO system can simplify the recall process by ensuring that older stock, which is more likely to be affected by a recall, is used first. This can make it easier to identify and remove affected products, as they are more likely to be at the front and have been dispensed before newer stock.

801. When using a FEFO system, what is crucial for maintaining accurate stock rotation?
a. Regularly changing the prices of medications
b. Keeping all medications in refrigerated storage
c. Clearly labeling each item with its expiration date and lot number
d. Only ordering new stock when all existing stock has been used

Answer: c. Clearly labeling each item with its expiration date and lot number. Explanation: Clear labeling of each medication with its expiration date and lot number is crucial in a FEFO system to ensure that items are used in the correct order, reducing the risk of dispensing expired medications and facilitating efficient recall management.

802. What challenge might a pharmacy face when implementing a FEFO system for medications with long shelf lives?
a. Increased risk of theft
b. Difficulty in tracking expiration dates over extended periods
c. Decreased need for customer consultations
d. Rapid turnover of stock leading to frequent reordering

Answer: b. Difficulty in tracking expiration dates over extended periods. Explanation: Medications with long shelf lives can pose a challenge in a FEFO system because tracking their expiration dates over extended periods requires diligent monitoring and organization to ensure that the stock is rotated appropriately and used before it expires.

803. How can technology assist in maintaining a FEFO system in a pharmacy?
a. By automatically reordering stock when supplies are low
b. By using barcodes or RFID tags to track expiration dates and automate stock rotation
c. By providing virtual consultations to patients
d. By reducing the need for physical inventory checks

Answer: b. By using barcodes or RFID tags to track expiration dates and automate stock rotation. Explanation: Technology, such as barcode or RFID systems, can greatly assist in maintaining a FEFO system by tracking the expiration dates of medications and automating the process of stock rotation, ensuring that items are used in the correct order and reducing manual errors.

804. In what scenario might a pharmacy deviate from the FEFO principle?
a. When a medication is on sale
b. If a medication's packaging is damaged but still intact
c. When a specific lot of medication is requested by a healthcare provider
d. For high-demand items during peak hours

Answer: c. When a specific lot of medication is requested by a healthcare provider. Explanation: A pharmacy might deviate from the FEFO principle if a healthcare provider requests a specific lot of medication, perhaps due to specific patient needs or clinical considerations, even if it means bypassing older stock.

805. What is the impact of a well-maintained FEFO system on patient safety?
a. It increases the risk of dispensing expired medications
b. It ensures patients receive medications with adequate shelf life, enhancing treatment efficacy
c. It reduces the variety of medications available to patients
d. It prolongs the time it takes to dispense medications

Answer: b. It ensures patients receive medications with adequate shelf life, enhancing treatment efficacy. Explanation: A well-maintained FEFO system ensures that patients receive medications with adequate shelf life, minimizing the risk of dispensing expired or nearly expired medications, which can compromise treatment efficacy and patient safety.

806. How should a pharmacy address FEFO in a manual inventory system?
a. By relying solely on visual inspections for expiration dates
b. By documenting expiration dates in a log and organizing stock accordingly
c. By increasing the stock of fast-moving items only

d. By eliminating slow-moving items from the inventory

Answer: b. By documenting expiration dates in a log and organizing stock accordingly. Explanation: In a manual inventory system, documenting expiration dates in a log and organizing stock accordingly is crucial to maintaining a FEFO system. This methodical approach ensures older stock is used first and helps prevent the use of expired medications.

807. What is the recommended temperature range for storing most medications in a pharmacy setting?
a. 2°C to 8°C (36°F to 46°F)
b. 15°C to 30°C (59°F to 86°F)
c. 30°C to 40°C (86°F to 104°F)
d. Below 0°C (32°F)

Answer: b. 15°C to 30°C (59°F to 86°F). Explanation: The recommended temperature range for storing most medications in a pharmacy is between 15°C to 30°C (59°F to 86°F). This range ensures the stability and efficacy of medications under typical storage conditions.

808. In a situation where a refrigerator used to store vaccines fails overnight, what immediate action should be taken with the vaccines?
a. Discard all vaccines immediately without further assessment
b. Quarantine the vaccines and consult vaccine stability guidelines before making a decision
c. Use the vaccines as quickly as possible before they degrade further
d. Return the vaccines to the supplier for a refund

Answer: b. Quarantine the vaccines and consult vaccine stability guidelines before making a decision. Explanation: If a refrigerator storing vaccines fails, the vaccines should be quarantined and not used until stability guidelines and data logs are consulted to determine if the vaccines remained within a safe temperature range. This ensures that compromised vaccines are not administered.

809. Which device is essential for continuous monitoring of temperature in a pharmacy's medication storage area?
a. Barometer
b. Thermocouple
c. Digital thermometer with a min/max function
d. Anemometer

Answer: c. Digital thermometer with a min/max function. Explanation: A digital thermometer with a min/max function is essential for continuous monitoring of temperature in a pharmacy's medication storage area. It records the highest and lowest temperatures reached, helping to ensure that medications are stored within the required temperature range at all times.

810. How should humidity levels be managed in a pharmacy to preserve medication integrity?
a. Keeping humidity levels as high as possible to prevent medication drying
b. Maintaining a stable humidity level, ideally between 30% and 60%
c. Allowing natural fluctuations in humidity without control
d. Using dehumidifiers only during the summer months

Answer: b. Maintaining a stable humidity level, ideally between 30% and 60%. Explanation: Maintaining a stable humidity level, ideally between 30% and 60%, is crucial in a pharmacy to preserve medication integrity. Too much humidity can cause medication degradation, while too little can lead to drying out of certain formulations.

811. When receiving a shipment of temperature-sensitive medications, what verification process should be followed?
a. Checking the color change indicators or temperature logs included in the shipment
b. Tasting a sample of the medication to check for degradation
c. Waiting for 24 hours to see if the medication's appearance changes
d. Relying solely on the shipment's arrival within the expected time frame as proof of stability

Answer: a. Checking the color change indicators or temperature logs included in the shipment. Explanation: Verifying the integrity of temperature-sensitive medications upon receipt involves checking color change indicators or temperature logs included in the shipment. These indicators provide a direct measure of whether the medications were exposed to temperatures outside their safe storage range during transit.

812. What is the consequence of storing a medication at a temperature higher than recommended?
a. The medication will become more potent over time
b. The medication's shelf life will significantly increase
c. Potential degradation, leading to reduced efficacy or increased toxicity
d. The medication will become less potent but remain safe to use indefinitely

Answer: c. Potential degradation, leading to reduced efficacy or increased toxicity. Explanation: Storing a medication at a temperature higher than recommended can lead to potential degradation of the medication, resulting in reduced efficacy or increased toxicity. This can compromise patient safety and treatment effectiveness.

813. In the context of temperature monitoring, what is the purpose of a "buffered" temperature probe?
a. To increase the temperature within the storage unit
b. To measure the temperature of the storage unit's external environment
c. To simulate the temperature experienced by stored products more accurately
d. To decrease the humidity within the storage unit

Answer: c. To simulate the temperature experienced by stored products more accurately. Explanation: A "buffered" temperature probe, often surrounded by a material similar to medication packaging, is used to simulate the temperature experienced by stored products more accurately, providing a more representative reading of the conditions medications are actually exposed to.

814. What action should be taken if a humidity-sensitive medication is exposed to high humidity levels during storage?
a. Place the medication in a freezer for 24 hours to restore its integrity
b. Quarantine the medication and assess for any visible signs of degradation
c. Continue to dispense the medication as high humidity does not affect medications
d. Dry the medication using a hairdryer before dispensing

Answer: b. Quarantine the medication and assess for any visible signs of degradation. Explanation: If a humidity-sensitive medication is exposed to high humidity levels, it should be quarantined and assessed for any visible signs of degradation, such as clumping or changes in appearance, to determine if it remains safe and effective to use.

815. How often should temperature and humidity logs be reviewed in a pharmacy setting to ensure compliance with storage guidelines?
a. Annually during the pharmacy's inventory audit
b. Monthly, at a minimum, or more frequently as dictated by policy
c. Only when a medication-related problem is reported by a patient
d. Every six months, in alignment with general maintenance schedules

Answer: b. Monthly, at a minimum, or more frequently as dictated by policy. Explanation: Temperature and humidity logs in a pharmacy setting should be reviewed monthly, at a minimum, or more frequently as dictated by policy or regulatory requirements. Regular review helps ensure ongoing compliance with medication storage guidelines and early identification of any storage condition issues.

816. What is the impact of improper humidity control on effervescent tablets?
a. It enhances their flavor and dissolution rate
b. It has no significant effect as long as the temperature is controlled
c. It can cause premature tablet disintegration or reduced efficacy
d. It increases the tablets' shelf life by preventing oxidation

Answer: c. It can cause premature tablet disintegration or reduced efficacy. Explanation: Improper humidity control can lead to premature disintegration or reduced efficacy of effervescent tablets. High humidity can trigger the effervescent reaction prematurely, compromising the integrity and effectiveness of the medication.

817. Which of the following best describes the appropriate storage condition for a medication requiring refrigeration?
a. Stored at room temperature away from direct sunlight
b. Kept in a freezer at temperatures below 0°C
c. Maintained at 2°C to 8°C in a dedicated medication refrigerator
d. Placed in a dry area with humidity control

Answer: c. Maintained at 2°C to 8°C in a dedicated medication refrigerator. Explanation: Medications requiring refrigeration should be stored at temperatures between 2°C and 8°C, typically in a dedicated medication refrigerator, to ensure their efficacy and stability. Freezing these medications or storing them at room temperature could compromise their effectiveness.

818. How should controlled substances be stored in a pharmacy to comply with security requirements?
a. On open shelves for easy access
b. In a securely locked, substantially constructed cabinet
c. In the refrigerator next to vaccines
d. At the pharmacy counter within reach of the pharmacist

Answer: b. In a securely locked, substantially constructed cabinet. Explanation: Controlled substances must be stored in a securely locked, substantially constructed cabinet or safe to prevent unauthorized access and to comply with regulatory requirements. This ensures both security and compliance with legal standards.

819. What is the significance of using "tall man" lettering in medication storage?
a. To indicate medications that are to be stored at high shelves
b. To highlight the differences in look-alike/sound-alike medication names
c. To designate medications that require special handling
d. To identify medications that are on the pharmacy's formulary

Answer: b. To highlight the differences in look-alike/sound-alike medication names. Explanation: "Tall man" lettering is used to help distinguish look-alike/sound-alike medication names by capitalizing certain letters, which can reduce the risk of medication errors by making similar names more distinguishable.

820. In the context of pharmacy security, what is a "biometric access control system" used for?
a. Monitoring temperature and humidity in medication storage areas
b. Identifying and tracking the movement of customers within the pharmacy
c. Restricting access to medication storage areas to authorized personnel via unique biological traits
d. Ensuring that all prescriptions are digitally signed by the prescriber

Answer: c. Restricting access to medication storage areas to authorized personnel via unique biological traits. Explanation: A biometric access control system uses unique biological traits, such as fingerprints or retinal scans, to restrict access to sensitive areas like medication storage rooms, ensuring that only authorized personnel can enter.

821. What is the primary purpose of maintaining a "perpetual inventory system" for controlled substances?
a. To automate the reordering of stock when levels are low
b. To track the quantity on hand and movement of controlled substances continuously
c. To generate automatic billing to patients
d. To record temperature and humidity levels in storage areas

Answer: b. To track the quantity on hand and movement of controlled substances continuously. Explanation: A perpetual inventory system for controlled substances is maintained to continuously track the quantity on hand and movement (such as dispensing or receiving) of these substances, ensuring accurate records and compliance with regulatory requirements.

822. When storing medications that are sensitive to light, what is the best practice?
a. Keeping them in clear containers for easy identification
b. Storing them in amber-colored or opaque containers to block light
c. Placing them near windows to ensure they are exposed to natural light
d. Using transparent shelving units to enhance visibility

Answer: b. Storing them in amber-colored or opaque containers to block light. Explanation: Medications sensitive to light should be stored in amber-colored or opaque containers to protect them from light exposure, which could degrade the medication and reduce its effectiveness.

823. What role does an "automated dispensing system" play in medication storage and security?
a. It serves as a backup system for power outages
b. It provides a platform for online prescription orders
c. It secures medications and dispenses them based on authorized access and prescriptions
d. It monitors patient adherence to medication regimens

Answer: c. It secures medications and dispenses them based on authorized access and prescriptions. Explanation: Automated dispensing systems secure medications and control access, dispensing them only as authorized by prescriptions or provider orders, thereby enhancing both security and efficiency in medication management.

824. Why is it important to segregate "hazardous medications" from other inventory in a pharmacy?
a. To prevent theft of high-cost medications
b. To ensure easy access during emergency situations
c. To avoid cross-contamination and ensure safe handling
d. To comply with aesthetics and organizational policies

Answer: c. To avoid cross-contamination and ensure safe handling. Explanation: Hazardous medications should be segregated from other inventory to prevent cross-contamination, ensure safe handling practices are followed, and protect pharmacy staff and patients from exposure to potentially harmful substances.

825. How does "barcoding technology" enhance medication storage and security in pharmacies?
a. By providing detailed information about the manufacturer
b. By enabling precise tracking and verification of medications at the point of dispensing
c. By displaying prices more prominently to customers
d. By reducing the need for refrigeration for certain medications

Answer: b. By enabling precise tracking and verification of medications at the point of dispensing. Explanation: Barcoding technology enhances medication storage and security by allowing precise tracking of medication inventory and verification at the point of dispensing, reducing the risk of errors and ensuring that the correct medication is provided to the patient.

826. What is the best practice for storing multi-dose vials to prevent contamination?
a. Storing them with the cap off for easy access
b. Keeping them at room temperature regardless of the medication type
c. Dating the vial upon first use and following recommended storage guidelines
d. Placing them in high-traffic areas to ensure they are used before single-dose vials

Answer: c. Dating the vial upon first use and following recommended storage guidelines. Explanation: Multi-dose vials should be dated upon first use and stored according to the manufacturer's recommendations to prevent contamination. This includes adhering to any specific temperature requirements and discarding the vial after the recommended use period or beyond-use date to ensure patient safety.

827. What information must be recorded in a controlled substance vault logbook each time a medication is accessed?
a. The name of the medication, quantity taken, date, and name of the person accessing it
b. The price of the medication and the reason for its use
c. The expiration date of the medication and the temperature of the vault
d. The supplier of the medication and its intended use in the pharmacy

Answer: a. The name of the medication, quantity taken, date, and name of the person accessing it. Explanation: The controlled substance vault logbook must meticulously record each instance of access, including the specific medication name, the quantity taken or added, the date of the transaction, and the full name of the individual accessing the vault. This ensures traceability and accountability for all controlled substances.

828. How frequently must the inventory of controlled substances in the vault be audited and reconciled with the logbook entries?
a. Daily
b. Weekly
c. Monthly
d. Biannually

Answer: c. Monthly. Explanation: The inventory of controlled substances within the vault should be audited and reconciled with the logbook entries on a monthly basis. This regular audit helps in identifying any discrepancies early and ensures compliance with regulatory standards.

829. In the case of a discrepancy found during the audit of the controlled substance vault, what immediate action should be taken?

a. Adjust the logbook to match the physical count
b. Investigate the discrepancy, document the findings, and report to the appropriate regulatory body if necessary
c. Dismiss minor discrepancies as counting errors
d. Immediately dispose of excess controlled substances

Answer: b. Investigate the discrepancy, document the findings, and report to the appropriate regulatory body if necessary. Explanation: Any discrepancies found during an audit must be thoroughly investigated, documented, and, if necessary, reported to the appropriate regulatory body. Adjusting logbook entries without investigation compromises the integrity of the controlled substance management system.

830. What additional security measure is recommended for the controlled substance vault?
a. Keeping the vault unlocked during business hours for easy access
b. Using a biometric access system such as fingerprint or retina scan
c. Storing the vault keys in an easily accessible location
d. Sharing the vault access code with all pharmacy staff

Answer: b. Using a biometric access system such as fingerprint or retina scan. Explanation: Implementing a biometric access system, such as fingerprint or retina scanning, adds an additional layer of security to the controlled substance vault by ensuring that only authorized individuals can gain access, thereby enhancing the control and accountability of substance handling.

831. What should be done with outdated or damaged controlled substances found in the vault?
a. Return them to the manufacturer for a refund
b. Dispose of them immediately in the pharmacy trash
c. Securely store them until they can be properly disposed of through a DEA-approved process
d. Donate them to a charity that accepts medications

Answer: c. Securely store them until they can be properly disposed of through a DEA-approved process. Explanation: Outdated or damaged controlled substances should be securely stored in a designated area within the vault until they can be disposed of in accordance with DEA regulations, which may involve the use of a reverse distributor or participation in a DEA take-back event.

832. How should access to the controlled substance vault logbook be managed?
a. The logbook should be digital and accessible to all pharmacy staff for efficiency
b. The logbook should be kept within the vault and only accessible to the pharmacist-in-charge
c. The logbook can be stored outside the vault as long as it is locked up at night
d. All staff members should have their own copy of the logbook for convenience

Answer: b. The logbook should be kept within the vault and only accessible to the pharmacist-in-charge. Explanation: The controlled substance vault logbook should be securely stored within the vault itself and only be accessible to the pharmacist-in-charge or designated authorized personnel. This ensures that the logbook is always accounted for and that entries are made accurately and responsibly.

833. What is the protocol for making entries in the controlled substance vault logbook?
a. Entries can be made in pencil for easy correction
b. Entries should be made in ink and any corrections must be initialed and dated
c. Electronic entries are preferred and can be edited without a trace
d. Corrections should be made using correction fluid for a clean appearance

Answer: b. Entries should be made in ink and any corrections must be initialed and dated. Explanation: Logbook entries must be made in permanent ink, and any corrections should be clearly initialed and dated by the person making the correction. This ensures the integrity and traceability of the logbook entries, which is crucial for accountability and compliance purposes.

834. In the event of theft or significant loss of controlled substances from the vault, what is the required action?
a. Report the incident to the DEA within 7 days using Form 106
b. Conduct an internal investigation before deciding to report
c. Report the incident to the local police only
d. Write off the loss as shrinkage in the next inventory report

Answer: a. Report the incident to the DEA within 7 days using Form 106. Explanation: Any theft or significant loss of controlled substances must be reported to the DEA within 7 days of discovery using Form 106. This prompt reporting is critical for regulatory compliance and for initiating an investigation into the loss.

835. What best practice should be followed when transferring controlled substances into the vault?
a. Document the transfer in the logbook immediately before physically moving the substances
b. Transfer substances in large batches at the end of the month for efficiency
c. Have two authorized staff members present during the transfer for verification
d. Transfer substances without documentation if they are from a trusted supplier

Answer: c. Have two authorized staff members present during the transfer for verification. Explanation: When transferring controlled substances into the vault, it is a best practice to have two authorized staff members present—one to handle the substances and another to verify and document the transfer. This dual control method enhances the accuracy and integrity of the inventory management process.

836. How should discrepancies in the controlled substance vault logbook be documented?
a. By erasing the original entry and writing the correct information
b. By documenting the discrepancy in a separate file outside the logbook
c. By making a clear note in the logbook, including details of the discrepancy and corrective action taken
d. Discrepancies should not be documented in the logbook to avoid legal implications

Answer: c. By making a clear note in the logbook, including details of the discrepancy and corrective action taken. Explanation: Any discrepancies identified in the logbook should be clearly documented within the logbook itself, including a detailed account of the discrepancy, investigation findings, and any corrective actions taken. This transparent approach ensures accountability and provides a traceable record of how discrepancies are addressed.

837. What is the recommended procedure for disposing of expired controlled substances in a pharmacy setting?
a. Flushing them down the sink or toilet
b. Returning them to the original manufacturer
c. Using a DEA-authorized reverse distributor
d. Placing them in regular trash with other non-pharmaceutical waste

Answer: c. Using a DEA-authorized reverse distributor. Explanation: The DEA recommends that pharmacies dispose of expired controlled substances by using a DEA-authorized reverse distributor. This ensures secure and compliant disposal, preventing diversion and environmental contamination.

838. When documenting the disposal of expired medications, what information is essential to record?
a. The name and address of the pharmacy technician disposing of the medication
b. The medication's brand name, strength, quantity, and expiration date
c. The weather conditions on the day of disposal
d. The cost price of the medication at the time of purchase

Answer: b. The medication's brand name, strength, quantity, and expiration date. Explanation: Proper documentation of expired medication disposal should include the medication's brand name, strength, quantity, and expiration date to ensure traceability and compliance with regulatory requirements.

839. What is the significance of using a "witness" during the disposal process of expired medications?
a. To ensure the disposal process is entertaining
b. To verify the correct execution of disposal procedures and prevent diversion
c. To provide emotional support to the staff disposing of the medications
d. To assist in the physical process of medication destruction

Answer: b. To verify the correct execution of disposal procedures and prevent diversion. Explanation: Having a witness during the disposal of expired medications ensures that the disposal procedures are correctly followed and helps prevent the diversion of medications by providing accountability and verification.

840. In the context of expired medication disposal, what does the term "non-retrievable" mean?
a. The medication cannot be sold or returned to the manufacturer
b. The medication is placed in a location where it cannot be accessed by unauthorized persons
c. The form of the medication is permanently altered to prevent its use
d. The medication is stored indefinitely in the pharmacy's archive

Answer: c. The form of the medication is permanently altered to prevent its use. Explanation: "Non-retrievable" means that the physical or chemical form of the medication is permanently altered in such a way that it cannot be transformed back into a usable form, ensuring that it cannot be used or diverted.

841. For non-controlled expired medications, which disposal method is considered environmentally responsible?
a. Incineration in a licensed facility
b. Disposal in regular landfill waste
c. Burying in a secured location within pharmacy premises
d. Diluting with water and pouring down the drain

Answer: a. Incineration in a licensed facility. Explanation: Incinerating non-controlled expired medications in a licensed facility is considered environmentally responsible because it ensures that the medications are destroyed in a manner that minimizes environmental impact, unlike landfill disposal or pouring down the drain, which can lead to pollution.

842. When using a medication disposal kiosk, what type of medications are typically prohibited?
a. Over-the-counter medications
b. Non-prescription liquid medications
c. Controlled substances and hazardous drugs
d. Expired dietary supplements

Answer: c. Controlled substances and hazardous drugs. Explanation: Medication disposal kiosks often prohibit the disposal of controlled substances and hazardous drugs due to specific regulatory requirements for handling and disposal of these medications to prevent diversion and ensure environmental safety.

843. How should a pharmacy manage the disposal of expired medication samples?
a. By offering them to employees for personal use
b. By following the same procedures as for full-sized commercial medication packages
c. By donating them to charitable organizations
d. By repackaging them for future use

Answer: b. By following the same procedures as for full-sized commercial medication packages. Explanation: Expired medication samples should be disposed of following the same regulatory procedures and guidelines as full-sized commercial medication packages to ensure compliance and safety.

844. What role do community "take-back" programs play in the disposal of expired medications?
a. They allow patients to return unused or expired medications to pharmacies for resale
b. They provide a safe and secure method for the public to dispose of medications, reducing the risk of misuse
c. They recycle expired medications into new pharmaceutical products
d. They exclusively handle the disposal of veterinary medications

Answer: b. They provide a safe and secure method for the public to dispose of medications, reducing the risk of misuse. Explanation: Community take-back programs offer a secure way for individuals to dispose of their unused or expired medications, helping to reduce the risk of accidental ingestion, misuse, or environmental harm.

845. In dealing with expired cytotoxic drugs, what additional safety measures should be taken during disposal?
a. Wearing full-body protective suits
b. Utilizing spill kits and personal protective equipment (PPE)
c. Disposing of them in regular pharmacy waste bins
d. Administering an antidote prior to disposal

Answer: b. Utilizing spill kits and personal protective equipment (PPE). Explanation: When disposing of expired cytotoxic drugs, additional safety measures such as using spill kits and appropriate PPE (e.g., gloves, gowns, eye protection) are necessary to protect staff from potential exposure to these hazardous substances.

846. What is a critical consideration when disposing of expired liquid medications?
a. Ensuring the liquids are frozen before disposal
b. Mixing the liquids with absorbent materials before disposal
c. Diluting the liquids with large volumes of water
d. Re-bottling the liquids into smaller containers

Answer: b. Mixing the liquids with absorbent materials before disposal. Explanation: When disposing of expired liquid medications, mixing them with absorbent materials can help contain the liquid and prevent leaks or spills during the disposal process, enhancing safety and compliance with disposal regulations.

847. What is the primary focus of a prospective drug utilization review (DUR)?
a. Reviewing the patient's medication history after dispensing to identify any discrepancies
b. Evaluating a patient's planned medication therapy before the medication is dispensed
c. Analyzing prescription trends over the past year for quality improvement
d. Conducting patient surveys on medication effectiveness post-therapy

Answer: b. Evaluating a patient's planned medication therapy before the medication is dispensed. Explanation: A prospective DUR focuses on evaluating a patient's medication therapy before dispensing the medication. It aims to ensure the appropriateness of the prescription, prevent medication errors, and identify potential drug interactions or contraindications.

848. In a retrospective DUR, what type of data is primarily analyzed?
a. Future medication orders and prescriptions
b. Medication therapy plans before dispensing
c. Historical prescription data and patient outcomes

d. Predictive analytics for medication trends

Answer: c. Historical prescription data and patient outcomes. Explanation: A retrospective DUR involves analyzing historical prescription data and patient outcomes to assess the effectiveness of drug therapy, identify patterns of medication misuse, and develop strategies for improving medication use policies and patient care.

849. Which scenario best exemplifies a prospective DUR in action?
a. A pharmacist reviews a patient's medication profile for potential drug interactions before filling a new prescription.
b. A healthcare team meets monthly to discuss adverse drug reactions reported in the last quarter.
c. A pharmacy technician enters prescription data into a database for future analysis.
d. An insurance company analyzes claims data to identify high-risk medication use.

Answer: a. A pharmacist reviews a patient's medication profile for potential drug interactions before filling a new prescription. Explanation: This scenario is a classic example of a prospective DUR, where the pharmacist actively reviews the patient's current medication regimen for potential interactions or contraindications before dispensing a new medication, ensuring the safety and efficacy of the therapy.

850. What is the main goal of conducting a retrospective DUR?
a. To prepare for future medication orders
b. To educate patients on medication adherence
c. To improve pharmacy dispensing efficiency
d. To enhance medication therapy and patient outcomes based on past experiences

Answer: d. To enhance medication therapy and patient outcomes based on past experiences. Explanation: The main goal of a retrospective DUR is to analyze past medication use and outcomes to identify trends, issues, or opportunities for improvement in medication therapy, ultimately enhancing patient care and outcomes.

851. During a prospective DUR, which factor is crucial for the pharmacist to consider?
a. The cost-effectiveness of the prescribed medication
b. The patient's insurance coverage for the prescribed medication
c. The patient's allergy history and current medication regimen
d. The pharmaceutical company's reputation for the prescribed medication

Answer: c. The patient's allergy history and current medication regimen. Explanation: In a prospective DUR, it's crucial for the pharmacist to consider the patient's allergy history and current medication regimen to identify any potential allergic reactions or drug interactions, ensuring the safety and appropriateness of the prescribed therapy.

852. How does technology support prospective DUR processes in modern pharmacies?
a. By automatically dispensing medications without pharmacist intervention
b. By providing telehealth consultations instead of in-person pharmacy visits

c. By using electronic health records and decision support systems to flag potential issues
d. By emailing patients their prescription history for self-review

Answer: c. By using electronic health records and decision support systems to flag potential issues. Explanation: Technology supports prospective DUR processes through the use of electronic health records (EHRs) and decision support systems that can automatically flag potential drug interactions, contraindications, or other issues before the medication is dispensed, aiding the pharmacist in making informed decisions about the therapy.

853. What role does patient counseling play in prospective DUR?
a. It is not related to DUR processes
b. It provides an opportunity to clarify the patient's understanding of their medication therapy
c. It is only necessary when a medication error has been identified
d. It is solely the responsibility of the prescribing physician

Answer: b. It provides an opportunity to clarify the patient's understanding of their medication therapy. Explanation: Patient counseling is a critical component of prospective DUR, as it provides the pharmacist with an opportunity to clarify and reinforce the patient's understanding of their medication therapy, usage instructions, and potential side effects, ensuring the safe and effective use of the medication.

854. In the context of retrospective DUR, what is an example of an intervention that might be initiated based on the findings?
a. Immediate alteration of a patient's current medication without consulting the prescriber
b. Development of educational programs for healthcare providers on identified prescribing trends
c. Direct contact with patients to discuss their medication therapy without prescriber consent
d. Ceasing all medication therapy for a condition based on a single adverse event report

Answer: b. Development of educational programs for healthcare providers on identified prescribing trends. Explanation: Based on the findings of a retrospective DUR, an appropriate intervention might include the development of educational programs or initiatives aimed at healthcare providers to address identified prescribing trends, errors, or opportunities for therapy optimization, enhancing overall medication safety and effectiveness.

855. How does a retrospective DUR contribute to pharmacy quality assurance programs?
a. By focusing solely on the financial aspects of medication dispensing
b. By providing data-driven insights into medication use patterns and outcomes
c. By eliminating the need for prospective DURs
d. By reducing the workload of pharmacy staff in medication dispensing

Answer: b. By providing data-driven insights into medication use patterns and outcomes. Explanation: A retrospective DUR contributes to pharmacy quality assurance programs by offering valuable, data-driven insights into medication use patterns, patient outcomes, and potential areas for improvement in prescribing and dispensing practices, ultimately contributing to enhanced quality of care and patient safety.

856. What is a key strategy in preventing diversion of controlled substances within a pharmacy?
a. Implementing an open-access policy for all pharmacy staff
b. Using manual logs for tracking medication movement
c. Conducting regular and random audits of controlled substances
d. Storing all medications on open shelves for easy access

Answer: c. Conducting regular and random audits of controlled substances. Explanation: Regular and random audits of controlled substances are crucial for identifying discrepancies and potential diversion early. This proactive approach ensures accountability and helps in maintaining accurate records of medication movement.

857. Which technology is most effective in monitoring and preventing diversion in real-time within the pharmacy?
a. Paper-based prescription tracking
b. Automated dispensing systems with individual user access
c. Unmonitored drop boxes for medication disposal
d. Non-digital, lock-and-key storage cabinets

Answer: b. Automated dispensing systems with individual user access. Explanation: Automated dispensing systems equipped with individual user access ensure that each transaction is recorded and attributed to a specific user, providing a clear audit trail that can help identify potential diversion activities.

858. In the context of diversion prevention, why is it important to provide continuous education and training for pharmacy staff?
a. To ensure staff are aware of new medications only
b. To keep staff updated on the latest entertainment trends
c. To maintain awareness of diversion tactics and the importance of compliance
d. To encourage staff to self-manage their work schedules

Answer: c. To maintain awareness of diversion tactics and the importance of compliance. Explanation: Continuous education and training for pharmacy staff on diversion tactics, regulatory compliance, and the pharmacy's policies and procedures are essential to reinforce the importance of vigilance and adherence to protocols designed to prevent diversion.

859. What role does a "two-person verification system" play in preventing diversion when handling high-risk medications?
a. It slows down the workflow and increases patient wait times
b. It requires two staff members to verify each step in the handling of high-risk medications to prevent unauthorized access or tampering
c. It doubles the workforce needed, increasing operational costs
d. It is used only during inventory counts for accuracy

Answer: b. It requires two staff members to verify each step in the handling of high-risk medications to prevent unauthorized access or tampering. Explanation: A two-person verification system is a critical control measure where two authorized staff members verify each step in the handling of high-risk medications, reducing the risk of diversion by ensuring accountability and oversight.

860. How does "restricted access to controlled substances" contribute to diversion prevention in pharmacies?
a. By allowing all pharmacy staff unrestricted access to enhance workflow
b. By limiting access to controlled substances to authorized personnel only, reducing opportunities for unauthorized handling
c. By restricting patient access to prescription information
d. By locking up all pharmacy supplies, not just controlled substances

Answer: b. By limiting access to controlled substances to authorized personnel only, reducing opportunities for unauthorized handling. Explanation: Restricting access to controlled substances to a limited number of authorized personnel is a fundamental strategy to minimize the risk of diversion by reducing the number of individuals who can handle these medications.

861. What is the significance of maintaining accurate and up-to-date inventory records in diversion prevention?
a. It is only necessary for financial reporting and has no impact on diversion prevention
b. Accurate records ensure that discrepancies are quickly identified, indicating potential diversion
c. Inventory records are less important than sales records in preventing diversion
d. Up-to-date records are only required for controlled substances, not for all inventory

Answer: b. Accurate records ensure that discrepancies are quickly identified, indicating potential diversion. Explanation: Maintaining accurate and up-to-date inventory records, especially for controlled substances, is crucial in diversion prevention as it allows for the timely identification of discrepancies, which could indicate diversion or theft.

862. How do "prescription drug monitoring programs" (PDMPs) aid in the prevention of medication diversion?
a. By providing entertainment to pharmacy staff during downtime
b. By tracking controlled substance prescriptions, aiding in the identification of suspicious prescribing and dispensing patterns
c. PDMPs are not useful in diversion prevention and are only for research purposes
d. By monitoring over-the-counter medication sales exclusively

Answer: b. By tracking controlled substance prescriptions, aiding in the identification of suspicious prescribing and dispensing patterns. Explanation: PDMPs are state-run databases that track the prescribing and dispensing of controlled substances, helping healthcare providers and pharmacies identify and prevent potential prescription drug abuse and diversion by highlighting suspicious activities.

863. What is the impact of implementing a "closed-circuit television" (CCTV) system in pharmacy areas where controlled substances are stored and dispensed?

a. It provides a distraction for pharmacy staff
b. It serves as a deterrent to potential diverters and provides a means of investigation in the event of a discrepancy
c. CCTV systems are only useful for marketing purposes in pharmacies
d. It increases privacy concerns and is therefore not recommended

Answer: b. It serves as a deterrent to potential diverters and provides a means of investigation in the event of a discrepancy. Explanation: CCTV systems in areas where controlled substances are stored and dispensed act as a deterrent to diversion by increasing the perceived risk of getting caught and can provide valuable evidence in the investigation of discrepancies or suspected diversion incidents.

864. In what way does "employee wellness and support programs" contribute to diversion prevention?
a. By offering financial incentives for reporting colleagues suspected of diversion
b. By addressing potential underlying issues, such as substance abuse, that may lead to diversion
c. By providing recreational activities to distract staff from workplace stresses
d. These programs are unrelated to diversion prevention

Answer: b. By addressing potential underlying issues, such as substance abuse, that may lead to diversion. Explanation: Employee wellness and support programs can play a significant role in diversion prevention by providing support for personal or professional issues, including substance abuse, that might otherwise lead an individual to consider diversion as a coping mechanism.

865. When a pharmacy system flags a potential drug-drug interaction requiring an override, what should be the first course of action?
a. Automatically override the alert without further review
b. Contact the prescribing healthcare provider for consultation
c. Proceed with dispensing as the system errors are common
d. Advise the patient to reduce the dosage to avoid the interaction

Answer: b. Contact the prescribing healthcare provider for consultation. Explanation: When a system flags a potential drug-drug interaction, the first course of action should be to consult with the prescribing healthcare provider. This allows for a professional review of the potential interaction, ensuring patient safety and the appropriateness of the therapy.

866. In the event of an allergy alert during medication processing, what is the best practice for a pharmacy technician?
a. Ignore the alert if the patient has taken the medication before
b. Override the alert and proceed with dispensing
c. Document the alert and refer the issue to the pharmacist for further review
d. Change the medication to an alternative without consulting the pharmacist

Answer: c. Document the alert and refer the issue to the pharmacist for further review. Explanation: When an allergy alert occurs, the pharmacy technician should document the alert and refer the matter to the pharmacist for further evaluation and decision-making, ensuring the patient's safety and addressing the potential allergic reaction appropriately.

867. What action should be taken if a prescription requires an override due to a high dosage alert?
a. Decrease the dosage to the system's recommended level and dispense
b. Dispense the medication as prescribed without addressing the alert
c. Consult with the pharmacist to review the prescription and patient's medical history
d. Contact the patient to suggest a lower dosage

Answer: c. Consult with the pharmacist to review the prescription and patient's medical history. Explanation: A high dosage alert warrants a review of the prescription and the patient's medical history by the pharmacist to assess the appropriateness of the dosage. This ensures that any deviations from standard dosages are clinically justified and safe for the patient.

868. How should a pharmacy handle a situation where a patient's medication profile shows a contraindication with a new prescription?
a. Proceed with dispensing and monitor the patient for adverse reactions
b. Recommend an over-the-counter alternative to the patient
c. Initiate a clinical intervention to discuss the contraindication with the prescriber
d. Remove the contraindicated medication from the patient's profile if it's no longer active

Answer: c. Initiate a clinical intervention to discuss the contraindication with the prescriber. Explanation: When a patient's medication profile indicates a contraindication with a new prescription, a clinical intervention should be initiated to discuss the issue with the prescriber. This collaborative approach ensures that all medications are safe and appropriate for the patient.

869. What is the recommended approach when a system alert indicates a potential duplication of therapy?
a. Dispense both medications as they may have different active ingredients
b. Override the alert if the patient insists they need both medications
c. Review the patient's medication history and consult with the pharmacist
d. Suggest to the patient to alternate between the two medications

Answer: c. Review the patient's medication history and consult with the pharmacist. Explanation: A potential duplication of therapy alert requires a review of the patient's medication history and consultation with the pharmacist. This ensures that the patient is not at risk of receiving unnecessary or harmful duplicate therapies.

870. When encountering a formulary substitution alert, what is the appropriate action?
a. Automatically substitute with the recommended formulary option
b. Ignore the alert if the prescribed medication is available in stock
c. Discuss the substitution with the pharmacist and contact the prescriber for approval

d. Inform the patient of the substitution without consulting the prescriber

Answer: c. Discuss the substitution with the pharmacist and contact the prescriber for approval. Explanation: A formulary substitution alert should prompt a discussion with the pharmacist, followed by contact with the prescriber for approval of the substitution. This ensures that any changes to the medication regimen are clinically appropriate and agreed upon by the prescriber.

871. In the case of a pediatric patient, how should a weight-based dosing alert be addressed?
a. Estimate the dose based on average pediatric weights
b. Override the alert if the medication is commonly used in pediatrics
c. Verify the patient's weight and consult with the pharmacist for dose adjustment
d. Advise the caregiver to adjust the dose at home

Answer: c. Verify the patient's weight and consult with the pharmacist for dose adjustment. Explanation: For pediatric patients, a weight-based dosing alert should lead to verification of the patient's current weight and consultation with the pharmacist to adjust the dose accordingly, ensuring the safety and efficacy of the medication for the child.

872. What is a critical step in managing a therapeutic duplication alert for a patient with a complex medication regimen?
a. Simplifying the medication regimen by removing one of the duplicative therapies
b. Holding a medication therapy management (MTM) session with the patient
c. Consulting with the pharmacist to evaluate the necessity of both medications
d. Automatically discontinuing the medication added most recently

Answer: c. Consulting with the pharmacist to evaluate the necessity of both medications. Explanation: Managing a therapeutic duplication alert, especially for patients with complex regimens, involves consulting with the pharmacist to critically evaluate the therapeutic necessity and safety of both medications, ensuring optimal patient care.

873. How should a pharmacy technician proceed when an alert indicates a medication is not covered by the patient's insurance?
a. Advise the patient to pay out-of-pocket for the medication
b. Automatically substitute the medication with an over-the-counter equivalent
c. Consult with the pharmacist to explore therapeutic alternatives or prior authorization
d. Ignore the alert and process the prescription, assuming the patient will handle the insurance issue

Answer: c. Consult with the pharmacist to explore therapeutic alternatives or prior authorization. Explanation: When an insurance coverage alert occurs, consulting with the pharmacist to explore therapeutic alternatives or the process for obtaining prior authorization ensures that the patient's therapy is not interrupted and that all options for coverage are considered.

874. In the context of pharmacy informatics, what is the primary benefit of real-time alerts for drug interactions?
a. They provide historical data analysis for research purposes.
b. They notify the pharmacist of potential drug-drug interactions at the point of dispensing.
c. They track patient medication adherence over time.
d. They automate the inventory management process.

Answer: b. They notify the pharmacist of potential drug-drug interactions at the point of dispensing. Explanation: Real-time alerts are designed to provide immediate feedback to pharmacists about potential drug-drug interactions during the prescription processing phase, enhancing patient safety by allowing for timely intervention.

875. How does analyzing prescription patterns benefit pharmacy practice?
a. It enables the prediction of future medication trends.
b. It identifies potential medication misuse or diversion.
c. It reduces the need for patient consultations.
d. It simplifies the medication compounding process.

Answer: b. It identifies potential medication misuse or diversion. Explanation: Analyzing prescription patterns helps in identifying unusual or irregular prescribing or dispensing activities, which could indicate medication misuse or diversion, allowing for appropriate interventions to enhance medication safety.

876. What is the significance of allergy alerts in a pharmacy management system?
a. They streamline the billing process for allergy medications.
b. They prevent the sale of over-the-counter allergy remedies.
c. They alert pharmacists to patient-specific allergens when dispensing medications.
d. They monitor the storage conditions of allergenic substances.

Answer: c. They alert pharmacists to patient-specific allergens when dispensing medications. Explanation: Allergy alerts in pharmacy management systems are crucial for patient safety, as they provide pharmacists with instant notifications about a patient's known allergens, reducing the risk of allergic reactions to prescribed medications.

877. In what way do real-time alerts for duplicate therapies aid in patient care?
a. By ensuring that all medications are billed accurately
b. By alerting the pharmacist when a patient is prescribed similar medications that could be redundant
c. By tracking the number of prescriptions filled per day
d. By notifying patients when their prescriptions are ready for pickup

Answer: b. By alerting the pharmacist when a patient is prescribed similar medications that could be redundant. Explanation: Real-time alerts for duplicate therapies help pharmacists identify when a patient has been prescribed medications that are therapeutically similar, preventing unnecessary duplication and potential adverse effects.

878. How can analyzing dispensing patterns improve pharmacy operations?
a. By identifying fast-moving items for promotional sales
b. By highlighting inconsistencies in medication adherence among patients
c. By optimizing stock levels based on usage trends
d. By reducing the frequency of medication compounding

Answer: c. By optimizing stock levels based on usage trends. Explanation: Analyzing dispensing patterns allows pharmacies to optimize their inventory based on actual usage trends, ensuring that high-demand medications are always in stock while reducing excess inventory of less frequently dispensed items.

879. What role do real-time alerts play in managing high-risk medications?
a. They facilitate automatic refills for high-risk medications.
b. They provide immediate feedback on potential risks when dispensing high-risk medications.
c. They allow for the remote monitoring of patients taking high-risk medications.
d. They enable the tracking of expiration dates for high-risk medications.

Answer: b. They provide immediate feedback on potential risks when dispensing high-risk medications. Explanation: Real-time alerts are particularly important for high-risk medications, as they provide pharmacists with immediate warnings about potential risks, such as narrow therapeutic indices or significant side effects, enhancing patient safety.

880. How does pattern analysis contribute to the identification of prescription fraud?
a. By comparing the handwriting on prescriptions
b. By detecting unusual prescribing patterns that may indicate fraudulent activity
c. By verifying the legal status of prescribers
d. By tracking the geographic distribution of prescribed medications

Answer: b. By detecting unusual prescribing patterns that may indicate fraudulent activity. Explanation: Analyzing prescribing patterns can reveal anomalies or trends that deviate from normal practices, such as excessive quantities or frequent prescriptions for controlled substances, which may suggest prescription fraud.

881. What advantage does integrating real-time interaction alerts with electronic health records (EHRs) provide?
a. It reduces the need for manual data entry.
b. It ensures that interaction alerts are based on a patient's complete medication history.
c. It automatically updates the patient's billing information.
d. It simplifies the process of transferring prescriptions between pharmacies.

Answer: b. It ensures that interaction alerts are based on a patient's complete medication history. Explanation: Integrating real-time interaction alerts with EHRs ensures that alerts are informed by a patient's complete medication history, including prescriptions from different providers, enhancing the accuracy and relevance of the alerts.

882. How can the analysis of medication utilization patterns improve patient outcomes?
a. By identifying areas where patient education on medication adherence could be improved
b. By increasing the pharmacy's revenue through targeted marketing
c. By simplifying the medication compounding process
d. By reducing the time pharmacists spend on patient consultations

Answer: a. By identifying areas where patient education on medication adherence could be improved. Explanation: Analyzing medication utilization patterns can highlight issues with medication adherence, enabling targeted interventions such as patient education or adherence support programs, ultimately improving patient outcomes.

883. What is the primary goal of implementing both real-time alerts and pattern analysis in pharmacy practice?
a. To increase the efficiency of inventory management
b. To enhance patient safety and medication therapy management
c. To streamline the prescription refill process
d. To facilitate the transition to paperless operations

Answer: b. To enhance patient safety and medication therapy management. Explanation: The primary goal of implementing both real-time alerts and pattern analysis is to enhance patient safety by providing immediate warnings about potential issues and to improve medication therapy management by identifying trends that may impact patient care or reveal opportunities for intervention.

884. When should a pharmacy professional report an adverse drug event to MedWatch?
a. Only when the adverse event results in patient hospitalization
b. After obtaining consent from the patient involved
c. When an adverse event is serious, unexpected, or has significant clinical relevance
d. Only if the adverse event has been previously reported and confirmed

Answer: c. When an adverse event is serious, unexpected, or has significant clinical relevance. Explanation: MedWatch, the FDA Safety Information and Adverse Event Reporting Program, encourages healthcare professionals to report adverse events that are serious, unexpected, or have significant clinical relevance to help ensure the safety of medical products.

885. What is the primary purpose of the Institute for Safe Medication Practices (ISMP)?
a. To regulate the pharmaceutical industry's marketing practices
b. To provide legal representation for patients harmed by medication errors
c. To specialize in understanding and preventing medication errors through education and advocacy
d. To track and report pharmaceutical sales data

Answer: c. To specialize in understanding and preventing medication errors through education and advocacy. Explanation: The Institute for Safe Medication Practices (ISMP) is a nonprofit organization specializing in medication error prevention and safe medication use through education, advocacy, and expert guidance to healthcare professionals.

886. In conducting a root cause analysis using a fishbone diagram, what does the "bone" labeled "Processes" typically represent?
a. Financial aspects impacting healthcare delivery
b. Steps involved in the patient care process where errors might occur
c. Architectural design flaws in healthcare facilities
d. Inherent patient conditions that contribute to adverse events

Answer: b. Steps involved in the patient care process where errors might occur. Explanation: In a fishbone diagram for root cause analysis, the "bone" labeled "Processes" represents the various steps or stages in the patient care or medication use process where errors might occur, helping to identify potential areas for improvement.

887. How can national reporting systems like MedWatch contribute to pharmacy practice?
a. By providing financial incentives for error-free practices
b. By compiling and analyzing data on adverse events to improve medication safety
c. By directly intervening in pharmacy operations to prevent errors
d. By serving as a legal watchdog to prosecute medication errors

Answer: b. By compiling and analyzing data on adverse events to improve medication safety. Explanation: National reporting systems like MedWatch compile and analyze data on adverse drug events, which can then be used to inform healthcare professionals about potential risks, ultimately contributing to safer pharmacy practices and patient care.

888. What is an essential component of a fishbone diagram used in root cause analysis?
a. A chronological timeline of the patient's care journey
b. A central "spine" that represents the problem or adverse event being analyzed
c. Patient testimonials and personal experiences
d. Predictive modeling algorithms

Answer: b. A central "spine" that represents the problem or adverse event being analyzed. Explanation: The central "spine" of a fishbone diagram is crucial as it represents the specific problem or adverse event being analyzed. From this spine, various "bones" branch out, categorizing potential contributing factors to be explored.

889. When using a fishbone diagram, how are contributing factors to a problem typically categorized?
a. By the severity of their impact on the problem
b. Into broad categories such as People, Processes, and Environment
c. Alphabetically for ease of reference
d. By the chronological order in which they occur

Answer: b. Into broad categories such as People, Processes, and Environment. Explanation: In a fishbone diagram, contributing factors to the central problem are typically categorized into broad areas like People, Processes, Equipment, Materials, Environment, and Methods to systematically identify and analyze potential root causes.

890. After identifying a potential medication error, what is the FIRST step in utilizing a fishbone diagram for root cause analysis?
a. Implementing immediate corrective actions to prevent recurrence
b. Defining and writing down the specific problem or error to be analyzed
c. Interviewing all staff involved in the error
d. Revising pharmacy policies and procedures

Answer: b. Defining and writing down the specific problem or error to be analyzed. Explanation: The first step in utilizing a fishbone diagram for root cause analysis is to clearly define and document the specific problem or medication error being analyzed. This clear definition provides a focused starting point for the analysis.

891. In the context of medication safety, what role do ISMP's Medication Safety Alerts play?
a. They serve as legal documents to prosecute medication errors
b. They are marketing materials for pharmaceutical companies
c. They provide timely information on identified medication risks and error prevention strategies
d. They offer financial advice to pharmacies on reducing operational costs

Answer: c. They provide timely information on identified medication risks and error prevention strategies. Explanation: ISMP's Medication Safety Alerts are critical communications that provide healthcare professionals with timely information on emerging medication risks, error-prone conditions, and practical error prevention strategies to enhance medication safety.

892. How should a pharmacy act upon receiving a safety alert from ISMP regarding a medication it dispenses?
a. Ignore the alert if no errors have occurred in the pharmacy
b. Review and assess pharmacy practices related to the alert and implement recommended changes
c. File the alert without review, assuming it is not applicable
d. Wait for direct instructions from regulatory bodies before taking action

Answer: b. Review and assess pharmacy practices related to the alert and implement recommended changes. Explanation: Upon receiving a safety alert from ISMP, a pharmacy should proactively review and assess its current practices related to the alert and implement any recommended changes or enhancements to prevent potential medication errors and enhance patient safety.

893. What is a key benefit of reporting medication errors and adverse drug reactions to national systems like MedWatch?
a. It provides immediate financial compensation to affected patients
b. It contributes to a broader understanding of medication risks and informs safety improvements

c. It absolves healthcare professionals from liability in case of medication errors
d. It serves as a primary source of evidence in legal disputes over medication errors

Answer: b. It contributes to a broader understanding of medication risks and informs safety improvements. Explanation: Reporting medication errors and adverse drug reactions to national systems like MedWatch is crucial as it contributes to the collective understanding of medication risks, helps identify patterns or trends in errors, and informs the development of strategies and guidelines to improve medication safety across the healthcare system.

894. What is the primary purpose of a non-punitive internal reporting system for medication errors?
a. To allocate blame to the individual responsible for the error
b. To document errors for legal purposes only
c. To encourage reporting of errors and near-misses to improve patient safety
d. To track the performance of pharmacy staff for annual reviews

Answer: c. To encourage reporting of errors and near-misses to improve patient safety. Explanation: Non-punitive internal reporting systems are designed to encourage the reporting of errors and near-misses without fear of retribution. This approach fosters an environment where staff can openly share and learn from mistakes, ultimately enhancing patient safety by preventing future errors.

895. How does an internal reporting system contribute to the analysis of medication errors?
a. By providing real-time alerts to pharmacists about potential errors
b. By compiling data that can be analyzed to identify common causes and trends
c. By automatically correcting errors as they are reported
d. By offering financial incentives for error-free performance

Answer: b. By compiling data that can be analyzed to identify common causes and trends. Explanation: An internal reporting system collects data on medication errors, which can then be analyzed to identify patterns, common causes, and system failures. This analysis is critical for implementing targeted interventions to prevent recurrence of similar errors.

896. In the context of error reporting, what does the term "culture of safety" refer to?
a. A set of guidelines that prioritize the physical safety of the pharmacy premises
b. An environment where team members feel responsible for patient safety and empowered to report errors
c. A regulatory framework mandating the use of safety equipment in pharmacies
d. A marketing strategy that promotes the pharmacy as a safe place

Answer: b. An environment where team members feel responsible for patient safety and empowered to report errors. Explanation: A culture of safety in healthcare, including pharmacy practice, emphasizes the importance of patient safety and creates an environment where staff are encouraged and feel safe to report errors and near-misses, contributing to continuous quality improvement.

897. What role do feedback loops play in an internal error reporting system?
a. They provide automatic discounts to patients who experience a medication error
b. They ensure that individuals who report errors receive direct punishment
c. They offer a mechanism for communicating the findings and changes implemented as a result of error analysis
d. They decrease the amount of documentation required for error reporting

Answer: c. They offer a mechanism for communicating the findings and changes implemented as a result of error analysis. Explanation: Feedback loops in error reporting systems are crucial for closing the loop between error reporting and improvement actions. They ensure that staff are informed about the outcomes of error reports, including any system changes or educational initiatives undertaken to prevent future errors, fostering a learning environment.

898. How does a non-punitive approach to error reporting affect staff attitudes towards reporting errors?
a. It may increase fear of retribution and decrease error reporting
b. It typically leads to a decrease in overall staff morale and job satisfaction
c. It encourages more open and frequent reporting of errors and near-misses
d. It has no significant impact on reporting behaviors or attitudes

Answer: c. It encourages more open and frequent reporting of errors and near-misses. Explanation: A non-punitive approach to error reporting removes the fear of blame and retribution, encouraging staff to more openly and frequently report errors and near-misses. This openness is essential for identifying and addressing systemic issues to enhance patient safety.

899. What is the significance of root cause analysis in the context of an internal reporting system?
a. It determines the financial impact of each error on the pharmacy
b. It identifies the deepest underlying cause of an error to prevent recurrence
c. It focuses on finding the individual responsible for an error
d. It calculates the probability of an error occurring again without intervention

Answer: b. It identifies the deepest underlying cause of an error to prevent recurrence. Explanation: Root cause analysis is a systematic process used to identify the fundamental cause(s) of an error. By understanding these underlying issues, pharmacies can implement changes to processes, systems, or training to prevent similar errors in the future.

900. How can technology enhance the effectiveness of an internal error reporting system?
a. By replacing the need for human judgment in error identification
b. By providing an anonymous platform for reporting and analyzing errors more efficiently
c. By automatically penalizing staff who make errors
d. By limiting error reporting to only the most severe incidents

Answer: b. By providing an anonymous platform for reporting and analyzing errors more efficiently. Explanation: Technology can support internal error reporting systems by offering a secure and often anonymous way for staff to report errors. It can also facilitate the efficient collection, analysis, and dissemination of data on errors, contributing to more effective and timely interventions.

901. What is a key component of an effective error reporting system in terms of organizational support?
a. Mandatory disciplinary actions for reported errors
b. Strong leadership commitment to learning from errors and implementing changes
c. A policy of public disclosure of all errors to promote transparency
d. Outsourcing error analysis to external agencies to ensure objectivity

Answer: b. Strong leadership commitment to learning from errors and implementing changes. Explanation: Effective error reporting systems require strong support from leadership, demonstrating a commitment to using reported errors as opportunities for learning and improvement. This leadership support is crucial for fostering a culture of safety and continuous quality improvement.

902. In what way does continuous education and training relate to error reporting and analysis?
a. It is only necessary for new employees as part of their orientation
b. It provides ongoing opportunities to learn from errors and update practices based on emerging evidence
c. It is used as a punitive measure following an error report
d. It focuses exclusively on reinforcing punitive measures for errors

Answer: b. It provides ongoing opportunities to learn from errors and update practices based on emerging evidence. Explanation: Continuous education and training are integral to an effective error reporting system, as they ensure that all staff members, from new hires to seasoned professionals, have regular opportunities to learn from reported errors and to update their knowledge and practices in line with the latest evidence and safety protocols.

903. Which of the following dosage forms is designed to dissolve slowly over time for prolonged release of medication?
a. Chewable tablets
b. Effervescent tablets
c. Enteric-coated tablets
d. Extended-release capsules

Answer: d. Extended-release capsules. Explanation: Extended-release capsules are specifically designed to dissolve slowly and release medication over an extended period, providing prolonged therapeutic effects and reducing the frequency of dosing.

904. What does the sig abbreviation "qid" indicate for medication administration?
a. Once daily
b. Twice daily
c. Three times daily

d. Four times daily

Answer: d. Four times daily. Explanation: The sig abbreviation "qid" stands for "quater in die," which is Latin for four times a day, indicating that the medication should be administered four times throughout the day.

905. Which dosage form is specifically designed to bypass the acidic environment of the stomach and release its active ingredient in the intestine?
a. Sublingual tablet
b. Effervescent tablet
c. Enteric-coated tablet
d. Chewable tablet

Answer: c. Enteric-coated tablet. Explanation: Enteric-coated tablets are designed with a special coating that resists dissolution in the acidic environment of the stomach, ensuring that the tablet passes intact into the intestine where the coating dissolves and releases the active ingredient.

906. In prescription writing, what does the abbreviation "prn" signify?
a. Take as needed
b. Take before meals
c. Take after meals
d. Take at bedtime

Answer: a. Take as needed. Explanation: The abbreviation "prn" stands for "pro re nata," a Latin phrase that means "as needed." It indicates that the medication should be taken only when required for specific conditions or symptoms.

907. What is the primary advantage of administering medication in a suspension form?
a. Faster absorption compared to tablets
b. Extended duration of action
c. Suitable for patients with difficulty swallowing solid dosage forms
d. Enhanced stability of the active ingredient

Answer: c. Suitable for patients with difficulty swallowing solid dosage forms. Explanation: Suspensions offer a significant advantage for patients who have difficulty swallowing tablets or capsules, such as children or elderly patients, by providing the medication in a liquid form.

908. What does the sig abbreviation "ac" instruct the patient to do?
a. Take the medication with food
b. Take the medication before meals
c. Take the medication after meals
d. Take the medication at bedtime

Answer: b. Take the medication before meals. Explanation: The abbreviation "ac" stands for "ante cibum," which is Latin for "before meals," indicating that the medication should be taken before eating.

909. Which type of tablet is designed to dissolve rapidly on the tongue without the need for water?
a. Sublingual tablet
b. Effervescent tablet
c. Chewable tablet
d. Orodispersible tablet

Answer: d. Orodispersible tablet. Explanation: Orodispersible tablets (also known as orally disintegrating tablets) are designed to dissolve rapidly on the tongue, making them convenient for patients who have difficulty swallowing or who do not have immediate access to water.

910. For a patient who has difficulty swallowing, which form of medication might be most appropriate?
a. Capsule
b. Tablet
c. Suspension
d. Suppository

Answer: c. Suspension. Explanation: A suspension, being a liquid dosage form, is often most suitable for patients who have difficulty swallowing solid forms of medication like tablets or capsules.

911. What is the purpose of a "troche" dosage form?
a. To provide extended-release medication absorption through the skin
b. To dissolve slowly in the mouth for local or systemic effect
c. To provide rapid relief of nasal congestion through inhalation
d. To deliver medication directly to the lungs via nebulization

Answer: b. To dissolve slowly in the mouth for local or systemic effect. Explanation: A troche is a lozenge designed to dissolve slowly in the mouth, delivering medication for either a local effect in the oral cavity or systemic absorption through the mucosal lining.

912. In the context of sig abbreviations, what does "hs" instruct the patient to do?
a. Take the medication with food
b. Take the medication in the morning
c. Take the medication at bedtime
d. Take the medication every other day

Answer: c. Take the medication at bedtime. Explanation: The abbreviation "hs" stands for "hora somni," which is Latin for "at bedtime," indicating that the medication should be taken at or around the patient's bedtime.

913. In the PDSA cycle for continuous quality improvement, what does the "P" stand for and what is its purpose?
a. Plan: To develop a hypothesis based on identified issues.
b. Process: To outline the steps required to perform a task.
c. Prescription: To decide on the medication and dosage for treatment.
d. Prevention: To identify strategies to avoid errors.

Answer: a. Plan: To develop a hypothesis based on identified issues. Explanation: In the Plan-Do-Study-Act (PDSA) cycle, "P" stands for Plan. It involves identifying a goal or purpose, formulating a theory, defining success metrics, and putting a plan into action. The planning stage is crucial for setting the direction for quality improvement efforts.

914. When interpreting a prescription, what is a critical step if a pharmacist encounters illegible handwriting?
a. Guessing the medication based on the context of the prescription.
b. Consulting a drug reference book to match partial drug names.
c. Contacting the prescriber for clarification.
d. Asking the patient what medication they were expecting.

Answer: c. Contacting the prescriber for clarification. Explanation: When faced with illegible handwriting on a prescription, the safest and most appropriate action is to contact the prescriber directly for clarification. This ensures accurate dispensing and patient safety.

915. What role does the "Do" phase play in the PDSA cycle for continuous quality improvement in pharmacy practice?
a. Implementing the plan on a small scale to test its effect.
b. Documenting all errors without attempting to correct them.
c. Disseminating the plan throughout the entire organization immediately.
d. Discarding the original plan in favor of a more complex one.

Answer: a. Implementing the plan on a small scale to test its effect. Explanation: The "Do" phase involves executing the planned change on a small scale. This allows the team to test the effect of the change and gather data in a controlled environment, which is essential for evaluating the effectiveness of the improvement strategy.

916. In the context of deciphering prescriber handwriting, what tool or resource is most beneficial for pharmacy professionals?
a. A standard list of abbreviations approved by the pharmacy.
b. A handwriting analysis software.
c. A prescription translation service.
d. An online forum for pharmacists to discuss handwriting challenges.

Answer: a. A standard list of abbreviations approved by the pharmacy. Explanation: Having access to a standardized list of abbreviations approved for use in the pharmacy helps professionals accurately interpret common shorthand used by prescribers, reducing the risk of misinterpretation.

917. During the "Study" phase of the PDSA cycle, what is the primary focus?
a. Reviewing the data collected during the "Do" phase to evaluate the outcomes.
b. Studying the original plan to identify any potential improvements.
c. Studying the behavior of staff members and patients.
d. Conducting external research to find better solutions.

Answer: a. Reviewing the data collected during the "Do" phase to evaluate the outcomes. Explanation: The "Study" phase involves analyzing the data collected during the implementation ("Do") phase to understand the impact of the change and determine whether the intended outcomes were achieved. This analysis is critical for informed decision-making.

918. What strategy can help improve the legibility of future prescriptions from a prescriber known for poor handwriting?
a. Requesting all prescriptions from this prescriber to be sent electronically.
b. Implementing a policy that only allows typed prescriptions.
c. Suggesting the prescriber attend a handwriting improvement course.
d. Refusing to fill any prescriptions from the prescriber until handwriting improves.

Answer: a. Requesting all prescriptions from this prescriber to be sent electronically. Explanation: Encouraging or requesting that prescriptions be sent electronically from prescribers known for poor handwriting can significantly reduce interpretation errors, ensuring accurate dispensing and enhancing patient safety.

919. How does the "Act" phase finalize the PDSA cycle for continuous quality improvement?
a. By taking action based on what was learned in the "Study" phase to implement change.
b. By acting out different scenarios to determine the best course of action.
c. By legally binding the organization to follow the new process.
d. By taking disciplinary action against staff who resist the changes.

Answer: a. By taking action based on what was learned in the "Study" phase to implement change. Explanation: The "Act" phase involves making informed decisions based on the analysis conducted in the "Study" phase. It may mean adopting the change, modifying it for better results, or abandoning it if it did not lead to improvement.

920. In ensuring continuous quality improvement, how often should the PDSA cycle be repeated?
a. Only once, as repeating the cycle could lead to confusion.
b. Repeatedly, as part of an ongoing effort to enhance quality.
c. Bi-annually, to align with financial audits.
d. Only when significant errors occur.

Answer: b. Repeatedly, as part of an ongoing effort to enhance quality. Explanation: The PDSA cycle is iterative and should be repeated continuously as part of a commitment to ongoing improvement. Each cycle builds on the learnings from the previous one, fostering a culture of sustained quality enhancement.

921. For a pharmacy team struggling with interpreting a specific prescriber's handwriting, what collaborative step could be beneficial?
a. Developing a reference guide based on previous prescriptions from the prescriber.
b. Mandating that all pharmacy staff take a course in calligraphy.
c. Implementing a policy that bans handwritten prescriptions.
d. Using only generic names to avoid confusion with brand names.

Answer: a. Developing a reference guide based on previous prescriptions from the prescriber. Explanation: Creating a reference guide with common medications and instructions from the specific prescriber, based on past prescriptions, can aid the pharmacy team in accurately interpreting the prescriber's handwriting in future prescriptions.

922. What is the primary purpose of double-checking patient information during data entry in a pharmacy setting?
a. To ensure the correct patient receives the prescribed medication
b. To comply with pharmaceutical advertising regulations
c. To facilitate faster billing processes
d. To organize prescription records alphabetically

Answer: a. To ensure the correct patient receives the prescribed medication. Explanation: Double-checking patient information is crucial to avoid medication errors, ensuring that each prescription is accurately associated with the correct patient, thus safeguarding patient safety and care quality.

923. When entering a new prescription into the pharmacy management system, what critical information must be verified for accuracy?
a. The patient's favorite pharmacy location
b. The prescribing physician's vacation schedule
c. The medication name, strength, dosage form, and directions
d. The pharmacy stock levels of over-the-counter medications

Answer: c. The medication name, strength, dosage form, and directions. Explanation: Verifying the medication's name, strength, dosage form, and directions is essential to ensure that the patient receives the correct medication and dosage, which is fundamental to effective treatment and patient safety.

924. In the context of data entry, what is the significance of accurately entering the prescriber's DEA number for controlled substances?
a. It determines the pharmacy's inventory pricing.

b. It is necessary for scheduling staff shifts.
c. It is required for legal verification of the prescriber's authority to order controlled substances.
d. It is used to track the pharmaceutical company's sales representatives.

Answer: c. It is required for legal verification of the prescriber's authority to order controlled substances. Explanation: The DEA number is a unique identifier for healthcare providers authorized to prescribe controlled substances. Accurate entry is crucial for compliance with legal requirements and to prevent the misuse of controlled medications.

925. What role does the use of barcode scanning play in pharmacy data entry processes?
a. It is primarily used for employee time tracking.
b. It enhances the accuracy of medication selection and entry.
c. It is used to monitor patient adherence to medication.
d. It serves as the main method for patient identification.

Answer: b. It enhances the accuracy of medication selection and entry. Explanation: Barcode scanning in pharmacies is integral for enhancing the accuracy of medication selection and data entry, reducing the risk of human error, and ensuring that the correct medication and dosage are dispensed.

926. How does the use of electronic prescribing (e-prescribing) impact pharmacy data entry practices?
a. It eliminates the need for data entry.
b. It increases the time required for prescription processing.
c. It reduces the likelihood of transcription errors.
d. It requires manual verification of each prescription with the prescriber.

Answer: c. It reduces the likelihood of transcription errors. Explanation: E-prescribing directly sends prescriptions from the prescriber's system to the pharmacy's, reducing the need for manual entry and thereby decreasing the likelihood of transcription errors, improving efficiency and patient safety.

927. When inputting prescription data, what is the importance of accurately recording the SIG codes?
a. To determine the pharmacy's sales trends
b. To ensure the patient understands the non-medical advice
c. To provide clear and accurate dosing instructions to the patient
d. To keep track of the pharmacy's promotional offers

Answer: c. To provide clear and accurate dosing instructions to the patient. Explanation: SIG codes are shorthand for prescription instructions. Accurately recording these ensures that dosing instructions are clear, precise, and understandable, directly impacting patient adherence and therapy effectiveness.

928. In pharmacy data entry, what is the consequence of incorrectly inputting the patient's insurance information?
a. The prescription is automatically canceled.

b. The patient's medication is upgraded to a premium version.
c. Claims may be rejected, leading to billing issues and delays in medication dispensing.
d. The pharmacy's music playlist is changed.

Answer: c. Claims may be rejected, leading to billing issues and delays in medication dispensing. Explanation: Incorrect insurance information can lead to claim rejections from insurance providers, causing billing issues, potential out-of-pocket expenses for the patient, and delays in receiving their medication.

929. What precaution should be taken when entering data for a medication with a narrow therapeutic index?
a. Assigning the task to the newest pharmacy technician
b. Double verification by another pharmacist or technician
c. Immediate disposal of excess stock
d. Notification to the local marketing representatives

Answer: b. Double verification by another pharmacist or technician. Explanation: Medications with a narrow therapeutic index have a small range between therapeutic and toxic doses. Double verification ensures dosage accuracy, minimizing the risk of adverse effects or therapeutic failure.

930. How does integrating pharmacy management systems with electronic health records (EHRs) affect data entry?
a. It increases the reliance on paper prescriptions.
b. It reduces the need for manual data entry, decreasing the risk of errors.
c. It makes the pharmacy responsible for maintaining all patient medical records.
d. It restricts access to medication information to pharmacists only.

Answer: b. It reduces the need for manual data entry, decreasing the risk of errors. Explanation: Integrating pharmacy management systems with EHRs streamlines the information flow, reducing the need for manual data entry, thus decreasing the potential for errors and enhancing the efficiency and safety of the dispensing process.

931. When creating a patient profile, what critical information must be included to ensure medication safety?
a. Favorite pharmacy location and preferred pharmacist
b. Full name, date of birth, allergies, and current medication list
c. Previous pharmacists' names and locations
d. Patient's insurance policy number and expiration date

Answer: b. Full name, date of birth, allergies, and current medication list. Explanation: Essential information for a patient profile includes the patient's full name, date of birth, known allergies, and a comprehensive list of current medications. This information is crucial for identifying potential drug interactions, allergies, and ensuring appropriate dosing, thereby enhancing medication safety.

932. In updating medication records, what is the importance of noting the date of last medication review?

a. To track the frequency of pharmacy visits
b. To ensure medication regimens are evaluated periodically for efficacy and safety
c. To monitor the expiration dates of medications in stock
d. To calculate the patient's age accurately

Answer: b. To ensure medication regimens are evaluated periodically for efficacy and safety. Explanation: Documenting the date of the last medication review is important to ensure that the patient's medication regimen is periodically assessed for continued efficacy, safety, and to identify any need for adjustments. Regular reviews help to optimize therapeutic outcomes and minimize the risk of adverse effects.

933. How can a pharmacist identify duplicate therapies in a patient's medication regimen?
a. By checking for medications with the same brand name
b. By reviewing the therapeutic classes of the prescribed medications
c. By counting the total number of prescriptions
d. By comparing the colors and sizes of medication tablets

Answer: b. By reviewing the therapeutic classes of the prescribed medications. Explanation: Identifying duplicate therapies involves reviewing the patient's medication list to check for drugs within the same therapeutic class or with overlapping pharmacological actions. This helps in preventing redundant therapy, which can increase the risk of adverse effects and contribute to unnecessary healthcare costs.

934. What strategy can be employed when creating a patient profile to ensure comprehensive medication records?
a. Requiring patients to bring all medication bottles to each visit
b. Only recording medications dispensed at the pharmacy
c. Relying on patient memory for medication history
d. Using a standard form for all patients regardless of their condition

Answer: a. Requiring patients to bring all medication bottles to each visit. Explanation: Asking patients to bring all their medication bottles, including prescription drugs, over-the-counter medications, and supplements, to each visit ensures that the pharmacist has a comprehensive view of the patient's medication regimen. This practice aids in updating the patient profile accurately and identifying potential drug interactions or duplicate therapies.

935. When is it most crucial to update a patient's medication profile?
a. Annually, during routine check-ups
b. Whenever a new medication is prescribed or an existing one is discontinued
c. Only when the patient reports a problem
d. When the pharmacy changes its management system

Answer: b. Whenever a new medication is prescribed or an existing one is discontinued. Explanation: Patient profiles should be updated promptly whenever there is a change in the patient's medication regimen, including the start of a new medication or the discontinuation of an existing one. Timely updates are essential for maintaining an accurate medication record, which is crucial for ongoing patient care and safety.

936. In the context of patient profiles, how can pharmacists utilize technology to identify duplicate therapies?
a. By setting up automatic alerts for drugs within the same class
b. By using social media to track patient health trends
c. By emailing patients monthly for updates on their medication
d. By using manual logs to track patient prescriptions

Answer: a. By setting up automatic alerts for drugs within the same class. Explanation: Modern pharmacy management systems can be configured to provide automatic alerts when medications within the same therapeutic class are prescribed to a patient, helping pharmacists identify and address duplicate therapies efficiently. This technology enhances medication safety and optimizes therapy.

937. What role does patient education play in maintaining accurate medication records?
a. Educating patients on the importance of reporting all medications, including non-prescription drugs and supplements
b. Teaching patients to dispose of unused medications
c. Instructing patients on how to read prescription labels
d. Providing detailed information about the pharmacy's history and policies

Answer: a. Educating patients on the importance of reporting all medications, including non-prescription drugs and supplements. Explanation: Patient education is key in ensuring that individuals understand the importance of reporting all medications they are taking, including over-the-counter drugs and dietary supplements, to the pharmacist. This comprehensive information is vital for maintaining accurate medication records and preventing potential drug interactions.

938. How can collaboration with prescribers enhance the accuracy of patient medication records?
a. By agreeing on a standardized prescription format
b. By competing for patient loyalty
c. By sharing proprietary pharmacy data
d. By limiting communication to only complex cases

Answer: a. By agreeing on a standardized prescription format. Explanation: Collaboration with prescribers to use a standardized prescription format can significantly enhance the accuracy of medication records. Clear communication between prescribers and pharmacists ensures that prescriptions are accurately transcribed and updated in patient profiles, minimizing the risk of errors.

939. What is the significance of documenting 'reason for use' in a patient's medication profile?
a. It helps in tracking the pharmacy's inventory levels
b. It provides context for each medication, aiding in the identification of potential therapeutic duplications
c. It is used primarily for billing purposes

d. It assists in predicting future medication needs based on past trends

Answer: b. It provides context for each medication, aiding in the identification of potential therapeutic duplications. Explanation: Documenting the 'reason for use' for each medication in a patient's profile provides essential context that can help in identifying potential therapeutic duplications and ensuring that each medication is appropriate for the patient's current health conditions, thereby enhancing the safety and efficacy of the treatment regimen.

940. When reviewing a patient's medication list, what is a key indicator that a medication may no longer be needed?
a. The medication was prescribed more than a year ago
b. The patient has multiple medications for the same condition
c. There is no documentation of a recent review by a healthcare professional
d. The patient reports feeling better and no longer experiencing symptoms

Answer: c. There is no documentation of a recent review by a healthcare professional. Explanation: A lack of recent review by a healthcare professional may indicate that a medication needs reevaluation to determine its current relevance to the patient's therapy. Regular review and reconciliation of medication lists are essential to ensure that each drug remains necessary and appropriate for the patient's evolving healthcare needs.

941. When verifying a prescription for Warfarin, what is crucial to ensure regarding the dosage strength?
a. That it matches the most commonly prescribed dosage for convenience
b. That it is the highest available strength to ensure efficacy
c. That it aligns precisely with the prescriber's instructions due to its narrow therapeutic index
d. That it is the lowest available strength to minimize side effects

Answer: c. That it aligns precisely with the prescriber's instructions due to its narrow therapeutic index. Explanation: Warfarin has a narrow therapeutic index, making it crucial to ensure the dosage strength precisely matches the prescriber's instructions to avoid underdosing or overdosing, which could lead to ineffective treatment or severe adverse effects.

942. A prescription reads "Amoxicillin 500mg tid for 10 days." What is essential to verify regarding the quantity to be dispensed?
a. The quantity covers the duration of a standard antibiotic course
b. The quantity is the maximum allowed by insurance
c. The quantity is double the standard to ensure backup supply
d. The quantity is as minimal as possible to reduce cost

Answer: a. The quantity covers the duration of a standard antibiotic course. Explanation: It's essential to verify that the quantity dispensed covers the full duration of the antibiotic course as prescribed, in this case, 10 days at three times daily (tid), to ensure the effectiveness of the treatment and reduce the risk of antibiotic resistance.

943. For a prescription with the direction "ii gtts au qid," what is critical to confirm about the directions given to the patient?
a. The patient understands that "au" means in both ears
b. The patient knows to take the drops orally
c. The patient should apply the drops to the eyes
d. The patient must inhale the drops nasally

Answer: a. The patient understands that "au" means in both ears. Explanation: The abbreviation "au" stands for "auris utraque," which means "both ears" in Latin. It's crucial to ensure the patient understands the directions to apply two drops in both ears four times a day (qid) to ensure proper administration.

944. A prescription for insulin states "40 units sc bid." What must be verified regarding the drug form?
a. The insulin is in pill form for oral ingestion
b. The insulin comes in a pre-filled syringe for subcutaneous injection
c. The insulin is available as an inhalable powder
d. The insulin should be administered intravenously

Answer: b. The insulin comes in a pre-filled syringe for subcutaneous injection. Explanation: The direction "sc" signifies subcutaneous injection. It's vital to verify that the insulin is in a form suitable for subcutaneous administration, preferably in a pre-filled syringe or insulin pen, to ensure the patient can accurately dose and administer 40 units twice a day (bid).

945. In dispensing a medication that reads "1 po qd," what must be ensured about the medication's form?
a. It is in a liquid form for intravenous use
b. It is in a topical form for dermal application
c. It is in an oral form for ingestion
d. It is in a form suitable for rectal administration

Answer: c. It is in an oral form for ingestion. Explanation: The abbreviation "po" stands for "per os," meaning by mouth in Latin. Therefore, it's essential to ensure the medication is in a form intended for oral ingestion, such as a tablet or liquid, to be taken once daily (qd).

946. A patient receives a prescription for "Prednisone 10mg qam." What must be clarified regarding the timing of the dose?
a. The dose should be taken in the evening
b. The dose should be taken with each meal
c. The dose should be taken in the morning
d. The dose should be taken as needed for pain

Answer: c. The dose should be taken in the morning. Explanation: "qam" stands for "quaque ante meridiem," meaning every morning. It's crucial to clarify with the patient that the prednisone should be taken in the morning, possibly to mimic the body's natural corticosteroid rhythm and minimize potential insomnia.

947. For a medication labeled "Use topically bid," what is essential to verify regarding the application site?
a. The medication should be applied to the scalp only
b. The medication should be applied to the specified area, avoiding sensitive regions like the eyes
c. The medication is intended for oral use only
d. The medication should be injected subcutaneously

Answer: b. The medication should be applied to the specified area, avoiding sensitive regions like the eyes. Explanation: For topical medications, it's crucial to ensure the patient knows the specific application site and to avoid sensitive areas, if not specified, to prevent irritation or harm, applying it twice daily (bid).

948. When dispensing "Hydrochlorothiazide 25mg qd," what should be confirmed about the patient's regimen?
a. The patient takes the medication on an empty stomach
b. The patient consumes an adequate amount of potassium-rich foods or supplements
c. The patient avoids drinking water to prevent dilution
d. The patient takes the medication with a high-fat meal

Answer: b. The patient consumes an adequate amount of potassium-rich foods or supplements. Explanation: Hydrochlorothiazide can cause potassium depletion. It's important to confirm that the patient is aware of the need to consume adequate potassium, either through diet or supplements, when taking this medication once daily (qd).

949. In a prescription for "Omeprazole 20mg before breakfast," what must be ensured for optimal effectiveness?
a. The medication is taken immediately after a meal
b. The medication is taken on an empty stomach, 30 to 60 minutes before eating
c. The medication is taken with a large glass of orange juice
d. The medication is taken at bedtime

Answer: b. The medication is taken on an empty stomach, 30 to 60 minutes before eating. Explanation: Omeprazole, a proton pump inhibitor, works best when taken on an empty stomach, typically 30 to 60 minutes before meals, to effectively reduce stomach acid and improve absorption.

Made in United States
North Haven, CT
30 April 2024

51974356R00193